All the Famous People I've Known

Charles L. Connor

Copyright © 2022 Charles L. Connor

All rights reserved.

Cover photography by Lailah Ismael

Cover Art by Cheyenne Connor

Lailah (951) 533-9452

Charles/Autry (909) 642-3163

Printed in the United States of America. No part of this publication may be distributed or reproduced in any manner whatsoever without written permission except in the context of critical reviews and other non-commercial uses permitted by copyright law.

ALL THE FAMOUS PEOPLE I'VE KNOWN

INTRODUCTION TO THIS BOOK.

WHAT A TITLE, ALL THE FAMOUS PEOPLE IVE KNOWN, CAME ACROSS OR BEFRIENDED. I FELT SINSE I HAVE BEEN IN SHOW BUSINESS FOR 43 YEARS AND A LITTLE MORE THAT I SHOULD TELL OF MY TALES OF WHO I MET AND WHO LOVES FAMOUS PEOPLE? WELL, EVERYBODY DOES SO I WILL WRITE ABOUT THESE PEOPLE I HAVE KNOWN, BEFRIENDED OR CAME ACROSS. SOME OF THESE STORIES ARE AMAZING AND HARD TO BELEIVE. I WOULDNT BELEIVE SOME OF THESE STOREIS MYSELF IF I WASNT THERE BUT I WAS THERE AND THESE ARE ALL TRUE STORIES. I LEARNED THROUGH THESE PEOPLE THAT FAMOUS PEOPLE ARE SOMETIMES LESS CHARISMATIC AND MORE BORING THEN SOME OF THOSE WHO HAVENT SUCCEEDED IN THE BUSINESS AND WHO ARENT FAMOUS. I LEARNED PEOPLE ARE PEOPLE, ALL NO MORE AND ALL NO LESS. WE ALL ARE THE SAME. PEOPLE CALLED CELEBRATIES OR NOT CELEBRATIES IN THE SENSE OF THE MEANING OF THE WORD, THEY ARE JUST CATAGORIZED AS THAT IN A CATAGORY LABEL SOCIETY. I LEARNED THE CELEBRATY THING IS A MARKET THING AND EGO THING AND A STATUS THING. SOME OF THE BEST MUSICIANS I

EVER PLAYED WITH ARE NOT FAMOUJS AND BETTER THEN THOSE FAMOUS WHO I WORKED WITH. SOME OF THE WORST MUSICIANS I HAVE PLAYED WITH ARE FAMOUS FROM THE PAST SO I LEARNED NOT TO CATAGORIZE PEOPLE AND IN THIS CULTURE AND SOCIETY THAT MAKES FAMOUS PEOPLE SEEM BETTER THEN THIOSE NOT FAMOUJS AND THIS IS JUST NOT TRUE. I KNOW I HAVE EXPERIENCED AT LEAST 160 FAMOUS PEOPLE THAT I HAVE KNOWN OR CAME ACROSS OR BEFRIENDED..

I BELEIVE THE REASON WHY PEOPLE THINK FAMOUS PEOPLE ARE THE BEST IN THE WORLD IS BECAUSE SOCIETY AND THE ENTERTAINMENT BUSINESS ESPECIALLY CREATED THAT MYTH. FAMOUS PEOPLE ARE NOT THE BEST PEOPLE AND DEFINATELEY ARE AT THE BOTTOM OF THE LIST WHEN IT COMES TO KNOWING GOD AND BEING MORAL.

1. GEORGE PUTNAM.

2000, LAILAH AND I WERE SEARCHING FOR KIEV RADIO. LAILAH IS A GREAT FRIEND AND EX GIRLFRIEND AND STILL MY PERSONNEL MANAGER OF MY ENTERTAINMENT CAREER. WE WANTED TO DO A SHOW. NOW KIEV USED TO BE ON SUNSET BLVD OWNED BY HIS DAD. HIS NAME IS R.J. AND HIS DAD HAS SINSE DIED AND THIS WAS 1986 WHEN I WAS TRYING OUT FOR BEING A DISC JOCKY ON KIEV. I HAD TO LEARN THE EQUITMENT AND AT THAT TIME COULDNT FEEL IT AS WELL AS THE TEACHER SUCKED BADLY. RJ IS NOW THE OWNER OF THE RADIO STATIONS I AND LAILAH WILL BE GOING TO IN GLENDALE OFF BRAND AVENUE IN A SKYSCRAPER. I WAS THINKING THAT THEY HAVE SUCCEEDED ALOT SINSE THEY WERE ON SUNSET BUT THIS IS WRONG. THESE ARE A WHOLE BUNCH OF RADIO STATIONS THAT HAD NOTHING TO DO WITH THE SUNSET BLVD RADIO STATION NOW CALLED KCLA BUT I

DIDNT KNOW THIS AT THIS TIME BECAUSE I WAS FOLLOWING THE TRAIL. THE TRAIL CALLED KIEV RADIO.

TALKING TO RJ. RJ, THE SON OF FOUNDER OF KIEV ON SUNSET BLVD NOW IN CHARGE OF KRLA AND KEZY AMONG OTHERS IN GLENDALE WHERE WE ACCIDENTELY CAME ACROSS BEING WE WER LOOKING FOR KIEV FOUNDED ON SUNSET BLVD.

WELL, THE BOTTOM LINE IS WE WENT TO THE WRONG PLACE BUT IT TURNED OUT TO BE A BLESSING. KIEV BACK IN 1986 WAS 7 DOLLORS PER WEEK TO HAVE YOUR OWN 1/2 HOUR TO 1 HOUR SHOW BUT I DIDNT GO THROUGH IT AND RJ'S FATHER DID ASK ME STRAIGHT UP "ARE YOU EVER GOING TO DO THIS?" AND I ANSWERED "YES SOMEDAY". WELL R.J.S DAD DIED AND NOW SOMEONE ELSE TOOK OVER THIS PLACE ON SUNSET AND AS I SAID I FOLLOWED THE TRAIL TO KIEV RADIO STATION. NOW WE ARE IN GLENDALE AND ME AND LAILAH MEET R.J. IN THE LOBBY. RJ SEEMED LIKE A FRIENDLEY COOL GUY. THIS PLACE HAD 10 OR MORE RADIO SHOWS INCLUDING KIEV, KRLA AS WELL AS KEZY AND WHAT I THOUGHT KIEV, BASICALLY WE WENT TO THE WRONG PLACE AND IT WAS A COUPLE STEPS UP IN FACT LATER WHEN I WORKED AS A RADIO SHOW PERSONALITY IN THE SUNSET BLVD PLACE WHERE I FIRST DIDNT DO, PEOPLE WERE SAYING THEIR GOAL AND HOPE WAS TO MAKE IT TO GLENDALE AND BE ON KEZY OR KRLA AND WE ALREADY HAVE DONE IT BEING IT WAS 2007-08 WHERE WE DID 52 SHOWS, 1 SHOW IEACH WEEK FOR 52 WEEKS FROM APRIL 2007 TO 2008 AND I HAD ALREADY DONE KEZY AND KRLA IN 2000 TO 2002. SO BY HAVING A SHOW ON KCLA WHICH WAS KIEV BEFORE I ACTUALLY WENT DOWN THE LADDER SINSE I HAVE ALREADY DONE KRLA AND KCLA WHICH WAS THE HOPEFUL FUTURE GOALS OF THE PEOPLE WORKING BESIDE ME AND

IN OTHER BOOTHS AT KCLA OTHERWISE KNOWN AS KIEV BACK N THE PAST.

WHAT WE SAID WE WERE ABOUT. WHEN WE CAME IN WE WERE A LITTLE OVERWHELMED AND MY FIRST THOUGHT WAS WE WERE NOT GONNA GET A SHOW HERE BECAUSE IT WAS A MUCH MORE IMPRESSIVE LOOKING PLACE THEN KIEV WAS BEFORE WHEN I WENT ON SUNSET TO BE ON AND AUDITION FOR KIEV ON THE SUNSET BLVD PLACE.

WELL, I SAID TO RJ WE WERE BASICALLY AT THE WRONG PLACE AND HE SAID "NO, WHAT ARE YOU ABOUT?" WE TOLD HIM "WE WERE DOING A SHOW ON ALL THE BANDS AND SOLO ARTISTS WHO HAVE RECORDED MUSIC THAT WERE NOT HEARD YET BY THE MUSIC BUSINESS. THE SHOW WAS CALLED BANDS PASSED UP, UP TO NOW, WELL, RJ LOVED THE IDEA AND GAVE US A RATE WE COULD AFFORD. AT FIRST IT WAS 125 DOLLORS PER HOUR.

HOW WE PAID FOR OUR SHOW. WE WOULD GET OTHER ARTISTS TO PAY FOR A SPOT AND IN ONE HOUR WE WOULD DIVIDE IT INTO 3 20 MINUTE SESSIONS WITH OTHER ARTISTS WE CHARGED ONE HUNDRED FOR EACH 20 MINUTES. WE ASKED RJ IF WE COULD PROFIT LIKE THIS OFF THE ONE HOUR SPOT AND HE WAS FINE WITH IT SO WE WERE MAKING ABOUT 200 PROFIT OFF EACH ONE HOUR SHOW AND THE PEOPLE WE HAD ON THE SHOW NOT ONLY PAID FOR THE ONE HOUR COST OF THE ORIGIONAL COST OF THE ONE HOUR SPOT BUT ACTUALLY GAVE US 200 EXTRA AS A PROFIT BEING THAT 100 X 3 20 MINUTE SESSIONS EQUALS 300 DOLLORS. THE FIRST HUNDERED TO PAY FOR ONE HUNDRED PRICE OF ORIGIONAL COST OF THE SHOW AND THE OTHER 200 ALL PROFIT FOR US. ME AND LAILAH.

SO AROUND THE FIFTH SHOW I HEARD THAT GEORGE PUTNAM WAS ON. WE WERE EARLY AND GEORGE CAME

ON BEFORE US AND I DIDNT KNOW THIS NOR HAS LAILAH KNOWN THIS UNTIL WE GOT THERE EARLY TO SEE GEORGE ON HIS SHOW. WE WATCHED HIS SHOW THROUGH THE WINDOW AND THEN AFTER THAT WE MET GEORGE PUTNAM. I SAW LAST WEEK GEORGE PUTNAM AS THE MAIN U.S. ANCHORMAN OR ONE OF THEM ON AN AND ON A BUS BENCH IN THE MOVIE ENTITLED ONCE UPON A TIME IN HOLLYWOOD AND THIS REMINDED ME OF MY FRIEND GEORGE PUTNAM WHO I MET AND HE ALSO COMMENTED ON OUR SHOW SAYING IT WAS A GOOD IDEA TO HELP THE ARTISTS NOT HELPED THAT HAVE BEEN PASSED UP IN THE PAST.

GOERGE WAS IN HIS MID EIGHTIES WHEN DOING THIS SHOW AND HE HAS DIED SINSE THEN.

HE WAS A COOL GUY AND DOWN TO EARTH. MANY TIMES AFTER WE DID OUR SHOW WE THEN CHATTED WITH GEORGE ON VARIOUS OCCASIONS AND ALWAYS HAD SOME GOOD LAUGHS.

2. MARTIN HEWETT

MARTIN HEWETT WAS AN ACQUANTANCE. I KNEW AND GREW UP WITH HIS BROTHER JOHN AND THEY LIVED CLOSE TO CLAREMONT HIGH SCHOOL. MARTIN USED TO PARTY AT A JACOUSI WITH US AND VAN EVERS WHO IS METGER EVERS SON WAS THERE TOO. ONE DAY WORD WAS GOING AROUND THAT MARTIN WAS PLAYING A LEAD ROLE IN ENDLESS LOVE WITH BROOKE SHIELDS. THIS WAS AROUND 1982-83.

MARTIN WAS COOL ONE DAY THIS GIRL IN OUR CLICK SAID MARTIN IS LEAD IN A MOVIE OPPOSITE OF BROOKE SHIELDS. NEXT THING I KNOW I SEE THE MOVIE AND THEIR HE IS THE GUY WE PARTIED WITH A FEW TIMES AT THE

JACOUSIE ACROSS THE STRET AT THE APARTMENT COMPLEX.

3. KEVIN LYMAN. KEVIN LYMAN BECAME THE FOUNDER OF THE WARP TOUR. HE DID A FEW OTHER THINGS TOO AND I WOULD NOW AND THEN HEAR ABOUT MY OLD FRIEND KEVIN LYMAN. I FIRST MET KEVIN LYMAN IN KINDERGARDEN IN 1966. KEVIN FARTED ALOT THATS ALL I CAN TELL YOU AND IT SMELLED MORE POWERFUL AND STINKIIER THEN I HAVE EVER SMELT IN MY LIFE UP TO THAT POINT. I KNOW EVERYONE FARTS BUT KEVIN WAS KING OF THE FARTERS. AS WE GOT OLDER ME AND KEVIN PLAYED TOGETHER GOING TO EACH OTHERS HOUSES TO EAT DINNERS. WHAT ELSE BUT BOSTON BAKED BEANS. AFTER DINNER WE WOULD PLAY SOCCER IN THE HALLWAY WITH A ROLLED UP SOCK OR WHATEVER BALL WE COULD FIND AND WE WERE ON OUR KNEES AND THAT WAS HOW WE PLAYED SOCCER AFTER DINNER.

AS WE GOT OLDER KEVIIN STARTED TO HANG OUT WITH THE GUILFORD GANG. AND THINGS THEN STARTED TO CHANGE.

WHAT IS THE GUULFORD GANG. THE GUILFORD GANG CONSISTED OF GLEN EARLEMEYER, BILLIE AND ALAN PITTS, DOUG ROSS, JEFF AND DALE KERN, AS WELL AS TIMMY AND STEVE TIPPING, AND THE TOUGEST GUYS THERE THE MAILAZZO BROTHERS, MARK AND I BELEIVE THE OTHER WAS NAMED MIKE MALAZZO. WE PLAYED FOOTBALL AGAINST THE GUILFORD GANG. WE WERE CALLED THE CINDERELLA GANG BEING WE WERE FROM BASICALLY CINDERELLA DRIVE. IT WAS MIKE AND LANCE FOLDEN. THE PERRY BROTHERS, ME AND MY BROTHER JOHN, PHIL WOOTTON AS WELL AS JOHN HENDERSON WHO WAS AROUND 4 FEET FIVE INCHES TALL AND GERRY TAFOYA. WE WERE BASICALLY OUTNUMBERED AND PRETTY MUCH LOST EACH FOOTBALL GAME AND DIDNT

WANT TO BE A GANG AND WE WERE NOT. WE WERE CALLED THAT BY THE GULIFORD GANG WHICH WAS LIKE A SPORTS GANG NOT A CRIMINAL AND DRUG GANG. KEVIN WAS ON NOTRE DAME AVENUE WHICH WAS NOT WITH THE GUILFORD GANG AND NOT WITH THE CINDERELLA GANG AND SO KEVIN COULD HAVE PICKED OUR SIDE BEING HE WAS AS CLOSE TO CINDERELLA AS HE WAS GUILFORD. KEVIN PICKED THEM AND THIS SORT OF HURT OUR FRIENDSHIP.

KEVIN AND HIS MOM BEING DEN MOTHER IN OUR CUB SCOUT DEN 2. THE MOTTO ME AND KEVIN INVENTED WHICH WAS DEN 2 DEN 2 THATS THE PLACE FOR ME AND YOU. THAT WAS OUR GENIUS MOTTO.. JUST KIDDING IT DEFINATELEY WASNT GENIUS AT ALL.

MRS LYMAN. WELL, WHAT CAN I SAY, SHE WAS LOUD RUDE AND CRAZY. SHE WAS OUR DEN MOTHER FOR CUB SCOUTS AND WE MET AT KEVINS HOUSE AKA MRS LYMAN AND MR LYMANS HOUSE BECKY, BARBARA AND GREGG. THE BROTHER AND SISTERS OF KEVINS.

KEVIN AND HIS MOM AND FAMILY WERE JEWISH AND I GET ALONG WELL WITH JEWISH PEOPLE. THESE WERE THE FIRST JEWISH PEOPLE I EVER KNOWN.

AT SCHOOL WE WERE PLAYING MARBLES ME AND KEVIN AS WELL AS ALOT OTHERS AND ME AND KEVIN INVESTED IN A GRAPE BALL MARBLE. WHAT IS THAT YOU MAY WONDER AND ASK? GIANT MARBLES. ABOUT THE SIZE OF ALMOST A BASEBALL AND WHEN PLAYING IF YOU HAVE A GREAT BALL AND THEY HAVE A REGULAR BOULDER, THE BOULDER TO WIN HAS TO HIT THE GREAT BALL WHILE PLAYING MARBLES 8 TIMES AND THE GUY WITH THE GREAT BALL HAS TO ONLY HIT THE BOULDER 1 TIME. KEVIN AND I WERE IN THE SAME SCOUT TROOP WITH HIS MOM AS DEN MOTHER. DEN MOTHER IS THE BOSS AND ORGANIZER OF THE SCOUT

TROOP. AT ONE PACK MEETING WE DID THE JEWISH DANCE HA VAH NAKELA. iF YOU WONDER WHAT A PACK MEETING IS, A PACK MEETING IS WHERE ALL THE DENS GET TOGETHER FOR DANCE COMPETITIONS AND AWARDS AS WELL AS PERSONAL AWARD CEREMONIES AMONG OTHER THINGS LIKE DOING PLAYS AND ACTING SKITS ETC. ALL THE DENS MEETING TOGETHER TO GET TOGETHER FORMING WHAT IS CALLED A PACK MEETING. I IN LATER YEARS AROUND EARLY 2000S PUT MY SON CHARLIE IN A SCOUT TROOP AND IT WAS ALOT DIFFERENT. BACK IN OUR DAY BEING IN SCOUTS WE COULD PICK WHAT THINGS TO DO DO ACHIEVE AWARDS BUT IN MY SONS TIME NO ONE COULD GET AHEAD OF ANOTHER. NO COMPETITION BEING THAT ALL THE KIDS IN MY SONS SCOUT TROOP ALL DID THE SAME THINGS TO ACHIEVE THE EXACT AWARD AND AMOUNTS OF AWARDS TOGETHER AS A DEN. NO INDIVIDUALITY. I BELEIVE IT MORE HEALTHIER THAT THEIR ARE WINNERS AND LOSERS AND SOME BEAT AND ARE BETTER THEN OTHERS BECAUAE THIS IS THE WAY I WAS RAISED AND LIVED. THOUGH MY SONS SCOUT TROOP WAY WAS NO LOSERS AND NO WINNERS ONLY ALL DO THE SAME, I BELEIVE THIS BECAUSE IN LIFE ITS NOT ALL EVEN. THERE A WINNERS AND LOSERS IN LIFE AND ALOT OF COMPETITION SO WHY DO SCOUTS WHERE IT IS NOT COMPETITIVE AND NO WINNERS OR LOSERS? SCOUTS SHOULD PREPARE THEM FOR REAL LIFE. WHICH IS COMPETITION AND WINNERS AND LOSERS. AT ONE PACK MEETING FOR THE SCOUTS OUR DEN DID THE DANCE HAVA NAKILA WHCH IS A WELL KNOWN JEWISH DANCE. IT WA ALOT OF FUN AND WE WON THAT COMPETITION AGAINST ALL THE OTHER DENS COMPETING FOR THE BEST SKIT/DANCE.

ALSO AROUND THIS TIME KEVIN WAS ON THE INDIANS BASEBALL TEAM AND I WAS ON THE HUSKIES. WE WERE ALSO INVOLVED IN BASEBALL CARD TRADING. KEVIN AND I

HAD THE MOST CARDS OF EVERYONE I KNOWN AROUND THE NEIGHBORHOOD AND IN THOSE DAYS WE HADNT LEFT THE NEIGHBORHOOD UNLESS WITH OUR MOMS AND DADS ON A VACATION OR A RELATIVE OR MOM AND DADS FRIENDS VISITS. IN OTHER WORDS MY WHOLE LIFE AT AGE 9 WAS MY NEIGHBORHOOD. THE FRIENDS IN THE NEIGHBORHOOD AND THE COMPETITION OF PEOPLE THAT I PLAYED WITH THAT MAY NOT HAVE BEEN FRIENDS BUT COMPETITION FOR SPORTS ARE IN THE NEIGHBORHOOD ARE 1.FREND DANNY GORMAN, MY BROTHERS BEST FRIEND 2. ACQUANTANCE MIKE AND 3. FRIEND LANCE AND 4. ACQUANTANCE MICHELLE FOLDEN AND 5. FRIEND MONIQUE FOLDEN. ON OUR STREET CINDERELLA 6. FRIEND GERRY TAPOHOIA, 7. FRIEND JOHNNY SUN SMILES AND HIS 8, ACQUANTANCE-SISTER 9. FRIEND HARRY 10. ACQUANTANCE CRAIG MAUDLIN AND 11. ACQUANTANCE LEE MAUDLIN, THEY WERE ON LEWIS COURT ACROSS THE STREET. 12. ACQUANTANCE JIMMY AND 13. ACQUANTANCE-TOMMIE KNAPP AND 14. ACQUANTANCE ROBERT AND 15. ACQUANTANCE BILLY KNAPP AND THE HUFFMANS 16. ACQUANTANCE KAREN AND 17. FRIEND JOHN. THEY WERE ON LEWIS COURT 18. ACQUANTANCE LANAI BACHELDER. SHE WAS 2 HOUSES UP, THE MORENO BROTHERS 19.FRIEND ROBERT, 20. FRIEND ROY 21 ACQUANTANCE LUPE AND 22. FRIEND ARTHUR AND 23. ACQUANTANCE RICHARD. THEN 25. FRIEND KEVIN LYMAN ON NOTRE DAME AS WELL AS 26. FRIEND JIM BUNTE ON DE PAUL WITH AND NEXT TO THE MORENOS. 27. ENEMY RALPH CHAPPOINIE. NOT A FRIEND BUT A SPORTS COMPETITOR THEN ON MARYGROVE 28. FRIEND GREG HANDZIAC AND HIS BROTHER 29. ACQUANTANCE LITTLE RED WHO HAD THE HARDEST TO GET OUT HEADLOCKS EVER. THEN 30-31 ACQUANTANCE THE-PERRY BROTHER AS WELL AS 32.FRIEND JOHN SQUEEK HENDERSON AND 33.ACQUANTANCE GREG LYMAN, GREG IS BROTHER OF KEVIN ON NOTRE DAME 34.

ACQUANTANCE JOHN JOHN EAGLETON ON NOTRE DAME AND SQUEEK ON MARYGROVE. THEN OUR ENEMIES WHO WE PLAYED SPORTS AGAINST IN THE NEIGHBORHOOD. 35 ENEMY STEVE TIPPING 36 ENEMY JEFF KERN 37. ENEMY TIMMY TIPPING AND 8. ENEMY DALE KERN AND 39. ACQUANTANCE-DAYLENE KERN WHO SHE WAS NOT AN ENEMY 40. ENEMY BILLY AND 41.-SUPER ENEMY ALAN PITS AND 42. SUPER ENEMY MARK AND 43. ENEMY MIKE MALAZZO 44. FRIEND DOUG ROSS AND 45.ACQUANTANCE SCOTTY RAY WHO WAS ON DE PAUL THE REST WERE THE GUILFORD GANG AS WELL AS 46. ALSO 47. BEST FRIEND PHIL WOOTTON AND FRIEND GLEN EARLEMEYER 48 AND 49 THE WOOTTON BROTHERS, FRIEND-DON AND ACQUANTANCE TURNER,-THERE WAS 50 ACQUANTANCE MARTY YARBOROUG AS WELL AS THE ACQUANTANCE THE FLOYDS 51-52 AND 53. ACQUANTANCE-FLOYD ADAMS AND 54 FRIEND LENZEL BROWN AS WELL AS 55. ACQUANTANCE JOHNNY FELIX LIVING NEXT TO KEVIN LYMAN AND THE ACQUANTANCES FIEST BROTHERS 56 AND 57 AND 58 JFRIEND JASON ENEMY SHELLY AND ENEMY ALEX AND 59 FRIENDS, FRIEND HEATHER AND 60.FRIEND EON, SOME FOREIGN EXCHASNGE KIDS FROM HOLLAND. 61. ACROSS FROM INDIAN HILL ON BORDER OF POMONA AND CLAREMONT WAS FRIEND CRAIG REED, LATER ON A GOOD SKATEBOARD EXPLORER AND FRIEND 62. MY OLD ORIENTEL CHINEESE FRIEND THOMAS LEE AS WELL AS 63 LITTLE BROTHER FRIEND GEE GEE LEE AS WELL AS 64, OLDER BROTHER AND PROTECTOR FRIEND-MARK LI. 65 FRIEND JAMES AND 66.ACQUANTANCE DAVID BENSON 66 WHO I TRADED MY ORIGIONAL BEATLE ALBUMS FOR HIS OLD 60S AND 50S CARDS HE RECIEVED FROM HIS BROTHER ACQUANTANCE KENNY. ALSO THERE WAS FRIEND 67 JIMMY CAFFEE ON MARYGROVE AVENUE. I LIVED IN THIS NEIGHBORHOOD UNTIL I WAS 21 FULLY AND THEN OFF AND ON LIVED AT THE SAME HOUSE TILL I WAS 50. THOUGH I LIVED AND PAID RENT ALSO WITH MY NOW

WIFE GAILS APARTMENT- SINSE I WAS 32 AND THROUGHOUT THE 80S I WAS LIVING EVERYWHERE FROM HOMELESS IN POMONA TO HOMELESS AT VISTA PARK TO POMONA KAREN HARLENS HOUSE THROWING PARTIES FOR A LIVING TO LIVING AT PAT HICOX MY PARTNERS PRINT SHOP FOR 6 MONTHS TO LIVING AT SUNRISA APARTMENTS IN 1982. LMOST TO 83. BASICALLY I LIVED FULL TIME THERE UNTIL I WAS ALMOST 21 MEANING 20. I WAS BLESSED TO STAY AT THE SAME PLACE SO I CAN ESTABLISH LONG TIME FRIENDS. THE SAME FRIENDS FROM KINDERGARDEN TO 12TH GRADE AND THEN SOME. MY SON THOUGH LIVING WITH HIS MOM AND BROTHERS AND SISTERS LIVED AT 21 DIFFERENT PLACES BEFORE HE HIT AGE 18. I DONT AGREE WJTH THAT LIFESTYLE BUT IT WAS OUT OF MY POWER BEING ANNIE HAD FULL CUSTUDY WITH CHARLIE MY SON AT ONE TIME CHARLIE EVEN LIVED WALKING DISTANCE FROM MOMS WHERE I WAS STAYING PART TIME. IT IS QUITE A BLESSING TO HAVE 67 PEOPLE TO PLAY WITH AND COMPETE WITH AND GROW UP WITH FROM AGE 5. 8. -ALMOST EVERY HOUSE HAD KIDS AND ALWAYS MORE THEN ONE.

KEVIN AND THE INDIANS AND THE HUSKIES.

KEVIN WAS ON THE INTERMEDIATE LEAGUE TEAM ENTILED THE INDIANS AND I WAS ON THE HUSKIES. OUR WON-LOST RECORD WAS 3-17 AND WE BEAT THE FIRST PLACE TEAM 24-16 ON LAST GAME. II DONT KNOW HOW WE DID IT BUT WE DID WHEN PLAYING THE INDIANS I REMEMBER KEVIN WAS ON THIRD BASE AS I WAS PUT IN TO PITCH. I WALKED THE FIRST TWO BATTERS THEN GOT TWO STRIKES ON THE NEXT BATTER AS IT WAS BASES LOADED AND HE SWUNG BUT THE UMPIRE CALLED IT A BALL. I GOT SO MAD I STARTED A RAGEFUL SCENE AND THREW MY MIT DOWN AND WALKED OFF THE MOUND. KEVIN COULD HAVE RAN HOME TO SCORE BUT DIDNT. THIS IS THE ONLY MEMORY I

HAVE OF KEVIN WAS ON THIRD BASE. THEY BEAT US THAT DAY AND KEVIN DIDNT SCORE AS I GOT BACK ON THE MOUND AND STRUCK THE GUY OUT.

KEVINS BAR MITZ VAH. YES, I WAS INVITED TO KEVINS BAR MITZ VAH. I REMEMBER HIM READING STUFF IN JEWISH LANGUAGE. IT SOUNDED LIKE HE REALLY DID HIS HOMEWORK. WHEN I GOT THERE I SAW LITTLE SHOTS OF LIQUID. I ASKED THE RABBIS IF THAT WAS APPLE JUICE AND THEY LAUGHED AND SAID IT WAS. I TOOK ABOUT 4 SHOTS. IT TASTED LIKE ROT. GUESS WHY? IT WAS HARD LIQUOR. IM GUESSING WHISKY OR TAQUILA BEING IT WAS BROWN.

NOW I KNOW WHY THEY CALL IT ROTGUT.

IT WAS FUNNY TO THEM AND THEY WERE BUSTED UP WITH LAUGHTER AND I THEN REALIZED IT WAS ALCOHOL AFTER THE RABBIS TOLD ME IT WAS ALCOHOL FINALLY.I THEN WAITED TO FEEL THE BUZZ AND THERE NEVER WAS A BUZZ. NOT EVEN AFTER 4 OR 5 SHOTS OF HARD LIQUOR. I SHOULD HAVE KNOWN ALCOHOL WILL NOT BE GOOD FOR ME.

IN THE END I BECAME AN ALCOHOLIC. I AGAIN SHOULD HAVE KNOWN BY THE WARNING SIGNS OF WHAT JUST HAPPENED AT THE BAR MITZ VAH WITH THE 4-5 SHOTS OF HARD LIQUOR I JUST DRANK.

THE BASEBALL CARDS. LIFTING WEIGHTS AND WATCHING BILL WALTON.

I REMEMBER ONE THING WITH KEVIN ABOUT BASEBALL CARDS. WE WOULD TRADE AND NEXT WE WERE ACTUALLY STEALING CARDS IN FRONT OF EACH OTHER. IT WAS WEIRD BUT THATS WHAT WE DID. I REMEMBER KOUFAX GOING TO HIM BUT I GOT A WILLIE MAYS. IT WAS ALL GOOD.

WE LIFTED WEIGHTS WITH GREG WHO WAS KEVINS BROTHER AND MY BROTHER AND ME AND KEVIN AND MR LYMAN. IT WAS THE FIRST TIME I EVER LIFTED WEIGHTS AND I PRETTY MUCH LOST INTEREST IN IT AS DID KEVIN. SO MY BROTHER JOHN AND GREG AND MR LYMAN STILL KEPT IT UP IN THE LYMANS GARAGE FOR THE NEXT FEW YEARS.

ME AND KEVIN WERE SPORT PEOPLE AND LOVED TO PLAY AND EVEN MORE WATCH COLLEGE BASKETBALL AT THE TIME BILL WALTON WAS AROUND. ME AND KEVIN AND MR LYMAN WATCHED ON WEEKENDS THE BILL WALTON UCLA GAMES AS AND WHEN BILL WALTON WAS A COLLEGE STANDOUT.

I LATER LOST TOUCH WITH KEVIN ESPECIALLY WHEN HE WENT TOWARDS THE GUILFORD GANG RATHER THEN ME AND PHIL AND LANCE ON CINDERELLA AND WHERE WE WERE NOT A GANG THOUGH TO MAKE GUILFORD FEEL JUSTIFIED TO BE A GANG THEY CALLED US THR CINDERELLA GANG WHICH WAS NOT AT ALL TRUE. WE DEFINATELY WERE NOT A GANG.

LATER ON IN JUNIOR HIGH WE WERE STILL FRIENDS TO A LESSER DEGREE AND THEN BY HIGH SCHOOL I DIDNT REALLY EVER SEE KEVIN.

LATER IN COLLEGE AROUND 1983 WHEN ME AND KEVIN WERE AROUND 22, KEVIN WAS BORN ON APRIL 5TH 1961 AND I WAS APRIL 16TH 1961. 11 DAYS APART. IN COLLEGE ME AND KEVIN BECAME FRIENDS AGAIN.

WHAT I REMEMBERED FROM COLLEGE ABOUT KEVIN.

IT WAS 1983 AND MY DAD DROPPED ME OFF AT CITRUS COLLEGE TO GET SOME PAPERWORK FROM AN OPEN CLASS. I GET THE PAPERS AND THEN GO TO THE CAFETERIA TO SAY HI TO A LADY IM FRIENDS WITH THAT

WORKS THERE AND AS I AM LEAVING I RUN ACROSS KEVIN LYMAN. AS I SEE KEVIN IN THE CAFETERIA I REMEMBER HIM TO THIS DAY WEARING LONG JOHN FARM CLOTHS AND HE WAS REAL NICE AND FRIENDLEY AND I REMEMBER TO THIS DAY HIM TELLING ME HIS FUTURE THAT HE IS GOING TO THROW BIG CONCERTS OF LOCAL BANDS TO GET THEM NOTICED.

WELL , KEVIN DID THAT AND NOW HE IS A MILLILONAIRE AND THE FOUNDER OF THE WARP TOUR, USA BIGGEST CONCERT VENUE FOR THE LAST FEW YEARS. BASICALLY KEVIN LYMAN IS THE BILL GRAHAM THIS GENERATION.

IN 2012 ON NEW YEARS WAS THE LAST TIME I HEARD FROM ANYONE FROM KEVIN OR HIS FAMILY. ON THIS DAY JAN 1 2012 I DIDNT TALK TO KEVIN BUT I DID GET A VISIT FROM HIS SISTER BARBARA AND SHE WANTED TO HAVE ME GO TO ONE OF KEVINS PARTIES AT HIS RESIDENCE IN SAN MORENO AND SURPRISE HIM. BARBARA WAS BETTING HE WOULDNT RECORGNISE ME AND THEREFORE I COULD SURPRISE HIM AT THE PARTY. NEVER GOT TO GO TO THAT PARTY OR THOSE PARTIES. THOUGH IN 1980 I WENT TO ONE OF KEVINS PARTIES AT THE BEACH AT ELISO BEACH.

AND THAT IS MY HISTORY WITH KEVIN LYMAN AND HIS FAMILY.

4 AND 5, MIKE WEAVER AND VAN EVERS.

I TALK ABOUT EACH OF THE GUYS TOGETHER BECAUSE WE USED TO JACOUSI TOGETHER WITH WOMEN AND WIVES. MIKE HAD A GIRLFRIEND AND USED TO LIVE IN CLAREMONT ACROSS FROM MOMS IN SOME APARTMENTS, SOME REAL NICE APARTMENTS.

WE USED TO GO SWIMMING AND LAY OUT IN THE SUN AND JACOUSI THERE. WE USED TO JACOUSI WITH MIKE WEAVER AND VAN EVERS CAME TO THE JACOUSI WITH

FRIENDS OF MINE BRUCE DANIELS. WE ALL USED TO PARTY TOGETHER AND HAVE FUN--MIKE WAS A COOL GUY AND VAN IS TOO.

I DIDNT KNOW AT THAT TIME WHO MEDGER EVERS WAS AND PEOPLE KEPT SAYING VAN IS SON OF MEDGER EVERS AND I DIDNT CONNECT IT BUT YEARS LATER I LEARNED THE HISTORY OF VANS DAD WHO WAS UNFORTUNATELY ASSASSANATED IN THE SOUTH BACK IN THE 60S AND THE CIVIL RIGHTS ERA.

I SEEN MIKE THROUGHOUT MY LIFE AND SAID HELLO. HE HAD A WHITE CORVETTE AT THE TIME AND LAST TIME I SAW HIM WAS AT SEARS GETTING INTO HIS CORVETTE. A FEW YEARS LATER MIKE WEAVER WAS A HEAVYWEIGHT BOXING CHAMP FOR A TIME.

I SAW VAN AT VARIOUS PARTIES AND HE WAS IN OUR CIRCLE OF FRIENDS OR SHOULD I SAY IN MANY CIRCLES OF OUR FRIENDS.

I LAST SAW VAN WITH BRUCE AT A PARTY AT THE CLAREMONT COLLEGES. CLAREMONT MENS COLLEGE TO BE EXACT WE PARTIED AND HAD A GREAT TIME LIKE ALWAYS. BRUCE LATER PASSED ON I BELEIVE IN 2015. SO BASICALLY THE LAST TIME I HUNG OUT WITH VAN AND BRUCE WAS 1988 OR 89.

6. RODNEY KING

I HAVE CAME ACROSS RODNEY KING ALOT. AROUND 4 OR 5 TIMES. 1. WHEN I WAS IN   BERDOO COUNTY JAIL HE WAS THERE SWEEPING THE FLOORS. ANOTHER TIME WHEN HE HAD HIS WEALTH I WAS PANHANDLING IN LA VERNE AND HE WAS COMING OUT OF A SUSHI RERSTRAUNT AND HE WAS KIND ENOUGH TO GIVE ME 10 DOLLORS. A TEN DOLLOR BILL. I SAW HIM ON THE BUS IN LATER YEARS AND I WAS ABOUT TO ASK HIM IF I CAN DO AN

INTRVIEW WITH HIM BUT HE GOT OFF ON THE NEXT STOP. ALSO SAW HIM AT HAVEN COURTHOUSE AS WELL AS HIM ON A BUS STOP--A DOWN TO EARTH GUY AND REALLY NICE AND FRIENDLEY AND UNASSUMING. OH YES AND ONE OTHER TIME ON THE BUS AFTER MY GIRFRIEND GOT ARRESTED AND I RAN UP TO THE BUS WITH HER CLOTHS AS I TOOK FOR HER SAFE KEEPING RODNEY WAS THE GUY HELPOING ME GET ON THE BUS WITH ALL MY STUFF WHICH WAS LIKE 4 BAGS.

7. EDDIE VAN HALEN AND 8. VALERIE BERTENELLI

THIS WAS JUST DESTENY. MY SON AND VALERIES SON WAS IN THE SAME KARATE CLASS IN MONTCLARE CALIFORNIA. I WOULD SEE VALERIE EVERY WEEK AND I WAS THE CASHIER THERE AND DID IT TO GET A DISCOUNT FOR MY SONS KARATE CLASS AND EVERY TIME AND WEEK I WOULD SAY HI AND THEN I RECOGNIZED HER. SHE WAS AT THAT TIME WITH A BLONDE HAIR DO. THIS WAS 1999 TO 2002. IT WAS A WONDERFUL TIME IN LIFE BEING THAT MY DAUGHTER JOINED TOO AND SHE WAS JUST 4 AND 5 YEARS OF AGE AND CHARLIE MY SON WAS ALSO YOUNG HE WAS 7 TO 10 YEARS OLD. SON AND HER SON GOT ALONG GREAT AND WERE BEST OF FRIENDS IN THE CLASS.

VALERIE WAS COOL BUT SHE WAS DEFINATELEY IN COGNITO AND AT THIS TIME IN HER LIFE WAS ON THE DOWN LOW IF YOU WANT TO CALL IT THAT.

I REMEMBER ONCE SHE SAID SHE DIDNT HAVE A CD PLAYER SO I GAVE HER ONE AND THE KARATE TEACHER SAID, "SEE YOU STILL HAVE FANS". I DIDNT GIVE IT TO HER BECAUSE I WAS A FAN BUT I GAVE IT TO HER BECAUSE SHE SAID SHE DIDNT HAVE ONE.

I WAS TO GET ON A TV SHOW FOR SOME STUFF INVOLVING GIRLFRIENDS ETC AND IT WASNT A TRUE STORY AND IT

WAS ON THE SHOW CALLED FORGIVE AND FORGET. I ASKED VALERIE IF SHE WOULD BE ON THE SHOW WITH ME TO BE A FAKE AS AN ACT GIRLFRIEND AND SHE ASKED ME IF THE STORY IS TRUE AND I SAID NO AND SHE DIDNT DO IT. BUT SHE WAS NICE ABOUT IT. ONCE I WAS TO BABYSIT VALERIES AND EDDYS KID AS WELL AS MY KID OUTSIDE OF THE KARATE STUDEO AND SHE WAS REAL OVER PROTETIVE AND ALMOST THREATENING TO ME ABOUT MAKING SURE NOTHING BAD HAPPENS.

BUT SHE STILL WAS COO. ONCE I BROUGHT A FRIEND OF MINE NAMED JANET TO SHOW HER VALERIE BERTENELLI AND IT WAS QUITE UNCOMFORTABLE TO ALL OF US INCLUDING ME AND JANET AS WELL AS VALERIE BECAUSE VALERIE KNEW I WAS SHOWING HER TO JANET KIND OF IN AN ADULT SHOW AND TELL WAY WHICH NOW I LOOK BACK I FEEL I WAS WRONG TO DO THAT BUT NO HARM DONE AND JANET WAS QUITE STAR STRUCK BEING SHE WAS A FEW YEARS OLDER THEN ME AND VALERIE. VALERIE IS A YEAR OR TWO OLDER THEN ME. I WAS BORN I 1961 AND I BELEIVE VALERIE WAS BORN IN 1960 OR 59.

I WAS ALWAYS WONDERING WHERE EDDIE WAS AND THE BAND HAD BROKEN UP AND AT THIS TIME HAD NO SINGER. THERE LAST WAS A GUY GARY CHERONE. HE WAS FIRED SO THERE WAS NO SINGER AT THIS TIME SO I WROTE VALERIE A NOTE IF I CAN MEET EDDIE AND POSSIBLY AUDITION FOR VAN HALEN. SHE NEVER RESPONDED AND I BELEIVE SHE FELT I WAS USING HER WHICH I WASNT BUT I DID FEEL THAT SHE FELT THAT WAY BECAUSE AFTER THAT SHE HAD A LITTLE BIT OF A DIFFERENT ATTITUDE TOWARDS ME.

FINALLY EDDIE CAME TO A KARATE PRACTICE AND THEN HE CAME ALOT. ONCE EDDIE AND I WERE OUT IN THE SQUARE IN FRONT OF THE ENTRANCE TO THE KARATE STUDEO AND HE WAS SMOKING A CIGERETTE AND I HAD

RFECENTLY HEARD THAT HE HAD TONGUE CANCER. I ASSUMBED IT WAS FROM SMOKING SO I CARINGLEY SAID TO HIM, "YOIU SHOULDNT BE SMOKING" AND HE PLAYFULLY GAVE ME THE MIDDLE FINGER AND SMILED.

IT WAS ALL GOOD. EDDIE WAS A HUMBLE CARING GUY AND HE LOOKS QUITE DUTCH AT TIME BEING HE IS FROM HOLLAND.

THE KARATE FINALLY ENEDED AND I HADNT SEEN VALERIE SINSE SUMMER OF 2001 WHEN I LAST BROUGHT JANET THERE TO MEET HER. BY 2001, SUMMER THE KIDS HAD QUIT KARATE. MY KIDS THAT IS. IN 2008 I WENT THERE TO SEE IF THE PLACE WAS STILL INVOLVING KARATE AND IT WAS JUST NOT YOUNG OLYMPIONS WHICH WAS THE CORPORATON IT WAS UNDER WITH THAT NAME BACK THEN. NOW IT HAD A DIFFERENT NAME BUT THE KIDS WERE STILL IN THAT ROOM DOING KARATE.

ME AND MY 2 KIDS HAD A WONDERFUL TIME IN THOSE DAYS. I WILL NEVER FORGET THE MAGIC OF THOSE TIMES.

9. JEFFREY DAMNER

THIS WAS PRETTY MUCH THE ONLY FAMOUS PERSON I WISH I NEVER HAD MET. IT WAS IN 1985 AROUND THE SUMMER OR LATE SPRING MAY OR JUNE OR JULY. I WAS IN A DEPRESSION AND WAS IN CLAREMONT ON FOOTHILL BLVD.

IT WAS A LIQUOR STORE I WAS IN FRONT OF AND I WAS ON MY 4TH OR 5TH BEER AND FEELING PRETTY GOOD. ALL OF A SUDDEN THIS GUY CAME UP AND STARTING TALKING TO ME. HE WAS FRIENDLEY AND SORT OF A TOUGH PERSONNA. I GAVE HIM A BEER AND THEN ANOTHER.

HE SEEMED NORMAL AND SAID HIS NAME IS JEFF. HE SAID HE WALKED 25 MILES AND HE SAID HIM AND HIS DAD WERE

IN AN ARGUMENT. IT WAS NOT TRUE BECAUSE JEFFS DAD WAS NEVER IN CALIFORNIA I DONT BELEIVE.

WE GET ALONG REAL GOOD AND ARE BOTH GETTING GOOD BUZZES FROM DRINKING AND WE THEN DECIDE TO HANG OUT FURTHER AND LIVE IN THE OUTSIDE. IM MENTELLY ILL AT THIS TIME. WE GO TO DADS AND HE GIVES ME THE SHELL GAS CARD AND SAYS GOOD LUCK TO ME AND JEFF.

WE GET TO LAGOONA BEACH AND IT IS WARM AND BEAUTIFUL AND NOT CROWDED. IT IS STILL THE DAYTIIME AND JEFF IS IN A GREAT MOOD AND I AM HAVING FUN. WE ARE PANHANDLING FOR MORE ALCOHOL AND MAYBE COCAINE IF WE CAN FIND SOME.

NOW IT BECOMES NIGHT TIME AND JEFF ACTS DIFFERETLY. I LAY MY BLANKET DOWN OUTSIDE OF THE CAR TO SLEEP AND I SEE JEFF BEHIND ME STANDING OVER ME AND I GET THIS CHILLING VIBE EVEN TO THIS DAY 35 YEARS LATER AS THIS WAS 1985.

I THEN KNEW HE WAS GOING TO KILL ME IN A WEAKEN STATE, WHILE SLEEPING. YES, AT THIS TIME I SENSED THAT HE WAS GOING TO BASH MY HEAD IN WITH A BIG ROCK. THERE WAS COINCIDENTELY A BIG ROCK NRXT TO WHERE I WAS SLEEPING AND JEFF WANTED TO MOVE THE ROCK TO SUPPOSIDELEY CARE ABOUT ME BEING MORE COMFORTABLE WHILE SLEEPING. I SAW THROUGH IIT AND NOW HES KNOWN AS ONE OF THE WORST SERIAL KILLERS IN AMERICAN AND WORLD HISTORY.

I TOLD HIM THERE STRAIGHT UP. I GOTTA TAKE YOU BACK. HE WAS IN SHOCK AND WAS UPSET.

THE DRIVE HOME.

AS WE DROVE HOME HE WAS MAD AND IT SHOWED HEAVILY ON HIS FACE. HE WAS SO MAD THAT HE DIDNT TALK.

DROPPING HIM OFF.

I DROPPED HIM OFF IN WEST COVINA IN A LITTLE ONE ROOM APARTMENT TYPE SHACK SO HE LIED. HE HAD A PLACE-I SAID SEE YA LATER AND HE GOT OUT AND DIDNT SAY A WORD AND SLAMMED THE DOOR. HIS ANGER ON HIS FACE WAS SO ANGRY IF LOOKS COULD KILL I WOULD BE DEAD. AND THAT WAS THE EDND OF MY ACQUANTANCE WITH JEFF DAMNER.

10. NATALEE COLE.

I FIRST MET NATALEE ON HOLT BLVD SHE WAS HANGING OUT IN FRONT OF A HOTEL SHE WAS STAYING AT. NATALEE LIKES TO BE AWAY FROM THE GLITZ AND GLAM OF HOLLYWOOD AND I TRULY BELEIVE SHE CANT STAND IT BUT SHE DOES TOLORATE IT IN HER NATALEE PERSONALITY. NATALEE IN MY OPINION HAS MORE THEN ONE PERSONALITY AS DOES MOST OF THESE METHOD ACTORS I HAVE BEFRIENDED OR CAME ACROSS.

NATALEE ALSO HAS A PERSONALITY NAMED DORTHY AND DORTHY IS THE ONE WHO LIKES TO PARTY. AT THIS TIME WAS WAS IN THE WINTER OF 2001 I WAS COMING BACK FROM A BAND PRACTICE FROM A BAND CALLED CRY BABY. I WAS KEYBOARDIST AND I WAS CRUISING AROUND AND SAW NATALEE. WE BECAME FRIENDS. I ASKED HER IF SHE WOULD SING ON MY LET IT BE COVER VERSION OF THE BEATLES AND SHE SAID SHE DIDNT LIKE THE "NARE NARE" SOUNDS OF THE THE LEAD GUITAR" SO SHE DIDNT AND WOULDNT DO THAT. STUDEO WORK THAT IS. I FINISHED THE SONG ANYWAYS IN THE STUDEO IN 2003.

ME AND NATALEE HUNG OUT ABOUT 3 OR 4 TIMES MAYBE MORE IN THE POMONA AREA. I ALSO SAW HER ON THE BUS AND THERE WAS WHERE SHE WAS DRESSED LIKE A BOBBY SOXER FROM THE MID TO LATE 60S. SHE TOLD ME SHE WAS NATALEE AND THEN ASKED IF I WANTED TO MEET HER DORTHY PERSONALITY. I GOT OFF THE BUS WITH HER AND WE WERE TALKING AWHILE. SHE WAS THERE TO MEET HER DAUGHTER WHO WAS TO PICK HER UP.

NATALEE CAME TO MOMS HOUSE A COUPLE TIMES TOO AND WE HUNG OUT.

THEN IN TENNESSEE, THE DRAKE HOTEL NASHVILLE ACTUALLY MURPHYSBOUROUGH.

THIS WAS AN AMAZING COINCIDENCE WHEN I WENT TO TENNESSEE AND NORTH CAROLINA AS WELL AS TAKING THE 40 THROUGH BARSTOW TO FLAGSTAFF ARIZONA TO ALBERQUERQUE NEW MEXICO AS WELL AS ALBERQUERQUE, TEXAS AND OAKLAHIOMA CITY AMONG OTHER PLACES LIKE LITTLE ROCK ARKANSAS. WELL, WHEN I GOT TO TENNESSEE MY NEXT DOOR NEIGHBOR AT THE DRAKE HOTEL WAS NATALEE COLE AND A FRIEND. WE WOUND UP LIVING TOGETHER AND WE LIVED TOGETHER AROUND A WEEK. AT NIGHT SHE USED TO LIKE TO PLAY CARDS LATE AT NIGHT WITH THE HOMEYS. NATALEE HAS A STREET PERSONALITY AND SHE WAS IN THIS PERSONALITY. THE PERSONALITY SHE LIKES TO CALL HERSELF IS NOT NATALEE BUT DORTHY.

NATALEE WAS FUN AND WE WERE AGREEING TO MOVE TO ANOTHER HOTEL WHICH I PUT MONEY DOWN ON THE PLACE AND THEN I GOT STUFF FROM A FRIEND OF HERS AND WE WERE MOVING IN. THE DAY BEFORE I WAS LEAVING FOR NORTH CAROLINA I TOLD HER I WOULD BE BACK IN A WEEK AND SHE DIDNT BELEIVE ME AND SHE STOLE 105 DOLLORS FROM ME I HAD ON THE TABLE. I

COULDNT FIND HER SO I PUT HER STUFF OUT IN THE FRONT OF THE ROOM AND LEFT FOR NORTH CAROLINA

WHEN I GOT BACK FROM NORTH CAROLINA.

I COME BACK AND GO AGAIN TO THE DRAKE HOTEL IN NORTH CAROLINA. I SEE NATALEE WALKING TO ONE OF THE ROOMS I TELL HER SHE TOOK MY LAST 105 DOLLORS BEFORE I LEFT AND SHE SAID SHE WAS MAD THAT SHE NEEDED THE MONEY AND THAT SHE WAS UPSET THAT I AGREED TO HAVE ME AND HER LIVE TOGETHER AND THEN GO TO NORTH CAROLINA. TOLD HER I WOULD BE BACK AND THEN MOVE WITH HER. SHE GOT UPSET AND LEFT. WE GOT INTO AN ARGUMENT AND I TOLD HER I WOULD TELL PEOPLE THAT SHE WAS NATALEE. NATALEE WAS HIDING AND NOT SAYING WHO SHE WAS AND THOSE THAT DIDNT KNOW HER WOULD NOT KNOW IT IS NATALEE. I KNEW HER FROM ONTARIO AND FROM LOS ANGELES AND HOLT BLVD IN POMONA AND SO I KNEW IT WAS NATALEE. I SAID IF SHE DOESNT GIVE ME MY 105 DOLLORS OR I WOULD TELL ALL THE PEOPLE WHO SHE IS. I TOLD PEOPLE WHO SHE WAS THEN AND SHE ADMITTED WHO SHE WAS TO THE PEOPLE WHO WERE THEN STAR STRUCK AND THEN SHE LEFT IN A WHITE TRUCK. BEFORE SHE LEFT I TOLD HER SHE NEEDS TO GET BACK INTO MUSIC. ThAT THIS WAS MY OPINION AND I WAS GOING TO EXPRESS MY VIEWS ABOUT IT. I TOLD SHE SHOULD DO A TOUR AND GET ON AMERICAN IDOL TO BE A PERSON TO HAVE THEM DO HER PAST MUSIC ,THE CONTESTENTS THAT IS.

SHE DID AND A FEW MONTHS LATER I SAW NATALEE ON ONE OF THOSE IDOL SHIOWS AND HEARD SHE WENT ON A TOUR IN VIRGIN ISLANDS OR HAITI.

ALL IN ALL I FEEL SAID THAT WE COULDNT HAVE HUNG OUT LONGER. I ALWAYS FELT WE WOULD HAVE ANOTHER CHANCE AND WE NEVER DID AS SHE DIED IN 2016 OR 15.

I CARE ABOUT HER AND SHE WAS A COOL FRIEND. ONCE WE HAD A GREAT TIME EATING PULL PORK AND THIS WAS THE TIME WHERE I FIRST HEARD OF THE NAME PULL PORK.

NATALEE WAS A COOL FRIEND.

11. JASON BATEMAN

I LEARNED TO PLAY PIANO ON MR SMITHS, AKA MARK FERGERSONS MOTHERS PIANO WHEN SMITH LIVED IN UPLAND WITH HIS MOM. I COULDNT PLAY A NOTE UP UNTIL THIS MOMENT. I GOT ON MY KNEES IN FRONT OF THE PIANO AND PRAYED TO GOD JESUS CHRIST THE FATHER, SON AND HOLY SPIRIT TO PLAY. I GOT UP ANS IMMEDIATELEY STARTED PLAYING CHORDS ALONG WITH NEW COORDINATION IN MY FINGERS TO PLAY THAT I NEVER HAD BEFORE UP TO THIS MOMENT THAT I PRAYED TO GOD.

SINSE THIS MOMENT IN 1985 IN WHICH I WAS BLESSED BY GOD MIRACULASLEY TO PLAY AND FROM THERE I THEN PRACTICED AT THE PIANIO ROOM AT THE CLAREMONT COLLEGES.

1987. HEADING TO PRACTICE AT THE CLAREMONT COLLEGES.

AROUND EARLY 1987 ME AND ROLAND WERE PLAYING BASKETBALL WITH FRIENDS NEAR THE COLLEGES. ALL OF A SUDDEN IT STARTED TO POUR RAIN AND WE WENT TO FIND SHELTER. A GUY AT THE FRAT HOUSE ON TH4 CORNER OF COLLEGE AND 2ND STREET INVITED US TO COME IN AND DRY OFF. THERE HE GOT US A NEW SHIRT EACH AND THREW THE OTHER WET CLOTHS IN THE DRYER THERE. HE LEFT FOR A MOMENT TO PUT AWAY THE CLOTHS IN THE DRYER. WHILE HE WAS GONE FOR THAT MOMENT TWO GIRLS CAME IN AND DIDNT SAY ANYTHING LOOKED AT US LIKE THEY SAW TWO GHOSTS AND RAN OFF.

WE THOUGHT NOTHING OF IT UNTIL WE FOUND OUT WHAT THEY JUST DID. THEY CALLED THE POLICE ON US SAYING WE WERE BURGLERS.

COPS GET ON THE SCENE.

1 COP GETS ON THE SCENE WHO HATES ME ALREADY SO HE DIDNT HEAR THE TRUTH OR WANT TO HEAR IT. THE TRUTH WAS TOLD TO HIM FROM THE GUY WHO LIVED THERE THAT LET US IN. THE GUY TOLD COP LIONEL BROWN THE COP THAT HE INVITED US IN THE FRAT HOUSE TO DRY OFF FROM THE POURING RAIN STORM OUTSIDE THAT JUST STARTED ABOUT AN HOUR EARLIER.

ALL HE HEARD THAT IS LIONEL BROWN IS LIONEL JUST HEARD TWO GIRLS WERE SCARED OF CREEPY LOOKING GUYS WHOS HAIR WERENT COMBED. WELL, OUR HAIR WAS COMBED, ITS JUST THAT THE RAIN MESSED OUR HAIR UP BUT NO, LIONEL MADE ME SIGN A PAPER THAT I AM NEVER ALLOWED TO GO TO ANY PROPERTY OWNED BY THE CLAREMONT COLEGES. AT FIRST I SAID I WASNT GOING TO SIGN IT AND HE SAID IF I DIDNT SIGN IT I WOULD BE ARRESTED RIGHT THERE AND NOW, SO I WAS FORCED TO SIGN IT. I KNOW NOWADAYS COPS WERE NOT THIS CURRUPT BUT THIS IS 1987 32 YEARS AG0.

I SIGNED IT RELUCTANTLEY BUT I SIGNED IT. I HAD TO EVEN THOUGH IF I WOULD HAVE GOT ARRESTED FOR GOING IN THERE. IT WOULD HAVE BEEN DROPPED. I STILL DIDNT FEEL LIKE BEING ARESTED FOR A COUPLE DAYS FROM LIONELS ARREST RIGHT THERE.

NOW ITS A YEAR LATER.

I AM WALKING UP TO THE PIANO ROOM AND EVEN THOUGH I SIIGNED I CAN NEVER COME ONTO ANY PROPERTY OF THE CLAREMONT 5 COLLEGES WHICH INCLUDE THE PIANO ROOM WHERE I PRACTICE AT SINSE I STARTED PLAYING

PIANO AFTER BEING BLESSED TO LEARN HOW TO PLAY PIANO IN 1985 LEARNING AT MARK FERGERSONS HOHSE AND GARAGE, AKA MR SMITH.

WELL, I KNOW THAT THE COPS WILL NEVER KNOW I AM STILL GOING TO THE PIANO ROOM AS LONG AS I AM NOT CAUSING PROBLEMS OR STANDING OUT.

SO ON THIS DAY IN 1988 I WAS WALKING THERE AND COPS ARE BY THERE. THAT JS THE PIANO ROOMS AND THEY ARE THERE BECAUSE THESE COPS ARE PROTECTING A SET FOR A MOVIE CALLED TEEN WOLF 2.

AS I WALK BY THE COIPS TELL ME I CANT WALK THIS WAY AND TELL ME TO WALK TOWARDS THE MOVIE SET. I TOLD THEM THIS WOULD NOT BE A GOOD IDEA TO WALK THROUGH THE SET AND THNEY SAID NO, THAT THEY THE FILM CREW AND ACTORS ARE ON A BREAK.

IT WAS OFFICER JENKINS AS WELL AS A COUPLE OTHERS. THEY TOLD ME I MUST WALK IN THIS DIRECTION. THEY WERE LIEING AND JUST TRYING TO AMUSE THEMSELVES ON MY BEHALF.

I START WALKING ON THE SET AREA AND THERE I SEE STANDJNG THERE IS JASON BATEMAN THE ACTOR. I LOOK BACK AND THESE COPS ARE ROLLING ON THE GROUND LAUGHING. AS THIS MOMENT PEOPLE ON THE SET INCLUDING THE DIRECTOR ARE YELLING AT ME TELLING ME IM IN THE WAY AND NOT SUJPOSED TO BE ON THE SET.

I LOOK BACK AND TELL THEM THE COPS TOLD ME I HAVE TO GO THIS WAY AND I SEE JASON FEELING SORRY FOR ME. NOT UNDERSTANDING WHY COPS WOULD BE SO UNCOOL AND JERKS. THE COPS TOLD ME AFTER I GOT ON THE SET, "CHUCK THERE YOU GO YOU ALWAYS WANTED TO BE IN THE MOIVIES", I SAID NO I DONT IM IN MUSIC. THE COPS LOOKED BEWILDERED.

I THEN GET OFF THE SET AND WALK TO THE PIANO ROOMS. WHICH WAS WHERE I WAS ORIGIONALY HEADED IN THE FIRST PLACE.

ABOUT 20 MINUTES LATER I AM PRACTICING THE PIANO AND I HEAR A KNOCK ON THE DOOR OF THE PIANO ROOM AND I ANSWER IT AND IT IS THE CLAREMONT POLICE READY AND ARE GOING TO NOW ARREST ME FOR TRESSPASSING ALL BECAUSE OF WHEN I SIGNED A PAPER FROM LIONEL BROWN THE COP BACK AT THAT FRAT HOUSE A YEAR OR SO EARLLIER. THOUGH THIS IS AN ILLEGEL WAY FOR HIM TO SIGN THIS PAPER I STILL WAS ARRESTED. THATS THE WAY THE SYSTEM IS, IT IS TO MAKE SURE THE PERSON ARRESTED HAS NO RIGHTS. OR HARDLEY ANY AT ALL.

I AM NOW ARRESTED FOR TRESSPASSING.

AS I AM BEING TAKEN AWAY I SEE JASON BATEMAN LOOKNG SAD AND NOT UNDERSTANDING WHAT JS HAPPENING TO ME.

6 YEARS LATER IN 1994 I AM RENTING OUT MY MUSIC EQUITMENT AND STUDEO AT MOMS HOUSE. ONE THAT IS APPLYING TO PRACTICE THERE IS A GUY NAME JASON AND HIS BRO.

WHEN I OPEN THE DOOR I SEE THAT IT IS JASON BATEMAN AND HIS BRO. FOR THE NEXT FEW MONTHS JASON RENTS THE EQUITMENT AND PRACTICE ROOM FROM MOMS HOUSE AND HE IS IN THE BAND CALLED THE LOVE HOUNDS. JASON AND ME GET ALONG GREAT AND HE IS A REAL NICE GUY. THOUGH ANOTHER TIME I SAW HIM WAS WHEN HE WAS IN A SIT COM WITH HARLEN WILLIAMS AND IT WAS AN UNSECCESSFUL SIT COM AND IT WAS DROPPED MONTHS AFTER THIS. I WAS AN AUDIENCE MEMBER BEING PAID TO LAUGH AND APPLAUD WHICH WAS 35 DOLLORS A

SHOW AND TAX FREE. I SAY HI TO JASON AND HE AVOIDED ME AND GAVE ME A VIBE LIKE LEAVE HIM ALONE WHICH WAS PHONEY BECAUSE LATER THAT NIGHT I WOULD BE RENTING MY STUDEO ROOM OUT TO HIM. I LEANRED BY ALL MY DEALINGS WITH ACTORS FROM FRIENDS TO ACQUANTINCES THAT THEY ARE REAL PRETENCIOUS. BASICALLY JASON DIDNT WANT TO BE ASSOSSIATED WITH AN AUDIENCE MEMBER WHO WAS BEING PAID TO BE THERE WHICH IS LIKE A MOVIE EXTRA AS HE WAS THE STAR OF A SITCOM. PHONEY IS PHONEY IS.

12. EZE A.K.A, ERIC WRIGHT.

I MET EZE ON VARIOUS OCCASIONS. THE FIRST TIME WAS IN 1986.

1986, KAREN HARLENS HOUSE.

I WAS HOMELESS AT THE BEGENNING OF 1986 AND A LITTLE IN 1985 IN DECEMBER. ONE NIGHT I WAS WALKING DOWN TO 7-11 THE STORE ON SAN BERNADINO AVENUE AND INDIAN HILL AND I WAS LOOKING AT A RECYCLER MAGAZINE BUT DIDNT BUY IT DUE TO THAT I DIDNT HAVE ANY MONEY. I WAS WRITING DOWN GUITAR PLAYER NUMBERS AND AS I WAS LOOKING AT THIS RECYCLER MAGAZINE A GUY CAME UOP TO ME AND ASKED ME IF I WAS LOOKING FOR A GUITAR PLAYER. THIS MUST BE A MIRICLE OF GOD BECAUSE NO ONE COULD KNOW THIS. I TOLD HIM YES AND HOW DID HE KNOW. HE SAID SIMPLY THAT I LOOKED LIKE I WAS LOOKING FOR A GUITAR PLAYER.

ME AND ALEX HIT IT OFF GREAT AND THAT NIGHT AROUND 3 AM WE GO OVER TO HIS HOUSE AND PLAY MUSIC, HIM ON GUIAR AND ME SINGING. WE WROTE A COUPLE SONGS BEFORE THE MORNING LIGHT.

THE NEXT DAY I MET THE OWNER OF THE HOUSE ALEX TOK ME TO AND LIVED AT AND HER NAME WAS KAREN HARLEN. WE GOT ALONG GREAT ALSO AND BY THE END OF THE DAY I WAS LIVING THERE FOR SHE INVITED ME TO LIVE THERE.

NOW I AM LIVING AT KAREN HARLENS AND IT IS LATE JANUARY. ME AND ALEX HANG OUT AND GO TO CLUBS. WE WRITE MORE MUSIC AND IN THIS TIME I AUDITION FOR A BAND CALLED ATHENZ. THE ONE GUITARIST WAS A SPOILED KID AND HAS BEEN IN GUITAR PLAYER MAGAZINE FOR SOME AD AND HAD A HUGE EGO. HE WAS GOOD THOUGH. I BROUGHT THEM TO KARENS AND ASKED IF WE COULD PLAY IN THE GARAGE THAT WAS EMPTY. AFTER KAREN MET ALL THE GUYS SHE WAS OK WITH IT AND WE ALSO PAID HER 100 PER MONTH WHICH WAS 20 PER MEMBER FOR EACH DIVIDED CUT TO PAY HER.

WE STARTED PRACTICING THERE AS THE BAND ATHENZ AND MY FRIEND AND OTHER BAND MATER FROM THE ALEX AND CHUCK PROJECT IS QUITTING. YES, ALEX IS NOT THE KIND OF GUY TO SHARE HIS BAND MATES WITH ANOTHER BAND WHERE I BELEIVE IN BEING IN MORE THEN ONE BAND WHICH I HAVE DONE A FEW TIMES IN THE EARLY 80S.

ALEX THEN LEAVES BACK TO PUARTA RICO.

I MISS THAT GUY STILL BUT HE WAS NOT INTO ME BEING IN ANOTHER PROJECT SO I WAS THE LAST THING KEEPING HIM HERE IN THE STATES EVEN THOUGH KAREN WAS HIS GIRLFRIEND HE TOLD ME THE FIRST NIGHT HE WAS GETTING SICK OF HER. KAREN WAS 38 IN 1986 MAKING HER NOW 72. WOW TIME FLIES. I AM IN A BAND WHERE THE DRUMMER NAMED TONY IS IN THREE BANDS IN 2021 AND I DONT CARE ABOUT THAT. SOME PEOPLE ARE LIKE ME WHO DOENT CARE AND OTHER PEOPLE ARE LIKE ALEX WHO WANTS HIS LEAD SINGER TO BE ONLY IN HIS BAND.

THE BAND PRACTICES AND GETS READY FOR OUR FIRST GIG WHICH IS IN THE BACKYARD OF KAREN HARLENS.

THE NEIGHBIORS AND THEIR HELP.

MAN, THE NEIGHBORS WERE ALL BALL DUE TO THIS WAS A BLACK AREA OF POMONA, SOUTH OF SAN BERBADINO AND INDIAN HILL ON THE WEST SIDE.

ALL THESE FOLKS FELT I WAS THE GREAT WHITE HOPE AND ALL IN THE HOOD HAD DREAMS OF MAKING THESE PARTIES LEGENDARY AND THAT THEY BECAME BUT NOT AS LEGENDARY AS ONE OF THE PLAYERS PLAYING IN MY SHOWS RIGHT AT THIS TIME AND THAT NAME WAS EZA AND N.W.A..

THE PARTIES AND THE NEIGHBORS HELP.

I GO AROUND THE HIGH SCHOOLS TO PASS OUT FLYERS AND WE GET HUNDEREDS TO COME TO THE PARTIES. THE PARTIES ARE A SUCCESS AND MY BAND ATHENZ PLAYS THE FIRST THREE SHOWS AND THEN THEY TOLD ME THEIR PARENTS THINK IM NOT RIGHT FOR THE BAND. I DONT GET THAT BEING THAT I WROTE THE LYRICS AND VOCAL MELODIES AND GOT THEM THE SHOWS

BUT OH WELL.

WE ALL DECIDED EVEN THOUGH MY BAND BROKE UP THAT I WOULD GET OTHER BANDS TO PLAY THESE SHOWS IN THE FUTURE AT KAREN HARLENS AND FOR THE NEXT 16 WEEKS. S00 DOLLORS WE MADE AT LEAST EVERY WEEK FOR FOUR MONTHS WE HAVE SHOWS THAT OTHER BANDS PLAY. AT THIS TIME WHICH IS EARLY 1986 RAP WAS JUST BECOMING KNOWN IN SOUTHERN CALIFORNIA AND ESPECIALLY JUST BEING KNOWN WHERE WE LIVE IN THE POMONA VALLEY AREA.

I GOT CALLS FROM GUYS IN LOS ANGELES THAT SAYS THEY HEARD FROM MY NEIGHBOR THAT WE ARE THROWING PARTIES WITH AT LEAST 500 PEOPLE THERE AND THEY ARE WONDERING IF THERE ARE ANY OPENING SLOTS TO GET THEIR BAND TO PLAY. I SAID YES AND ASKED THEM WHAT THEIR BAND WAS ABOUT AND WHAT KIND OF MUSIC THEY DID AND THEY SAID RAP. THEY SAID THEY WOULD REALLY APPRECIATE THE SHOW AND HE SAID HIS NAME WAS ERIC BUT I CAN CALL HIM EZ.

THE BAND PLAYED THE NEXT WEEK-ERIC AKA EZ- ALSO TOLD ME THE NAME WAS N.W.A.

THEY PLAYED A COUPLE SHOWS AND I PAID THEM 50 DOLLORS AND THEY APPRECIATED THIS. THIS IS 1986 AND 50 DOLLORS THEN IS LIKE 250 DOLLORS NOW I WOULD SAY.

BELEIVE IT OR NOT I FELT SORRY FOR THEM BEING I DIDNT THINK THEY HAD MUCH TALENT AND IT WAS TRUE THAT IN THE MOVIE ABOUT N.W.A. THAT THEIR TALENT HADNT BLOSSEMED YET IN EARLY 1986. REMEMBER THIS WAS FEBUARY OF 1986.

ME AND ERIC AKA EZ GOT AL0NG WELL AND HAD NO PROBLEMS WITH HIM OR HIS BAND AND WE ALL GOT ALONG AND HAD GOOD SHOWS THEN.

LATER IN 1990 I RAN INTO ERIC AKA EZ AND HE WAS AT BEACH RECORDING STUDEOS DOING SOME WORK WITH HIS LATESRT PRIOJECT AND WE NEEDED A GUY TO SAY YO ON THIS ROCK N RAP SONG WHICH IS THE FIRST ORIGINAL FULL ROCK N RAP SONG IN HISTORY CALLED "AS SAMMY SAID-". ERIC WAS HAPPY TO DO IT AND I DIDNT HAVE TO PAY HIM ANYTHING.

LATER I HEARD HE DIED OF AIDES. I WAS SAD. ERIC TO ME WAS A COOL GUY WHO WASNT RACIST OR PREJUDICE AND

TREATED EVERYONE COOL THAT I WAS ASSOSSIATED WITH AND THAT I HEARD ABOUT. IF EZ-E EVER ACTED PREJUDICE IT WAS JUST AN ACT BECAUSE THE GUY I KNEW NAMED ERIC WRIGHT WAS A REAL FRIENDLEY AND DOWN TO EARTH NON PREJUDUCE GUY.

LATER IN 1993 I GOT THE TAPE THE CHRONIC AND HEARD SO MANY INSULTS ABOUT EZE AND I WAS SAD TO HEAR IT.

13. HOUSTON

I MET HOUSTON IN REDONDO BEACH AT A PLACE CALLED BEACH RECORDING STUDEOS. I NEVER KNEW HIS LAST NAME BECAUSE I DIDNT NEED IT. HE WAS THE ASSIGNED ENGENEER FOR THE RECORDING. HE FIRST SONG WE DID WAS "AS SAMMY SAID" WHICH WAS THE WORLDS FIRST ROCK N RAP TUNE THAT IS FULLY ORIGIONAL IN MUSIC HISTORY. THE REASON WHY I KNOW THIS IS ANTHRAX IS OFFICIALLY THE FIRST IN 1992. WELL WE DID THIS IN 1989..

ONCE HOUSTON HEARD THE SONG " AS SAMMY SAID" HE WAS HOOKED ONTO US AS OUR ENGENEER AND CO PRODUCER FOR THE NEXT 4 YEARS UP UNTIL LATE 1995. THE ONLY REASON WHY HOUSTON STOPPED BEING OUR ENGENEER AND CO PRIDUCER IS BECAUSE 1. JEFF DE ALLEN RIPPED OFF THE STUDEO AND I WAS LOOKED AS RESPONSIBLE BECAUSE I BROUGHT JEFF D ALLEN IN.AND 2. HE GOT A JOB WORKING WITH FREDDY FENDER AS HIS LEAD GUITARIST.

THE DAY I MET HOUSTON WAS THE FIRST DAY I DID ROCK N ROLL IN A 24 TRACK STUDEO. IT WAS A HARRISON MIXING BOARD AND THE QUALITY CAME OUT BETTER THEN THE HALF MILLION DOLLOR NEVE BOARD THE RECORD COMPANY BOUGHT. THAT RECORD COMPANY WAS STATUE RECORDS AND HOUSTON WORKED FOR THEM AS A STUDEO MUSICIAN/ENGENEER. WHEN WE DID THE ALBUM

THOUGH HOUSTON WAS ALSO CO PRODUCER. HE WAS ON TO IT.

HOUSTON WAS THE BEST ENGENEER I EVER HAD THOUGH HIS PROTAJAE KELLY WHO I WORKED WITH WHEN I CAME BACK TO PLANET HOLLYWOOD STUDEOS WHICH WAS STATUE RECORDS WAS ALSO EXCELLENT AND NOW KELLY IS THE HEAD ENGENEER AND LIKVED THERE. IT WAS IN NORTH HOLLYWOOD. THIS WAS 1998-99.

SO I WORKED WITH STATE FROM 1990 TO 1994 WITH HOUSTON AS ENGENEER AND CO PRODUCER AND CO-MASTERING. HOUSTON GOT ME AN EQ MASTER GENIOUS THAT LIVED IN AN ATTIC. IT WAS COOL AND TOOK TWO DAYS. HIS NAME WAS LEE SCOTT.

LEE MASTERED BADDCLOWN 1 ENTITLED IN YUR FACE AND BORIS MIDNEY MASTERED BADDCLOWN 2-ENTITLED LOST IN HOLLYWOOD. THE BADDCLOWN 2 WAS ACTUALLY THE LEFT OVER SONGS I DIDNT WANT TO PUT ON BADDCLOWN 1 BECAUSE BADDCLOWN 1 WAS A CONCEPT ALBUM MEANING THE SONGS WERE ABOUT A BASIC IDEA OF A LIFE STYLE IN ROCK N ROLL AT THAT TIME.

HOUSTON NEVER MISSED A SESSION AND SOMETIMES WHEN WE GOT THERE HE HAD BEEN DOING STUDEO WORK FOR RANDY MEISNER ALL NIGHT OR VINNIE VINCENT OF KISS OR GENE SIMMONS ON SOME VOICE OVERS FOR BEEVUS AND BUTTHEAD. THIS WAS THE HOTTEST STUDEO AROUND AND HOUSTON WAS IN CHARGE OTHER THEN WHEN THE RECORD COMPANY OWNER CAME IN NAMED JEFF ENGLAND. JEFF HAD DONE KEYBOARDS IN STEPPENWOLF AND DEEP PURPLE.

I LIKED JEFF BUT REALLY LOVED HOUSTON. HE PUT HIS BLOOD SWEAT AND TEARS AS I DID TOO IN BADDCLOWN ONE AND 2.

HOUSTON DID STUDEO WORK FOR ME ON MANY OF THE SONGS ON BADDCLOWN 1 AND BADDCLOWN 2. I REMEMBER ONE IN PARTICULAR, HE DID A LEAD ON A CHRISTIAN SONG ENTITLED HYMN 17. THE HYMN 17 WAS THE AMOUNT OF LETTERS IN OUR NAMES COMBINED WHICH WAS TONY, DEAN, CHUCK AND MIKE. 17 LETTERS WHICH CREATED THE SONG TITLE HYMN 17. ANYWAYS ON THE END OF THE SONG HOUSTON DID A WONDERFUL LEAD ON THE 1ST TAKE, HE SAID HE BEEN PRACTICING ALL WEEK AND WANTED TO PUJT IT ON BEFORE WE CAME BUT FELT THAT I WOULD RATHER HAVE WATCHED. HE WAS RIGHt. HE SAID THE HOLY SPIRIT GAVE HIM THE FEEL AND THAT WAS ALL HE WAS FEELING WAS THE HOLY SPIRIT WHILE PLAYING THAT LEAD.

ME AND HOUSTON HAD SOME ARGUMENTS AT TIMES AND ALOT OF THE SESSIONS WE HAD ALOT OF COCAINE TO DO. ONE OF THE ARTIST WAS A DRUG DEALER AND WOULD BRING OVER 1 OZ OF COCAINE AND THE REASON WHY WE DID THE COKE WAS TO GET THAT TRUE AND PURE ROCK FEEL AND IT WORKED. OF COURSE NOW I NOW THE TRUTH IS IN SOBRIETY WHEN IT COMES TO RECORDING MUSIC AND PLAYING, WRITING AND ORGANIZING SONGS AND SONG MELODIES.

HOUSTON WAS A WEEKEND TYPE PARTYER AND ONCE THERE WAS A PARTY AT THAT HOUSE THAT IN THE BACK WAS THE RECORDING STUDEO ROOM. THE RECORDING STUDEO WAS BIG AND ROOMEY. ENOUGH FOR A SEPERATE ROOM FOR ISOLATION FOR THE RECORDING ARTISTS AS WELL AS A 20 FOOT LONG 72 CHANNELL NEVE BOARD. ROOM FOR 10 GUESTS AS WELL AS A VOCAL BOOTH AND MORE ROOM FOR STORAGE AND UNPACKING.

THE PARTY I SAW HOUSTOIN DO WAS COOL AND WE WERE INVITED AND THAT WAS THE ONLY TIME I SEEN HOUSTON IN LIVE STAGE PERFORMANCE. I DONT THINK HE EVER

SEEN ME ON STAGE THOUGH. BACK THEN I WAS OBSESSED WITH THE RECORDING STUDEO AND SPENT 300 A MONTH OR MORE ON IT. I WAS BLESSED TO ONLYH HAVE TO AY HOUSTON 12 AN HOUR AND THE REST WAS FREE- THE USAGE OF THE STUDEO WAS FREE TO ME BECAUSE I WAS SIGNED WITH THEIR LABEL.

HOUSTON HAD A COOL AND FUNNY SENSE OF HUMOR AND HE HAD GREAT IDEAS FORM BADDCLOWN 1 AND BADDCLOWN 2. WE ARGUED ABOUT DIFFERENT GUITAR LEVELS AND THE POWER OF THE SOUND OF THE GUITAR. I WAS A BIT MORE HEAVIER MUSIC WISE AND HE WAS LIKE THE LED ZEPPELEN TRIP LIKE MORE MORE BLUES YET HEAVY SOUNDS AND I WAS INTO MORE THE LEVEL OF METALLICA THOUGH I DIDNT FOLLOW METALLICA FULLY THOGH I LIKED SOME OF THEIR SONGS. , I DO NOW BUT THEN I JUST WANTED THE HEAVIEST GUITAR POSSIBLE WITH MELODIES. THIS IS WHAT KURT COBAIN DID TOO AT THAT TIME AND WE WERE JUST PARALLENING BECAUSE I DIDNT KNOW OR EVER HEARD OF THE SEATTLE SCENE YET AND THIS WAS 1991 AND 1990. AS HISTORY HAS IT NERVANA AND SOUNDGARDEN MADE IT BIGGEST IN 1992 AND SO ON. THAT IS IN ROCK N ROLL

HOUSTON AND MY MANAGER WERE FRIENDS ALSO AND HOUSTON HARMLESSLEY FLIRTED WITH HER ALOT. ONCE WE DID A 24 HOUR SESSION. WE WERE ON WHAT HOUSTON CALLED THE BUMP RATE. NOW THE BUMP RATE IS WHEN N O ONE ELSE HAS BOOKED TIME FOR THAT SLOT WE COULD GET IT FOR FREE AND 12 DOLLORS FOR HOUJSTONS TIME. WELL, THIS WORKED GREAT AND ON THE 4-5 SESSIONS WE DID FOR THE FIRST ALBUM OF BADDCLOWN 1. I FELT I HAD TO BE TOTALLY HIGH ON COCAINE AND ALCOHOL WHEN I SING SO THAT FEEL OF DRUGS AND PARTYING WILL COME OUT IN MY VOCALS. HOUSTON DID A COUPLE HUNDERED DOLLORS OF COKE

AS WE ALL DID EACH TIME AND IT WAS ALL FREE, A FREE NEVE MIXING BOARD 72 CHANNEL AUTOMATIC FADER AND FREE OUNCE 2000 WORTH OF COCAINE. NOW NEXT ALL WE NEEDED WAS THE GIGS. BEING WITH STATUE RECORDS WERE WERE ABLE TO ACCESS FREE MILLION DOLLOR RECORDING STUDEO AND GOT FREE COCAINE BEING ONE OF THE GUITARISTS. I PAY TO ENGENEER FOR 12 DOLLORS AN HOUR AND THATS IT JUST FOR THE ENGENEERS TIME AKA HOUSTON, AKA FUTURE GUITARIST FOR FREDDY FENDER BAND.

WHEN HOUSTON WORKED WITH US FROM JULY 1990 TO DEC 1994 THERE WERE MANY DIFFERENT PLAYERS MAKING MANY DIFFERENT PLAYER CHANGES.

CHANGE 1-

1. RAUEL RANOA BASE, DANNY MC AARON DRUMS AND AARON MC DANNY ON GUITAR LEAD AND RHYTHEM.

2. MIKE FOOT LEAD GUITAR, JOHNNY HOLLYWOOD DRUMS AND RICK PATYK BASE.

3. STEVE RAY DAUGHERTY LEAD GUITAR AND RHYTHEM, KENNY MEOLA LEAD GUITAR AND RYTHEM TIM BURP WILLIAMS DRUMS, RICK PATYK BASE .

4. CHRIS GOOD LEAD AND RHYTHM GUITAR, RICK HARRISON FORD DRUMS RICK PATYK BASE.

5. TONY BRUNETTE RHYTHEM AND LEAD GUITAR, MIKE ANIUMAL SUMMERS DRUMS, DEAN WILLIAMS BASE.

6. JIM BOURNE BASE, AARON GADDAS LEAD AND RHYTHEM GUJITAR, GARY HARRISON DRUMS.

7 TIM MCWHIM BASE, DORY CORY DRUMS, AARON GADDAS DRUMS.

8. CRAIG MT. BALDY TRECUDDER DRUMS, BILL DE ALLEN BASE, ROBB WHITIKER LEAD GUITAR

22 MUSICIANS IN ALL AND GOD BLESS THEM. THEY DIDNT STAY AROUND BECAUSE WE BROUGHT THEM UP TO A LEVEL THEY THOUGHT THEY WOULD NEVER REACH AND EACH ONE JUST DIDNT HAVE TO CONFIDENCE TO GO ON A TOUR I GOT FROM A LADY NAMED MIMI VASHAWN. MIMI WAS GREAT AND HAD AN OFFICE NEAR GEFFIN RECORDS AS WELL AS SHE GOT US A TOUR CALLED THE CHITLINS CIRCUIT. I GOT THIS BECAUSE I TOLD HER I WAS WITH STATUE RECORDS AND BROUGHT UP HOUSTONS AND JEFFS NAME. THAT WAS MY IN NOT ONE OF THOSE 21 MUSICIANS WANTED TO GO. THEIR EXCUSES RANGED FROM EVERYTHING FROM THEIR SICK TO THEIR JOB CANT LEAVE TO "THEY ARE IN COLLEGE DUDE" AND THEY ARE MOVING AWAY WAS ANOTHER ONE/EXCUSE.

HOW ME AND HOUSTON ENDED.

WELL I TOLD YOU HE WENT TO FREDDY FENDER BUT SAID HE WAS STATIONED NEAR THE STUDEO SO HE PROMICED ON HIS OFF TIME HE WOULD RECORD US FOR OUR THIRD ALBUM WITH STATUE RECORDS.

DIDNT HAPPENAND HEAR IS WHY.

THE JEFF DE ALLEN INCIDENT. IT RUINED EVERYTHING.

JEFF WAS A GREAT BASSIST AND SONGWRITER, BUT A CROOK. THOUGH I DIDNT KNOW HE WAS GOING TO RIP ME OFF AND OH YES HE DID.

WE DID STUDEO WORK FOR 3 DAYS IN ERO. BILL WAS TO DO HIS BASE PARTS ON THE LAST DAY AND HE DID IT WELL AND PROFESSIONS. ONLY ONE PROBLEM, HE IS A CRIMINAL AND WORKS WITH STOLEN AND ALL TYPES OF

MUSIC EQUITMENT MEANING HE SELLS EQUITMENT FOR A LIVING.

AND DOES BASE ON THE SIDE AND HAD A BRAND WHEN I WORKED WITH HIM CALLED DE ALLEN. HIS LAST NAME. NOW HE HAS AGREED TO BE IN MY BAND ENTITLED BADDCLOWN.

SO ON THE LAST DAY WE HAD JEFF DO BASE AND HE LEFT AS HE LEFT WITH A COUPLE BAGS OF EQUITMENT WE THOUGHT WAS HIS. WELL, HE STOLE 4000 IN MICROPHONES FROM THE STUDEO. I DIDNT HEAR ABOUT IT TILL THE NEXT MORNING. HOUSTON CALLS ME AND IS SCREAMING WHY AND HOW DID I RIP HIM OFF. I DIDNT KNOW WHAT HE WAS TALKING ABOUT. WE FINALLY REALIZED IT WAS JEFF DE ALLEN BEING HE WAS THE LAST GUY WHO LEFT THE ROOM WITH BAGS FROM THE ROOM THAT HAD THE EQUITMENT THAT WAS STOLEN.

I TOLD HOUSTON I WOULD NEVER DO THIS AND HE SAID I WAS RESPONSIBLE, I SAID I AM MY OWN ADULT AND JEFF DID THIS WITHOUT ME KNOWING IT JUST LIKE THE SAME HOUSTON IS GOING THROUGH.

I TELL HOUSTON THAT I WILL CALL JEFF DE ALLEN AND TALK TO HIM ABOUT THIS AMOUNT. MAYBE HE WILL GIVE IT BACK.

THE TALK WITH JEFF ON THE PHONE.

JEFF, WHEN I TALKED WITH HIM ON THIS PHONE CALL LIED AND SAID HE DIDNT DO IT. YOU CAN HEAR IT IN HIS VOICE HE WAS LIEING. BILL SAID "CHUCK I DIDNT TAKE ANYTHING". I ASKED HIM IF HE HAS AND SELLS MUSIC EQUITMENT AND HE SAYS YES. I SAID THIS IS WHY HE DID IT. HE DENIED IT. HE LIED ALL THROUGH THIS PHONE CONVERSATION.

I CALLED BACK HOUSTON AND HE SAID HE BELEIVES ME THAT I DIDNT DO IT BUT STILL IT HAS TO FALL ON SOMEONE AND IT FALLS ON MY HEAD. MY HEAD MEANING ME, CHUCK.

I WAS DISMISSED FROM THE RECORD COMPANY. NOT ONLY DID JEFF RUIN THE EQUITMENT FROM THE RECORD COMPANY BY STEALING IT BUT HE GOT ME SO MY CAREER AS A RECORDING ARTIST WITH STATUE RECORDS WAS RUINED. I WAS FIRED FROM THE RECORD COMPANY THAT EXACT DAY.

I ASKED HOUSTON IF I CAN HAVE HIM AT LEAST FINISH MIXING THE MUSIC BEING WE JUST FINISHED ALL RECORDINGS OF THE MUSICIANS PARTS AND HE SAID HE WOULD TALK TO JEFF TJHE OWNER OF THE RECORD COMPANY.

HOUSTON CAME BACK AND SAID JEFF SIAD OK AND THE I ASKED HIM IF HE COULD DO AN EQ MASTER TO MASTER THE ALBUM WITH HIS FRIEND LEE SCOTT STILL AND HOUSTON SAID OK.

SO THANK GOD HOUSTON FINISHED THE ALBUM BADDCLOWN ONE BEING IT HAS TAKEN FOUR YEARS ALONG WITH 15 EXTRA SONGS THAT WILL LATER BE PUT ON BADDCLOWN 2 AS WELL AS EQ NASTERED BY BORIS MIDNEY.

HOUSTON WAS COOL

AT LEE SCOTTS IT WAS GREAT AND AS I SAID BEFORE WE DID IT ALL IN A LITTLE ATTICK ABOUT 5 FEET HIGH AND 10 FEET LONG AND IT WAS SUBPERB WITH THE SKILLS OF ME AND LEE SCOTT AND HOUSTON. ALL SKILLS BLESSED BY GOD FULLY.

THEREFORE BADDCLOWN 1 WAS DONE. I HAD TO BUY NEAR LEE SCOTTS HOUSE A TWO ALBUM CD OF PHYSICAL GRAFITTI WHICH WAS MY FIRST CD I EVER OWNED AND BOUGHT AND I QUICKLEY JUST GAVE IT TO HOUSTON AS A TIP AND A GIFT FOR HIS HARDWORK AND FRIENDSHIP ON THE ALBUM. I NEVER SAW HOUSTON AGAIN EXCEPT ON TV WHEN HE WAS PLAYING GUITAR WITH FREDDY FENDER.

14. ROBERT DOWNEY JR.

IN 2009 I GOT INTO AN ARGUMENT WITH A POLICE DISPATCHER IN CLAREMONT WHO IS WITH THE CLAREMONT POLICE. HER NAME IS KATHY WALLIS. I HAVE TO THANK HER FOR DOING THAT BECAUSE THIS LED TO ME DOING 16 SHOWS WITH ROBERT DOWNEY JR IN LOS ANGELES COUNTY JAIL.

HERES HOW IT ALL STARTED.

IN THER MAIL I RECEIVED A NOTICE THAT I WAS BEING SERVED A RESTRAINING ORDER FROM KATHY WALLIS AT CLAREMONT POLICE AS WELL AS ANOTHER GUY. I DONT REMEMBER HIS NAME BUT IT DEFINATELEY WAS 2 PEOPLE SERVING A RESTRAINING ORDER ON ME. ON THE OUTSIDE IT LOOKS LIKE ITS A RESTRAINING ORDER BUT REALLY THE MOTIVE FOR THIS WAS THAT CLAREMONT POLICE WAS TRYING TO GET A WAY TO STOP ME FROM COMPLAINING AND COMING IN AND COMPLAINING WHICH IS MY RIGHT BUT THEY FOUND A WAY TO STOP MY RIGHT THROUGH CONTRIDICTION CALLED A RESTRAINING ORDER X 2.

NEXT I HAD TO GO TO COURT ON THIS AND MEET A JUDGE. I WASNT FACING JAIL TIME NOR WAS THIS AN ARREST BUT IT WAS A WARNING THAT IF I COME ACROSS KATHY WALLIS OR GET 30 FEET CLOSE TO HER I WILL THEN BE ARRESTED FOR VIOLATION OF A RESTRAINING ORDER. AT THIS TIME IN MY LIFE I DONT EVEN KNOW WHAT KATHY WALLIS

LOOKS LIKE NOR DO I KNOW WHO SHE IS. I GUESS I GOT IN AN ARGIUMENT WITH HER AND SHE WENT SO FAR AS TO GET A RESTRAINING ORDER ON ME BUT TRULY I WOULDNT KNOW HER FROM THE NEXT PERSON.

THE JUDGE WHOSE NAME IS JUDGE YARTE WAS ORDERING ME TO NEVER DEAL WITH HER AND I WAS COOL WITH IT BEING I DONT KNOW WHO SHE IS BUT I DO KNOW THAT SHE WORKS AT THE CLAREMONT POLICE DEPARTMENT. SO THE POINT OF THE RESTRAINING ORDER AS I SAID BEFORE IS SO I DONT COME NEAR THE CLAREMONT POLICE STATION AND ITS JUST SO THAT SHE WORKS THERE, THAT IS KATHY WALLIS.

I AGREE TO THIS IN COURT THAT I WILL BE ARRESTED IF I GET CLOSE TO HER. I TRIED TO TELL THE JUDGE THAT I DONT KNOW WHO SHE IOS OR WHAT SHE LOOKS LIKE AND SHE WOULDNT LET ME SAY 1 WORD. IT HAD TO BE THROUGH MY LAWYER WHICH I DIDNT HAVE BEING I WASNT ARRESTED.

A YEAR LATER.

I HAD TO TALK ON A COMPLAINT ABOUT A SITUATION I DON T EVEN REMEMBER WHAT IT IS ART THIS POINT NOW AS I AM WRITING THIS BOOK BUT I TALKED TO A WATCH COMMANDER NAMED OFFICER SEEZIX. OFFICER SEEZIZ INVITED ME TO COME IN THE STATION. I TOLD HIM THAT I DONT WANT TO VIOLATE MY RESTRAINING ORDER BEING THAT KATHY WALLIS WORKS THERE AND I WOULD BE TOO CLOSE TO HER AND WOULD BE VIOLATED IF I WENT IN AND OFFICER SEEZIX SAID, "DONT WORRY CHUCK AS LONG AS IT IS FOR BUSINESS YOU WONT AND I WILL MAKE SURE YOU WONT BE VIOLATED."

WELL I MADE A HUGE MISTAKE. I TRUSTED AND BELEIVE HIM, NEVER TRUST A COP AND THAT IS A FACT AT LEAST

FOR ME. EVERY TIME I TRUST A COP I GET SCREWED AND HERE IT IS AGAIN

A LETTER.

THIS LETTER I OPEN AT THE APARTMENT SAYS THAT I HAVE VIOLATED A RESTRAINING ORDER. I CALL CLAREMONT POLICE AND TALK TO SEEZIX AND REMINDED HIM THART HE SAID I COULD COME IN AND WOULD NOT BE VIOLATED. HE LAUGHED AND SAIDS HE LIED AND THEN HE SAID HE DIDNT REALLY LIE BECAUSE WHEN I CAME IN IT IN HIS OPINION WAS NOT BUSINESS.

I TOLD HIM IT WAS BUSINESS BECAUSE I ASKED HIM WHAT OTHER REASON COULD IT BE THAT I WOULD TALK TO HIM AND GO TO CLAREMONT POLICE DEPARTMENT. HE SAID IT THE DECISION HAS ALREADY BEEN MADE AND LAUGHS AND SAYS IN A SARCASRTIC MANNER "GOOD LUCK AT COURt."

AT COURT THE SECOND TIME WITH JUDGE YHARTE. OH YES JUDGE YHARTE THIS JUDGE WHO LOOKS AROUND 27 AND SEEMS LIKE SHE JUST GOT OUT OF COLLEGE. SHE IS WHAT THEY CALL A HANGING JUDGE. IMEAN AND ON A TERRIBLE POWER TRIP BEYOND MOST PEOPLES IMAGINATIONS.

IN OTHERWARDS JUDGE YARTE SUCKED.

SO AS I GET THIS LETTER IN THE MAIL FROM CLAREMONT POLICE IT SAYS I HAVE TO COME TO THE STATION AND BE PROCESSED. IN OTHER WORDS OFFICIALLY ARRESTED.

THIS IS CRAZY. THE COP SEEZIX PROMICED ME AND SAID I COULD COME IN THE STATION WITHOUT BEING VIOLATED. HE LIED AND NOW I GO TO THE STATION WHERE THE FINGERPRINT ME AND ARREST ME AND LEAVE ME IN THE JAIL CELL WITH THE DOOR OPEN FOR 10 MINUTES AND

THEN I LEAVE THEY TOLD ME MY COURT DATE AND SO I GO THERE AND NOW I AM IN FRONT OF JUDGE YARTE A SECOND TIME.

THE SECOND TIME IN FRONT OF JUDGE YARTE.

WHEN I GO TO COURT THAT MORNING, I GET A CAPPICINO BECAUSE I NEVER THOUGHT IN A MILLION YEARS THAT I WOULD BE GOING TO JAIL FOR 43 DAYS FROM THIS MORNING ONTO THE NEXT 43 DAYS.

WHEN I GOT CALLED UP TO THE JUDGE SHE, JUDGE YARTE LOOKED UPSET AT ME AND THEN ASKED ME IF I KNEW WHAT THIS WAS ABOUT. I SAID YES, NOW THIS IS ANOTHER TRICK BECAUSE WHEN I SAY I KNOW WHAT IT IS ABOUT THAT THE UNWRITTEN RULE IS THAT IF I KNOW WHAT IT IS ABOUT THEN I MUST HAVE DONE IT WHICH IS NOT TRUE. THIS IS A LIE, I KNEW WHAT IT WAS ABOUT BECAUSE I READ THE ARREST THAT WAS SENT TO ME IN THE MAIL. NOW BELEIVE IT OR NOT I WASNT ALLOWED TO SAY A SINGLE WORD AFTER I SAID I KNEW WHAT IT WAS ABOUT AND THE FIRST TIME I WAS ALLOWED TO TALK WAS THE NEXT COURT APPEARENCE I 1 MONTH. I WAS UPSET AND WANTED A SPEEDY TRIAL WHICH IS MY RIGHT AND SHE SAID IT ISNT MY RIGHT BEING THIS IS A RESTRAINING ORDER VIOLATION NOT A STATE OR FEDERAL ARREST BUT KNOWING HOW CURRUPT THE JUDICIAL SYSTEM IS THIS IS PROBABLEY A LIE TOO BUT I COULDNT TALK OR SAY ANY DEFENCE OF MYSELF TILL THAT TIME. WELL, IT GOT POSTPONED OF COURSE FOR ANOTHER 13 DAYS MAKING IT 43 DAYS.

WHEN YOU HAVE NO POWER THEY THE COURT SYSTEM TAKES ADVANTAGE, LIES AND MANIPULATES AS IN THIS CASE.

I WAS PISSED OFF AND I HEARD A LITTLE STORY FROM THE ACTOR AND COMEDIAN EDDIE GRIFFIN WHEN ME AND HIM WERE IN THE SAN BERNADINO 51/50 WARD AT SOME HOSTBITAL IN SAN BERNADINO.

15. EDDIE GRIFFIN

EDDIE WAS IN THERE FOR BEATING UP HIS GIRLFRIEND AND WE WERE FRIENDS AND PLAYED MONOPOLY TOGETHER AND WON. EDDIE WAS THE RACE CAR AND I WAS THE THIMBLE.

EDDIE TOLD ME WHEN HE WAS LEAVING THE HOSTBITAL TO SAY I AM A CELEBRATY AND 51/50 AND IT WILL GET ME OUT OF JAIL WITHIN 72 HOURS ON A 72 HOUR HOLD. 51/50 IS A CODE, A LAW CODE MEANING YOU ARE TO BE OBTAINED FOR BEING A THREAT TO YOURSELF OR OTHERS.

SO I DID THIS

WHAT I SAID TO JUDGE JARTE WAS I GAVE HER THE MIDDLE FINGER OUT OF ANGER BEING I COULDNT BELEIVE THAT I GOTTA GO 40 PLUS DAYS IN JAIL. I THOUGHT I WOULD BE GONE THE DAY I WENT TO SEE HER. I COULDNT BELEIVE THAT THE LIE THAT CLAREMONT POLICER OFFICER SEEZIZ SAYS IS AUTOMATICALLY BELEIVED WITHOUT BEING CHALLENGED.

AND I COULD CHALLENGE IT IN 40 DAYS MINIMUM AND MAYBE MORE DAYS. YES, IT DID GET REPOSTPONED AND A NEW DATE WAS IN 43 DAYS BUT AT THIS TIME I FELT I WOULD BE BETTER OFF DOING WHAT EDDIE GRIFFIN TOLD NE TO DO BECAUSE IT WORKED FOR HIM. INSTEAD OF EDDIE BEING CHARGED WITH FELONY SPOUSEL ABUSE HE WAS OUT WITH NO CHARGES ON HIM AFTER 72 HOUR HOLD AT A PLACE MUCH BETTER THEN JAIL. YES THIS 51/50 WARD WAS CO ED AND HAD NO BARS. WE ALL GOT A ROOM FOR TWO FOR EACH ROOM.

WHAT I DID AND WHAT HAPPNED WHEN I TOOK EDDIE GRIFFINS ADVICE AND DID EXACTLEY AS HE SAID.

EDDIE SAID SAY IM A CELEBRATY AND IM A THREAT TO MYSELF OR OTHERS, TRANSLATION A CELEBRATY WHO IS 51/50.

SO I TOLD JUDGE YARTE THAT I WAS A CELEBRATY AND WAS 51/50 AND I AM A THREAT TO MYSELF OR OTHERS AND THE PROBLEM IS, IM NOT A CELEBRATY.

BUT THEY DID SOMETHING FOR ME AND IT WORKED OUT IN THE LONG RUN. IN THE LONG RUN I WAS POSITIONED NEXT TO ROBERT DOWENEY JR.

AND I WAS IN THER BED THAT WAS OCCUPIED BEFORE ME FROM A GUY NAMED DANA OF KROQ, A DISC JOCKY WHO HAS HAD 12 DRUNKIN DRIVING CHARGES.

WELL, TO MAKE A LONG STORY SHORT THE FIRST GUY I RAN ACROSS AT THE COUNTY JAIL DORM WAS ROBERT DOWNEY JR BUT BEFORE THIS I WAS AND SPENT 6 OR 7 DAYS IN SOLITARY CONFINEMENT AND ALMOST NAKED IN WHICH ALL I HAD TO WEAR WAS THIS WEIRD VELCROW TYPE DRESS THING. I WAS PRETTY MUCH NAKED AND KEPT IN ISOLATION FROM GENERAL POPULATION AND AFTER 7 DAYS OF THIS I WAS DEPRESSED BEING I DIDNT GET THE MEDS I AM USED TO HAVING NOR THE SARAQUIL THART PUTS ME TO SLEEP.

SARAQUIL 400 MG IS WHAT I WAS USED TO AND BY THE TIME I GOT INTO GENERAL POPULATION I WAS FINALLY ISSUED 200 MGS OF SARAQUL. I SHARED IT WITH ROBERT DOWNEY JR BECAUSE HE HAD SLEEP PROBLEMS THERE TOO. I WOULD GET THE MED AND PUT IT IN MY MOUTH PRETENDING THAT I INGESTED IT IN FRONT OF THE NURSES AND KEPT IT IN BASICALLY MY CHEEK.

WHEN I GOT BACK TO MY BUNK I GAVE SOME TO ROBERT DOWNEY JR.

14. ROBERT DOWNEY JR. CONCLUSION

EVERYBODY WAS SAYING "ROBERT DOWNEY JR IS A CHOLO". THIS MEANT HE WAS LOOKING LIKE A CHIOLO WITH A BIG MUSTACHE AS WELL AS HE SPOKE SPANISH ALOT. HES A NICE GUY AND WHEN HE MET ME HE WAS REALLY COOL AND WAS ASKING ME QUESTIONS, HE TOLD ME HE GOT TIRED OF THE HOME INCARCERATION AND PURPOSLEY TOOK OFF HIS ANKLE BRACLET AND HE SAID HE MISSED THE GUYS IN JAIL. NOW WE WERE NOT IN THE TOUHGEST PART OF JAIL, IT WAS THE MILDEST AND MELLOWEST PEOPLE. IT WAS LEVEL ONE OR 2. THE LEVELS GO UP TO LEVEL 10 AND THOSE BEING RAPISTS, MURDERERS AND SEX OFFENDERS, CHILD MOLESTERS ETC. I WAS WITH ROBERT LEVEL WHICH WAS LOW IN THE SENSE OF CELEBRATIES WOUJLD BE THERE OR MILD OFFENDER AND EVEN THOUGH ROBERT WAS IN JAIL FOR DOING HEROIN AND VOILATING PROBATION WHICH IS AROUND 1 LEVEL FIVE WELL, BEING HE IS FAMOUS AND ALL THAT HE GETS TO BE IN LEVEL ONE OR TWO,

THE DREAM.

BEFORE I EVER MET ROBERT DOWNEY JR OR SPENT TIME WITH HIM OR DID 16 SHOWS WITH HIM I HAD A DREAM. THIS DREAM WAS THAT THERE WAS A BUNK NEXT TO ME AND ON TOP WAS ROBERT DOWNEY JR. I TOO WAS IN A BUNK TO THE LEFT OF ROBERT AND I WAS ON THE BOTTOM BUNK. IN THE DREAM I WAS FEEDING ROBERT DOWNERY JR HEROIN. AFTER THIS DREAM I ASSUMBED THAT THIS SCENERO WAS IN THE MILITARY, YOU KNOW, BUNKS IN THE MILITARY. I NEVER EVER EVEN ONCE THINKING THAT THIS WAS JAIL.

SO THE ONLY DIFFERENCE WAS FROM THE DREAM WAS THAT I WAS GIVING ROBERT DOWNEY JR SARAQUIL INSTEAD OF HEROIN.

TJHIS IS A MIRICLE DREAM. I BELEIVE SOME DREAMS ARE NOT PROFECY AND MOST DREAMS ARE MADE TO MEAN NOTHING AND NOT BE TRUE. BUT THIS DREAM WAS A PROFECY OR WHAT WOULD YOU CALL IT.

HOW ME AND ROBERT STARTED THE SHOWS AND HOW WE GOT THE IDEA TO DO THE SHOWS.

ROBERT AND ME USED TO SIT AROUND AND TALK AND THEN HE AND ME CAME UP WITH THE IDEA TO START DOING LIKE A CHURCH BEFORE COUNT AND BEFORE WE GO TO BED. COUNT IS WHEN YOU HAVE TO BE AT YOUR BUNK AND YOU ARE COUNTED. YOU CANNOT LOOK UP AND YOU AS IS EVERYONE HAS TO LAY ON YOUR STOMACH ON THE BUNK FACING AWAY FROM THE GUARDS CHECKING WITH HEELS UP AND PALMS UP SO COPS CAN SEE THERE IS NO POSSIBILITY OF VIOLENCE AND RETALIATION AGAINST THE COPS/GUARDS THAT ARE DOING CHECK.

ONE DAY ME AND ROBERT DECIDED TO DO CHURCH FOR THE JAIL DORM. THE DORM HAD ABOUT 250 PEOPLE. ROBERT ASKED ME IF I COULD SING SOME SONGS AND I SAID I COULD WRITE A SONG FOR EACH SHOW DEPENDING ON WHAT THE TOPIC OF THE DAY WAS FOR CHURCH SO ON DAY ONE AND THEN THROUGH THE NEXT 16 DAYS WE WAITED AROUND STARTING EARLY AFTER BREAKFAST TO FIND WHAT THE TOPIC WAS FOR THE DAY FOR CHURCH.

A GUY CAME OVER TALKING ABOUT HOW UNFAIR IT WAS THAT HE DOESNT HAVE A CIITIZENSHIP BUT HAS HAD HIS OWN BUSINESS HERE FOR 25 YEARS AND FAMILY 100 YEARS AND HE GETS FLOWN TO KOREA AND DROPPED THERE THEN COMES BACK AND THERE THEY ARE WAITING

FOR HIM AGAIN AT HIS JOB AND HE HAS BEEN TRYING TO GET A CITIZENSHIP BUT DUE TO DUE PROCESS IT HASNT HAPPENED YET SO WE DO OUR FIRST SHOW ON A THEME ABOUT THAT WHICH IS A LESS HARDENED HEART AND I SING A FEW SONGS BUT ONE OF THEM BEING A SONG I WROTE CALLED "SIGN OF A HARDENED HEART" AND THERE WERE 6 PEOPLE ON THAT FIRST SERVICE AND ME AND ROBERT DIDNT CARE HOW MANY JUST WAS HONERED AND BLESSED SIX FELT WHAT WE WERE SAYING AND PREACHING AND DOING GODS CHRISTIAN MUSIC IN GODS NAME. NEXT DAY 10 MORE THEN THE DAY AFTER 20 MORE THEN DAY AFTER 10 AND SO ON AND BY THE 16 SHOW EVERY SINGLE PERSON IN THAT DORM. OVER 250 WERE ALL THERE STANDING ROOM ONLY AND THEN GUARDS CAME FROM OTHER BLOCKS AND IT WAS WONDERFUL. WE EVEN GOT A GUARD SAVED AND ACTUALLY LAID HANDS ON HIM IN THE NAME OF JESUS CHRIST. THE GUARD LET US AS WELL AS LATER MANY JOINED ON WHOM WE GOT SAVED THROUGH CHRIST TO HELP US LAY HANDS ON OTHERS BY THE END OF THE DAYS THE DORM WAS MORE POSITVIE THEN A CHURCH ON THE OUTSIDE.

EVEN A MUSLIM JOINED IN. THIS MUSLEM WAS AN ANGRY AND SERIOUS ONE AND USED TO HAVE A RITUAL OF PUTTING DOWN A BLANKET AND PRAYING. BY THE END OF THE SERVICE OF SERVICE 16 HE HAD FOUND CHRIST AND GAVE UP ON HIS MUJSLIM BELEIFS TO A HIGHER AUTHORITY, THE TRUE GOD JESUS THE FATHER, SON AND HOLY SPIRIT.

EACH CHURCH TIME I WOULD LEAD IN MUSIC MINISTRY AND ROBERT IN PREACHING. ITS SAD HE DOESNT PUT THAT MINISTRY INTO THE HOLLYWOOD THING/WORLD. HOPEFULLY ROBERT DOWNEY JR WILL COME OUT AS A TRUE CHRISTIAN THAT HE IS BUT HE IS IN THE HOLLYWOOD CLOSET AS A CHRISTIAN UNFORTUNATELEY. IM NOT

JUDGING JUST HOPING HE MINISTERS TO ACTORS AND THE HOLLYWOOD WORLD.

EACH DAY WE WOULD KNOW AND BELEIVE SOMETHING. SOME KIND OF TOPIC WILL COME OUR WAY AND EVERY DAY IT DID FROM HEARTBREAK TO OPPRESSION TO HUMILITY TO ABOUT EVERY TOPIC YOU COULD THINK OF FOR 16 SHOWS. I USED TO SEE ROBERT BEFORE EACH SHOW LOOK IN THE MIRROR TO PSYCH HIMSELF UP AND TALK TO HIMSELF AND YOU KNOW JAIL MIRRORS ARE SORT OF DISTORTED AND CLOWDY. I DONT KNOW WHY BUT THEY ARE, MAYBE ITS THE MATERIAL THE MIRROR IS MADE OF BUT I DO REMEMBER ROBERT LOOKNG IN A CLOWDY MIRROR AND THEN GET READY FOR THE SHOW, ALL FREE.

IN THE SHOWS PEOPLE WERE COMING UP WHO HAVENT YET BEEN SAVED THROUGH THE GRACE OF JESUJS CHRIST AND WOULD FALL TO THE GROUND AND CRY AT TIMES. WE WOULD ALL LAY HANDS ON THESE PEOPLE AND BY THE END OF THE 16 DAYS WE HAD SAVED 90 PERCENT OF THE PEOPLE IN THERE THROUGH GUIDENCE FROM OUR LORD JESUJS CHRIST. I HAVE NEVER SEEN THE SPIIRT OF DARKNESS LEAVE AND THE SPIRIT OF JESUS TAKE OVER THAT DORM SO FAST THEN THERE.

IT WAS A MIRICLE AND I REALIZED I WASNT MAD AT THE POLICE THAT PUT ME THERE OR THE VERDICT THE POWER HUNGRY JUDGE YARTE UNFAIRLEY DID AND GAVE TO ME. NO, IF THEY WOULDNT HAVE DONE THAT I WOULDNT HAVE MET ROBERT DOWNEY JR AND GOT TO WORK WITH HIM AS AND IN CHAIRTY WORK TO SAVE SOULS FOR JESUS. GOD TURNED A NEGATIVE SIUTUATION INTO A POSITIVE ONCE AGAIN.

PRAISE GOD.

ALL IN ALL AFTER DAY 16 GOING INTO 17 WE WERE ALL MOVED TO DIFFERENT PLACES. THERE I MET THE NEXT GUY.

DANA OF KROQ. I MET DANA WHO IS THE WELL KNOWN DISC JOCKEY OF KROQ IN L.A. COUNTY JAIL AS WE AND ME AND ROBERT DOWNEY JR WERE MOVED FROM THE DORM ME AND ROBERT HAD ENTERTAINED AND DID CHURCH FOR THE DORM FOR 16 DAYS IN ERO.

I HAD HEARD ABOUT DANA OF KROQ AND ALOT OF PEOPLE ARE SAYING HE IS A RADIO LEGEND WITH A DRINKING PROBLEM. I AT THE TIME I FIRST HEARD ABOUT HIM DIDNT KNOW WHAT HE WAS IN FOR AND DID NOT KNOW WHERE HE WAS AT. ALL I KNOW IS EVERYONE TOLD ME I HAVE THE BED DANA WAS IN BEFORE I WAS THERE AND IT IS ALL FOR CELEBRATIES. EVERYONE ASKED IF I WAS FAMOUS WHEN NEXT TO ROBERT DOWNEY JRS BUNK AND IN DANA PAST BUNK AND I SAID NO BUT I SAID IN WAS A CELEBRATY BECAUSE EDDIE GRIFFIN TOLD ME TO SAY THIS IF I EVER GET ARRESTED FOR SOME BULLS--------.

EDDIE TOLD ME THIS ART A 51/50 WARD SO I BELEIVE THAT GOD TURNS THINGS THAT ARE AT FIRST BAD INTO GREAT BLESSINGS. 1. AT THE 51/50 WARD I WAS PUT THERE FOR AN INSANE AND ILLEGEL REASON AND THAT REASON WAS THAT I TOLD THE COPS THEY WERE DRIVING ME CRAZY WHICH IS OF COURSE A WELL KNOWN FIGURE OF SPEECH AND THEY PUT ME IN THE 51/50 WARD FOR SAYING I WAS CRAZY WHEN I SAID THEY WERE DRIVING ME CRAZY. ALL THE PEOPLE AT THE 51/50 WARD SAID THAT WAS MESSED UP THAT THEY DID THAT TO ME AND EDDIE AGREED AND ME AND EDDIE BECAME FRIENDS BECAUSE OF THAT EXACT OPPRESSION I SUFFERED THE THE CURRUPTNESS OF THE COPS THAT PUT ME THERE UNFAIR REASON AND INSANLEY AND ILLEGELLY.

THEN BECAUSE I FOLLOWED EDDIE GRIFFNS INSTRUCTIONS TO SAY I WAS A CELEBRATY AS HE DID. WELL, IT DID WORK FOR ME AND THIS IS WHY I GOT TO BE NEXT TO ROBERT DOWNEY JR AND HAVE DANAS OLD SPOT/DORM BED.

IN THE NEXT PLACE BEING MOVED AFTER I WAS THERE FOR 16 DAYS NEXT TO ROBERT AS MY BUNKEE AND THEN 7 DAYS IN A 51/50- HOLD AT THE OLD COUNTY JAIL BEING DAY   DAY 24. I RUN INTO DANA.

16. DANA OF KEOQ. SO AT THIS NEXT PLACE LOS ANGELES COUNTY JAIL PLACED US WAS FAR FROM ROBEERT DOWNEY JR BUT NOW I AM IN THIS DORM WITH DANA OF KROQ. IM NOT A FAN AND NEVER HEARD OF HIM AT THIS POINT BEING I DONT LISTEN TO KROQ BUT ALOT OF PEOPLE DO ESPECIALLY THE COPS WORKING THERE AT LOS ANGELES COUNTY JAIL AND BECAUSE OF THIS DNA IS TREATED GREAT BY THE COPS. THATS HOW COPS ARE, THEY ARE STAR STRUCK MORE THEN THE AVERAGE STAR STRUCK PERSON BASICALLY.

ALMOST A RIOT. ME AND DANA WERE KICKING IT AND WAS GOING TO DO ANOTHER SHOW THAT NIGHT AND RIGHT WHEN WE WERE GETTING TOGETHER THE 40 PLUS PEOPLE WHO WANTED TO DO IT AND THIS WHITE GUY WAS ARGUING WITH A BLACK GUY AND SUPPOSIDLEY THE BLACK GUY TOOK ONE OF THE MATTRESSES THE WHITE GUY OWNED AND HE WOULDNT GIVE IT BACK BECAUSE THE BLACK GUY SAID IT WASNT HIS. ANYWAYS THE WHITE GUY IS TRYING TO GET ALL THE WHITES TO FIGHT THE BALCKS IN THE DORM. THERE ARE LIKE 30 WHITES AND 20 BLACKS AND THERE WAS ALMOST GOING TO BE A RIOT AT THIS MOMENT. ME AND DANA DIDNT WANT TO BE IN A RIOT FOR THIS GUYS PURPOSE AND THE WHITE GUY WAS SAYING IT WAS THE POLITICS OF THE DORM AND IN LA COUNTY JAIL THAT A RIOT MUST BE DONE AND FOUGHT

BECAUSE OF THE PURPOSE THAT ONE RACE. THIS BLACK GUY SUPPOSIDLEY STOLE FROM ANOTHER RACE FROM THIS WHITE DUDE. SO HE IS USING THIS TO GET A BIG RIOT GOING. I BACK OUT AND HIDE AWAY AS DOES DAN AND DANA SAYS "MAN I DONT WANNA FIGHT BECAUSE THIS GUY LOST HIS EXTRA MATTRESS". I AGREED WITH HIM AND ME AND DANA LEFT THE AREA AND STAYED FAR FROM THESE RIOTERS. WE HIID OUT BY THE SHOWERS. WHEN WE SAY WE LEFT THE AREA WELL THAT ISNT TOO FAR AWAY BEING THE AREA I AM TALKING ABOUT IS WHERE THE 8 TOYLETS AND TWO SHOWERS ARE AT 25 FEET AWAY FROM THIS FOOL WHITEBOY.

ANYWAYS THE RIOT STARTED AND ME AND DANA DID NOT JOIN IN OR PARTICIPATE.

WE WERE TALKING TO EACH OTHER BOTH AGREEING WERE NOT GOING TO FIGHT FOR SOME GUY WHITE OR NOT AND THE SITUATION HAD NOTHING TO DO WITH ME OR DANA, IT WASNT WORTH IT TO US AND WE DIDNT BELEIVE IN THE CAUSE.

DANA WAS A NICE AND FRIENDLEY AND HUMBLE GUY.

17 AND 18. MOON UNIT AND DWEEZIL ZAPPA

I WAS AT THE CLAREMONT COLLEGES AND IT WAS THE TUESDAY NIGHT ART SHOW. THE ART SHOW CONSISTED OF MODERN ART TRANSLATION MEANING ITS NOT ART REALLY OR IT IS BUT NIOT GOOD. LET ME EXPLAIN. LIKE TWO PEOPLE PACKED IN MUD, AN ART PIECE OR A BRANCH AND A BROKEN LIMB WITH PAINT RUNNING OFF IT ETC NOT TALENT ART BUT B.S. ART.

WE WOULD GO NOT FOR THE ART BUT FOR THE FOOD AND ALCOHOL. THE FOOD WAS DELICIOUS, CHEESES AND MEATS AND DRINKS LIKE BEER AND CHAMPAINE AMONG

OTHER DRINKS LIKE PUNCH AND ORDERED EVEN SOMETIMES CAVIAR.

THERE WOULD BE ALL THE LOCALS FROM THE CLARMONT VILLAGE, YOU KNOW, THE CLAREMONT VILLAGE HANGERS LIKE PEBBEER BROWN AND KIKI AND HENRY BARNES AMONG MARTIN MODELL WHO AUDITIONED FOR FRNK ZAPPAS BAND IN 1982 AND WOULD HAVE MADE THE SPOT EXCEPT HE DIDNT KNOW HOW TO READ CHARTS AND THAT WAS IMPORTANT WITH FRANK ZAPPA AND HIS PEOPLE AND BAND.

SPEAKING OF THE ZAPPAS. A COUPLE TIMES DWEEZIL ZAPPA WOULD BE GOING TO THESE TUESDAY ART SHOWS AND I DONT KNOW IF IT WAS BECAUSE HE WAS AT ONE OF THE CLAREMONT COLLEGES. THE COLLEGES CONSISTING OF 5 COLLEGES AND VERY LOVED IN THE USA. 1. HARVY MUDD 2.. PITZER 3. CLAREMONT MENS 4. SCRIPPS AND 5. POMONA COLLEGES.

OR I DONT KNOW IF HE WAS THERE BECAUSE FRANK ZAPPA USED TO LIVE IN CLAREMONT IN WHICH HE DID FINALLY LEAVING IN 1964, SO WHEN WE WERE FIRST LIVING HERE IN 1964 FRANK ZAPPA LIVED ACROSS THE STREET ACROSS FROM INDIAN HILL ON OAK PARK AVENUE 3 HOUSES ACROSS THE STREET.

WHATEVER REASON THEY WERE THERE IVE SEEN DWEEZIL A COUPLE TIMES AND HE WAS QUIET AND NOT TALKING BUT ON THIS NIGHT HIS SISTER WAS THERE TOO. I WAS BEING SARCASRTIC AND SAYING "WOW ITS DWEEZIL ZAPPA WOW AND HIS SISTER VALLEY GIRL". THEY GOT UP AND NICLEY ASKED ME IF THEY COULD TALK TO ME OUTSIDE ON THE STEPS AND I SAID SURE. DWEEZIL SAID SOMETHING TO THE COVERSATION LIKE "MAN WE CANT HELP BEING ZAPPAS KIDS". AND THEN MOON SAID "PUT YOURSELF IN OUR P45LACE HOW WOULD YOU LIKE IT. LIKE

IT IF SOMEONE WAS GETTING ON YOU FOR BEING A KID OF ZAPPA" I FELT UNCOMFORTABLE AND BAD AND SORT OF STUPID AND EMBARRASSED AND APOLOGISED AND THEY SAID COOL AND THAT WAS IT.

THEY WERE COOL PEOPLE, A LITTLE SARCASRTIC BUT DOWN TO EARTH FOR THE MOST PART. ALL IN ALL I HAD A POSITIVE ASSOSSIATION WITH THEM.

THE OTHER TIME I EVER DEALT WITH ANYONE FROM THE ZAPPA FAMILY WAS WHEN I CALLED BARKING PUMPKIN RECORDS AND THE OLDER BROTHER SAID STRAIGHT UP. WE DONT EXCEPT ARTISTS OUTSIDE OF OUR FAMILY.

JOHN KOLLADNER. 19 AND 20. TOM WHALLEY 21. MICHEAL KLINK.

THIS IS SHORT. I MET JOHN KILADNER THROUGH SENDING STUFF TO GEFFIN RECORDS. I WAS N A BAND WITH MIKE CORRIERE TRYING TO GET A MAJOR RECORD DEAL WITH GEFFIN AND MICHEAL KLINK OFFERED TO PRODUCE US FOR 30,000. WE DIDNT HAVE IT AND THAT WAS IT KNOWING MICHEAL KLINK. JOHN KOLLADNER BECAME A BIG A AND R GUY FOR GEFFIN AND THEN MOVED UP. KOLLADNER TURNED DOWN MY MUSIC A FEW TIMES AS WELL AS TOM WHALLEY DID TOO. TOM, WHEN WE KNEW HIM WAS WORKING FOR CAPITOL RECORDS AND WAS A AND R MAN AT THE TIME AND AGAIN WROTE ME THREE LETTERS OF REJECTION. TOO MUCH THIS AND TOO LITTLE THAT BLAH BLAH BLAH AS WELL AS WE LOST TOUCH WITH TOM TOO. TOM BECAME HEAD OF WARNER BROTHERS RECORDS. REPLACING TED TEMPLEMAN.

22/23. DICK CLARK AND LIONEL RICHEY.

THE REASON WHY I PUT THESE TWO GUYS TOGETHER IS BECAUSE I RAN ACROSS THEM AT THE SAME TIME. TWO DIFFERENT STORIES THOUGH.

ME AND LAILAH WERE DRIVING BACK FROM DEALING WITH SOMEONE AT OUR WORK IN HOLLYWOOD AND LAILAH SAYS, "LOOK THERES LIONEL RICHEY" AND I 'SAID AND DICK CLARK,"

SHE THEN DROPS ME OFF TO GO TO THEM. I DIDNT CARE MUCH ABOUT LIONEL RICHEY BUT I WANTED TO TALK TO DICK CLARK. AS I GOT CLOSER TO DICK CLARK WHO HIM AND LIONEL RICHEY WERE TOGETHER TALKING IN FRONT OF THE BMI BUILDING AND SO I AM GIUESSING THIS IS WHY LIONEL WAS THERE. TO GET A CHECK OR SOMETHING. AS I GOT CLOSER ON THE HOLLYWOOD SIDEWALK SORT OF WALKING FAST TO THEM. LIONEL TALKS OFF LIKE A SCARED RABBIT THEN I CAME UP TO DICK CLARK AT THIS TIME NO ONE BUT ME RECOGNIZED HIM AND WELL LAILAH TOO RECOGNISED HIM. AS I STARTED TALKING TO HIM ALOT OF OTHER PEOPLE RECOGNISED HIM. I ASKED HIM IF HE CAN LOOK AT MY MUSIC AND PUT ME ON HIS SHOW OR SOMETHING AND HE TOLD ME TO CONTACT HIS COMPANY IN BURBANK.

WHAT ME AND LAILAH TRIED TO DO WITH DICK CLARK AND HIS PRODUCTION AND HIS RECORD COMPANY.WAS HAPPY AND LOOKING FOREWARD TO POSSIBLY WORKING WITH DICK CLARK BEING HE TOLD ME TO GO TO HIS OFFICE IN BURBANK. IT WAS A PRETTY BIG PLACE AND IT HAD A LOWER FLOOR BELOW THE GROUND. ONCE I SAW DICK AT THE CHALK BOARD TALKING TO PEOPLE WITHOUT HIS HAIRPIECE ON.

I WENT TO THE PLACE ABOUT 10 TIMES SENDING STUFF TO DICK CLARK AND WEARING ,MY BADDCLOWN MAKEUP AS A CLOWN. THEY SEEMED TO LIKE THE CLOWN GET UP BUT NEVER CALLED ME BACK AND FINALLY AFTER I ASKED WHY NO ONE WILL TALK TO ME THEY SENT ME A LETTER CLAIMING THEY ARE CLICK RECORDS WHICH IS ABOUT OLDIES BUT GOODIES FROM THE 50S AND NOTHING ELSE.

WELL, I WISH HE DICK CLARK AND HIS STAFF COULD HAVE TOLD ME THIS UP FRONT AND NOT TO WASTE OUR GAS AS WELL AS OUR TIME FOR THESE 10 UN-NECESSARY TRIPS. DICK SHOULD HAVE SAID OUT ON THE SIDEWALK WHEN I MET HIM THAT HE DOESNT DO ANYTHING BUT OLDIES AND GOODIES.

AFTER GETTING THE REJECTION LETTER FROM DICK CLARK PERSONALLY OR AT LEAST IT SAID THAT AND IT WAS HIS SIGNATURE. WELL, AFTER THAT REJECTION LETTER WE WERE DONE WITH DICK. ALWAYS TO THIS DAY WONDER WHY DICK JUST SAID WHEN I TALKED TO HIM ON SUNSET BLVD THAT HE ONLY DOES OLDIES BUT GOODIES BUT HE DIDNT. HE LET US GO ALMOST 10 TIMES DOWN THERE GIVING MUSICAL MATERIAL. THAT USED UP ALOT OF TIME AND MONEY AND THAT WAS A PLAIN OLD WASTE.

24.   KAREEM ABDUL JABBAR.

ONE DAY IN 1984 I WAS SLEEPING IN MY LIMO. I GUESS TAKING A NAP AND IT WAS AT THE SHELL GAS STATION I USED TO WORK AT 5 YEARS EARLIER OR SO IN 1979. THE GAS STAITON WAS LOCATED ON INDIAN HILL BLVD AND THE 10 FREEWAY.

I WAS PARKED NEXT TO THE PHONE BOOTH AND I DONT KNOW WHY BUT I WAS JUST THERE. AS I WOKE UP I LOOKED OVER AND HERE WERE THESE VERY TALL PEOPLE ABOUT 5 OR 6 PEOPLE AROUND 6 FOOT 8. THE ONLY BLACK ONE WAS THE TALLEST AND HE WAS KAREEM. I JUMPED OUT OF THE CAR AND I SAID TO HIM, "HI KAREEM YOU ARE THE GREATEST BASKETBALL PLAYER OF ALL TIME". AT THIS TIME HE WAS IN THE LEAGUE STILL I THINK ON HIS 16TH YEAR. HE DIDNT SAY ANYTHING BUT SMILED. I NEXT STARTED WALKING NEXT TO HIM AND HE WAS REAL TALL, TALLER THEN 7-2 IN MY OPINION. I BELEIVE HIM TO BE AROUND 7-4. AGAIN I SPOKE AND SOMEONE ELSE WAS

PUMPING THE GAS THOUGH HE PAID. HE THEN SAT ON ONE OF THE ISLANDS WHERE THE PUMP WAS AND HE WAS ALMOST AS TALL AS ME THEN I SAID I" AM A SINGER IN A BAND AND ONE DAY I WILL PLAY THE FORUM TOO." HE LAUGHED BUT DIDNT SAY ANYTHING AND THAT WAS IT.

KAREEM NEVER TALKED AND I WAS ALITTLE DISAPPOINTED IN WHY AND WHAT WAS HIS REASON NOT TO TALK. IS IT BECAUSE HES BETTER THEN ME OR COULD IT BE SHY OR COULD IT BE AFRAID OF A LAWSUIT? IM NOT LIKE THAT AND WOULD NEVER DO SOMETHING LIKE THAT BUT HE DOESNT KNOW SO I RESPECT THAT AND UNDERSTAND THAT.

25-AND 26. GARY COLEMAN AND ROBERT GULLIMEA.

I FIRST SAW DAVID ENKE PLAYING A JAZZ TYPE ROCK INSTRUMENTEL WITHOUT ANY VOCALS AT ALL. I BELEIVE BECAUSE THERE WERE NOT MANY VOCALISTS AROUND THIS AREA OF CLAREMONT AT THIS TIME WHICH WAS MID 1982. I SAW THE DRUMMER TOO.. HIS NAME WAS MARTIN MODALL AND THIS GUY WAS THE BEST DRUMMER AROUND. WHY? BECAUSE HE CAN PLAY JAZZ. DRUMMERS FOR SOME REASON ARE THE BEST. EVEN THOUGH I DONT FIND JAZZ AS THE BEST SOUND AND OR MUSIC BUT FOR SOME REASON IF A DRUMMER CAN FEEL JAZZ HE CAN DO ANY TYPE OF MUSIC. LATER MARTIN AUDITIONED FOR FRANK ZAPPA AS A PERCUSSIONIST AND DIDNT MAKE THE BAND ONLY BECAUSE HE COULDNT READ CHARTS, WHATS FUNNY IS I DID MY VERY FIRST CHART AFTER 40 YEARS OF SIGHT PLAYING TODAY FOR MY DAUGHTER CHEYENNE FOR A PIANO PIECE CALLED FREE FOR HER TO LEARN ON THE PIANO.

LATER I WAS INTRODUCED TO DAVE ENKE BY MERRILL ANDERSON. AT THIS TIME BOTH OF THEM WERE GOING TO

POMONA PITZER COLLEGE. AT THIS TIME IN 1981 AROUND MAY MERRILL WAS ONE OF MY GIRLFRIENDS,

GETTING TOGETHER AND WORKING WITH DAVE ENKE.

I REMEMBER IN 1982 I WAS LOOKING FOR A GUITARIST THAT CAN PLAY ROCK AND OTHER SOFT TYPE OF ORIGIONAL. I FINALLY FOUND AN ORIGIONAL GUITARIST NAMED DAVE ENKE. LIKE THE BAND ONE WITH ROLAND AND ME AS A DUET IN ONE ME AND DAVE WERE LIKE THAT TOO.

WHEN I GOT TOGETHER TO AUDITION FOR DAVE IT WORKED MAGICALLY. ME AND DAVE PRACTICED IN MOM AND DADS BACKYARD EVEN THOUGH I WAS LIVING AT TRISHAS AND MY APARTMENT AT THE SUNRISA APARTMENTS IN POMONA. WELL THE VIBE FELT BETTER PRACTICING AT MOM AND DADS EVEN THOUGH I LIVED SOMEWHERE ELSE.

ME AND DAVE WROTE ABOUT 20 SONGS TOGETHER AND IT WAS EASY BEING HE WROTE THE MUSIC AND I WROTE THE VOCAL MELODY AND LYRICS AS WELL AS WE BOTH ARRANGED THE MUSIC TO OUR BOTH LIKES AND TASTES. IN OTHER WORDS A MUSICAL COLLABORATION.

THR PLACES ME AND DAVE PLAYED. WE PLAYED AT CITRUS COLLEGE ABOUT 10 TIMES AND PLAYED CAL POLY POMONA AS WELL AS MANY OTHER PLACES. BACKYARD PARTIES ETC AND WALTERS COFFEE SHOP.

THE WASH. THE WASH IS A PLACE ART THE CLAREMONT COLLEGES. THE MIDDLE OF THE WASH LOOKS LIKE A LITTLE LION ARENA LIKE THE OLD JULIUS CEASEAR DAYS BUT THE BANDS PLAY THERE BECAUSE THERE ARE ELECTRIC OUTLETS BUT ME AND DAVE WERE ACOUSTIC AND ALSO ELECTRTIC BUT NEVER PLAYED AN ELECTRIC GUITAR GIG THERE. WE WOULD ALWAYS JUST GO AND

PLAY OUT ON THE LAWN. THERE WAS GRASS ON THE OUTSIDE OF THIS CEASAR LOOKING PLACE. IT WAS BEAUTIFUL.

SO WITHOUT PLANNING IT, WE MADE IT A HABIT EVERY FRYDAY AT THIS PARTY WE STARTED WITH 1 KEG TO PLAY RANDOMLEY WITH ANYONE ELSE WHO WANTS TO DO THE SAME. ME AND DAVE WOULD JUST SIT ON THE GRASS AND PLAY AND SING AND PLAY GUITAR. WE WOULD PLAY OUR ORIGINALS AND ONE DAY WE HEARD THIS NOISE OF ALOT OF PEOPLE IN THE BACKGROUND. WE KEPT PLAYING AND FINALLY SOME PEOPLE FROM THAT CROWD CAME OVER. THEY WERE RUDE AND SNOOTY AND TOLD US TO TURN DOWN OUR MUSIC. WE SAID WE COULDNT TURN IT DOWN BECAUSE IT IS ACOUSTIC AND SAID NO AND SAID WE DIDNT APPRECIATE THEIR UNFRIENDLEYNESS SO THESE PEOPLE DECIDED TO TRY IT ANOTHER WAY. THEY INVITED US TO WATCH THE MOVIE SET AND SAID THAT THEY WERE DOING A FILM AND WE ARE WELCOME TO WATCH SO ME AND DAVE AND A FEW OTHERS DECIDED TO WATCH AND THERE WAS GARY COLEMAN AND ROBERT GULLIMEA AND THE MOVIE WAS ABOUT GARY COLEMAN BEING AN ANGEL OR SOMETHING TO THAT EFFECT.

ANYWAYS I WENT RIGHT UP TO GARY COLEMAN, NOT WHEN HE WAS ACTING BUT WHEN HE WAS IN BETWEEN SCENES TO SHOOT. FIRST I SAW HIM STANDING THERE TELLING PEOPLE WHAT TO DO AS HE PICKED HIS NOSE AND ATE HIS BUGGERS THEN HE WALKED BY US AND HE SAID . "LOOK DAD A LIZARD."

I THEN TRY TO CATCH THE LIZARD TO HELP GARY AND GARY THEN SAYS TO ME AS I GAVE THE LIZARD TO GARY. HE SAYS "I WANNA CATCH MY OWN LIZARD." ME AND GARY GOT ALONG AFTER THAT AS I PUT THE LIZARD DOWN AND HE DID CATCH IT AND WE BECAME ACQUANTANCES. WE PLAYED SOME MUSIC ME AND DAVE THAT IS AND DAVE ON

GUITAR ANDF ME SINGING AND THEN GARYS STRICT FATHER SAID TO HIM. 'GARY BACK ON THE SET NOW' AND GARY WAS NOT HAPPY. GARY WAS THE OWNER OF THE PRODUCTION COMPANY BECAUSE HE TOLD ME THAT. I FINALLY PICKED UP GARY AND HELD HIM IN MY ARMS AND HE WAS COOL WITH THAT BECAUSE I ASKED HIM IF I COULD PICK HIM UP. HE SAID OK AND THEN GUARDS PULLED STICKS AND GUNS ON ME AND MADE ME PUT HIM DOWN.

LATER ON AS WE WERE LEAVING FOR THE NIGHT GARY WAS IN A TRAILOR AND YELLED, "HEY GUYS" AND WE SAID HEY. HE GOES "NA NANNAN NAN NA NNA NA" AND WE IGNROED THAT STUFF AND SAID IF HE WANTS TO KNOW US HE HAS TO GIVE RESPECT. WE DONT DO THE STAR THING AROUND HERE,

WE ALSO SAW ROBERT GULLIMEA AND TRIED TO SAY HI TO HIM AND HE SNBBED US.

27. GEORGE HAMILTON AND 28. KIM KARDASHION AND 29. CHLOE KARDASION AND 30. TONI BRAXTON

THESE ARE CALLED THE SNUBBERS.

29 AND 30. KIM AND CHLOE KARDASHION. I SAW THESE GIRLS AT TARGET. I WAS PANHANDLING AND I SAID. HEY YOU LOOK LIKE THAT CHICK ON THAT SHOW. THIS WAS LIKE 2010 AND I DIDNT KNOW THEIR NAMES AND THE I SAID HEY YOU LOOK LIKE THE SISTER AND THEY SMILED AND DIDNT SAY A WORD AND THEY DIDNT GIVE ME ANY MONEY WHEN I PANHANDLED. THEY THOUGHT THEY WERE BETTER THEN ME.

WHATS FUNNY IS IN REALITY THOSE TWO GIRLS CANT DANCE SING OR ACT OR DO ANYTHING BUT BE FAMOUS. ME ON THE OTHER HAND I HAVE WRITTEN OVER 2000 SONGS 28 VIDEOS AND OVER 1000 MUSIC PERFORMANCES FROM RADIO TO TV TO LIVE. AND IM NOT FAMOUS.

SO WHAT IS FAME?

28. GEORGE HAMILTON.

DAVID COHEN WAS MY VIDEO PRODUCER IN OUR FIRST VIDEO ENTITLED HER GAME WHICH I WORKED WITH DAVID IN 1990 TO MAKE THIS VIDEO. WE WORKED OUT OF BEVERLY HILLS AS WELL AS HOLLYWOOD AND THE GREEN DOOR. A CLUB IN MONTCLARE CALIFORNIA.

NOW IT IS 1995 AND DAVE IS THE PERSONAL ASSISTANT TO GEORGE HAMILTON ON THE GERARGE HAMILTON SHOW.

I WAS A MOVIE EXTRA AND WAS PART OF AN AGENCY THAT WAS GETTING ME SOME SHOWS TO BE A MOVIE EXTRA AS WELL AS BEING AN AUDIENCE PARTICIPANT IN SHOWS AND ONE OF THESE SHOWS WAS FOR THE GEORGE HAMILTON SHOW. I WAS AN AUDIENCE PARTICIPANT AND WHAT THIS ENTAILS IS I GOTTA LAUGH WHEN THE LAUGH LIGHT TURNS ON AND APPLAUD WHEN THE APPLAUD LIGHT TURNS ON.

I SAW THE GEORGE HAMILTON SHOW THIS DAY AND JANET LEE WAS ON IT FROM PSYCHO. JAMIE LEE CURTIS MOTHER AND TONY CURTIS EX WIFE AS WELL AS LL COOL J WAS ON IT AND ELANA HAMILTON. AFTER THE SHOW I WENT OVER TO TALK TO DAVID COHEN SINSE I HAVENT SEEN HIM SINSE 1990. AS I WENT OVER THERE I HAD TO GO INTO A LITTLE SWINGING DOOR AROUND 3 FEET HIGH AND ON THE OTHER SIDE OF THE DOOR WAS DAVID AND GEORGE HAMILTON. I WASNT INTERESTED IN SPEAKING TO GEORGE HAMILTON BUT WAS INTERESTED IN SPEAKING TO DAVID COHEN. AS I GO IN THROUGH THE DOOR I REALIZE THIS DOOR IS THE UNWRITTEN DIVIDER BETWEEN THE AUDIENCE AND GEORGE HAMILTON. GEORGE, AFTER I SAID HEY TO HIM HE RAN OFF LIKE HE THOUGHT I WAS GOING TO HURT HIM WHICH OF COURSE IS PURE PARANOIA ON HIS PART. I WAS JUST THERE TO TALK TO

DAVID COHEN AND WASNT EVEN INTERESTED IN TALKING TO GEORGE.

AFTER THAT I REALIZED EVEN MORE THAT THESE ENTERTAINMENT PERSONALITIES ARE EXTREMELY PHONEY AND STUCK UP AND WEIRD AND PARANOID.

31. TONI BRAXTON AT TARGET, MONTCLARE.

I WAS COMING FROM TARGET AND I SAID HEY YOUR BEAUTIFUL YOU LOOK LIKE AND SHE FINISHES WITH "YEAH IM TONI BRAXTON, i AM HER AND LEAVE ME THE F------ ALONE".

31. MARK MCGUIRE

THE FIRST TIME I SAW MARK MCGWIRE WAS WHEN HE WAS PLAYING SOCCER AGAINST MY BROTHERS TEAM. MY BROTHER JOHN WAS THE GOALE AND MARK WAS A FORWARD ON THE OTHER TEAM. I REMEMBER THINKING HE IS OFF SIDES AND TOO CLOSE TO THE OPPOSING GOALIE WHICH IS MY BROTHER.

HE IS AROUND 30 FEET FROM MY BROTHER A.K.A. 10 YARDS AWAY AND I REMEMBER HIM WEARING GLASSES AND HE WAS AN AKWARD GUY, PRETTY TALL AND HAD A MOP OF RED HAIR. PHIL WOOTTON KNEW HIM AND WE USED TO CALL HIM "MOP" MCGWIRE.

ONCE AT THE JUANITAS BURRRITO PLACE IN POMONA WE SAW MARK THEN AND THIS WAS AFTER HE WAS ROOKIE OF THE YEAR AND MY FRIEND DANNY ADAMS RAN UP TO HIM WITH A BASEBALL BAT AND THE PURPOSE OF THIS WAS DANNY WANTED TO GET AN AUTOGRAPH FROM MARK TO PUT THE AUTOGRAPH ON THE BAT. MARK FREAKED OUT AND RAN. HE THOUGHT DANNY WAS GOING TO HIT HIM WITH THE BAT. RIGHT THEN DANNY SAYS "NO MARK, REMEMBER ME?". "I WENT TO GRADE SCHOOL WITH YOU".

DANNY ADAMS AND MARK THEN REMEMBERED AND SIGNED THE BAT AND WAS REAL COOL. MARK LEFT AN AUTOGRAPHED PICTURE FOR THE RESTRAUNT JUANITAS AND THE PICTURE SAID THE BEST BURRITOS EVER IN THE WORLD AND I AGREE WITH THAT. JUANITAS ARE SPECIAL AND HAVE THEIR OWN STYLE OF BURRITO AND IT IS AND WAS THE BEST BURRITOS I EVER HAD TOO. EVER IN THE WORLD.

ANOTHER TIME WE WERE ALL PLAYING SOFTBALL AT MEMORIAL PARK IN CLAREMONT WHICH THIS IS THE CITY I WAS RAISED ON AND SO WAS MARK RAISED IN CLAREMONT THOUGH ON HIS ROOKIE CARD HE SAID HE WAS FROM POMONA WHICH IS THE SAME EXACT FEEL I HAVE TOO. I SAY POMONA TOO BECAUSE CLAREMONT ARE REAL POSER PHONEY PEOPLE. THIS IS MY TRUE OPINION.

WE ARE IN THE MIDDLE OF THE GAME AND MARK COMES OVER AND MY NEXT DOOR NEIGHBOR MADE A JOKE ABOUT ME SAYING HED RATHER BE DEAD THEN RED IN THE HEAD.

WELL, I TOLD MARK THIS THAT DON WOOTTON SAID THAT HED RATHER BE DEAD THEN RED IN THE HEAD BECAUSE I HAD RED HAIR AND OF COURSE MARK HAS RED HAIR TOO. WELL MARK LAUGHINGLY SAYS "WHAT DID YOU SAY DON?". DON EMBARRISSINGLEY LAUGHS AND SAYS "jUST KIDDING BIG MARK.'

LATER MARK JOINED ONTO THE GAME AND HE HIT THE BALL OUT OF THE ENTIRE PARK INTO THE HOUSES ACROSS THE STREET BEHIND MEMORIAL PARK.

WE SAID TO MARK, "MARK WE THOUGHT YOU WERE A PITCHER AT DAMIAN HIGH SCHOOL" AND MARK SAYS "WELL I HIT A LITTLE TOO."

YEAH ENOUGHT TO BREAK ROGER MARIS SEASON RECORD OF 61 HOMERS.

MARK AT THAT TIME WAS OM THE GOLF TEAM AT DAMIAN AND WAS ON THE BASEBALL TEAM AS A PITCHER. WOW MIRICLES DO HAPPEN.

ONCE AT HOLIDAY HEA;LTH SPA AROUND 1984.

MARK WAS WORKING OUT THERE AS DID ME AND ROLAND WHO LATER BECAME BILLY BRAGG I TOLD ROLAND ID GIVE HIM A JOINT IF HER ASKED THAT GUY IF HE WAS NAMED MOP MCGWIRE AND HE DID IT AND MARK AGREED. WE THINK ITS BECAUSE HE THOUGHT ROLAND SAID MARK NOT MOP SINSE IT SOUNDS ALOT ALIKE.

MARK WAS A NICE GUJY.

32. COURTNEY LOVE AKA MICHELLE HARRISON

I WENT TO HOLLYWOOD TO THE RAINBOW CLUB WITH TWO EX GIRLFRINEDS NAMED TJ. AND PATRICIA AND PATRICIA WAS GERMAN AND TJ WAS JAPANEESE. WE WERE AT THE RAINBOW ROOM AND THEY DECIDED TO GET ALOT OF ATTENTION IN THE FRONT ROOM. I DECIDED TO GO TO THE VIP ROOM. NOW THE VIP ROOM IS A PLACE YOU PAY 5 DOLLORS FOR AND YOU THINK YOUR A VIP I GUESS. I DONT KNOW WHY I WENT THERE BUT I DID AND IT WASNT FOR THAT REASION I KNOW THAT. WHEN I GOT THERE, THERE WAS ONLY 1 OTHER PERSON THERE AND SHE WAS A BLONDE SKINNY GIRL IN A DRESS. SHE WAS EXPOSING HER VAGINA TO ME AND I FELT MAYBE THATS HER WAY OF SAYING HI AND WANTING TO GET TO KNOW ME AND IT WAS. THIS WAS TRUE AND TURNED OUT TO BE JUST THAT.

I CAME UP AND TALKED TO HER AND WE HIT IT OFF GREAT. SHE HAD A GREAT PERSONALITY AND WHILE WE WERE TALKING THE DISC JOCKY RADIO GUY WAS PLAYING A TAPE. THE FIRST SONG I HEARD FROM THE TAPE WAS THE SONG WELCOME TO THE JUNGLE WHICH OF COURSE IS THE GREAT SONG BY GUNS AND ROSES THE BAND. AT

THIS TIME IT WAS PLAYING COURTNEY LOVE TOLD ME THE TAPE I AM HEARING IS A TAPE SHE GAVE THE DISC JOCKY GUY. I REMEMBER THERE WAS JUST 2 PEOPLE PLUS THE DISC JOCKY THERE. ME AND COURTNEY LOVE AND THE DISC JOCKEY. I TOLD COURTNEY THE SONG WAS GREAT AND SHE SAID "YEAH THE BAND IS NAMED GUNS AND ROSES AND I JUST GOT DONE DOING AXL". I DIDNT KNOW WHAT AXL WAS SO I WAS LIKE WONDERING, DOING AN AXEL? -SHE SAID "NO.AXL IS THE NAME OF THE LEAD SINGER OF THIS BAND". SHE SAID IT IS A DEMO TAPE SHE GOT FROM AXL WHO GOT IT FROM GEFFIN RECORDS AND I ASKED IF THEY WERE SIGNED TO GEFFIN AND COURTNEY SAID "YEAH I BELEIVE ITS A STARTER CONTRACT". THIS WAS THE SUMNMER OF 1987 AND I REMEMBER SEEING GUNS AND ROSES PROMOTING THEIR BAND AND THEIR SHOWS IN HOLLYWOOD IN THIS LOCAL MAGAZINE CALLED BAM MAGAZINE AND I REMEMBER THEIR BAND AD WAS ON THE OTHER SIDE OF THE PAGE AS OUR BAND AD AT THAT TIME BUT A LITTLE EARLIER LIKE MAY OF 1987.

SO ME AND COURTNEY LEFT THE VIP ROOM AND THE RAINBOW CLUB AND I WENT LOOKING FOR MY TWO FRIENDS BUT THEY LEFT ME SO I WAS STUCK WITH COURTNEY LOVE AT THAT TIME SHE SAID HER NAME WAS SHASTA AND HER REAL NAME WAS MICHELLE HARRISON AND THAT HER STAGE NAME IS COURTNEY LOVE AND SHE WILL BE A ROCK STAR. I SAID GOOD LUCK AND REMEMBER HER TELLING ME THIS THE NEXT DAY AFTER I STAYED THE NIGHT WITH HER.

WE FIRST WENT TO DENNYS FOR AROUND AN HOUR AND THIS DENNYS WAS ON SUNSET BLVD BY THE FREEWAY. ITS STILL THERE TO THIS DAY. WHEN WE SAT DOWN WE ORDERED FOOD AND A DRINK. THERE WAS A BEAUTIFUL GIRL FROM FLORIDA FLIRTING WITH ME, ASKING ME TO TAKE HER AWAY AND I LOOKED AT SHASTA AKA MICHELLE

AKA COURTNEY WITH A LOOK LIKE SHE BETTER BE ROMANTIC TO ME TONIGHT BECAUSE I AM PASSING UP AN OPPORTUNITY WITH SOME BEAUTIFUL GIRL FROM FLORIDA WHO IS INTO THE ALL AMERICA BLONDE SURFER ROCKER TYPE LIKE THE KIND OF GIRL I DREAM ABOUT.

WE THEN LEAVE AND GO TO ONE OF THE CANYON DRIVES AND SHE TAKES ME TO A PLACE SHE KNOWS ABOUT WHICH IS OFF OF THE CANYON DRIVE AND WE WALK A BIT DOWN A GULLY AND INTO A SECLUDED PLACE. I REMEMBER PARKING THE CAR OFF THE ROAD AND IT WAS QUITE A ROMANTIC PLACE.

WHAT ME AND MICHELLE TALKED ABOUT IN THE CANYON.

WE TALKED ABOUT HER BEING IN THE SID AND NANCY MOVIE AND TALKED ABOUT HER FUTURE DREAMS AND MINE AS WELL AS HER SAYING SHE WAS A STRIPPER AS WELL AS BEEN TO ALASKA AND THAT SHE WANTS TO HAVE A DAUGHTER. WE WERE SITTING BASICALLY ON A ROCK. IT WAS IN A VALLEY AREA AND IT WAS QUITE ROMANTIC. IT WAS LIKE SHE WAS PROPHOCISING HER FUTURE. SHE TALKED ALOT BUT LISTENED TOO.

AFTER A COUPLE HOURS TALKING WE WATCHED THE SUNSET COME UP AND THEN WENT TO THE HOTEL AS I WENT TO THE HOTEL I SAW A HEROIN ADDICT SHOOT UP HEROIN IN AN ALLEY NEXT TO THE HOTEL THEN WHEN WE WENT UP TO HER HOTEL I SAW A RAT RUN DOWN THE HALL. THESE TWO THINGS ARE SO STEREOTYPE THAT I THOUGHT THIS WAS LIKE A MOVIE I WAS IN OR SOMETHING ALSO FINDING 20 AND THEN 12 DOLLORS ON TWO DIFFERENT OCCASIONS THIS NIGHT BEFORE I FELT SHE WAS GOOD LUCK. WE THEN WENT INTO THE HOTEL AND I SAW ALL THESE KIDS. THEY LOOKED LIKE RUNAWAYS AND WERE ALL SLEEPING ON HER FLOOR. THERE WAS NO FURNITURE AND I THOUGHT SHE WAS NICE TO LET THESE

KIDS SLEEP ON THE FLOOR. THIS ALSO REMINDED ME LATER OF THE MOVIE SID AND NANCY WHEN ALL WERE SLEEPING ON THE FLOOR IN THAT MOVIE WHILE THE SEX PISTOLS BAND WAS ON THEIR FIRST SMALL TOUR.

I REMEMBER SHASTA A.K.A. MICHELLE AND ALSO KNOWN AS COURTNEY LOVE DRIVING ME IN THE CAR THE LAST NIGHT LISTENING TO THE WHOLE GUNS AND ROSES TAPE AS WELL AS I REMEMBER THERE WERE ALL THESE DRUMS IN THE BACK IOF THE CAR. IT WAS A HATCHBACK SO THERE WAS A THIRD SEAT IN THE BACK THAT HELD THE DRUMS.

I LOVED ALL THE GUNS AND ROSES SONGS AND WHEN I GOT BACK I ORDERED THE 33 RECORD THAT HELD ALL 9 SONGS. I REMEMBER PARADISE CITY AMONG OTHERS AND REALLY LOVED THE ALBUM. GUNS AND ROSES WERE NOT YET FAMOUS OR HAD MADE IT AND SO WHEN I ORDERED THE 33 RECORD NO ONE HAD HEARD OF THE ALBUM AT THE MUSIC PLUS STORE.

TH FLOOR WAS TOO CROWDED FOR ME AND COURTNEY TO BE INTIMATE SO WE WENT INTO THE CLOSET INSIDE AND CONNECTED TO THE BATHROOM.

I SLEPT BUT SHE DIDNT. WE WERE INTIMATE. THE NEXT DAY AFTER WAKING UP I WANTED TO LEAVE BUT WOULDNT BE RUDE. ALL THE KIDS WERE GONE AND IT WAS JUST ME AND SAUNDIE. I BELEIVE SHE WAS HER BISEXUAL LOVER. BUT MICHELLES ATTITUDE WAS,

 THEY ARE TOGETHER UNLESS SHE FINDS A GUY SO SAUNDIE WAS NOT WITH HER AS WHEN I WAS AND I REMEMBER SAUNDIE JUMPING OUT OF THE BATHROOM WHILE WE WERE IN THE FRONT ROOM TOPLESS AND SCREAMED LIKE SHE WAS STARTLED. WE TALKED SOME MORE AND THIS IS WHERE SHE SAID SHE WAS GOING TO

BE COURTNEY LOVE A ROCK STAR. I WISHED HER LUCK. WE TALKED ABOUT HER BAND BABALON SOMETHING. AND SHE SHOWED ME HER TATOO THAT SAYS COURTNEY LOVE.

WE NEXT WENT TO THE SIZZLER RESTRAUNT AND THERE MICHELLE STARTED A FOOD FIGHT AND WE WERE KICKED OUT.

AFTER THIS PAT MY GUITARIST CAME TO PICK ME UP. THE DAY BEFORE PAT WAS SUPPOSED TO COME WITH ME ON THIS DATE WITH PATRICIA AND T.J. MY TWO EX GIRLFRIENDS BUT HE HAD A DATE WITH HIS FUTURE WIFE. I AM GLAD PAT DIDNT GO OR I WOULD NOT HAVE BEEN ABLE TO HANG OUT WITH COURTNEY LOVE THE WHOLE NIGHT BEING TJ AND PATRICIA LEFT ME THERE AND IF PAT WOULD HAVE CAME THAT NIGHT HE WOULDNT HAVE LEFT ME THERE AND I WOULD HAVE LEFT WITH PAT THEREFORE NOT SPENDING THE NIGHT WITH MICHELLE AKA COURTNEY LOVE. AS PAT AND ME WERE DRIVING OFF I SAW COURTNEY AND HER FRIEND SAUNDIE WAVING TO ME. I FELT LIKE THAT WAS THE LAST TIME I WOULD EVER SEE HER BEING I HAD A GIRFRIEND AT HOME AND I TOLD COURTNEY THAT AND SHE UNDERSTOOD AND THEN SAID SHE WAS AVAILABLE AGAIN TO GO OUT.

A WEEK LATER SHE CALLED AND SAID SHE WANTED TO MAKE LOVE OUTSIDE OF GAZZARIES IN THE OPEN IN THE PARKING LOT ON THE SIDE. I SAID OK BUT NEVER SHOWED. I TOLD HER I WOULD TAKE THE BUS TO SEE HER.

SHE WAS KIND ENOUGH TO GIVE ME A CALLING CARD TO CALL HER BUT I DIDNT CALL HER AGAIN MY LOSS AND IMAGINE IF I WOULD HAVE MARRIED HER THERE WOULD BE NO KURT AND COURTNEY 4 YEARS LATER IN 1991.

AND THE REST IS HISTORY FOR HER.

33 SOUPIE SALES 34. BILLY BARTY. 35. TIMOTHY HUTTON

SOUPIE SALES. WHEN I WAS 5 WE WENT TO SEARS AND THERE WAS SOUPIE SALES AS A GUEST AT SEARS AND FOR 5 DOLLORS YOU COULD THROW A PIE IN HIS FACE AND THIS IS WHAT ME AND MY BROTHER JOHN DID. JOHN WAS 3 1/2 AND I WAS ALMOST 6. I THREW MY PIE AND HIT HIM SMACK IN THE FACE. MY BROTHER WAS TOO SMALL TO THROW SO HE GOT TO SQUISH IT IN HIS FACE. 5 DOLLORS IN THOSE DAYS IS LIKE 50 NOW. SOUPIE WAS A FRIENDLEY AND NICE GUY AND HUMBLE TOO.

35. BILLY BARTY WHEN MY FAMILY, MY MOM AND DAD AND JOHN WERE DRIVING ON SUNSET BLVD. WE RAN INTO BILLY BARTY LITERELLY. WE ALMOST RAN HIM OVER BECAUSE WE AT FIRST DIDNT SEE HIM BECAUSE HE WAS SO SMALL-BUT WE DIDNT HIT HIM. MY DAD APOLOGISED AND BILLY WAS OK WITH IT.

36. TIMOTHY HUTTON. I RAN INTO TIMOTHY 3 TIMES ONE TIME HE WAS COMING OUT OF HIS MANAGEMENT THAT JUST WORKS ON HIM. SEE WE WERE COMING IN TO SOLICITE MY MUSIC AND THEY WERE SNOBS AND SO WAS TIIM. HE ACTED LIKE WE WERE INVADING HIS SPACE. WHEN WE WENT IN THERE WE DIDNT KNOW IT WAS A MANAGEMENT FOR JUST TIMOTHY HUTTON. ITS SAD THESE SNOBBY HOLLYWOOD PEOPLE CANT JUST SAY WHAT THE WANT TO SAY RATHER THEN BE SNOBBY.

THE NEXT TIME I SAW HIM HE WAS FILMING A MOVIE ON THE BOARDWALK OF VENICE BEACH AND THEN ONE TIME BY TOWER RECORDS I ALMOST CRASHED INTO HIM. HE LOOKED LIKE HE WAS MAD AND STARED AT ME IN A HATEFUL WAY. I CANT TELL YOU THAT I LIKE TIMOTHY HUTTON. HE IS ONE OF THESE HOLLYWOOD ACTOR TYPES.

36. STEVEN TYLER.

WE WERE IN LAS VEGAS AND AS ME AND MY WIFE GAIL WERE WALKING THROUGH A CORRIDOR WHERE THERE ARE MORE SLOTS GAIL SEES AND SAYS HEY THERE IS SOMEONE WHO LOOKS JUST LIKE STEVEN TYLER. I SAID IT IS STEVEN BECAUSE HIS TATOO ON HIS SHOULDER/ARM AREA SAYS AEROSMITH. SHE DOESNT BELEIVE IT AND THINKS IT IS A LOOK ALIKE. I SAID NO I KNOW HE HAS A TATOO OF AEROSMITH ON HIS ARM AND IT IS HIM.

LATER I WALK THROUGH THE CORRIDOR AND I GO TO A SLOT MACHINE AND I DIDNT KNOW WAS STEVEN TYLER WAS PLAYING SLOTS ON THE NEXT MACHINE. IT WAS JUST RANDOM AND A COINCIDENCE. TALK TO HIM AND WE TALK ABOUT EVERYTHING BUT MUSIC. I DIDNT THINK HE WOULD WANT TO TALK ABOUT THAT SO I DIDNT.

HE WAS GOOD LUCK BECAUSE I WON 100 DOLLORS WHEN I WAS PLAYING NEXT TO HIM. STEVE TYLER IS A DOWN TO EARTH FRIENDLEY GUY WITH NO HEAD TRIPS OR HANG UPS.

37. ED TOWNSAND 38. PERRIS HILTON 39. NIKKI HILTON 40. ETHAN HAWK

ONCE WHEN ME AND MY MANAGER LAILAH WERE ON HOLLYWOOD AND VINE. ON THAT CORNER. WE WENT INSIDE TO TALK TO A COMPANY. I WAS IN CLOWN MAKEUP AND THIS ATTRACTED ED TOWNSANDS SON.

I WAS COMING OUT OF THE ELEVATOR AND THIS GUY CAME UP TO ME AND SAID HE LIKED THE CLOWN GET UP. I SAID THAT WAS FOR MY BAND BADDCLOWN. HE TOLD ME HE WAS THE SON OF ED TOWNSAND. HE SAID HIS DAD WAS THE CO-WRITER OF THE SONG ENTITLED "LETS GET IT ON" BY MARVIN GAYE. I REALLY RESPECTED THAT BECAUSE I LOVE THAT SONG. ONE OF MY FAVORITES FROM THOSE DAYS.

I WENT INTO THE ROOM TO MEET ED TOWNSAND AND HE INVITED ME TO A PARTY BEING THROWN ON HOLLYWOOD BLVD.

I WENT AND WHEN I GOT THERE HE WAS WONDERING WHY I DIDNT WEAR MY MAKE UP. I SAID IN WOULD HAVE IF IF WOULD HAVE KNOWN TO DO SO. I THOUGHT SINSE THE PARTY WAS ABOUT SOMEONE ELSE THAT I WASNT TO GET ATTENTION WITH THE CLOWN GET UP. HE THOUGH WAS WEARING THE MAKE UP OF A CLOWN.

HE TOLD ME TO HAVE A GOOD TIME AND THEN I SAT DOWN.

AS I SAT DOWN I LOOKED UP AND HERE WERE THESE 2 GIRLS. THEY ALMOST LOOKED LIKE TWINS AND THEIR NAMES WERE PERRIS AND NICKI HILTON. I NEVER HEARD OF THEM AND THEY WERENT FAMOUS YET. THIS WAS 2003. TO ME THEY LOOKED LIKE PHONEY HOLLYWOOD PELICAN TYPES WITH THE LONG NECKS AND SKINNY BODIES. I THEN WAS ALSO SITTING NEXT TO A GUY IN THE SAME SEATING ARRANGEMENTS. HIS NAME WAS ETHAN HAWK. HE TRIED TO GET FREE ALCOHOL AND THE GUY WOULD NOT LET HIM GET FREE ALCOHOL. HE SAID HE WAS FAMOUS AND I TALKED TO HIM AND ASKED HIM WHAT HE DID. HE COULDNT BELEIVE I NEVER HEARD OF ETHAN HAWK BUT I HADNT. I DO NOW AND RESPECT HIM AS A GREAT ACTOR.

AT THE END OF THE PARTY I TOOK THE BUS HOME AND THANK GOD THERE WAS A BUS BECAUSE IT WAS VERY LATE AROUND 1 AM.

41. DON SUTTON 42. STEVE GARVEY 43. JIMMY CARTER, PRESIDENT OF THE UNITED STATES 44. STEVE YEAGER

42. DON SUTTON WAS AT DODGER STADIUM AND WAS SCHEDULED TO PITCH THAT NIGHT. WE WERE THERE TOO IN SOME GREAT SEATS BEHIND THE DODGER DUGOUT AND

ABOUT ONLY 2-3 ROWS BACK. MY MOM AND DAD AND MY BROTHER AND DAD WERE AT THE GAME. I WENT DOWN BY THE DUGOUT TO SEE THE DODGERS UP CLOSE. 43. STEVE GARVEY WAS THERE AS WELL AS ALL THE DODGERS ARE THIS TIME WHICH WAS AROUND 1974 WAS GREAT, STEVE WAVED TO US. STEVE GARVEY YEARS LATER AT A BASEBALL CARD SHOW SIGNED A BALL THAT I BOUGHT AND STEVE LIKED MY STAGE NAME AUTRY ODAY.

ALSO WHILE WE WERE BY THE FIELD BEHIND THE DUGOUT DON SUTTON WAKED BY AND I SAID TO MY MOM, "HEY MOM LOOK, THERE IS DON SUTTON". MY MOM RIGHT THERE SAID TO DON SUTTON. "OH MR SUTTON WILL YOU SAY HI TO MY SONS CHARLES AND JOHN ?" AND DON SUTTON SAID "SURE HI CHARLES AND JOHN". HE THEN SHOOK OUR HANDS. DON SUTTON IS NOW IN THE BASEBALL HALL OF FAME AND I LOVE THAT GUY TO THIS DAY. I WAS ALWAYS FANS OF HIS AND FOLLOWED HIS CAREER FROM 1969 TO 1987. i THOUGHT HE STARTED IN 1966. I DIDNT GET INTO KNOWING ABOUT BASEBALL TILL 1968 WHEN I WAS 7 THOUGHT I PLAYED BASEBALL SINSE I WAS IN KNDERGARDEN BUT DIDNT GET INTO FOLLOWING MAJOR LEAGUE BASEBALL UNTIL 1968. DON SUTTON WAS A NICE FRIENDLEY DOWN TO EARTH GUY.

THE DOCTORS OFFICE IN 1968 OFF OF HOLT BLVD.

IT WAS 1968 AND I WAS 7 YEARS OLD AND ON THE TV IN THE DOCTORS WAITING ROOM WHICH THE DOCTORS OFFICE WAS A HOUSE WITH A FRONT AND THEN THE BACK OFFICE FOR THE DOCTOR. WELL AT 7 IN THE WAITING ROOM I SAW ON TELEVISION A PICTURE OF A TIGER AND A PICTURE OF A RED BIRD CALLED A CARDINAL. YES TRANSLATION, THIS WAS THE WORLD SERIES OF 1968 AND I NEVER HEARD OF MAJOR LEAGUE BASEABALL SO THIS WAS THRE START OF MY LOVE FOR MAJOR LEAGUE BASEBALL AND EVEN JAPANEESE WITH ICHERO SUZUKI

ROOKIE CARD. NOW I HAVE OVER 200,000 CARDS, MOSTLEY BASEBALL INCLUDING A 2ND YEAR MICKY MANTLE AND A WILIE MAYS ROOKIE CARD AND A SECOND YEAR WAYNE GRETSKY.

SO I LOVED GOING TO BASEBALL GAMES AT DODGER STADIUM AND ANGEL STADIUM. PROBABLEY SEEN 100 GAMES WHEN THE PRICES WERE AROUND 4.50 PER PERSON.

STEVE YEAGER. AFTER I SAT NEXT TO STEVE YEAGER THROUGH THE WHOLE BALLGAME. I REALIZED THAT IT MAY BE SOMETHING TO THE FACT THAT BALL PLAYERS WHIO ARENT THAT GOOD ARE MEAN TO KIDS AT THE BALL GAME SITTING NEXT TO THEM. YES, FOR THE WHOLE GAME I SAT RIGHT NEXT TO STEVE YEAGER. THERE WAS A DIVIDER BETEWEEN ME AND HIM BEING HE WAS IN THE BULLPEN AND I WAS TJHE LAST SEAT BEFORE THE BULLPEN STARTED.

I SAID HI TO STEVE YEAGER AND HE GRUMBLED AND TOLD ME HE DIDNT WANT TO TALK. HE WAS THE MEANEST BALL PLAYER I EVER MET. THIS WAS AROUND 1973 AT DODGER STADIUM. THE WHOLE GAME I FELT UNCOMFORTABLE UNTIL I TRADED SEATS WITH MY DAD WHO SAT NEXT TO HIM WHERE STEVE DIDNT SAY ANYTHING TO HIM EITHER.

STEVE WAS A MEAN GUY AND UNFORTUNATELEY IT MADE ME SEE GROWN UPS DIFFERENTLEY BECAUSE AT THAT TIME I HAD NEVER MET A MEAN GROWN UP LIKE THAT BEFORE .

ISNT ITS FUNNY THE MEAN ONES ALWAYS SUCK AT THIER SPORT.

JIMMY CARTER

ME AND MY SON CHARLIE AND MY MANAGER AND MY FRIEND LAILAH HEARD JIMMY CARTER THE PAST U.S. PRESIDENT WAS DOING A BOOK SIGNING AT A BOOK STORE IN HOLLYWOOD.

WE WENT AND IT WAS INTERESTING. FIRST WE WAITED IN A LINE FOR A COUPLE OF HOURS.

WE HAD ALREADY SPENT TIME DOING SOME VIDEO FOOTAGE IN HOLLYWOOD. ME AND MY SON BOTH. WE WERE BOTH DRESSED AS CRAZY AND SORT OF SCAREY CLOWNS.

THIS DIDNT WORK TOO GOOD AT THE BOOK SIGNING OF JIMMY CARTER.

JIMMY CARTERS BODYGUARD.

IF LOOKS COULD KILL ID BE DEAD. I WOULD THINK SINSE MY SON IS IN MAKE UP THAT THEY WOULD THINK WE JUST GOT DONE DOING A JOB BUT NO THESE BODYGUARDS ESPECIALLY THE ONE CLOSEST TO JIMMY THOUGHT ME AND MY 3 YEAR OLD SON WAS GOING TO KILL JIMMY OR HURT HIM OR WHATEVER THEIR PARANOID SELVES ARE THINKING.

WE WERE ABOUT 3 FEET FROM CARTER AND 2ND IN LINE AT THIS TIME AND BY THIS TIME AND THE GUARDS ESPECIALLY THE ONE CLOSEST TO JIMMY WAS BREATHING DOWN MY NECK. IT BOTHERED ME BAD AND GOT INTO MY SPACE BUT I JUST PUT UP WITH IT. I NOTICED JIMMY IS SAYING NOTHING TO ALL THE PEOPLE SO I THOUGHT HE WOULD BE THE SAME WITH ME AND MY SON AND LAILAH.

WHEN WE GOT UP THERE.TO GET THE BOOK SIGNED.

I HAND THE BOOK TO JIMMY AND HE SAYS TO ME, "I LIKE YOUR FACE, IT LOOKS GREAT". I SAID THANKS AND I SAID

"YOU ARE MY FAVORITE PRESIDENT", AND HE FOR SOME REASON LOOKED SAD AFTER I SAID THAT AND THIS WAS THE TRUTH. WHEN JIMMY CARTER WAS PRESIDENT IT WAS THE HAPPIEST TIME THAT I EVER HAD IN LIFE AND THAT WAS THE END OF THAT. THE BODYGUARD GOT OUT OF MY FACE AND I WAS THE ONLY PERSON JIMMY TALKED TO, SORT OF SNOBBY ON HIS BEHALF BUT THATS HOW FAMOUS PEOPLE ACT, LIKE THEY ARE TOO GOOD OR SOMETHING WHEN JIMMY SHOULD REMEMBER THAT WE VOTED HIM TO BE PRESIDENT AND WITHOUT OUR VOTES HE WOULD NOT HAVE BEEN PRESIDENT. I FIRST BECAME A LEAD SINGER WHEN JIMMY WAS PRESIDENT, I FIRST HAD SEX WHEN JIMMY CARTER WAS PRESIDENT AND I GOT POULAR AT SCHOOL FOR THE FIRST TIME WHEN JIMMY WAS PRESIDENT PLUS I GOT ON MY FIRST SKATEBOARD TEAM WHEN JIMMY WAS PRESIDENT AS WELL AS I WENT TO MY FIRST PARTY WHEN JIMMY WAS PRESIDENT. YES, JIMMY WAS PRESIDENT JAN 15TH 1977 TO JAN 15TH 1980. THESE WERE THE BEST DAYS AND HEARS OF MY LIFE. I ALWAYS TRULY LOVE JIMMY CARTER AND IT WAS THE ICING ON THE CAKE THAT I MET HIM AND THAT THE ONLY FAN HE TALKED TO WAS ME BEING HE WASNT I GUESS ALLOWED TO TALK TO THE FANS, JUST SIGN THE BOOKS.

44. ALEX VAN HALEN.

IT WAS BLACK ANGUS 1984 AND THERE WAS A GUY WEARING SUNGLASSES AT BLACK ANGUS. IT WAS ALEX VAN HALEN. HE WAS VERY FRIENDLEY AND STOOD NEXT TO ME THE WHOLE TIME WE WERE WATCHING A VAN HALEN VIDEO ENITLED "PRETTY WOMEN". THE VIDEO WAS ON A BIG SCREEN ABOVE THE DANCE FLOOR.

HE WAS SMILING AND HAPPY AND VERY COOL. I REMEMBER TALKING SMALL TALK TO HIM. I BELEIVE HE HUNG OUT WITH ME ABOVE ALL OTHERS THERE WAS BECAUSE I LOOKED MORE ROCK N ROLL THEN ANYONE

THERE. ALL IN ALL ALEX VAN HALEN WAS A REAL FRIENDLEY AND COOL PERSON. I ALSO SAW ALEX WHEN VAN HALEN PLAYED CLAREMONT HIGH SCHOOL IN 1976-77. I NEVER LOOKED AT ANYONE BUT THE DRUMMER AS I STOOD ON THE LEFT SIDE OF ALEX ABOUT FIVE FEET FROM HIM AS HE WAS SEMI ROPED OFF ITH ROPE. ALEX WAS JAMMING HARD AND LOOKING LIKE HE IS WORKING OUT AS WELL AS SWEATING LIKE CRAZY JUST LIKE THE FUTURE ARENA GIGS ALEX WILL PLAY WITH VAN HALEN.

45. BOBBY LEE ANTHONY.

BOBBY LEE IS THE BROTHER OF MICHEAL ANTHONY THE BASSIST FOR VAN HALEN. I SEEN BOBBY PLAY AT GAZZARIS IN 1980 IN THE BAND ASYLUM SUITE. LATER ON A GIRLFRIEND OF HIS, A PAST GIRLFRIEND NAMED MICHELLE WAS AUDITIONING FOR A PART IN A VIDEO I WAS DOING. THAT WAS 1988 AND I MET BOBBY LEE IN AND AROUND 2005. HE CAME OVER TO AUDITION ME AS A VOCALIST FOR HIS BAND. HE TOLD ME HE LIVES WITH HIS BROTHER MICHEAL IN GLENDORA AGAIN THE BASSIST OF VAN HALEN SINSE 1974..

WHEN BOBBY CAME OVER HE BROUGHT HIS GIRLFRIEND AND HE HAD A FULL SET OF HAIR STILL AND WE WERE IN OUR REARLY 40S SO THIS IS COOL. WE TALK AND HE ASKS ME IF I WANNA KNOW THE TRUE STORY ABOUT THE BEGENNINGS OF VAN HALEN AND I SAID SURE.

HE TOLD ME THAT WHERE GENE SIMMONS OF KISS AND TED TEMPLEMAN WERE THERE WAS AT GAZZARIS AND NOT THE STARWOOD OR TROUBODOUR LIKE HISTORY SAID. HE SAID THAT ONLY 2 PEOPLE WERE AT THE SHOW AND THEY DIDNT RECOGNISE THE TWO PEOPLE AND THE TWO PEOPLE BEING GENE SIMMONS OF KISS AND TED TEMPLEMAN. AT THIS TIME NO ONE KNEW WHAT GENE LOOKED LIKE BEING THIS WAS BEFORE HE SHOWED HIS

SELF WITHOUT THE KISS MAKEUP. HE SAID THAT WAS ALL THE PEOPLE THEY NEEDED BEING THAT GENE PAID FOR A 45 DEMO AS WELL AS TED TEMPLEMAN SIGNED ON TO PRODUCE VAN HALEN. HE SAID MR ROTH, DAVID LEE ROTHS FATHER PAID FOR THE PRODUCER COSTS OF THE THOUSANDS OF DOLLORS NEEDED.

IT WAS AN AMAZING STORY BUT NOT YET DONE. HE TOLD ME MIKE HIS BROTHER AND BASSIST WENT IN THE CAR WHERE BOBBY WAS PICKING HIM UP AND MIKE THREW UP AND SAID HES QUITTING THAT NIGHT. BOBBY SAID" DONT QUIT" AND THIS IS WHY TO THIS DAY THEY ARE SUCH CLOSE BROTHERS. EVEN WHEN MIKE WANTED TO QUIT BOBBY TRIED WITH ALL HE COULD TO GET MIKE NOT TO QUIT. AND THE REST IS HISTORY.

FINALLY I WAITED FOR THE NEXT STEP OF THE AUDITONED AND CALLED UP MIKE ANTHONYS HOUSE AS WELL AS WHERE HIS BROTHER IS AT AND HE SAID HE WAS BUSY BECAUSE THERE WAS A DEATH IN THE FAMILY AND THAT WAS THE LAST TIME I EVER TALKED TO MIKE WHO FIRST ANSWERED THE PHONE AND BOBBY HIS BROTHER.

46. JOAN RIVERS

ME AND LAILAH MY MUSIC MANAGER AND GIRLFRIEND AT THAT TIME IN 1988 WAS GOING TO THE 9000 BUILDING ON SUNSET BLVD TRYING TO GET INTEREST FROM WARNER CHAPPELL PUBLISHING AND ALSO HAD A LAWYER I MET IN THE ELEVATOR THERE NAMED HARRY WEISS. ELEVATORS IS A PLACE WHERE PEOPLE MEET PEOPLE SOME TIMES. I MET MY LAWYER HARRY WEISS THERE AS WELL AS ED TOWNSAND AND OTHERS. AGAIN ED TOWNSAND WAS THE ONE WHO CO WROTE THE GREAT SONG "LETS GET IT ON" BY HIM AND CO WRITTEN WITH MARVIN GAYE.

HARRY WEISS SAID I REMIND HIM OF FRANK SINATRA. I DONT KNOW HOW HE SEES THAT COMPARISON BUT I GUESS IT WAS THE COMPARISONS OF OUR MOTAVATION AND DRIVE.

JUST LAST WEEK MY DRUMMER SAID A CO WORKER SAID I REMIND HIM OF NEIL YOUNG . MY MUSIC THAT IS.

I WAS OUTSIDE SITTING ON THE CURB ACROSS FROM THE 9000 BUILDING WAITING FOR LAILAH TO GET WORK DONE IN THAT BUILDING AND A LADY IN A BLUE MUSTANG COMES UP TO ME AND SAYS- "DO YOU NEED ANY CLOTHS HONEY". I SAID HUH? SHE AGAIN ASKED IF IM HOMELESS AND NEED SOME CLOTHS. RIGHT THEN I NOTICE SHE IS TRYING TO PICK UP ON ME AND ASKS ME IF I WANT TO GO TO HER HOUSE AND GET CLOTHS AND TRY THEM ON. RIGHT THEN LAILAH MY MANAGER AND THEN GIRLFRIEND COMES OUT AND SAYS HI AND THE LADY DRIVES OFF DISCOURAGED. I WAS NOT HOMELESS BUT I GUESS THE IMAGE OF ME SITTING ON THE CURB WAS THAT I LOOKED HOMELESS AND NEEDED CLOTHS. I DONT KNOW, LAILAH SAID THAT WAS JOAN RIVERS. I SAID IT DIDNT LOOK LIKE HER REALLY AND I FELT SHE MAY HAVE BEEN MISTAKEN.

LAILAH SAID FOR SURE IT WAS JOAN RIVERS.

A COUPLE NIGHTS LATER I WAS WATCHING THE TONIGHT SHOW WITH JOAN RIVERS AS HOST AND SHE SAID SHE HAD A BLUE MUSTANG. I KNOW THEN THAT WAS JOAN JUST LIKE ALOT OF FAMOUS PEOPLE THEY CAN DISGUISE THEMSELVES HYPTNOTICALLY OR WHATEVER IF THEY DONT WANT YOU TO KNOW ITS THEM. JULIA ROBERTS AND HALLE BERRY CAN DO IT REAL GOOD. ITS LIKE THEY CAN REARRANGE THEIR MOLECULES IF YOU CAN BELEIVE THAT.

I ALWAYS FELT JOAN RIVERS WAS CUTE AND BEAUTIFUL AND CUTE AND SEXY WHEN YOUNGER AND SHE STILL WAS

ATTRACTIVE. I WOULD HAVE GONE WITH HER IF THE TIMING WAS BETTER AND IF I WASNT SEEING LAILAH AS MY GIRLFRIEND AT THAT TIME.

I ALWAYS WONDERED WHAT COULD HAVE BEEN BECAUSE I DONT REMEMBER WHAT YEAR IT WAS BUT IT WAS AFTER JOANS HUSBAND DIED. SO I THINK IT WAS 1988 BUT COULD HAVE BEEN 1989 OR 1990 BUT I REMEMBER IT WAS AFTER JOANS HUSBAND EDGER DIED WHICH IS WHY SHE WAS TRYING TO PICK UP ON ME. SHE WAS SINGLE I AM SUPPOSING.

47. AUDIE DESBROW. DRUMMER FOR THE BAND GREAT WHITE.

BECAUSE OF ME GIVING A SONG CALLED FEED THE CHILDREN TO A COMPANY I WAS GIVING MONEY TO TO HELP OUT POOR CHILDREN NAMED CHRISTIAN CHILDRENS FUND. I WAS ON A PANEL TO ASK QUESTIONS FOR THE COMPANY CHRISTIAN CHILDRENS FUND. THIS WAS IN RIVERSIDE AND THERE WERE OTHER PEOPLE ON THE PANEL TOO. ONE WAS THE DRUMMER FOR TTHE BAND GREAT WHITE NAMED AUDIE DESBROW.

HE INTRODUCED HIMSELF TO ME AND SAID HE LIKED THE IDEA I HAD ABOUT THE CHRISTIAN CHILDREN FUNDS QUESTION. THAT QUESTION WAS SHOULD THE NAME CHRISTIAN CHILDREN FUND BE CHANGED TO CHILD FUND BECAUSE THE STARVING MUSLEMS WILL NOT ACCEPT FOOD FROM CHRISTIANS AOR THE PROMOTION OF JESUS CHRIST. I SAID NO. NEVER TO SELL OUT THE NAME OF JESUS CHRIST. THAT SOMEHOW THROUGH GOD JESUS CHRIST THE FATHER, SON AND HOLY SPIRIT THE MUSLIMS WILL BE FED.

AUDIE SAID HE LIKED THAT ANSWER AND FROM THEN WE BECAME FRIENDS. WE TALKED ALOT AND I FOUND OUT AS

HE TOLD ME HIS EX GIRLFRIEND GOT PREGNANT BY THE GREAT BOXER WHO IS HISPANIC NAMED OSCER DE LAHOYA HE WAS A WORLD CHAMP HISPANIC MIDDLE WEIGHT BOXER. AUDIE SAID HE THE BOXER DID NOT TAKE CARE OF THE CHILD SO AUDIE TOOK CARE OF THE CHILD.

AUDIE NOW IS PLAYING AGAIN WITH GREAT WHITE AS OF 2020-BUT THIS IS IN 2003 AND LATE 2002. I ASKED AUDIE IF HE CAN DO SOME STUDEO WORK FOR ME AND HE SAID OK. HE CAME OVER TO THE HOUSE AND DID THREE SONGS ON PERCUSSION. I HAD HIM HOOKED UP TO A ROCKMAN WHICH IS A LITTLE AMP THAT STRAPS ONTO HIS BELT AND CAN GO INTO HIS EARS WITH EARPHONES.

THE THREE SONGS WERE EZ-AS-123 AND GET HIGH AND ANOTHER I CANT REMEMBER. I PAID HIM 60 DOLLORS. QUITE A DEAL BECAUSE BOBBY BLOTZER CHARGED ME 500 A DAY AS WELL AS JUAN CROCIER THE BASSIST OF RATT TO WORK WITH JAKE E LEE WHEN I VISITED JUAN CROCIER IN PALOS VERDE/SAN PEDRO.

AUDIE WAS A CHRISTIAN AND A FRIEND. WE ALSO DID AN INTERVIEW WITH HIM AS WELL AS EARLIER IN THE DAY WE WERE ON A COMMERCIAL OF TOGOS RESTRAUNT WHERE I GOT AUDIE THAT JOB TOO AS WELL AS I WAS PAID 100 FOR THAT. WE TESTED PIECES OF EACH TOGO SANDWICH AND THEN WAS ASKED WHAT OUR FAVORITES WERE. AUDIE LATER INVITED ME TO AUDITION FOR HIS NEW BAND WHICH HAD SOME MEMBERS OF GREAT WHITE THERE.

HE ALSO TOLD ME HE BROKE JACK RUSSELLS RIBS IN A FIGHT. JACK RUSSELL WAS THE FOUNDER OF GREAT WHITE THE BAND AS WELL AS THE LEAD VOCALIST. HE TOLD ME JACK WAS.

A PYRO AND HE BELEIVED HE STARTED THAT FIRE ON PURPOSE. I DONT KNOW IF THATS TRUE OR NOT BUT IT IS WHAT HE TOLD ME.

AUDIE AT THAT TIME HAD QUIT GREAT WHITE AND AFTER THAT I TURNED HIM ONTO ANOTHER GUY NEEDING STUDEO WORK WITH A DRUMMER AND HIS NAME WAS GARY OLDMAN IN HIS PRIOJECT OLD MAN. GET THE HOOK?

I NEVER SAW AUDIE AGAIN BUT I HEARD HE DID DO THE STUDEO WORK AND GOT PAID BY GARY OLDMAN FOR THE PROJECT AND BAND OLD MAN.

AUDIE WAS A GOOD GUJY AND A GOOD CHRISTIAN TOO.

48. GARY OLDMAN.

I MET GARY TROUGH AN AD IN THE RECYCLER. HE WAS LOOKING FOR A LEAD VOCALIST TO BE IN HIS BAND AS WELL AS DO STUDEOWORK ON HIS SONGS.

ON THE PHONE HE TOLD ME HIS BAND WAS NAMED OLD MAN. HIS STAGE NAME FOR THE BAND WAS VINCE CRADLE.

WE ARRANGED TO MEET AND HE CAME TO OUR APARTMENT IN FONTANA. WE TALKED AND THEN I INVITED HIM IN AND WE TALKED MORE. HE HAD A ROCK HAIRCUT ETC. LATER I FOUND OUT IT WAS A HAIRPIECE.

HE SAID HIS NAME WAS VINCE CRADLE. HE WAS REALLY GARY OLDMAN THE ACTOR BUT LIKE MANY ACTORS ONLY USE THEIR PERSONNA FOR ACTING AND NOT FOR REAL LIFE.

THE NEXT MEETING I TOOK THE BUS TO THE RIVERSIDE TRANS CENTER AND HE PICKED ME UP IN HIS CAR. WE

WENT TO HIS RIVERSIDE HOME WHICH WAS NICE AND QUAINT.

HE HAD A 24 TRACK RECORDING STUDEO THERE AND IT WAS IMPRESSIVE WITH ALL THE NEEDED EFFECTS.

I IMMEDIATELEY DID TWO TRACKS OF VOCALS ONTO HIS MIUSIC WHICH WAS GOOD AND ALL WAS THERE BUT THE LEAD VOCALS AND LYRICS ALONG AND FOR THE LEAD VOCALS.

AFTERWARDS WE TALKED AND I TOLD HIM I HAD JUST GONE OUT WITH JULIA ROBERTS FOR 7 MONTHS AND I SAID SHE WAS CRAZY AND HE ASKED ME, "YOU KNOW WHY DONT YOU?". I SAID BECAUSE SHES INSANE BY THE PEOPLE AND HE SAID THAT IS TRUE. THIS IS WHEN HE TOLD ME HE WAS GARY OLDMAN AND I SAID I KNEW IT ALREADY JUST DIDNT WANT TO ASK HIM BECAUSE IT MAY BOTHER HIM. HE TOLD ME HIS WORKING HOURS ARE EARLY MORNING BECAUSE OF MAKE UP AND HE LOVES HIS JOB AND HAS THE WEEKENDS SO WE DID THE WEEKENDS AND DID 6 SONGS. I HAD TO TELL HIM I DIDNT WANT TO SING THE WORDS "IM THE DEVILS ONLY BROTHER". THAT SEEMED AGAINST THE RESPECT TO LOVE GOD AND IT SOUNDED SATANIC BEING I THOUGHT OR PROMOTED I WAS BROTHER OF THE DEVIL SO HE FIRED ME.

HE NEEDED SOMEONE TO SING THAT AND HE SAID IT DIDNT MEAN WHAT IT WAS IMPLYING AND I JUST DIDNT WANT TO BE PART OF IT SO AGAIN I WAS FIRED.

WE REMAINED FRIENDS THOUGH AND MY MOM GOT ALONG GOOD WITH HIM SO WELL GARY USED TO CALL MY MOM "MOM".

I TOLD HIM THE NAME OLD MAN WAS A SMART NAME BEING HIS NAME IS OLDMAN.

I TOLD HIM HE WAS ONE OF MY FAVORITE ACTORS AND HE DIDNT FEEL TOO COMFORTABLE ABOUT THAT.

WE REMAINED FRIENDS AND WENT OUT WITH GIRLS TOGETHER AS WELL AS WENT TO VINCES SPAGHETTI A FEW TIMES BECAUSE WE BOTH LOVE THAT PLACE. IT IS IN ONTARIO ON HOLT BLVD.

WE ALSO USED TO DRINK COFFEE TOGETHER AND MANY DIDNT KNOW HE WAS GARY OLDMAN EXCEPT ONE LADY NAMED JOY LOVE WHO LOVED GARY ALOT AND ANYWAYS HE REALLY DIDNT LIKE BEING KNOWN AS GARY OLDMAN.

WE STAYED FRIENDS UNTIL I LOST TOUCH WITH HIM AFTER MOM DIED IN 2012. IN THE LAST DAYS OF MOMS LIFE ESPECIALLY THE LAST WEEKEND I WAS REAL DEPRESSED ABOUT MOM DECLINING AND GARY WAS THERE TO BE MY FRIEND AND COMFORT ME. HE HELPED ME TO GET A HOUSE KEEPER FOR MOM AND IN THE LAST WEEK MOM AGREED TO GET ONE BUT UNFORTUNATELELY THAT WEEKEND MOM PASSED AWAY AT THE POMONA VALLEY HOSTBITAL.

IN THE END I SOLD GARY A BC RICH GUITAR FOR 100 DOLLORS AND THIS WAS THE LAST TIME AND WEEKEND I EVER SAW HIM. A FEW YEARS LATER HE WON HIS FIRST OSCER.

HE TOLD ME HE USED TO GET PAID 40,000 PER MOVIE AND THAT WAS IT.

49. GARY SENESE

I WAS AT CIRCUIT CITY AND THE PEOPLE WERE NOT WORKING WELL WITH MY SITUATION SO I GOT UPSET AND TOLD THEM I WAS A PROFESSIONAL MUSICIAN AND NEED TO SPEAK TO THE POLICE ABOUT THIS.

SO THEY SENT ME GARY SENESE.

NOW IN THE INDUSTRY TO TEACH ACTORS THE REALITY OF BEING IN THE POLICE THEY PUT THE ACTORS ON THE FORCE AND HELP THEM TO LEARN THEIR CRAFT OF ACTING AS A COP.

GARY CAME DOWN AND WAS A REAL NICE GUY, TOO GOOD TO BE A COP. AT FIRST I DIDNT RECOGNISE HIM BECAUSE I WASNT EXPECTING THIS AT ALL.

HE TOLD ME HE WAS THERE BECAUSE HE WAS AT A POLICE ACADEMY IN SAN BERNADINO. I SIAD HE REMINDED ME OF CHRISTIAN SLATER AND HE SAID "HOW ABOUT GARY SENESE". I SAID YEAH AND THEN LOOKED AT HIS TITLE ON HIS UNIFORM AND IT SAID SENESE. THIS WAS GARY SENESE. WE TALKED FOR ABOUT AN HOUR OUTSIDE OF THE CIRCUIT CITY STORE AND HE WAS NOT AT ALL LIKE A COP, HE WAS COOL AND FRIENDLEY WITH NO COP TRIPS THOUGH HE DID SEE MY IDENTIFACATION AND TOOK IT BECAUSE IT WAS EXPIRED.

THATS FUNNY. I TOLD HIM I LOVED HIM IN FORREST GUMP AS WELL AS HARRY TRUMAN. I THOUGHT HE DID GREAT AS AN ACTOR IN THOSE MOVIES AND HE SAID THANKS. THIS WAS AROUND 2005 WHEN CIRCUIT CITY WAS STILL AROUND. CIRCUIT CITY I BELEIVE AT LEAST IN CALIFORRNIA IS NOW NONEXISTENT.

I TOLD HIM I HAVE HUNG OUT WITH AND DATED HALLE BERRY AS WELL AS JULIA ROBERTS WAS MY EX FIANCEE FROM 2002 AND HE BELEIVED ME UNLIKE MOST PEOPLE. THE REASON WHY HE BELEIVES ME IS HE KNOWS THAT FAMOUS PEOPLE ARE NO BIG DEAL BUT SOCIETY PUTS THEM ON A PEDISTLE. SO HE ASKED ME HOW THEY WERE AND I SAID JULIA IS LIKE A CLOWN AND HALLE IS SORT OF SERIOUS GARY SAID HE THOUGHT THEY WERE THE

OPPOSITE THAT HALLE BE A CLOWN AND JULIA WOULD BE SERIOUS.

AFTER THE CONVERSATION ENDED WE SHOOK HANDS AND HE WISHED ME GOOD LUCK AND I WISHED HIM GOOD LUCK WITH HIS PRACTICING BEING A COP AND HIS ACTING AND FUTURE COP JOB AND I KNOW HIS COP JOB SUCCEEDED BECAUSE I SAW A COP SHOW SLOT MACHINE WITH HIM/ GARY ON THE SLOT MACHINE.

NEVER SEEN HIM SINSE.

50. JULIA ROBERTS.

THIS IS NOT JUST A STORY ABOUT KNOWING AND GOING OUT WITH JULIA ROBERTS BUT HOW ACTORS ARE AND HOW STRANGE THEY ARE. THE BOTTOM LINE IS, IS THAT PEOPLE ARE PEOPLE AND I JUST DONT GET WHY THEY MAKE ACTORS THE GREATEST PEOPLE IN THE WORLD AND THE TOP IN LEVELS OF SUCCESS BUT JULIA IS A DIFFERENT TYPE MEANING SHE WANTS THAT BUT ALSO LIKES ANNONIMITY. SHE WANTS EVERYTHING HER WAY AND NO OTHER WAY.

THEY ALWAYS HYPE THE ACTORS UP WITH PHRASES LIKE "SHE IS THE NEW IT GIRL", OR "SHE IS THE NEW SUPER STAR OF THE NEW GENERATION". ALL THIS HYPE TRICKS PEOPLE OUTSIDE OF THE ENTERTAINMENT AND ACTING BUSINESS.

1991 I FIRST MET JULIA ROBERTS WHILE HER THEN BOYRFRIEND AND FUTURE ACTOR JASON PATRIC WAS BODYGUARADING HER AS WELL AS HER BOOYFRIEND WHILE JULIA WAS DOING HER WEIRD THING WHICH IS RUN AROUND AND NOT BE NOTICED WHO SHE IS AND THEN 11 YEARS LATER I WOULD BE IN THE SAME POSITION OF JASON PATRIC AS HER BODYGUARD NOW TOO.

JULIA TOLD ME LATER ON WHEN I MET HER AGAIN IN 2002 THAT ALL HER BOYFRIENDS USE HER TO FURTHER THEIR CAREER BUT I FOUND OUT JULIA DID THE SAME THING TO HER BROTHER WHICH MEANT SHE USED HIM TO GET INTO SHOW BIUSINESS. I TOLD JULIA SHE SHOULD BE NICE TO HER BROTHER AND SHE SAID NO THAT THEY DONT GET ALONG.

SO AS I SAW HER THAT DAY IN 1991 I DIDNT THINK IT WAS JULIA ROBERTS BECAUSE WHY WOULD JULIA BE OUT THERE WITH NO BRA ON JUST WEARING A TANKTOP AND ACTING LIKE A FREE BIRD WACKY PERSON.

SO I SAT NEXT TO HER AND I ASKED HER IF SHE EVER THOUGHT ABOUT BEING A JULIA ROBERTS DOUBLE IN MOVIES AND SHE DIDNT SAY ANYTHING BUT LAUGH WITH THAT BIG SMILE AND THAT BIG LAUGH.

SHE SEEMED LIKE SHE WAS INSANE BEING THE WAY SOCIETY SEEMS PEOPLE THAT ARE FAMOUS WOULD BE LABELLED EXCENTREC IF THEY ARE INSANE BUT A NON CELEBRATY WOULD BE CALLED AND LABELLED INSANE IF THEY ARE ACTING INSANE. SO NOT THINKING IT WAS JULIA I TRIED TO HELP HER BY ASKING PEOPLE FOR MONEY TO GIVE HER TO MAKE A PHONE CALL TO HER RELATIVES WHOM SHE LIED AND SAID SHE HAD IN THE MIDWEST AS WELL AS I PANHANDLED HER MONEY MOSTLEY COINS IF NOT ALL COINS FOR HER TO GO TO AND ON A BUS BACK TO WHERE I THOUGHT SHE WAS FROM WHICH WAS I LATER FOUND OUT SHE WAS ALL LIEING 100 PERCENT AND IT WAS JULIA ROBERTS.

AS I WENT OUT WITH HER IN 2002 11 YEARS LATER I ASKED HER WHY SHE DIDNT HANG OUT WITH ME LIKE SHE IS NOW AND SHE SAID BECAUSE BACK THEN SHE THOUGHT I WAS A PSYCHO. THATS CALLING THE COFFEE BLACK.

JULIA ONCE TOLD ME IF SHE WANTED TO SHE COULD GET ME KILLED BY A HIT MAN.

NOW THE FIRST MEETING 11 YEARS LATER MARCH 26TH 2002.

IT WAS OF ALL PLACES BELEIVE IT OR NOT AT THE MONTCLARE TRANS CENTER WHICH IS A CENTER FOR BUSSES, THE RTD BUS LINES TO BE EXACT.

I WAS TAKING THE BUS TO PICK UP MY SON TO TAKE HIM TO CUB SCOUTS.

AS I WAS WAITING FOR THE BUS I BELEIVE IT WAS THE 66 BUSLINE HERE COMES THIS GIRL WITH 7 BAGS AND ACTING AND REMINDING ME OF LUCY AS A HOBO IN THE I LOVE LUCY SHOW. SHE FIRST WALKS A BIT WITH ALL THESE BAGS THEN LAYS ON THE BUS BENCH THEN GETS UP AND DOES ALOT OF MANUVERS I FOUND FUNNY AND ENTERTAINING AND I KEPT WATCHING HER. I DIDNT RECOGNISE HER AS JULIA ROBERTS.

SHE FINALLY WALKED UP TOWARDS ME AND SHE SAID TO ME, "A BLACK GUY STOOD ME UP". I DIDNT KNOW REALLY AT ALL WHAT SHE WAS TALKING ABOUT SO IGNORED HER AND SHE SAID HI AND SAID OTHER THINGS THAT REALLY DIDNT MAKE SENSE AT THAT TIME. LATER ON I FOUND OUT THE BLACK GUY THAT STOOD HER UP WAS DENZEL WASHINGTON BUT HE REALLY DIDNT STAND HER UP, THAT WAS IN HER MIND BECAUSE DENZEL WAS MARRIED AND DIDNT STAND HER UP BUT HE JUST WASNT AVAILABLE FOR JULIA TO GO OUT WITH BECAUSE HE WAS MARRIED. THE MEETING WITH DENZEL WAS AT SOME AWARDS I BELEIVE THE OSCARS OF 2002.

NEXT SHE ASKS IF I CAN GET HER A DRINK. AT FIRST I SAID NO THEN I DECIDED TO NOT GO TO CUB SCOUTS BECAUSE MY SON DIDNT REALLY LIKE CUB SCOUTS ANYWAYS. MY

SON WOULD PROBABELY BE HAPPY I DONT COME OVER TO TAKE HIM TO CUB SCOUTS THAT DAY.

WE GOT ON THE BUS THEN GOING THE OTHER DIRECTION BACK TO A LIQUOR STORE I KNEW ABOUT THAT WAS ON THE WAY BACK TO MOMS HOUSE WHERE I WAS STAYING HALF THE TIME AND THEN STAYING THE OTHER HALF OF THE TIME WITH MY NOW WIFE GAIL WHO WAS MY GIRLFRIEND AT THE DAY BEFOERE THIS. WE HAD JUST BROKE UP THAT MORNING BELEIVE IT OR NOT SO I WAS SINGLE AND THE FIRST DAY I WAS SINGLE. I RUN IN TO JULIA ROBERTS. SOUNDS LIKE GOOD LUCK, WELL MAYBE IT IS AND MAYBE IT ISNT, YOU DECIDE.

WHILE WE WERE GETTING ON THE BUS AS AS I AGREED TO TAKE HER TO BUY SOME ALCOHOL SHE HELD MY HAND AND SAID "YOU LIKE ME FOR ME DONT YOU" AND I WAS LIKE WHATEVER AGAIN NOT KNOWING WHAT SHE WAS TALKING ABOUT AND WHY HER MOTIVE WAS WITH THOSE WORDS. SHE SAID "YOU DONT KNOW ME DO YOU". I SAID I DIDNT.

AT THIS TIME I DIDNT RECOGNISE HER AS JULIA ROBERTS. I REMEMBER SHE WAS SQUINCHING HER EYE AS SHE WAS TALKING TO ME. I GUESS THIS IS AN ACTORS TECHNIQUE TO BE UNRECOGNISED A LITTLE BIT MORE. ON THE BUS AFTER SAYING THE WORDS SHE SAID TO ME ASKING IF I KNOW HER AND I SAID NO SHE STARTED TO HOLD MY HAND CLUTCHING IT INSECURITY I THOUGHT AT THE TIME.

WHEN WE GOT TO THE LIQUOR STORE I BOUGHT HER SOME GOLDSCHLAGGER BOTTLE. A LITTLE SMALL ONE. SHE SAID IT HAD GOLD IN THE BOTTOM OF THE BOTTLE. I DIDNT BELEIVE HER BUT THERE WAS GOLDEN PARTICLES IN THE DRINK. WE THEN WALKED TOWARDS MOMS HOUSE. AS WE WALKED SHE FLASHED HERSELF, HER BREASTS AND I SAW THE MOLE IN THE MIDDLE OF HER CHEST AND

THIS MADE ME REMEMBER IN 1991 THAT THE JULIA ROBERTS LOOK ALIKE HAD A MOLE THERE TOO. REALIZE NOW THEY WERE THE SAME AND ONE. I KNEW IT WAS JULIA ROBERTS. BELEIVE THIS IS WHY SHE FLASHED ME TO LET ME KNOW SHE IS THE SAME PERSON AS LAST TIME AND THAT SHE IS JULIA ROBERTS AND I BELEIVE SHE WANTED ME TO KNOW THIS NOW AT THIS TIME. AS WE WALKED I SAID "ITS YOU FROM LAST TIME IN 1991" AND SHE SAID "YES". SHE THEN STARTED TALKING LIKE A DEAF GIRL AND THEN LATER SAID AS WE WERE WALKING THAT THEY SHOULD HAVE TABLOID NEWSPAPERS FOR NON FAMOUS PEOPLE, ALSO SHE SAID SHE HAD JUST GOTTEN BACK FROM ITALY.

WHEN WE GOT TO THE HOUSE AT MOMS I HAD TO SNEAK HER IN BECAUSE MOM WOULDNT ALLOW HER PROBABLY TO STAY THERE, SO WE DIDNT TAKE ANY CHANCES AND I SNUCK HER IN.

AS SHE STAYED THERE I SLEPT NEXT TO HER ON THE FLOOR AS SHE GOT THE COUCH AND THE COUCH WOULD OPEN UP BUT SHE JUST WANTED TO SLEEP ON THE COUCH WITHOUT IT OPENING UP TO A BED.

SHE WANTED ME TO CALL HER ANTONETTE AND SAID BECAUSE SHE IS LIKE MARIE ANTONETTE SO I ASKED HER IF I SHOULD CALL HER JULIA AND SHE SAYS REALLY MAD "NO, I WANT TO BE CALLED ANTONETTE". I SAID WHAT DOES SHE WANT FOR A LAST NAME THAT IS IF HER FIRST NAME IS ANTONETTE WHATS THE LAST NAME. SHE SAID SHE DOESNT KNOW YET.

SO WE STAYED THERE FOR 3 NIGHTS AND IT WAS ROMANTIC. AT LEAST I KNOW SHE FELT THAT AND RESPECTED THAT I DIDNT TRY TO HAVE SEX WITH HER SO SOON AND SHE WAS IMPRESSED AND REALLY LIKED THAT I SLEPT ON THE FLOOR AS SHE DID SLEEP ON THE COUCH.

ON THE FORTH MORNING AFTER THE THIRD NIGHT WE GOT A HOTEL FOR 3 DAYS AT THE HA PENNY INN. YES THAT IS THE HA PENNY INN. IT WAS WEIRD BECAUSE THE WHOLE TIME I WAS WITH JULIA SHE WAS ON JUST ABOUT EVERY MAGAZINE AND TABLOID AROUND. THATS THE PRESS AGENTS JOB AND OTHERS I REALLY DONT KNOW THE NAME OF THEIR TITLES BUT I KNOW THERE ARE ALOT OF THESE PEOPLE WORKING FOR JULIA TO MAKE HER FAMOUS. THAT THE SOCIETY FAME GAME, WHATEVER TO ME, ITS STRANGE TO ME.

I CAN SEE THROUGH THE HEARTLESS GODLESS GAME. GODLESS MEANING THE HOLLYWOOD FOLKS FIND IT TABOO TO TALK ABOUT JESUS CHRIST, THE FATHER SON AND HOLY SPIRIT, THEY ARE A DEVILISH BUNCH, THOSE HOLLYWOOD FOLKS. LOOK AT HARVEY WEINSTEIN. YOU THINK HES THE ONLY ONE LIKE THAT? ARE YOU KIDDING? I BEEN MESSED WITH BY GUYS IN THE BUSINESS WHEN GRACE BOREKI WHO IS THE HEAD OF PLAYGIRL MAGAZINE AND EDITOR IN THE EARLY 80S SENT ME TO PEOPLE I WONT SAY THEIR NAME BUT FOLKS WHO ARE GAY DOING THE CASTING COUCH THING. I AINT GAY SO I JUST ABOUT THROUGH THIS GUY THROUGH THE WINDOW. THIS IS ONE OF A FEW INCIDENTS THAT HAS HAPPENED TO ME ON THE SO CALLED CASTING COUCH AND I MEAN IT IS REAL, QUITE REAL.

ANUYWAYS BACK TO JULIA. WE SPENT THREE DAYS IN THIS HA PENNY INN HOTEL AND THE FIRST DAY SHE STARTED ACTING STRANGE NOT TOUCHING THE DOORS UNLESS SHE HAD A KLEENEX ON IT. I GUESS THATS NOT STRANGE NOW DURING THE CORANA VIRUS THING BUT THIS WAS IN 2002. JULIA WAS 34 AND WOULD BE 35 ON OCTOBER 28TH , JUST COINCIDENTELY WE BROKE UP THAT DAY AND THAT WAS THE LAST DAY I EVER SAW JULIA ROBERTS ON HER BIRTHDAY AND IT WASNT MEANT TO BE

THAT WAY IT JUST WAS OR MAYBE SHE MADE THIS HAPPEN. I WILL TELL YOU THE STORY LATER.

THE FIRST DAY AT THE HOTEL ME AND MY MANAGER WENT TO HOLLYWOOD TO DO MUSIC BNUSINESS AND SHE DIDNT WANT TO GO SO SHE STAYED AT THE HOTEL-

THE SECOND DAY.

AFTER DAY ONE WHEN I GOT BACK SHE WOULDNT LET ME TOUCH HER. II GUESS IT IS BECAUSE SHE SAW ME LEAVE WITH ANOTHER GIRL/LADY BUT THE TRUTH IS THE LADY I WENT WITH WAS MY MANAGER WHO IS MARRIED TO SOMEONE ELSE. A GUY NAMED ERNIE WHO IS 6 FOOT 5 AND I AM STRICKLEY PLUTONIC WITH LAILAH MY MUSIC PERSONEL MANAGER AT THAT TIME.

JULIA FINALLY REALIZED THIS BUT I GUESS IT IS HARD FOR HER AT FIRST TO BELEIVE THAT A GUY CAN BE PLUTONIC WITH A GIRL/LADY/WOMAN.

ANYWAYS ON THE SECOND DAY WE SAW JULIA ON T.V. AS WE WERE LAYING IN BED. JULIA WANTED ALCOHOL AND I ONLY HAD ENOUGH MONEY FOR THREE DAYS

DAY 3. SHE WAS DEPRESSING AND MOODY. I WAS NOT HAVING FUN AND FEELING SAD. I WAS WONDERING TO MYSELF IF SHE HAS A DRINKING PROBLEM.

I AM ALSO THINKING ABOUT MY EX GIRFRIEND GAIL WHO I STILL LOVE ALOT. ME AND GAIL AT THE TIME OF OUR BREAKUP WERE TOGETHER FROM JAN 5 1993 TO MARCH 25 2002. OVER 9 YEARS. IN THE LONG RUN ME AND GAIL GOT MARRIED AND I HAVE BEEN MARRIED TO HER SINSE GOING ON 28 YEARS NOW. WELL, ON JAN 5 2021 IT WILL BE 28 YEARS.

NOW WE ARE OUT OF THE HOTEL HA PENNY INN AND WE GO BACK TO MOMS AND THIS TIME I ASK MOM IF SHE CAN STAY THERE AND JUST DOWN STAIRS AND SHE FINALLY AND RELUCTANTLEY SAYS YES. I TOLD MY MOM THAT IT WAS JULIA ROBERTS AND SHE SAID SHE DOESN T CARE IF ITS THE QUEEN OF ENGLAND. SHE HAS TO FOLLOW THE RULES OF THE HOUSE WHICH SHE DOESNT AT ALL AND LATER I WILL HAVE TO DO SOMETHING ABOUT THAT BY PUNISHING HER TO A DEGREE. ANTONETTE I WILL CALL HER DOES NOTHING BUT PRETTY MUCH DRINK AND SLEEP TILL 5 IN THE AFTERNOON AND BED AROUN D 7 AM. I AM NOT ON THIS SCHEDULE SO IT IS BOTHERING ME AND I AM GETTING EXHAUSTED.

ON THE 7TH DAY AGAIN ME AND LAILAH DID WORK AROUND THE AREA AND THIS TIME JULIA WANTED TO GO. JULIA ALSO HAD A TALK WITH MY MOM WHEN I DROPPED MY SON OFF AT BALLET PRACTICE. IT WAS JUST HER AND MY MOM AND THEY DIDNT GET ALONG. JULIA WAS RAMBLING ABOUT HER AGENT AND MANAGEMENT BEING TERRIBLE AND THIS BORED MY MOM. MY MOM IS A TRUE DOWN TO EARTH LADY WHO WAS BORN IN KANSAS AND LIVED IN SUE CITY IOWA. THEN SINSE 1955 HAS LIVED IN L.A. FROM 1955 TO 1960 THEN IN 1960 MY MOM AND DAD WENT FROM LOS ANGELES TO ALHAMBRA UNTIL 1964 WHERE WE MOVED TO CLAREMONT UNTIL MOMS DEATH IN 2012. THE HOUSE WAS SOLD IN 2013. MOM AND DAD WERE MARRIED IN THE MID TO LATE 1940S.

AND SINSE THEN I HAVENT HARDLEY BEEN IN CLAREMONT OTHER THEN CHECKING MY P.O. BOX.

IN THESE DAYS IN APRIL OF 2002 UP UNTIL MY BIRTHDAY ON APRIL 16TH 2002 JULIA LIVED DOWN THERE AND TOTALLY MESSED UP THE HOUSE PILING JUNK UP TO THE BED HEIGHT OF 1 FOOT OR MORE. IT WAS TERRIBLE AND SHE DIDNT CARE ABOUT ANYTHING BUT THE DRINK AND

SLEEP. SHE WAS GETTING BORING THOUGH I GOT CREATIVE AND DID AN ALBUM CALLED 16 SONGS AND EXPRESSIONS FOR JULIA. I HAD WRITTEN IN THE 7 MONTHS WITH HER AND 6 OF THOSE MONTHS THERE DAILY. I HAD WRITTEN 16 SONGS ABOUT HER IN THE 7 MONTHS FROM MARCH 26TH 2002 UNTIL OCTOBER 28TH 2002. JULIAS BIRTHDAY TO BE EXACT.

WHEN JULIA WAS 34 I KNEW HER WELL BUT THE DAYS SHE TURNED 35 IT WAS OVER.

NOW WE ARE IN EARLY TO MID APRIL AND JULIA IS REAL COOL ON MY BIRTHDAY.

ON MY BIRTHDAY. LEAH REMINI CALLED ME ON MY BIRTHDAY IN 1992 TO SAY HI AND WISH ME A HAPPY BIRTHDAY AND NOW 10 YEARS LATER JULIA IS TREATED ME LIKE A KING BUT ONLY ON THE ONE DAY, MY BIRTHDAY. I AM TURNING 41 IN 2002 AND SHE IS SOBER AND SITTING ON MY LAP. SHE IS ROMANTIC AND KISSING ME WITH SOFT SWEET KISSES AND I BELEIVE WE ARE IN LOVE. I DONT KNOW IF SHE IS IN LOVE AS I THINK BACK BEING THESE ACTORS CAN ACT YOU KNOW. IT IS GREAT BUT AFTER THIS DAY WE WILL MOVE OUT AGAIN BECAUSE JULIA ABUSED THE ROOM SO BAD MOM KICKED US OUT SO NOW WE ARE ON OUR OUT ON 4-17-2002.

BEFORE WE LEAVE THOUGH WE TAKE A TRIP TO THER SPEARMINT RHINO, A SEMI STRIP CLUB AND MAN WHAT A TRIP.

BELEIVE IT OR NOT WE DIDNT HAVE A CAR SO WE WALKED THERE. SHE WAS COMPLAINING ABOUT THE LONG WALK BUT WHEN WE GOT THERE IT WAS BETTER. AS WE WERE GOING THERE I WAS SURE THAT JULIA WAS USING ME AS A BOYFRIEND/BODYGUARD.

THE SPEARMINT RHINO VISIT. WE WALKED ABOUT 2 MILES OR 3 AND WE WENT IN. AT THE DOOR THEY ASKED IF IT WAS JULIA ROBERTS AND AS JULIA TAUGHT ME I SAID NO SHE IS A LOOK ALIKE. JULIA WAS DRESSED GREAT AND LOOKED WONDERFUL. AS SHE WENT IN THEY GAVE HER FREE DRINKS AND TREATED HER GREAT. THEY LET HER PLAY POOL AHEAD OF THE LINE AND TREATED HER EXTRA SPECIAL BUT NOT ME. THE WAITRESSES WERE ALSO STRIPPERS AND THEY ACTED LIKE THEY DIDNT LIKE ME LIKE I WASNT GOOD ENOUGH FOR JULIA. ANYWAYS SHE GOES INSIDE THE BATHROOM AND IS TOPLESS AND SHE IS CHANGING WITH THE SRTIPPER GIRLS SO I GO IN AND GRAB HER AFTER I GET HER TO PUT HER SHIRT ON. THE BOUNCERS SEE THIS AND KICK ME OUT FOR GOING IN THE BATHROOM. THEY WERE ASSUMING I WAS BEING A PEEPING TOM BUT IN REALITY I DIDNT WANT HER IN THAT ENVIREMENT. IT WAS NOT NORMAL BUT BASICALLY JULIA AKA ANTONETTE IS NOT AT ALL NORMAL. I COULD CARE LESS ABOUT SEEING THE GIRLS IN THE LADIES RESTROOM.

I WROTE A SONG ABOUT JULIA CALLED THE WEIRDEST GIRL IN THE WORLD. I PLAYED IT FOR HER AND SHE DIDNT LIKE THE LYRICS AT ALL THOUGH IT WAS ALL TRUE.

WE THEN WALKED HOME THERE WERE TONS OF TAXI CABS COMING AND I DONT KNOW WHERE THEY CAME FROM . I BELEIVE THE BOUNCERS WANTED JULIA TO GET HOME SAFE BUT NOT TO WORRY I WAS HER BODYGUARD/ BOYFRIEND. I COULD TAKE CARE OF HER SAFETY.

WHILE WALKING BACK JULIA TOOK A PEE AND ALSO AS WE WALKED HOME SHE NAGGED AND COMPLAINED ABOUT THE WALK UNTIL WE GET TO THIS GAS STATION ON MILLS AVENUE I BELEIVE OR IT COULD HAVE BEEN PADUA AVENUE.

WHEN WE GOT THERE SHE SAID IN 10-9-8-8-7-6-5-4-3--ETC. A COP WILL COME AROUND THE CORNER AND THERE WAS A COP AND YES SHE WAS RIGHT THERE WAS A COP ON THE 10TH SECOND COMING AROUND THE CORNER ONTO FOOTHILL. LATER I REALIZED JULIA HAD SOME BUTTON THAT GOT COPS TO COME ON A CALL. AS THE COPS GOT THERE THEY KNEW ME AND SAID HI TO ME AND HI TO JULIA. THEY SAID HI JULIA AND SHE SAID SHE WASNT JULIA THAT SHE WAS ANTONETTE.

AS WE GOT HOME SHE SLEPT TILL 4 THE NEXT DAY SHE HAD A HABIT OF LISTENING TO COUNTRY MUSIC ALMOST ALL NIGHT.

I WAS WRITING ALOT OF MIUSIC ABOUT HER LIKE THE SONGS "1 TRUE FACE" AND "I WANNA TELL YOU". ALL IN ALL I DID 16 SONGS FOR HER AND THE ALBUM TO BE CALLED 16 SONGS AND EXPRESSIONS FOR JULIA.

NEXT WE WERE TO LIVE AT THE SAND AND SAGE HOTEL IN FONTANA, WE HAD ALOT OF FUN AT THE SAND AND SAFGE AND I USED ALL MY SSI MONEY TO PAY FOR THE HOTEL AS WE WERE THERE INTO EARLY MAY, FROM APRIL 18TH OR 19TH TO MAY 1 OR 2. BECAUSE I REMEMBER GETTING MORE SSI MONEY SO AFTER PAYING CHILD SUPPORT TO GAIL MY EX WHO WAS MY GIRLFRIEND LAST SINSE MARCH 25TH 2002. I THEN HAD MORE MONEY FOR MORE HOTEL RENTELS FOR ME AND JULIA.

AS WE WERE AT THIS SAND AND SAGE HOTEL WE WERE VERY CLOSE AND ROMANTIC. JULIA DRANK ALOT AND ONCE I BROUGHT MY SON THERE TO HAVE US ALL EAT PIZZA SO I TOOK THE BUS TO PICK UP MY SON AS HE SPENT THE NIGHT WITH US AT THE HOTEL. CHARLIE MY SON DIDNT MIND SLEEPING ON THE FLOOR.

GOING TO SOME BARS IN DOWN TOWN FONTANA.

FIRST WE WENT TO A CLOTHING STORE LIKE CLOTHS TIME AND SHE BOUGHT A WHOLE OUTFIT FOR THIS DATE WE WERE TO HAVE TONIGHT. THIS WAS LATE APRIL AND I PAID FOR ALL HER CLOTHS SHE BOUGHT AND WAS HAPPY TO DO IT. AS SHE WENT BACK TO THE HOTEL SHE HAD TO HAVE A PERFECT HIGH ON ALCOHOL AND LOOK PERFECT. SHE TOOK A LONG TIME IN THE BATHROOM AND I KNOW THERE WAS ALOT OF ALCOHOL IN THAT BATHROOM. IN FACT I TOOK A PICTURE OF THE BATHROOM LATER ON. WOW IT WAS MESSY. JULIA IS THE MESSYEST PERSON I HAVE EVER KNOWN BUT FINALLY AS SHE CAME PUT SHE LOOKED GREAT SHE LOOKED LIKE THE PRETTY WOMEN THING. IN FACT ROY ORBASON CAME ON OUR RADIO AND SANG PRETTY WOMEN AND IT MADE JULIA REAL MOTIVATED TO GO OUT THIS NIGHT TONIGHT.

AS WE LEFT THE HOTEL. WE WALKED TO DOWN TOWN FONTANA. WE WERE ON FOOTHILL AND DOWN TOWN FONTANAS WAS A LITTLE BELOW AAROW HIGHWAY, SO NOT A FAR WALK.

JUKLIA SEEING THE HOMELESS GUY IN THE TREES AND ACTING CRAZY.

YES JULIA WAS ACTING LIKE A HORSE RUNNING AROUND. JULIA LOVES TO ACT AND IN FACT WE ARGUED SO MUCH FOR A COUPLE DAYS THAT IF WE HAD A CAMERA WE COULD HAVE DONE THE MOVIE WHOS AFRAID OF VIRGINIA WOLF PART 2.

SHE SAW A HOMELESS GUY IN THE TREES AND CRIED FOR HIM. JULIA WAS A TRIP.

AS WE GET TO BAR 1 SHE GETS A COUPLE DRINKS AND THEN WE LEAVE BECAUSE SHE DOESNT LIKE THIS BAR SO WE GO TO BAR 2. WE PLAYED POOL AND I DID KEREYOKI. NO ONE WATCHING OR LISTENING BUT ME AND JULIA.JULIA

WAS PROUD OF MY VERSION OF DEEP PURPLES SONG HUSH. WE THEN TALKED TO THE BARTENDER AND SHE RECOGNISED JULIA AND SAID "IM GONNA MAKE THIS HOLLYWOOD CHICK A FONTANA DRINK SHE WILL NEVER FORGET". OH YES JULIA WAS BUZZED AFTER THAT DRINK . THE BARTENDER TOLD ME SHE MADE HER A TAQUILA SUNRISE/ZOMBIE MEANING REGULAR 3 SHOTS OF TIQUILA FOR THE SUNRISE PART OF THE DRUNK AND 6 SHOTS FOR A ZOMBIE. JULIA WAS BUZZED AND HUGGING EVERYONE AND HAVING A GREAT TIME.

NEXT BAR 3. FIRST THE OWNER CAME OUT AND SAID THEY AFRE CLOSED. I TOLD HER TO DO HER JULIA LOOK AND SHE AGREED BECAUSE SHE WANTED TO GO TO THIS BAR BEING THERE WAS A POOL TABLE HERE TOO AS WELL AS A DART BOARD JULIA LIKES TO DO.

AS SHE KNOCKED ON THE DOOR AGAIN THE BARTENDER OPENED UP AND SAID OH MY GOSH ITS JULIA ROBERTS AND SHE LET US IN. WITHIN 30 MINUTES 100 PEOPLE SHOWED UP BECAUSE IT GOT AROUND WORD OF MOUTH THAT JULIA ROBERTS WAS AT THIS BAR BUT NO ONE BOTHERED HER AND WERE VERY NICE TO HER AND NO ONE ASKED FOR AUTOGRAPHS. THAT IS HOW THE INLAND EMPIRE IS, NOT STARSTRUCK, AT LEAST NOT IN OL DOWN TOWN FONTANA. AS SHE LEAVES THIS BAR TO GO TO THE SECOND ONE SHE WAVES BY AND HUGS MANY PEOPLE. MOSTLEY GUYS. JULIA TOLD ME SHE GETS ALONG BETTER WITH GUYS THEN WITH WOMEN.

JULIA HAS NOW BEEN TO THREE BARS ALL IN BASICALLY THE SAME AREA IN DOWN TOWN FONTANA. JULIA IS NOW GOING BACK TO THE SECOND BAR. SHE IS IN THE FRONT AND TOTALLY DRUNK. SHE IS MAKING A SCENE AND WONT GET UP.

HERE COMES THE POLICE. THE POLICE COME AND WE ALL TRY TO LIFT HER BUT SHE WONT BUDGE.

I TELL THEM IT IS JULIA ROBERTS AND A BLACK MEAN COP SAYS "IF THIS IS NOT JULIIA ROBERTS YOU WILL BE ARRESTED FOR GIVING A FALSE NAME." JULIA DIDNT WANT ME TO GO TO JAIL SO SHE WAS ABLE TO PROVE SHE WAS JULIA ROBERTS BY GIVING A PHONE NUMBER TO HER MOM OR SOMEONE IN ANAHEIM.

ONCE THE OTHER COP FINDS OUT IT IS JULIA ROBERTS. HE IS STARSTRUCK. COPS USUALLY ARE THE MOST STARSTRUCK PEOPLE IN THE WORLD THAT I HAVE SEEN.

SO JULIA GRABS THIS COPS PRIVATE AREA AND HE DOESNT ARREST HER. THEN SHE JUMPS ON THE COP CAR AND TAKES OFF HER SHIRT AND IS TOPLEESS. NOW SHE IS ARRESTED. I THOUGHT SHE WOULD BE ARRESTED THE SAME WAY ANYONE ELSE WHO WOULD DO THAT STUFF. I THOUGHT SHE WOULD BE ARRESTED FOR THREE FELONIES, ASSAULT ON A POLICE OFFICER AND VANDALISM ON A POLICE CAR AND INDECENT EXPOSURE. I REMEMBER TO THIS DAY THE LOOK SHE HAD IN THE BACK OF THE POLICE CAR AS SHE WAS HAULED OFF, SHE LOOKED SOBER AS A JUDGE.

BUT NO SHE IS CHARGES WITH ONE THING, DRUNK IN PUBLIC.

SO I WALKED BACK TO THE HOTEL AND WAS REALLY IN A HYPER MOOD SO I LEFT AND WAITED TO CATCH THE BUS AS FAR AS I COULD GO TO GET TO SAN BERNADINO WEST VALLEY COUNTY JAIL WHICH IS WHERE JULIA WILL BE HELD.

I TAKE THE BUS AS FAR AND AS CLOSE AS IT CAN GO TO COUNTY JAIL WHERE JULIA IS. I WALK THE REST OF THE WAY WHICH IS AROUND 3 MILES DOWN ETAWANDA AVENUE.

THE BUS DROPPED ME OFF AT ETIWANDA AND AAROW HIGHWAY I BELEIVE OR FOOTHILL.

AS I WENT IN I TRIED TO ASK IF JULIA ROBERTS OR ANOTHER NAME ANTONETTE HOGUE. I WAS WONDERING WHICH NAME SHE WAS ARRESTED ON. I FOUND OUT SHE WAS UNDER THE NAME ANTONETTE HOGUE BUT THEY KNEW HER REAL NAME BEING THEY FINGERPRINTED HER AND HAD TO CHECK WHAT HER FINGERPRINTS SAY.

OH I FORGOT A COUPLE DAYS WHERE JULIA WAS STAYING FOR 3 DAYS WITH ANNIE THE MOTHER OF MY SON CHARLIE FOR FREE AND THIS IS WHERE SHE GOT THE IDEA FOR THE LAST NAME OF HOGUE WHICH ANNIES LAST NAME WAS HOGEN.

SO STARTING IN MAY AFTER I TRIED TO PICK HER UP FROM JAIL. WELL, I DIDNT PICK HER UP AND HERE IS THE STORY.

AS I GOT INTO WEST VALLEY JAIL IN THE WAITING ROOM, I WENT TO THE WINDOW AND THEY WERE UNFRIENDLEY AND MEAN. WHAT DO YOU EXPECT? IT TS JAIL. I WAITED AND WAITED AND SAID IT WAS JULIA ROBERTS AND SOME DIDNT BELEIVE BUT SOME KNEW SHE WAS THERE I GOT CALLED IN BY A SECURITY COP. A COUNTY JAIL GUARD AND HE ASKED ME IF I WAS LOOKING FOR A "PRETTY WOMEN"?. OH YEAH I GOT IT AND THEN HE WAS MEAN AND ASKED ME WHY DO I GOT TO GO OUT WITH HER AND I DONT GOT A CAR. HE ASKED WHY CANT HE GO OUT WITH HER. HE THEN SAID I WAS A .LOW LIFE HE ASKED AGAIN WHY DID AND IS SHE GOING OUT WITH ME AND NOT SOMEONE LIKE HIM. I TOLD HIM THE TRUTH. I SAID BECAUSE SHE LIKES MUSICIANS AND IS NOT ATTRACTED TO COPS. HE THEN KICKED ME OUT OF THE WAITING ROOM. I HAD BEEN THERE FOR 20 HOURS WAITING FOR HER. I LOVED HER AT THIS TIME AND WAS VERY DEDICATED TO HER AT THIS TIME.

AS I LEFT SOME LESBIANS PICKED ME UP IN THEIR CAR AND TOO ME TO THE HOTEL WHERE ME AND JULIA WERE STAYING AT WHICH WAS THE SAND AND SAGE HOTEL.

AS I GOT TO THE HOTEL JULIA WAS ALREADY THERE AND SHE WAS ACTUALLY SWEEPING AND CLEANING THE PLACE. I WAS HAPPY TO SEE HER AND WE CELEBRATED AND HAD A GREAT DAY TOGETHER. SHE WAS SOBER TOO.

IT WAS A NICE CHANGE

THE REST OF THE DAY ME AND JULIA HAD A WONDERFUL INTIMATE TIME. I BELEIVE IT WAS HER WAY OF THANKING ME THAT I WENT TO GET HER AND TRY WITH ALL MY MIGHT TO GET HER TO GO LEAVE WEST VALLEY COUNTY JAIL.

AFTER THIS WE STAYED ANOTHER TWO WEEKS UNTIL MID MAY OR EARLY MID MAY LIKE AROUND THE 12TH OF MAY AND NEXT SHE AND I WENT BACK TO MOMS AND STAYED THERE FOR JUST 3 DAYS.

AT MOMS FOR THE NEXT THREE DAYS SHE TOLD ME SHE DIDNT WANT TO GO OUT WITH ME IN PUBLIC AS HER DRESSED UP MEANING AS HER LOOKING LIKE AND BEING THE ONE AND ONLY JULIA ROBERTS. SHE WAS STILL UPSET WHEN I PULLED HER OUT OF THE BATHROOM OF THE SPEARMINT RHINO STRIP CLUB WHEN SHE WAS ACTING LIKE AND IMITATING THE STIPPER/WAITRESSES IN THE BATHROOM.

WE GOT INTO AN ARGUEMENT AS SHE BOUGHT 2 SIX PACKS FOR HER TO DRINK BY HERSELF. SHE LEFT AND WENT INTO SOME BUSHES AND A PIT LIKE HOLE AREA NEAR THE RAMADA INN HOTEL IN CLAREMONT DOWN THE STREET.

I WENT LOOKING FOR HER AND SHE WAS HIDING AS SHE WAS DRINKING BY HERSELF. I PULLED HER OUT AND SHE

GOT MAD AND THEN I TOOK HER BACK TO MOMS AND SHE WOULDNT GO IN. SHE CALLED A PHONE NUMBER OF A HISPANIC FRIEND SHE MET WHILE DRINKING AND SHE PICKED HER UP AND I SAID SO LONG. I WAS TIRED AND HER SLEEP HABITS WERE MESSING UP MY SLEEP HABITS.

AS SHE LEFT I FELT TIRED AND RELEIVED. I THEN WENT TO SLEEP FOR THE FIRST TIME IN TWO DAYS. I CLEANED UP THE MESS SHE MADE AND THEN WROTE SOME MORE MUSIC ABOUT HER. I BELEIVE IT WAS AROUND THE 10TH SONG I WROTE FOR HER. IT, AS I SAID BEFORE WAS GOING TO BE 16 SONGS AND EXPRESSIONS FOR JUIIA WHICH AGAIN WAS THE NAME OF THE ALBUM WHEN THE ALBUM WAS FINISHED.

I STILL HAVE THE ALBUM MASTER ON 8 TRACK ON MASRERED C.D. IN MY TREASURE CHEST WHERE ALL THE C,D.S OF MY ALBUMS WERE PRODUCED AND RECORDED.

AS JULIA WAS GONE FOR A LITTLE WHILE AFGAIN I FELT I COULD REST. SHE CAME BACK AS I WAS SLEEPING. SHE SAID TO ME SHE SAW A GUY PLAYING GUITAR TRYING TO MAKE SOME MONEY. SHE SAID I SHOULD TRY IT SO I DID, BUT NOT YET. AS JULIA CAME BACK MOM AGAIN WANTED HER GONE SO WE LEFT AND WE SPENT A COUPLE DAYS AT THE SAND AND SAGE HOTEL. THIS TIME SHE WAS ABLE TO GET MONEY AND PAY FOR IT BECAUSE I HAD RAN OUT OF MONEY SO AS I GOT TO THIS HOTEL IN THE MORNING WHERE SHE WAS AT WE DECIDED TO LEAVE AROUND NOON AND WALK TO WALMART WHERE I HAD MY GUITAR AND FOR THE FIRST TIME IN MY LIFE I DID IT. I PLAYED GUITAR IN THE STREETS. IT WAS AT WALMART IN FRONT OF THE STORE AND WE ASKED AND THEY SAID OK IN THE STORE AND WE ACTUALLY MADE ENOUGH FOR A DAY IN THE HOTEL. I SLEPT FROM 2-6 AND AGAIN IN THE MIDNIGHT TIME IN THE NIGHT. NOW LATER ON I WILL BE ACTUALLY ARRESTED AT THE DRIVING OUTLET OF

WALMART AT ETIAWANDA IN 2002 AND 2009. ONLY THOSE TWO TIMES DID I GET ARRESTED IN MY LIFE FOR DOING THAT AND BELEIVE IT OR NOT IT WAS IN ERO. I HADNT DONE STREET MUSIC ON ETAWANDA WALMART AND FOOTHILL FROM 2002 WHEN I FIRST GOT ARRESTED UNTIL 2009 WHEN I GOT ARRESTED AGAIN TWO TIMES IN ERO ARRESTED AND AT THE SAME EXACT PLACE SO I GAVE UP ON PLAYING STREET MUSIC AND DOING SHOWS IN THE STREET AT THAT SPOT WHERE I WAS ARRESTED 2 TIMES IN ERO. THAT LAST ARREST IN 2009 WAS THE LAST TIME I PLAYED STREET MUSIC IN RANCHO CUCUMONGA OR ETAWANDA AND AT THAT WALMART OUTLET AND THE 15 FREEWAY.

I PLAYED THE WAL MART THERE FOR ABOUT 4 HOURS AND AS I WAS DOING THIS JULIA WENT INSIDE THE WALMART AND CAME OIUT WITH 50 BURGERS WITHOUT BREAD FROM THE MAC -DONALDS INSIDE. WE ATE A FEW LATER BUT MOST WENT TO WASTE UNFORTUNATELEY.

WE THEN SETTLED AT THE INDIAN MOTEL WHICH WAS ONLY 25 PER NIGHT. SO I HALFED THE DAYS WITH LIKE I SAID A SLEEP EARLY AND THEN ANOTHER AT 2 AM TO 11 AND THEN WE WERE OUT OF THERE. WE DIDNT HAVE A HOME FOR A COUPLE DAYS AND WE ROAMED AROUND UNTIL I MADE MORE MONEY AT THE TARGET ON SLOVER AVENUE IN COLTON/FONTANA BORDER. DOWN ON SIERRA AND SLOVER ON THE CORNER THERE IS A TARGET STORE AND I MADE ANOTHER 30 AND WROTE ANOTHER SONG ABOUT JULIA CALLED ROCK HARD ROCK ON.

AFTER THIS EVENING WE WALKED AROUND 10 MILES TO GET BACK TO THE HOTEL, THE SAND AND SAGE OR MAYBE A CHEAPER ONE. WE WERE UP ALL NIGHT WALKING. WE PAST A DRUG STORE THAT LOOKED LIKE AN OLD SCHWABS IN LOS ANGELES THAT WAS IN FONTANA OLD TOWN DISTRICT BY THE BARS WE FREQUENTED A FEW WEEKS

EARLIER AND SHE SAID "NOW THAT IS WHAT I LOVE TO DO". SHE WAS POINTING AT THE BARS STOOLS ON THE COUNTER WHERE THEY WERE SELLING OLD ICE CREAM SUNDAYS AND ICE CREAM CONES.

WE KEPT WALKING FURTHER. AS WE WALKED FURTHER SHE SAID SHE WANTED TO CHECK OUT THE OLD MEXICAN TEX MEX BURRITO RESTRAUNT. SO SHE WENT IN AND SHE SAID "ARE YOU GUYS REAL TEX MEX PEOPLE"- AND EVERYONE DIDNT SEEM TO HAPPY TO HEAR THAT THERE. I QUICKLEY TOOK HER OUT OF THERE AND WE THEN PROCEEDED TO WALK A FEW MORE MILES.

NOW WE ARE ON CITRUS AVENUE AND AAROW HIGHWAY.

JULIA SAYS SHE HAS TO PEE SO SHE DOES AND THEN COMING FROM THE 7-11 ON THE CORNER OF CITRUS AND AAROW HIGHWAY WHERE SHE USES THE RESTROOM AND SHE AND ME NOW START WALKING UP CITRUS AVENUE TO FOOTHILL. RIGHT BEFORE WE GET TO THE CORNER OF FOOTHILL AND CITRUS ABOUT 100 YARDS AROUND THREE HOUSES DOWN FROM CITRUS AND FOOTHILL A FEW OF THE TEX MEX GUYS IN A SMALL CAR ABOUT 4 OR 5 OF THEM HAVE GUNS AND PULLED ONE OUT ON JULIA. I RAN INTO A HOUSE AREA ON THE DRIVEWAY OF ONE OF THE HOUSES TRYING TO GRAB A BROOM AND AS I DID THAT JULIA YELLS AT ME, "WHAT ARE YOU DOING YOU ARE STEALING A BROOM FROM A HOUSE YOU ARE BREAKING THE LAW," DUH, WOW. NEXT THING THE GUYS ARE ABOUT READY TO JUMP OUT OF THE CAR AND KIDNAP JULIA UNLESS I CAN USE THIS BROOM AS A WEAPON. RIGHT AROUND THE CORNER OF FOOTHILL AND CITRUS COMES 4 POLICE CARS. IT WAS JULIA USING THIS BUTTON THAT I NEVER FOUND OUT WHERE IT WAS OR WHAT IT LOOKED LIKE-BUT IT WAS SOME ALARM SHE PRESSED WHICH WAS ABLE AT THE POLICE STATION OR RADAR FIND OUT WHERE JULIA IS AND MAN THEY GOT DOWN THERE IN SECONDS.

ABOUT UNDER 2 MINUTES I BELEIVE-BECAUSE THE PROBLEM OF THE TEX MEX RAPISTS AND KIDNAPPERS DIDNT START SINSE ABOUT 2-3 MINUTES FROM THE GUYS GETTING THERE.

THE COPS GOT THERE AND ROUNDED THE GUYS UP. WE LEFT AND SHE THANKED THEM. JULIA THEN TOLD ME I WAS AN EMBARRASSMENT AND THAT SHE COULD HANDLE THESE SORT OF SITUATIONS. GEE, I THOUGHT I WOULD AT LEAST GET A THANKS FOR RISKING MY LIFE TO DEFEND HER, NOT ME, THEY DIDNT WANT TO HAVE SEX AND KIDNAP AND RAPE ME.

NO, INSTEAD SHE DISSED ME. THE POLICE CAR GOT THERE SO FAST BECAUSE JULIA I FOUND OUT LATER HAD A BUTTON SOMEWHERE ON HER OR IN HER OR WHATEVER THAT IS FOR CELEBRATIES TO PROTECT THEM AND SHE USED THE BUTTON AND THIS IS WHY THE COPS GOT THERE IN LESS THEN 3 MINUTES AND KNEW WHAT THEY WERE AFTER. JULIA CONTACTED THEM AHEAD OF TIME.

AS WE KEPT WALKING WE WENT ALL THE WAY TO CITRUS AND FOOTHILL SO FROM SLOVER AND SIERRA AND EVEN BEFORE THAT THE 10 FREWWAY TO SLOVER AND SIERRA, THE TARGET STORE WHERE I PANAHANDLED AND THEN TO IN N OUT BURGER THEN WALK ALL THE WAY TO FOOTHILLL AND CHERRY AVE. ABOUT 8 MILES WE WALKED. WE COULDNT FIND A HOTEL SO SHE GOT IN A CAR WITH A PERSON SHE KNEW AND I TOOK THE BUS TO GAILS WHERE I USED TO LIVE AND WHERE SHE IS MY EX BUT BACK BEFORE 3-25-02 SHE WAS MY GIRLFRIEND FROM 1-5-93 TO 3-25-02 SO SHE LET ME SLEEP OVER THERE AND I SLEPT FOR A LONG TIME BEING JULIA KEPT ME UP EVERYNIGHT AT THE HOTELS AS WELL AS MOMS HOUSE.

I WAS GLAD TO SEE HER ONE SO I CAN REST. SHES GOT MY NUMBER AND I BELEIVE SOON SHE WILL CALL AND SHE DID.

THE NEXT CALL. SHE CALLED AND SAID SHE HAD A HOTEL IN WEST COVINA BEHIND THE CITRUS COURTHOUSE AND SHE TOLD ME TO COME AND THAT SHE NEEDS ME BAD SO I CAME TO VISIT AND FROM THEN ON HANG OUT WITH HER FOR AS LONG AS SJHE WANTED. SHE AGREED SHE WOULD NOT BE SO SLOPPY IF LIVING AT MOMS AGAIN OR ANY NEW HOTELS WE LIVE IN AND NOT DRINK AS MUCH AND NOT BE AS RUDE. I SAID OK AS LONG AS SHE KEEPS HER WORD AND PROMICE TO NOT DO THOSE THINGS ANYMORE.

I HAD TO WALK ALONG WAY TO THIS HOTEL THAT YOU WOULD NEVER SEE UNLESS SOMEONE TOLD YOU IT WAS THERE AND JULIA TOLD ME WHERE AND IF SHE WOULDNT HAVE I WOULD NEVER HAVE FOUND THE HOTEL. YOU PASS THE CITRUS COURTHOUSE AND TURN A RIGHT AND THEN ALEFT AND FOLLOW THAT LEFT AND KEEP GOING TO THE END WHERE THERE IS NO BUSHES AND JUST A HOTEL IN THE WEIRDEST SPOT. JULIA LIKED THIS SPOT AND HAD BEEN THERE NOW FOR 3 DAYS. I ASKED WHY DIDNT SHE CONTACT ME EARLIER AND SHE SAID SHE THOUGHT ABOUT IT AND IS SORRY. I FORGAVE HER.

AS I WENT TO HER HOTEL I HUGGED AND KISSED HER AND SHE LOOKED DIFFERENT. ACTUALLY BEAUTIFUL. SHE HAD BEEN TO HER AGENTS AND WAS GOING TO WORK ON A FILM CALLED FULL FRONTEL.

SHE SAID SHE MAY BE IN NEW YORK FOR A WEEK ON A CHARITY EVENT ABOUT TERET SYNDRONE.. I WAS LIKE, "GOOD LUCK."

AFTER SHE WAS GONE FOR A WEEK ANE I AGAIN NEEDED THE BREAK. JULIA IS THE TYPE OF PERSON ESPECIALLY IN

THE BEGENNING THAT WANTS TO BE WITH YOU 24 HOURS A DAY AND NO LESS.

IT IS NOT NORMAL. BUT OF COURSE JULIA IS NOT NORMAL.

ME AND MY WIFE OF 27 YEARS MINUS THE TIME I WAS WITH JULIA HAVE A WAY OF UNDERSTANDING AND THAT IS WE ARE NOT AROUND EACH OTHER THAT MUCH. THIS WAY WE DONT GET SICK OF EACH OTHER. IF I COULD HAVE DONE THIS PHILOSOPHY ME AND JULIA COULD HAVE STAYED TOGETHER FOREVER.

I ASKED JULIA WHAT OUR NEW TRIP AND OR ADVENTURE WAS GOING TO BE. WELL , SHE TOLD ME SHE WOULD TELL ME ONCE WE GET ON THE BUS.

THE BUS TO L.A.

WE WENT TOWARD LOS ANGELES AND THEN FURTHER TO VENICE BEACH. ON THE BUS ME AND JULIA GOT INTO AN ARGUMENT AND SHE TOLD ME SHE HAS AN IMAGE TO UPHOLD AND ALL ALONG SHE IS DISGUISED IN THRIFT STORE FUNKY CLOTHING.

WHEN WE GOT TO VENCICE WE HAD TO CARRY A TON OF HER STUFF LIKE 5 BAGS OF STUFF SHE HAD WHICH WAS MOSTELY CLOTHS AND ALCOHOL.

WE WALKED ON THE STRIP AS IT WAS GETTING DARK. AT FIRST I TRIED TO HAIL A TAXI TO TAKE US 100 YARDS FOR 5 DOLLORS AND HE WOULDNT GIVE US A RIDE THEN WE MADE IT AS I SAID ON THE STRIP AND THESE SNOTTY PEOPLE. I ESPECIALLY REMEMBER A MAN THERE AND I WAS PLAYING GUITAR AS A MONEY MAKER AND THE SNOTTY GUY THREW ME A PENNY AND SAID GO HOME BOY. I TOLD HIM TO NOT BE A SNOB BECAUSE I AM WITH JULIA ROBERTS. JULIA SHOWS HIM IT IS HER AND HE TOTALLY IS

IN AWE AND NICE NOW AND GAVE ME A 10 DOLLOR BILL. HOW PEOPLE CHANGE, HOW PEOPLE CHANGE.

NEXT I START PLAYING GUITAR FOR MONEY WITHOUT A SIGN AND THIS GUY IN A WHEELCHAIR COMES UP AND TELLS ME TO STOP PLAYING BECAUSE THAT IS HIS TURF. I ARGUE WITH HIM AND HE TRIES TO SICK HIS DOG ON ME. I JUMPED ON A MAIL BOX AND SO THE DOG COULDNT GET ME.

JULIA THEN CAME BACK FROM WHERE EVER SHE WAS COMING FROM. I BELEIVE A STORE THAT SELLS ALCOHOL.

SHE TELLS THE GUY IN THE WHEEL CHAIR TO PLEASE NOT HAVE HIS DOG ATTACK ME AND HE AGREES BECAUSE HE KNOWS JULIA. JULIA HAS A HOUSE NEAR THERE. THIS IS WHY JULIA KNOWS A FEW PEOPLE.

NEXT IS THE GUITARIST CC DIVELLE WHO WANTS TO FIGHT ME. WE DONT FIGHT AND I DO GIVE HIM A PIECE OF MY MIND TO HIS CRAZY SELF.

I TOLD JULIA THAT WE NEED TO WALK FURTHER SO ON THE STRIP WE WALK FURTHER AND WIND UP AT THE END OF THIS LONG WALK. ALL I REMEMBER 18 YEARS LATER WHICH IS NOW IS THAT WE SAT THERE AND SOME HOBOS CAME BY AND ACTED FRIENDLEY. THEY WERE A COUPLE , A GUY AND A GIRL YOUNGER THEN US AS I WAS 41 AND JULIA 34. AND THEY WERE PROBABLY IN THEIR MID 20S. JULIA ASKED ME TO GET HER SOME STUFF AND A SHOPPING CART FOR ALL OF OUR 5 BAGS AS WELL AS THE ALCOHOL WHICH BY NOW SHE HAS ACUMULATED AN ALCOHOL BOTTLE AMOUNT LARGER THEN MY MOM AND DAD EVER HAD ALTOGETHER IN 50 YEARS. SHE HAD 8 FIFTHS OR BIGGER OF GIN RUM, VITANO, WINE AND LITTLE GOLDSCHLAGGER BOTTLES AS WELL AS A 5TH OF SOUTHERN COMFORT, ALSO A 5TH OF TIQUILA AND A 5TH

OF VODKA. ANOTHER GUY ADDED ON TO THE CONVERSATION AND HE WAS A PROFESSIONAL MOVIE EXTRA. HE RECOGNISED JULIA AND JULIA FOR THAT DIDNT LKE HIM. I DONT KNOW WHY BECAUSE I LIKED HIM.

I THEN LEFT JULIA AND THE TWO PEOPLE AND THE MOVIE EXTRA GUY AND WENT TO A LOCAL STORE JULIA TOLD ME THERE WAS AROUND THE CORNER AND AS I DID THIS A BODY GUARD OF JULIAS THERE TO SAY HELLO AND I DONT KNOW WHAT RELATIONSHIP HE HAD TO JULIA BUT I DO REMEMBER HE HAD NO NECK AND WAS A JOCK TYPE WHO DIDNT LKE ME FOR NO REASON OR PROBABLEY THE REASON WAS I WAS WITH JULIA AND HE COULD BE JEALOUS. ANYWAYS AS I LEFT FOR THAST STORE IN WHAT JULIA CALLED WALKING DISTANCE I SAW THE BOUNCER/ BODYGUARD DUDE TALK TO JULIA.

THE STORE.

I GOT THERE AND I BELEIVE IT WAS A SAFEWAY AND THE SHOPPING BASKETS YOU COULDNT TAKE BECAUSE THE WHEELS WOULD LOCK BECAUSE IT HAD A MAGNETIC LOCK ASSOSSIATED WITH THE WHEELS. I COULDNT TAKE THE BASKET BUT I DID ANYWAYS AND HOPING THAT IF I GOT THE BASKET OUT OF THE AREA THE WHEELS WOULDNT LOCK ANYMORE AND THIS IS THE CASE. IT DIDNT LOCK ANYMORE AFTER I DRUG THE BASKET ABOUT 1/2 A MILE.

AS I GOT BACK TO JULIA SHE WAS LOOKING VERY UNHAPPY AND HER HOBO FRIENDS WERE GONE. I FIGURED WHAT HAPPENED. SHE TRUSTED THE HOBOS AND THE HOBOS STOLE THE ALCOHOL. ALL OF IT. I WAS GLAD BECAUSE I BELEIVE IF SHE WOULD HAVE DRANK ALL THAT HARD LIQUOR SHE ACCUMULATED IN THE PAST FEW DAYS SHE WOULD HAVE SCEROSIS OF THE LIVER. SHE WAS MAD AND COULDNT BELEIVE THE HOBOS SHE TRUSTED TOOK HER ALCOHOL. OF COURSE YOU CANT

TRUST ANYONE IN THESE DAYS, ESPECIALLY A DESPERATE HOBO AND ESPECIALLY A COUPLE DESPERATE HOBOS.

SHE WANTED TO GET OUT OF THE AREA AND I NOTICED SHE WAS MEAN TO THE MOVIE EXTRA THAT KNEW HER STILL.

I TOLD THE MOVIE EXTRA GUY THAT I WAS SORRY FOR HER ACTIONS AND LEFT. ME AND JULIA TOOK THE BUS BACK. THE BUS DROPPED US ACROSS FROM THE LOS ANGELES COUNTY COURTHOUSE ON BROADWAY OR NEAR THERE AND FROM THERE WE WALKED THROUGH A LITTLE PART OF L.A. SKID ROW. WHEN JULIA WAS UNDERNEATH THE LIGHTS OF THE STREETLIGHTS SHE ILLUMINATED AS A SUPER HOBO WITH HER THRIFT SHOP CLOTHS SHE WAS WEARING, SHE REALLY SHINED AND I TOOK A COUPLE PICTURES OF HER THERE STANDING THERE. WE WOULD TAKE ANOTHER BUS THAT TOOK US TO INDIAN HILL AND HOLT BLVD IN POMONA AND FROM THERE WE DECIDED TO GET A HOTEL AT THE HOTEL 6 IN CLAREMONT. WE GOT A HOTEL THERE FOR 3 DAYS AND THEN WENT BACK TO MOMS. I CALLED ANNIE TO SEE IF SHE CAN HELP GET JULIA SOMEWHERE AND SHE SAID SHE COULDNT. AFTER WHATS GOING ON OVER TWO MONTHS NOW BEING IT IS BECOMING JUNE I DECIDED TO DROP JULIA AT A MOTEL IN FONTANA CALLED THE RED AAROW HOTEL AND THERE SHE GOT A HOTEL FOR 4 DAYS AS I PAID FOR IT AND THEN WENT TO GAILS AND MY DAUGHTERS AND PLAYED WITH HER AND HAD FUN WITH THEM FOR THE NEXT 4 DAYS. JULIA THEN CALLED BEGGING ME TO PICK HER UP. SHE SAID SHE WAS STILL IN THE RED AAROW HOTEL AND PAID FOR ANOTHER DAY BECAUSE HER FRIEND JOHN PAID FOR IT. JOHN WAS AN EX MOVIE ACTOR AND HELPED HER WITH HIS MONEY SO WE SPENT THE NEXT DAY THERE AS I HUNG OUT WITH HER. LATER ON SHE TOLD ME SHE WANTED TO HANG OUT WITH THESE TWO GUYS THAT ARE OUTSIDE OF THE HOTEL.

I ASKED WHO THEY WERE AND SHE SAID THEY WERE COOL. JULIA HAS NO STREET SMARTS SO I SHOULD HAVE NOT TRUSTED HER ANSWER. NEXT SHE ASKED IF I WOULD GO WITH HER WITH THE TWO GUYS TO GET METH. SHE SAID SHE NEVER DONE METH AND THESE GUYS SAID THE METH WAS GREAT. I SAID THESE GUYS ARE DRUGGIES AND OF COURSE THEY WILL SAY THE METH IS GREAT. SHE INSISTED ON TRYING METH SO THE GUYS GOT SOME FOR HER. WE WENT BACK TO THE HOTEL AND THE GUYS ASKED IF THEY COULD HAVE SOME OF THE METH SO WE GAVE THEM SOME AND IT WAS FOR THEIR EFFORTS OF THEM GETTING IT FOR US.

NEXT THE GUYS WAITED OUTSIDE OF JULIAS HOTEL. I GUESS I COME TO FIGURE THEY WERE HOMELESS GUYS. NEXT THE GUYS ASKED IF THEY COULD SEE JULIA TOPLESS THEY WILL GIVE ME MONEY. I ANGRELY SAID NO AND SCOOTED THE GUYS OUT AND THAT WAS THE END OF THE GUYS. JULIA THANKED ME FOR PROTECTING HER. I SAID AND ASKED HER TO STOP CAUSING PROBLEMS BY ATTRACTING LOW LIFE PEOPLE.

SHE SAID HOW DARE I JUDGE PEOPLE. I SAID I WASNT JUDGING AND THAT I KNOW FOR A FACT THEY ARE SCUMBAG PEOPLE. WHEN YOU HAVE NO STREET SMARTS YOU THINK ALL PEOPLE ARE GOOD AND THE SAME AND THIS WAS WHY JULIA ALMOST GOT RAPED, KLLED AND HAD HER LIQUOR STOLEN FROM HER ON ANOTHER OCCASION AT VENICE BEACH. SHE TRUSTED THESE PEOPLE I ALREADY KNEW WERE BAD FROM MY INSTINCTS AND STREET SMARTS SHE DOESNT HAVE. THIS IS WHY JULIA NEEDED ME, BASICALLY AS A BODYGUARD AND OCCASIONAL SEX 11 TIMES IN 7 MONTHS NOT TOO GOOD A SEX LIFE. BUT AT TIMES JULIA WAS GREAT AT SEX, IN HER DIFFERENT CHARACTORS AND PERSONAITIES.

I STAYED THE NIGHT WITH HER AND THE NEXT MORNING AFTER SHE RAN AROUND ALL HYPER BECAAUSE SHE TRIED THE METH FOR THE ONE AND ONLY TIE I WAS AROUND HER. SHE WAS IN A BAD MOOD LIKE METH PEOPLE ARE THE DAY AFTER THEY HAVE THIS EUPHORIC NIGHT.

SHE WAS MEAN AND GRUMPY AND TRIED TO MAKE ME CLEAN UP HER MESSY HOTEL THAT I PAID FOR AND SHE MADE THE MESS. I DID CLEAN IT FOR HER.

I WAS AT THIS TIME FALLING OUT OF LOVE WITH HER BECAUSE I REALIZED SHES A FAKE.

NOW WHAT DOES A FAKE MEAN TO ME? A FAKE IS A PERSON WHO REALLY ISNT THE WAY THEY PRETEND TO BE. PRETENDING IS ANOTHER FORM OF ACTING AND IS ACTUALLY THE BASICS OF WHAT ACTING IS. PRETENDING TO BE SOMETHING IN ALOT OF ACTORS CASES AT LEAST, I HOPE IN ALOT OF ACTORS CASES THEY LEAVE THE PRETENDING TO THEIR ACTING JOB. NOT JULIA, SHE TAKES PRETENDING EVERYWHERE AND BEING IM A MISICIAN AND NOT AN ACTOR IM NOT INTO THIS PRETENDING THING. JUST LIKE ROBERT DOWNEY JR WAS A FAKE BEING HE AND ME GOT ALONG AND SHARED BUNKS ALMOST FOR 20 DAYS OR SO AND THEN HE WAS SAYING WE SHOULD GET A CHURCH OUTSIDE OF JAIL TO START WITH ME AT THE MUSIC PART AND HIM AS A PREACHER AND HE AND I DIDNT. 16 SHOWS FOR THE INMATES AND ME AND ROBERT WERE GREAT FRIENDS SO I THOUGHT UNTIL WE ALL HAD TO BE MOVED FROM OUR SITUATION, AFTER WE WERE MOVED ROBERT WOULDNT EVEN TALK TO ME OR BE IN THE SAME AREA AS ME. ROBERT WAS ONLY NICE I FELT BECAUSE HE HAD TO BECAUSE EVERYONE IS WEAKER OR STRONGER AND HE FELT TO BE NICE TO ME BECAUSE I MAY HAVE BEEN STRONGER THEN HIM TO HIM PHYSICALLY IN HIS EYES. SO AS YOU BEFRIEND A STRONGER PERSON

YOU ARE NICE TO THEM. ONCE ROBERT LEFT OUR SITUATION WE WERE POSITIONED TO BE IN WHICH WAS ME ON THE LOWER BUNK AND HIM ON THE HIGHER BINK NEXT TO MY BUNK HE AVOIDED ME AND NEVER TALKED TO ME AGAIN. ROBERT ONLY WAS NICE TO ME OUT OF SURVIVAL AND I WAS REAL AND WEATHER OR NOT I WAS STRONGER THEN HIM I WOULD NEVER COMPARE ,MYSELF TO HIM IN WHO IS THE STONGEST, I AM FROM REALITY NOT THE FAKE ACTORS WORLD. I WAS REAL AND REALLY THOUGHT ROBERT WAS A FRIEND BECAUSE HE WAS ACTING LIKE THIS WHEN I DID THE 16 SHOWS AND HAD 3 HOUR TO 4 HOUR LONG TALKS WITH HIM LATE AT NIGHT BEFORE THE LIGHTS GO OUT IN THE DORM. I THOUGHT ROBERT WAS REAL ABOUT STARTING UP A CHRISTIAN CHURCH WITH ME AND HIM MINISTERS AND ME DOING THE MUSIC MINISTRY AND HIM THE PREACHING MINISTRY BUT NO IT WAS ALL FAKE. I CANT SAY THE PREACHING WAS FAKE AND I DONT THINK HIS PREACHING WAS FAKE. THIS IS THE ONLY THING REAL I BELEIVE ROBERT WAS AS A PREACHER FOR JESUS CHRIST THE FATHER, SON AND HOLY SPIRIT YET WHEN HE COMES BACK TO THE HOLLYWOOD WORLD HE NEVER BRINGS UP PREACHING OR JESUS CHRIST. BECAUSE I BELEIVE ROBERT DOWNEY DOESNT BRING UP GOD JESUS CHRIST THE FATHER SON AND HOLY SPIRIT AND DOESNT PREACH BECAUSE HE KNOWS THAT HE WOULD LOSE POPULARITY IN THE ATHIEST HOLLYWOOD WORLD.

THAT PART OF ROBERT WAS REAL. ANYWAYS BACK TO THE FAKE JULIA.

ON TIME AT THE SAND AND SAGE HOTEL JULIA WAS ACTING AND I MEAN ACTING STRANGE AND SHE STOPS AND SAYS TO ME "ACT, JUST TRY TO ACT."

I WAS LIKE NOT INTO IT BECAUSE SHE GETS AND HAS BEEN OVERPAID AND SHE IS TRYING TO GET A GUY WHO IS

NOT AN ACTOR TO ACT FOR FREE AND NOT ONLY FOR FREE BUT FOR THE AMUSEMENT OF HER AKA JULIA.

SO BECAUSE SHE WAS SO RUDE THAT MORNING AFTER I DID CLEAN UP HER HOTEL. SHE STAYED MORE DAYS AND I LEFT BY BUS TO SEE GAIL. LATER I WENT TO MY SONS AND THEN TO SEE MY MOM. I TOOK THE BUS EACH TIME AND IT WAS ON THE SAME DAY. I WENT FROM RANCHO CUCUMONGA TO CLAREMONT AND AS I PASSED THE HOTEL WHERE JULIA WAS STAYING CALLED AND ENTITLED THE RED WING HOTEL I SAW HER ON THE OUTSIDE OF THE HOTEL SITTING IN A SHORT LAWN CHAIR ABOUT THREE INCHES HIGH TO THE GROUND WHERE SHE SAT ON THE CHAIR. SHE LOOKED LIKE AN INDIAN.

JULIA TOLD ME HER BLOOD LINE INCLIUDED WHITE AND JEWISH AND INDIAN AND SWEEDISJH AS WELL AS AUSTIAN AMONG OTHERS. I DIDNT KNOW WHETHER TO BELEIVE HER UNTIL LATER WHEN I WENT OUT WITH AND HUNG OUT WITH HALLE BERRY AND SHE HAD 8 RACES IN HER WHICH MADE ME REALIZE THAT THIS IS WHY THEY ARE SUCH GOOD ACTORS BECAUSE THEY HAVE MANY BLOODLINE RACES THAT IN TURN ARE DIFFERENT PERSONALITIES, SO THIS IS WHY HALLE HAS SO MANY LOOKS, BECAUSE SHE CAN GO INTO ANY RACE OF HER BLOODLINE SHE WANTS TO AND OBVIOUSELEY SAME WITH JULIA. THIS ALSO WORKS WITH HALLE BERRY BEING SHE HAS 8 NATIONALITIES IN HER BLOODLINE.

I AT THIS TIME NEEDED A SHORT BREAK FROM HER BEING LIKE I SAID SHE IS THE KIND OF PERSON WHO WANTS TO BE AROUND YOU 24 HOURS A DAY AND WE HAD MANY TIMES WHERE WE WERE TOGETHER 72 TO 96 HOURS IN ERO. ONCE AT THE SAND AND SAGE HOTEL AND ONCE AT MOMS AT LEAST 72-96 HOURS IN ERO EACH TIME NOT EVEN ABLE TO LEAVE FOR 10 MINUTES.

ITS LIKE JULIA WANTED ME AS A PRISONER, SORT OF BUT JUST KIDDING.

ONCE I ESCAPED TO A MEXICAN BURRITO PLACE I NEVER HAVE BEEN TO SINSE BUT AT THAT TIME I REMEMBER IT WAS MY WAY TO GET AWAY FOR 1 HOUR.

JULIA IS HIGH HIGH MAINTENENCE AND ONCE SHE SAID SHE WASNT WHEN SHE SAID "IM NOT THAT EXPENSIVE. I ONLY COST FOR A LITTLE FOOD AND DRINK AND RENT". WELL, THATS ALOT FOR ME WHO WORKS AS A MUSICIAN MOSTLEY OUT OF WORK LIKE ME.

AT THIS TIME THE ROOM I WAS LIVING WITH WITH JULIA AT MOMS WAS ALSO A RECORDING STUDEO, 8 TRACK AS WELL AS A PRACTICE STUDEO IN WHICH I MAKE MY MONEY RENTING MY EQUITMENT OUT FOR SHOWS AND RENTING THIS ROOM AND EQUITMENT OUT FOR BANDS TO HAVE A PLACE TO PRACTICE AND ALSO THE ROOM WAS FOR ME TO WRITE MUSIC AND EVERYTHING ELSE THAT HAS TO DO WITH MUSIC INCLIUDING INTERVIEWS AS WELL AS VIDEO SEESSIONS AS SOME OF THE SCENES IN SOME OF MY VIDEOS WAS ABOUT THAT ROOM.

NOW WE ARE COMING TO THE POINT WHERE I AM STARTING TO THINK JULIA MAY BE A LITTLE WEIRD, SO SHE IS BACK WITH ME AND IT IS JUNE 1ST. SHE HAD BEEN GONE FOR A WEEK AND THIS WAS AFTER SHE WAS ARRESTED A SECOND TIME OVER AT THE FONTANA TRANS CENTER.

THE FONTANA TRANS CENTER ARREST........... IT STARTED WHEN JULIA CALLED ME AFTER BEING GONE FOR A WEEK. A GUY ACTUALLY CALLS ME FIRST ON THE PHONE AND THEN JULIA SPEAKS TO ME. HE SAYS SHE IS READY TO HAVE ME PICK HER UP AND THAT HE HAS NO MORE MONEY TO LET HER STAY. I SAID THANKS AND I UNDERSTAND. HE

SAID SHE LOOKS JUST LIKE JULIA ROBERTS AND I SAID "YES UNCANNY". HE THEN SAYS "WOULDNT IT BE AMAZING IF IT WAS HER? WHAT A TREAT". I SAID "YEAH , THAT WOULD BE A TRIP BUT ITS NOT. "IS A LOOKALIKE " HE AGREED. I THEN TOOK THE BUS TO PICK HER UP. AS I KNOCKED ON THE DOOR AT THE RED WING HOTEL IN FONTANA HE SAID SHE IS STILL GETTING READY. I SAID "OH NO BECAUSE I KNOW WHEN JULIA GETS READY IT TAKES ABOUT 3 HOURS" AND I WAITED AND I WAITED AND I WAITED AND FINALLY SHE CAME OUT ABOUT AFTER 3 HOURS. I TOLD HER THE LAST BUS IS COMING AND THAT ISNT TRUE THERE WERE STILLTHREE BUT I SAID IT TO GET HER OUT OF THERE. THANK GOD SHE FINALLY CAME OUT AFTER ALMOST 4 HOURS AND I WAS TIRED AND SHE WAS DRUNK.

AT THE FONTANA TRASNS CENTER IN LATE MAY ALMOST JUNE 1ST.

I PICKED UP JULIA AS SHE FINALLY CAME OUT AND SHE LOOKED GREAT. SHE ALWAYS DOES WHEN SHE SPENDS THAT MUCH TIME GETTING READY, 3 HOURS ON HERSELF.WE TAKE THE BUS AND AS SHE IS ON THE BUS WITH ME SHE CRIES AND SAYS HER MAKE UP ARTIST DIED. I SAID SORRY TO HEAR IT. WE THEN WENT TO THE TRANS CENTER BECASUE WE WERE HEADED TO EAT AT MILLES WHICH IS A RESTRAUNT IN FONTANA ON SIERRA AVENUE BELOW AAROW HIGHWAY.

AS WE GET TO THE FONTANA TRANS CENTER THERE IS JULIA ON THE BUS PULLING OUT A FIFTH OF SOME DRINK I CANT REMEMBER WHAT IT IS BECAUSE IT REALLY ISNT IMPORTANT. I NOTICED SHE WAS ALREADY DRUNK SO I AM THINKING THAT SHE HAD DRANK ANOTHER FIFTH BEFORE THIS ONE AND NOW I AM WORRYING SHE IS GOING TO GET INTO SOME KIND OF TROUBLE AT THE FONTANA TRANS

CENTER BECAUSE THEY HAVE A ZERO POLICY FOR THAT KIND OF THING, DRINKING.

JULIA OPENLEY STARTS DRINKING AND OF ALL THE LUCK THERE IS A YOUNG OVERZEALOUS SECURITY GUARD WHO I NEVER SEEN OR I ACTUALLY NEVER SEE SECURITY GUARDS AROUND THE FONTANA TRANS CENTER BUT LOW AND BEHOLD HERE IS THIS GUY AND HE DOESNT LIKE HER. HE DOESNT RECOGNISE HER AS JULIA AND THERE ARE ONLY A FEW PEOPLE THERE, ONE A BLACK GUY WITH A BIG BOOMBOX AND ME AND THE GUARD AND JULIA AND THAT IS ABOUT IT. THE BLACK GUY GETS A HUG BY JULIA AND JULIA SAYS SHE SORRY WHAT HAPPENED TO HIS PEOPLE. THE BLACK GUY SORT OF LIKES HER ANYWAYS EVEN THOUGH SHE MADE THE DUMB REMARK. THE GUARD IS GETTING ANNOYED AND THEN SHE GOES INTO THE BATHROOM WHERE SHE IS NOT SUPPOSED TO GO BECAUSE THE BATHROOM IS OFF BOUNDS BECAUSE IT IS BEING RESTORED AND THERE IS A SIGN THAT SAYS SO, WHICH IS QUITE APPROPRIATE FOR THE GUARD TO COME OVER AND HARRASS HER AND NOW I KNOW THERE IS GONNA BE TROUBLE WITH THE COMBINATION OF THIS OVERZEALOUS YOUNG DUDE WANTING TO MAKE HIS FIRST ARREST AND JULIA AND HER ALCOHOLIC REBELLIOUS ATTITUDE. I KNEW SOMETHING SOON WAS GOING TO GO DOWN. THE SIGNS WERE ON THE WALLS OF THE BATHROOMS SAYING NO ENTRY AND LOW AND BEHOLD JULIA ENTERS AND PEES AND THEN DRINKS AND IS SINGING IN THERE.

AS SHE COMES OUT THE COP GRABS HER AND PLACES HANDCUFFS ON HER. I TOLD HIM THERE IS NO REASON FOR THAT AND THAT I WILL TAKE HER AWAY AND JULIA IS NOW BEING COMBATIVE LIKE THE LAST TIME AND SHE WILL NOT MOVE HER LEGS AND HE IS DRAGGING HER. I LEAVE BECAUSE I KNOW IF I AM THERE LIKE LAST TIME I MAY GET IN TROUBLE. LAST TIME I ALMOST GOT ARRESTED FOR ME

SAYING ITS JULIA AND THE COP SAYS IF ITS NOT JULIA I
WLL BE ARRESTED FOR GIVING A FALSE NAME AND
LUCKILY JULIA PROVED SHE WAS SHE.

NOW I KNOW I WILL BE ARRESTED BEING AROUND HER SO I
LEAVE AND TAKE HER BAGS. AS I TAKE HER BAGS ON THE
BUS THE FIRST PERSON ON THE BUS TO HELP ME IS
RODNEY KING. IM TELLING YOIU THE TRUTH.

AS I LOOK BACK FROM THE BUS SEEING JULIA IN CUFFS
AGAIN I SEE THREE COP CARS FROM FONTANA COMING
AND I THEN SEE A VIEW OF JULIA BEING DRAGGED INTO
THE COP CAR BECAUSE SHE WONT WALK OR USE HER
LEGS. I SAID THIS TIME I WILL NOT MEET HER AT THE
COUNTY JAIL AND AT THIS TIME I WAS PRETTY THROUGH
WITH HER.

JUNE 2002.

JULIA GETS OUT OF JAIL THIS TIME AND I DONT ASK
QUESTIONS BECAUSE I DONT WANNA KNOW. SHE SAID
AND ASKED ME "THERE SHOULD HAVE BEEN
HELOCOPTERS ETC". I SAID "NO JULIA NOT FOR A
MSDEMEANER", JULIA SAYS "YEAH BUT ITS ME."

AFTER ALL THIS I MEET JULIA AT MILLIES. SHE CALLS ME
AND WANTS TO MEET THERE. AS I GO THERE I ALMOST
GET INTO A FISTFIGHT WITH THE BUS DRIVER WHO IS A
BLACK GUY AND A RACIST. I GET OFF THE BUS AT THE
TRANS CENTER A WALK TO MILLIES. JULIA IS NOT THERE.
SHE IS LATE 2 HOURS AND AS I WAS ABOUT TO LEAVE HERE
SHE COMES. AS WE WERE AT MILLIES A WAITRESS
RECOGNISED JULIA AND ASKED HER IF SHE WAS JULIA AND
I SAID NO SHES A LOOK ALIKE. SHE APPRECIATED ME
SAYING THAT I DO REMEMBER THAT.

WE THEN GO TO MOMS AND STAY A WEEK. AS WE STAY AT
MOMS SHE MESSES UP AGAIN AND WE HAVE TO LEAVE

MOMS. I GET ANOTHER HOTEL IN FONTANA AND WE DO MORE STREET MUSIC TO PAY FOR THE HOTEL AT TARGET ON SLOVER ON BORDER OF COLTON AND FONTANA.

WE THEN STAY UP ALL NIGHT AND I REMEMBER BEING REAL TIRED BUT SHE WAS HAPPY AND ALERT. I REALIZED SHE IS NOT TIRED BECAIUSE SHE IS USED TO THESE ACTOR HOURS THAT SHE DOES WHEN SHE DOES HER MOVIES AND SHOWS.

BACK TO CLAREMONT AND GOING TO AN AGENCY IN HOLLYWOOD FOR MY SON TO AUDITION AND THEN DROPPED AT MOTEL 6 IN CLAREMONT FOR 3 DAYS. I REMEMBER THAT JULIA DIDNT LIKE LITTLE CHILDREN THAT MUCH I MEAN IN BETWEEN 1-8. NATAWNEE IS LAILAHS DAUGHTER AND I DO REMEMBER NATAWNE GETTING ON JULIAS NERVES.. ALSO I FORGOT TO SAY ONCE WHEN WE WERE VISITING CHARLIE MY SON IN RANCHO CUCUMONGA I AND JULIA PLAYED HIDE AND SEEK WITH CHARLIE IN THE BACK AND JULIA WAS AT BEST TOLORATING THE SITUATION. SHE ASKED MY SON WHICH MOVIE DID HE LIKE BETTER "THE MEXICAN" OR " OCEANS 12. HE SAID HE LIKED THE MOVIE "THE MEXICAN" BETTER AND SHE LIKED THAT AND BONDED WITH MY SON OVER THAT BECAUSE SHE AGREED THAT SHE ALSO LIKED THAT MOVIE BETTER THEN "OCEANS 12."   JULIA TOLD ME THAT THE GUY IN THE MOVIE OF OCEANS 12 GEORGE CLOONEY PUT LSD IN HER DRINK AND PCP. ALSO THEY PLAYED ALOT OF PRANKS ON HER. SHE REALLY TOLD ME THIS.

LAILAH PICKED US UP FROM MOMS. IT WAS LAILAH AND NATAWNEE ME AND JULIA AND CHARLIE MY SON FOR THIS AUDITION. WE MADE IT TO L.A. ABOUT 6 P.M. WHICH WAS THE TIME OF THE AUDITION. JULIA WAS HIDING OUT BECAUSE SHE DIDNT WANT TO BE RECOGNISED. WHATEVER.

AFTER WE WERE DONE LAILAH DROPPED US OFF AGAIN OFF AT THE MOTEL 6 AND WE STAYED THERE A COUPLE NIGHTS. WHILE THERE I WENT TO MOMS TO GO TO THE RECORDING STUDEO BECAUSE I WROTE ANOTHER SONG ABOUT JULIA CALLED WHAT ELSE OTHER THEN "JULIA."

AFTER THOSE TWO DAYS SHE RAN OFF WITH A GIRL SHE MET WHILE WE WERE DOING STREET MUSIC THE DAY BEFORE ON THE FREEWAY AT THE 10 AND INDIAN HILL BLVD THE EAST OFF RAMP MEANING GETTING OFF FROM THE EAST ONTO INDIAN HILL.

AFTER SHE RAN OFF WITH THIS HISPANIC GIRL I WAS WITHOUT HER FOR ABOUT A DAY. THAT LAST TIME OUT ON THE STREET JULIA WAS HELPING ME TO GET MONEY AS SHE WAS RUNNING OUT IN THE STREET TO GET MONEY FROM THOSE WITH THEIR HANDS OUT THE WINDOW WITH A DOLLLOR OR MORE IN THEIR HANDS AND SOMETIMES JUST CHANGE BUT TO ME MONEY IS MONEY. I REMEMBER SHE WAS REALLY INTO A DIFFERENT PERSONNA AND THIS PERSONNA SAID TO ME, "WHATS YOUR NAME AGAIN? THAT IS REALLY WHAT SHE SAID TO ME.

SHE THEN CALLED ME THE DAY AFTER SHE WAS GONE AND SAYS SHE MISSES ME AND CALLS ME HANDSOME. WHICH IS WHAT SHE DOES ALOT IN A CERTAIN MOOD IS CALL ME HANDSOME. SHE SAYS SHES AT THE MOTEL 6 AND ON THE SECOND FLOOR AND WANTS ME TO COME UP NOW AND AGAIN SAYS "I WANT YOU NOW HANDSOME". I WENT AND GOT THERE IN 1 HOUR OR SO I WENT TO THE SECOND FLOOR AND WHEN I GOT IN IT WAS HOT AS FIRE. SHE HAD THE TEMPITURE UP AS HIGH AS IT CAN GET HOT WISE, IT WAS UNBEARABLE.

SHE WAS THE MOST ROMANTIC I HAVE EVER BEEN WITH HER FROM THAT MOMENT ON AND ALL BEFORE. THIS WAS THE PEAK OF OUR ROMANCE. WE STAYED FOR TWO

NIGHTS HER GETTING THAT GIRL TO PAY FOR BOTH NIGHTS. IT WAS FUN AND LIKE ALWAYS YOU NEVER COULD TELL WITH JULIA.

AFTER THAT SHE STAYED ANOTHER DAY THERE AND I WENT TO MOMS TO DO SOME RECORDING.

IT WAS FUNNY BECAUSE I KNEW SORT OF WHERE SHE WAS GOING TO BE, PROBABLEY AT HER HOTEL BUT KNOWING HER SHE WAS PROBABLEY AROUND AND TO THIS DAY I WILL NEVER FORGET WHEN I WAS WALKING IN THE OLD SAMBOS PARKING LOT IN BETWEEN THE OLD SAMBOS BUILDING AND THE LIQUOR STORE BY THE PAY PHONE AND I SEE JULIA SUNBURNT AND WALKING AROUND AND SHE RUNS UP TO ME AS I AM ON THE PHONE AND SHE SAYS "HI CHUCK" AND THEN SHE WALKS OF AS I GIVE HER A COUPLE DOLLORS FOR HER TO BUY A GOLD SCHLAGGER. YOU KNOW, THOSE SMALL BOTTLES.

NEXT TIME I SEE HER IS AT THE PAYPHONE AGAIN. THIS IS WHERE THE RELATIONSHIP STARTS TO END.

TALKING TO GAIL ON THE PHONE.

AS I SEE JULIA HERE I GO TO THE PHONE AND GAIL TRICKS ME INTO HER TALKING TO JULIA. GAIL TELLS ME ALL OF OUR SEXUAL EXPLOITS IN THE LAST MONTH. I WASNT CHEATING SO JULIA BECAUSE SHE LEFT AND LIVED WITH A GUY FOR THAT WEEK. JULIA HEARD GAIL AND WAS VERY SAD. SHE WALKED TO MOMS HOUSE WITH ME WHERE NEXT TO THE GARAGE ON THE SIDE OF THE YARD SHE THREW UP BECAUSE IT MADE HER SICK WHAT GAIL TOLD HER. I REALIZED JULIA SORT OF LOVED ME IN HER OWN SELFISH WAY.

WE THEN WENT TO THE PARK AND SHE GOT RIPPED AND AT THIS PARK TRIP WE ARGUED AND BEFORE OUR ARGUMENT I TOOK SOME PICTURES OF HER AND SHE GOT

MAD AND THAT WAS BASICALLY THE REASON FOR OUR ARGUMENT THERE AT THE PARK.

WHILE WE WERE SITTING AT THE PARK SOMEONE OR MORE THEN SOMEONE CALLED POLICE. HERE COMES OFFICER TABER WHO IS A CLAREMONT COP I DO NOT CARE FOR. HE IS DOWN ON JULIA AND ACTUALLY WHEN I TOOK THIS ONE PICTURE IT REALLY IS THE ONLY ONE THAT LOOKS LIKE JULIA ROBERTS.

SHE DIDNT GET ARRESTED BUT THEY MADE HER SIT ON THE SIDEWALK CURB AND HER FEET BEING IN THE STREET SHE DIDNT LOOK LIKE JULIA. JULIA SAID AND DUSTIN HOFFMAN I REMEMBER SEEING SAID THAT THE OUTFIT AND OR UNIFORM YOU PUT ON IS 99 PERCENT YOUR LOOK AND THAT SOUNDS LIKE JULIA TO THE TEE. WHEN SHE WEARS THRIFT STORE FUNKY CLOTHS SHE DONT LOOK LIKE JULIA BUT IF SHE WEARS REGULAR CUTE CLOTHS TIME CLOTHS ETC SHE LOOKS EXACTELEY LIKE THE WAY SHE WAS IN THE MOVIE PRETTY WOMEN.

SO NOW IT IS MID JUNE AND WE ARE BACK LIVING AT MOMS FOR AWHILE. JULIA PROMICED SHE WOULD BE ON HER BEST BEHAVIOR AND NOT MESS UP THE FAMILY ROOM WHERE WE WERE LIVING AT IN THAT ROOM.

AND SHE KEPT HER WORD UNTIL JULY BUT DURING THESE LAST TWO WEEKS OF JUNE WE HAD ALOT OF ROMANCE BUT SHE WENT CRAZY ONCE AND GOT DRUNK AND MOM SAID SHE HAD TO GO OUT SO I GOT HER A SLEEPING BAG AND SHE SLEPT ON THE SIDE OF THE HOUSE.

AND THEN A COUPLE DAYS AFTER THAT SHE GOT RIPPING DRUNK AND WOULDNT TURN DOWN HER COUNTRY MUSIC SO I HAD TO PUT HER IN THE GARAGE BUT I GAVE HER A NICE LTTLE NEST TYPE PLACE TO SLEEP AND I REMEMBER SEEING HER THE NEXT DAY AND SHE SAID SHE DESERVED

THAT AND WE THEN MADE UP. WE MADE UP ALOT OF TIMES AND THATS A GOOD THING ABOUT JULIA SHE FORGIVES AND FORGETS PRETTY EASY SO I THINK AT THIS TIME.

NEXT THE COURTHOUSE APPOINTMENT AT FONTANA COURTS. JULIA WAS ABLE TO SCHEDULE A COURTDATE AT THE FONTANAS COURTHOUSE FOR HER ARREST IN APRIL.

ON THE BUS.

WE WERE GETTING ON THE BUS, THE 65 BUS METRO I BELEIVE WHICH TAKES US TO ANOTHER BUS TO GET US TO THE COURTHOUSE. WE WERE RUNNING LATE AND SHE WAS WORRIED. I TOLD HER SHE SHOULD USE HER JULIA ROBERTS PERSONNA TO GET HELP AND AN OK FROM THE COURTS TO BE LATE. SHE WENT A STEP FURTHER. SHE, WHEN I WAS OFF THE BUS TO USE THE RESTROOM FOR 1 MINUTE TALKED TO THE BUS DRIVER TO TAKE HER STRAIGHT TO THE COURTHOUSE.

ONCE I HEARD THIS AND SAW THE STARSTRUCK DOPEY EYED LOOKING BUS DRIVER I REALIZED JULIA WAS TAKING ADVANTAGE OF THIS POOR SCHMUCK.

I TOLD JULIA THAT IF SHE DOES TAKE THIS BUS OFF ROUTE STRAIGHT TO THE COURTHOUSE THAT HE CAN LOSE HIS JOB. I SAID NO TO THIS DEAL AND SHE WAS MAD BUT HAD TO DO IT. IT MADE SENSE. TRULY THIS GUY WILL LOSE HIS JOB. I TOLD JULIA HOW WOULD SHE LIKE TO LOSE HER JOB FOR DOING A FAVOR FOR SOMEONE THAT IS USING YOU. SHE WAS MAD BUT OKAYED IT. WE GOT THERE LATE AT THE COURTHOUSE AND SHE SAID SHE WOULD HANDLE IT AND DIDNT WANT ME TO COME IN THE COURTHOUSE WITH HER SO I DIDNT. JULIA DIDNT CARE WHEN I SAID HE COULD BE FIRED.

AS I KICKED BACK AN HOUR OR TWO I REALIZED THAT I WILL SEE JULIA SOMEWHERE SINSE I ALWAYS DO. SO I STARTED WALKING UP ALDER AVENUE TO FOOTHILL TO CATCH A BUS THATS GOING TO GAILS MY EX GIRLFRIEND SINSE I STARTRED GOING OUT WITH JULIA.

ON THE BUS STOP AND WHAT A GUY SAID ABOUT WHATS GOING ON AT THE COURTHOUSE.

I WALKED UP TO THIS GUY AT THE BUS AND HE TURNS TO ME AND ASKS WHERE I AM COMING FROM. HE SAYS" DID YOU SEE THE ONE"? I SAID "THE ONE"? HE SAID "THE ONE WE ALL KNOW". I SAID "OH YEAH HER. NO, SHES A LOOK ALIKE". HE DISAGREED. "NO , THEY ALL SAID JULIA ROBERTS". I SAID, "OH OKAY ITS HER COOL",

I THEN CAUGHT THE BUS AND HOPED SHE WOULDNT FIND ME FOR AWHILE.

SHE CALLED THE NEXT DAY AND TOLD ME. "THEY KNEW ME THEY ALL CALLED ME HULIA."

I ASKED IF SHE PAID OR GOT THE TICKET TO THE NEXT STEP AND SHE SAID "YES THEY DROPPED IT BECAUSE I AM HULIA". THAT H STANDS FOR THE SPANISH PRONUNCIATION OF JULIA BECOMING IN SPANISH TRANSLATED HULIA.

NOW WE ARE GOING BACK TO THE CLAREMONT HOTEL FOR 5 DAYS THEN WE DECIDE TO SPEND MORE TIME AT MOMS. MOM WAS WONDERFUL AND AGREED TO LET HER STAY BUT ON THE 4TH DAY SHE WAS GETTING CRAZY WITH MANY THINGS.

1. HER FUZZY SLIPPERS , BREATHE RITE CONTRAPTIONS , 5 DIFFERERENT DRINKS PLUS ALCOHOL NOT INCLUDED WITH THE FIVE AND THEN ON THIS DAY 4 SHE FALLS ASLEEP DRUNK IN THE BATHROOM AND LEANS HER BACK

AGAINST THE OLD FASHION HEATER. THE NEXT DAY SHE HAS BURN MARKS ACROSS HER BACK.

THROUGHOUT THIS WHOLE TIME I WAS SEEING JULIA ALL OVER THE TABLOIDS SO I SEE HER WITH HER EX BOYFRIEND DANNY MODER SO SHE SAYS ITS AN EX AND THEY ARE ON THE FRONT COVER. I SAY "I THOUGHT YOU ARE BROKEN UP WITH THIS GUY" AND I WAS MAD AND SHE SAID "ALL PHOTOS ARE ALWAYS 6 MONTHS BEHIND IF I AM NOT THE MAJOR STORY."

THIS IS WHERE I START TAKING PICTURES AND SENDING THEM TO LIZ SMITH AT BOCA RATON FLORIDA.

1. LIZ SMITH, BOCA RATON 2. THE LOUD ALL NIGHT MUSIC. 3. THE DRINKING AND 4. SLEEPING TILL 6 PM AND BED AT 12 NOON AND YELLING AND SINGING ALL NIGHT.

WELL, WHAT I WOULD DO FOR HER ON A WHIM OF HERS IS GET HER ALFREDO SAUSE-, SMALL AMOUNT OF CHIPS BECAUSE SHE KEPT SAYING SHE HURT HER THROAT LIKE THE SUGER RAY LEONARD SURGERY, WHATEVER THAT MEANS.

ALSO SHE LOVES BUTTER AS WELL AS MASHED POTATOES WHICH I WOULD WALK DOWN WHEN SHE ASKS TO GET HER MASHED POTATOES AND TONS OF BUTTER FROM THE CORNER OF SAN JOSE AND INDIAN HILL CALLED BAKERS SQUARE. ALSO ONCE I WALKED ALL THE WAY TO HOLD BLVD 5 MILES DOWN TO GET HER ALFREDO SAUSE IN THE MIDDLE OF THE NIGHT LIKE 3 AM. THE STORE IS THE ONLY ONE OPEN ALL NIGHT. WHEN I GOT BACK SHE GOT MAD AT ME BECAUSE SHE TOLD ME THERE WERE CHUNKS OF MUSHROOMS IN IT AND SHE MASHED IT ON THE FLOOR BREAKING AND SPREADING ALFREDO SAUSE ALL OVER THE CARPET WHICH I HAD TO CLEAN UP. ALSO SHE MESSED THE HOUSE UP. I KICKED HER OUT AND MADE

HER SLEEP THIS TIME ON THE WEST SIDE OF THE HOUSE OUTSIDE WITH A SLEEPING BAG AND IF SHE DIDNT LIKE IT THE ULTAMATUM IS GO AND LEAVE AND DONT COME BACK. SHE CHOSE THE BEST SIDE OF THE HOUSE TO SLEEP. I LATER JOINED HER AND WE MADE LOVE. SHE APOLOGISED AND I THEN CLEANED THE ROOM AND THE CARPET.

THROUGH THIS SITUATION I TOOK OVER 100 PICTURES. I CALLED LIZ SMITH WHO IS THE HEAD OF THE ENQUIROR. SHE WAS FACINATED AND REALIZED THAT I AM NOT TO BE KNOWN AND I WAS COOL FOR THAT I NEVER WANTED TO BE FAMOUS FOR ANYTHING LIKE GOING OUT WITH JULIA. SHE SAID I SHOULD JUST PROTECT HER WHILE SHE IS ON HER BINGE OF BEING OUT EVERY 11 YEARS. SHE REMEMBERS WHEN JASON PATRIC WAS IN THE SAME POSITION THAT I AM IN NOW AND SHE UNDERSTANDS AND WISHED ME LUCK. I LATER WENT TO BEN GAGE WHO IS A LAWYER WHO SPECIALIZEDS IN CELEBRATY PHOTOS.

THE BEN GAGE STORY.

I CALLED THE LAWYER REFERREL SERVACE AND ASKED FOR CELEBRATY LAWYERS AND THEY WERE LIKE "OH WE GOT ONE FOR YOU". I MEANT A LAWYER WHO SPECIALIZES IN CELEBRATY THINGS. THEY GOT IT WRONG AS THEY MISUNDERSTOOD ME AND GOT ME A LAWYER WHO IS A CELEBRITY IN OTHER WORDS, A CELEBRATY LAWYER.

HIS NAME IS BEN GAGE AND HE IS ALSO A CELEBRITY UNDER HIS STAGE NAME GARY BUSCI.

THE CALL TO BEN GAGE.

I FINALLY REACHED BEN GAGE AND HE SET AN APPOINTMENT TO SEE THE PICTURES OF JULIA ROBERTS. WHAT I DIDNT KNOW IS HE WAS ON HER SIDE. HE SAID HIS MOTHER WAS ESTHER WILLIAMS AND HIS DAD WAS THE

FATHER OF THE GUY ON RENAGADE AND THAT WAS HIS STEP BROTHER. LORENZO LAMAS AND HIS DAD FERNANDO LAMAS.

I DIDNT BELEIVE HIM BUT HE WAS TELLING THE TRUTH-I SAW IT IN HIS PROFILE ON THE COMPUTER.

IT WAS 51. GARY BUSCI.

I DROVE TO SAN DIEGO TO MEET HIM AND AS I WAS DOING THIS JULIA WAS AT MOMS AND WAS SLEEPING. SHE DIDNT KNOW ANYTHING ABOUT THIS LITTLE ADVENTURE AT ALL. WHEN I GOT TO BEN GAGES I WAITED IN A ROUND ROOM FOR ABOUT 1/2 AN HOUR AND HE SAW THE PICTURES AND SAID HE WILL TAKE THE CASE AND WILL SELL THESE PICTURES BUT WANTS 1000 UPFRONT. I SAID SORRY AND SAID I WAS HERE BELEIVING IT WOULD BE ON A CONTINGENT BASIS. HE SAID HE IS A LAWYER AND HE DOESNT DO THAT BUT BELEIVES HE CAN SELL THE PICTURES AND WOULD MAKE MORE THEN 1000. I DIDNT TRUST HIM AND REALIZED IF I WENT WITH HIM AS MY LAWYER IT WOULD TAKE ME OUT OF POCKET 1000 DOLLARS JUST TO START SO NOW I WOULD BE MINUS 1000. NO THANKS. I WAS ALSO TIRED FROM THE DRIVE TO SAN DIEGO.

I DROVE BACK AND THAT WAS IT ON ATTEMPTS TO SELL PICTURES TO THE ENQUIROR OR ANYONE ELSE. BEN GAGE THE LAWYER SAID THAT HE CAN SELL THEM AT PLAYBOY MAGAZINE BEING SHE WAS BOTTOMLESS ON ONE PICTURE AND 1 BREAST WAS OUT ON ANOTHER PICTURE.

I DIDNT PERSUE PLAYBOY MAGAZINE AND DIDNT TRY ANYMORE TO SELL PICTURES OF JULIA. I ONLY WAS GOING TO DO IT BECAUSE JULIA HAS BEEN SUCH A NOT COOL PERSON.

NOW IT IS BECOMING JULY AND I ON JULY 2 AND 3 DID SOME SHOWS AT THE FREEWAY AND JULIA WAS HELPING ME PICK UP CASH FROM THE CARS OUT OF THE STREET COMING OFF THE OFFRAMPS.

I MADE ENOUGH SO ME AND JULIA CAN HAVE A GOOD TIME CELEBRATING THE 4TH OF JULY.

BUT BEFORE ALL THIS WE GOT INTO AN ARGUMENT AND THE COPS CAME TO THE HOUSE. THE COPS ADMIRED MY BAND EQUITMENT AND THEN JULIA OUT OF NOWHERE LIED AND SAID I BURNT HER BACK. THIS WAS A TOTAL LIE FOR SHE DID IT TO HERSELF DRUNK FALLING ASLEEP LAYING AGAINST THE OLD FASHION HEATER BUILT INTO THE WALL IN THE FRONT BATHROOM.

THE COPS WERE ABOUT TO ARREST ME WITH THE HANDCUFFS TAKEN OUT OF THEIR WASTE AND ABOUT TO CUFF ME AND THANK GOD MY MOM HEARD THIS BECAUSE THE ROOM DOWN THE TWO STEPS CALLED THE FAMILY ROOM WAS THE ROOM THAT WE WERE IN AND YOU CAN HEAR REAL EASILY FROM THE LIVING ROOM IN WHICH MOM WAS THERE.

MOM SAID "SHES LIEING. I KNOW SHE TOLD ME ALSO THAT SHE DID THIS TO HERSELF IN THE BATHROOM WHILE SHE WAS DRUNK". THANK GOD JULIA AGREED THAT SHE LIED SO I WAS WONDERING IF SHE WAS GOING TO GET ARRESTED FOR LIEING TO THE POLICE. NO SHES JULIA ROBERTS SHE GETS SPECIAL TREATMENT.

AFTER THIS IS WAS THINKING OF HOW I CAN GET JULIA OUT OF MY LIFE OR AT A DISTANCE.

4TH OF JULY. ON THE 3RD ME AND JULIA MADE UP BUT I REALLY WANTED HER OUT FOR GOOD OR AT A DISTANCE BECAUSE BEING TOO CLOSE TO HER ALMOST GOT ME

ARRESTED FOR HER LIES SAYING THAT I BURNT HER BACK WITH THE HEATER.

SHE ROLLED UP AGAINST IT AND PASSED OUT DRUNK AS THIS HAPPENED.

NOW IT IS THE 4TH OF JULY AND WE MAKE IT ONLY AS FAR AS ACROSS THE STREET FROM MOMS AS WE ARE WALKING TO THE EVENT. THE EVENT CONSISTS OF FIREWORKS AT THE GRANDEST LEVEL AND IT IS A YEARLY PARTY UP AT THE CLAREMONT COLLEGES. WE CAN SEE IT FOR FREE THOUGH WITHOUT PAYING BY BEING ON THE OUTSKIRTS AND JULIA WANTED THIS AMYWAYS FOR PRIVACY REASONS.

AS WE WERE WALKING TO THE FIREWORKS WE ARGUE AND SHE AGAIN PRESSES HER BUTTON THAT BRINGS THE COPS. THE COPS HAVE TO COME BECAUSE IT IS PAID FOR THIS BUTTON SHE HAS. THE COPS CANT COMPLAIN THEY HAVE TO ALWAYS COME NO MATTER HOW SMALL THE COMPLAINT. IN THIS CASE IT WAS A SMALL COMPLAINT WE WERE VERBELLY ARGUING ABOUT SOMETHING SO SMALL I CANT EVEN REMEMBER WHAT IT IS. THIS WAS THE THIRD TIME JULIA USED THIS BUTTON

1. IN AN ARGUMENT AFTER SPEARMINT RHINO CLUB DATE.

2. WHEN TEX MEX PEOPLE WERE ATTEMPTING TO KIDNAP AND RAPE JULIA.

3. THIS TIME ARGUING GOING UP TO THE 4TH OF JULY PARTY AND FESTIVAL.

THE COPS COME THE SAME COP THAT I DONT GET ALONG WITH, TABER. ONCE AGAIN IT WILL BE HIM AND THE NEXT DAY AGAIN IT WILL BE TABER.

THOUGH THIS DAY THEY COME AND HAVE ME SIT ON THE CURB AND THEN THEY LEAVE. THERE WAS NO LAW BROKEN AND ACTUALLY NOTHING HAD BEEN DONE THAT NEEDED COPS BUT JULIA I GUESS IS EXCERSIZING HER USAGE OF THIS BUTTON OR HOWEVER SHE GETS THEM THERE.

THE THREE COP CARS LEFT AND I NOTICED EVERYTIME SHE USES THE BUTTON AT LEAST THREE COP CARS COME.

AT THE 4TH FIREWORKS.

ME AND JULIA FINALLY GOT TO THE FIREWORKS. AFTER THE COP STOPPED ME AND PUT ME ON THE CURB BY THE OLD SAFEWAY ACROSS FROM THE STREET FROM MOMS.

NEXT WE GET THERE AND SHE IS IN THE HIDING HERSELF PERSONALITY. A LITTLE EARLIER WE TOOK PICTURES AND A GUY WHO TOOK THER PICTURES RECOGNISED JULIA AND ASKED IF HE CAN TAKE TWO PICTURES. ONE WITH MY INSTAMATIC AND ONE FROM HIS CAMERA FOR HIM AND I SAID YES AND LOOKED AT JULIA IF SHE WAS OK WITH IT AND SHE WAS COOL WITH THE DECISION. HE LET ME HOLD A TORCH AND IT LOOKED COOL AND WE ACTUALLY LOOKED HAPPY. LITTLE DID I KNOW THIS WOULD BE THE DAY BEFORE JULIA WAS TO LEAVE MOMS FOREVER.

I TOOK SOME PICTURES OF HER WITH THE FIREWORKS ABOVE HER HEAD IN THE BACKGROUND. WE THEN LEFT AFTER AN HOUR. THE FIREWORKS ONLY LASTS ABOUT 1 HOUR.

WE GO HOME AND JULIA IS UP ALL NIGHT WITH THE COUNTRY MUSIC SHE LIKES BLASTED SO HIGH IT WAKES MOM. I HAD TO TAKE THE RADIO AWAY BECAUSE SHE WOULDNT STOP NO MATTER EVEN WHEN MOM ASKED. WITH THE COMBONATION OF THIS AS WELL AS HER LIEING

AND SAYING I TRIED TO BURN HER BACK, I KNEW SHE HAD TO GO.

THE NEXT MORNING WAS JULY 5TH. I GOTTA HELP MOVE GAIL MY EX TO A NEW APARTMENT IN ANOTHER AREA IN FONTANA. THE SAME STREET WHERE JULIA ALMOST GOT KIDNAPPED BY THE TEX MEX GUYS EARLIER THE MONTH BEFORE.

JULY 5TH. JULIA KNEW I HAD TO MOVE GAIL TO ANOTHER APARTMENT FROM MAPLE HILL APARTMENTS TO CITRUS GARDENS. BOTH APARTMENTS ARE IN FONTANA.

FIRST OF ALL GET READY FOR DRAMA AND SECOND OF ALL I DIDNT GET A BIT OF SLEEP BECAUSE JULIA HAD THE MUSIC ON ALL NIGHT AND WOULDNT TURN IT DOWN AND BY THE TIME I TOOK THE RADIO FROM HER IT WAS 6 AM IN WHICH I HAD TO CATCH THE 8 A.M. BUS AND START WORKING AROUND 10 AM, BUT I COUJLDNT LEAVE IMMEDIATELY.

LET ME EXPLAIN.

I TOLD JULIA SHE HAD TO LEAVE BECAUSE I DIDNT TRUST HER WITH MY 86 YEAR OLD MOTHER. I FELT SHE CAN DO ANYTHING TO HER INCLUDING KILL HER. I REALLY LOST TRUST IN JULIA AFTER SHE LIED AND SAID I BURNT HER BACK WHEN SHE IN TRUTH BURNT HER OWN BACK FALLING ASLEEP DRUNK AND LAID AGAINST THE HEATER IN THE WALLAFTER SHE LOCKED THE BATHROOM DOOR IN WHICH I COUJLDNT GET IN TO HELP HER AND DIDNT EVEN KNOW WHERE SHE WAS. I FINALLY PICKED THE LOCK TO THE DOOR AND FOUND HER SKIN AGAINST THE WALL HEATER, AN OLD FASHION WALL HEATER BUILT IN THIS HOUSE WHEN THE HOUSE WAS BUILT IN 1958. JULIA WOULDNT LET ME GO WHEN I WAS TO LEAVE TO HELP

GAIL. SHE DIDNT WANT ME TO HELP GAIL SO SHE USED SEX AS A LEVERAGE SAYING "TAKE ME NOW HANDSOME'.

I DIDNT FALL FOR IT. SHE THEN TOLD ME TO GIVE HER DRINKS SHE NEEDS FOR THE MORNING WHICH WAS WARM MILK, ENSURE, THE ENERGY WEIGHT LOSS DRINK, WATER, ICE WATER, BREATHE RITES FUZZY SLIPPERS, HAIR CLIPS ETC AS WELL AS AN ALCOHOLIC BEVERAGE AND A SEPERARTE BOTTLE OF JUICE SHE HAD IN THE FRIDGE. ALL IN ALL 6 OR 7 DRINKS. I COULDNT GET HER OUT OF THE HOUSE AND I COULDNT LEAVE UNTIL SHE LEFT. SHE WOULD PUT HER LEGS UP IN FRONT OF HER AND BACK UP ON THE COUCH WHICH WAS A BED BUT I MADE IT TO GET HER OUT. AS SHE IS NOW SITTING ON THE COUCH AND PUTTING HER LEGS UP IN RETALLIATION TO FIGHT ME TO NOT LEAVE THE HOUSE. I GRABBED HER LEGS AND SHE KICKED AND SHE JUST WOULDNT LEAVE.

SO I CALLED THE POLICE.

WHAT THE POLICE SAID ON THE PHONE.

WELL IN THOSE DAYS BEFORE PHIL SPECTER KILLING AND BEFORE WEINSTEIN AND COSBY. BASICALLY NORMAL PEOPLE IN SOCIETY BELEIVE CELEBRATIES ARE ALMOST PERFECT. WHAT A SHAM, NOT EVEN, SO WHAT THE LADY DISPATCHER SAID ON THE PHONE FROM THE POLICE STATION WAS.

"OH COME ON CHUCK YOU KNOW YOU AND JULIA WILL WORK IT OUT."

I SAID "I DONT WANT TO WORK ANYTHING OUT, I WANT HER OUT OF THE HOUSE AND NEED HELP OF POLICE". WOW WAS THAT DISPATCHER STAR STRUCK LADY HURT. ITS LIKE IF YOU ARE AGAINST SOMEONES FAVORITE CELEBRATY YOU HURT THAT PERSON THEMSELVES THAT WAS TYHE STARSTRUCK FAN.

FINALLY THE COPS GOT THERE.

WHAT THE POLICE FOUND OUT WAS.

JULIA IS WEIRD. THE REASON WHY IS WHEN THE COPS GOT THERE THEY WERE EXPECTING TO SEE A MOVIE STAR GET UP, NOT SO. SHE WAS IN A ROBE WITH FUZZY SLIPPERS AND BREATHE RITES IN HER NOSE AS WELL AS 7 DRINKS AFOUND HER WITH ONE OR MORE IN EACH HAND. SHE WAS ACTING FLIRTACIOUS TO THEM AND THEY LOOKED AT ME WITH PITY BELEIVE IT OR NOT. I SAID I NEED HER TO GO. THEY ASKED WHY. I SAID I HAVE TO GO MOVE MY FRIEND FROM ONE APARTMENT TO ANOTHER AND I DIDNT TRUST HER IN THIS ALCOHOLIC STUPER TO BE NEAR MY MOM WHEN I WAS NOT AROUND THEY GOT HER TO LEAVE.

AS SHE WAS LEAVING SHE SAID TO ME "I SWEAR TO GOD IF I LEAVE NOW IM NEVER COMING BACK". I SAID OK. SHE WALKED OFF AND AS SHE WALKED OFF THE COPS AND ME BOTH LOOKED AT HER WALKING AWAY WITH BAGS AND ME AND THE COPS WERE LOOKING IN BEWILDERMENT WHY IS SHE DOING THIS WHEN SHE IS WEALTHY AND SUCCESSFUL.

I WILL TELL YOU WHY. SHE WANTS TO PROVE TO HERSELF SHE CAN SURVIVE WITHOUT ACTING AND THIS SHE CANT, JUST LIKE ALL OF US CANT REALLY SURVIVE IF WE QUIT OUR LIVES OR WE WILL SURVIVE BUT IT IS LIKE STARTING OVER AND WHO WANTS TO DO THAT? ACTORS.

THERE ALWAYS DOING THIS. THIS IS NOT MY INVENTION OR PHILOSOPHY, NO I JUST WATCHED AND REPORTED.

I THEN MOVED GAIL INTO THE APARTMENT WE ARE NOW IN 18 YEARS LATER IN 2020 STILL WE ARE HOPING WE CAN LEAVE ONE DAY BUT AGE AND TRADITION KEEPS US HERE.

JULIA CALLED ME A COUPLE DAYS LATER AND SAID SHE MISSED ME AND WANTED TO HAVE ME VISIT WHERE SHE IS NOW. SHE IS NOW AT A HOTEL CALLED THE ALI BABA HOTEL. IT IS A BIG GAWDY PALACE LOOKING PLACE AND ITS PRETTY REASONABLE TO STAY THERE. THE HOTEL IS A REGULAR SIZE, 1 ROOM AND A RESTROOM AND AN OUT OF THE RESTROOM SINK AND OTHER NECESSITITES THE TOYLET AND SHOWER IS IN THE OTHER ROOM ENTITLED THE BATHROOM.

I VISITED HER A FEW TIMES AND I ALWAYS BROUGHT HER A GIFT, ALCOHOL. ALOT OF TIMES WE WONDERED WHAT OUR RELATIONSHIP NOW WAS BEING I AM NOT BEING CONTROLLED BY HER IT DOESNT SEEM LIKE WE ARE AN ITEM. A COUPLE TIMES SHE WOULD JUST CALL ON THE PHONE AND TALK. SHE WOULD BE DRUNK AND SHE ONCE SAID SHE WAS WITH THE DEVIL IN HER ROOM AND IT WAS THE REAL DEVIL. I TOLD HER TO SLEEP IT OFF. THE DEVIL DOESNT EXIST I TOLD HER AND SHE WAS ACTING NUTS. OTHER CALLS SHE WOULD SAY SHE WANTS TO MEET AND ONE TIME I WENT DOWN THERE AND SHE SAID SHE DIDNT ASK ME TO COME DOWN. I WENT STRAIGHT BACK HOME.

I USED TO ALWAYS TELL PEOPLE AROUND THERE THAT JULIA ROBERTS WAS THERE AT THAT HOTEL AND IT BROUGHT UNWANTED FANS TO JULIA. SHE WAS MAD AT ME FOR SAYING THAT AND TELLING PEOPLE WHO AND WHERE SHE WAS.

ONCE I CALLED THE HOTEL AND THE ORIENTEL OWNER SAID "OOH HULIA ISNT AVAILABLE." FOR SOME REASON HISPANIC AND ORIENTEL PROUNOUNCE JULIA AS HULIA. AND THIS IS REALLY TRUE. THE NAME OF THE HOTEL IS COSTA MESA WAS THE ALI BABA HOTEL. IT LOOKED LIKE A BIG PALACE THING IF YOU KNOW WHATI MEAN. IT LOOKED SOMEWHAT LIKE IT WAS THE TYPE OIF STRUCTURE OF A MAGIC LAMP.

FINALLY ON OCT 27TH 2002 SHE ASKED ME TO COME THE NEXT DAY SO I DID AND PLANNED IT. I GOT THERE AROUND 6 PM AND FIRST BEFORE I GOT THERE I BOUGHT SOME ALCOHOL FOR HER AS A GIFT IN DOWN TOWN ANAHEIM. THE HOTEL WAS IN COSTA MESA AND A BIT OF A WALK.

WHEN I GOT THERE SHE WAS QUICK AND THANKED ME AND DIDNT WANT TO TALK ANYMORE I WASNT THINKING BUT THIS IS JUILIAS BIRTHDAY OCTOBER 28TH 1967. SHE IS NOW 35 THIS DAY. I DIDNT SAY HAPPY BIRTHDAY. I DIDNT KNOW AT THIS TIME THAT THIS DAY WAS HER BIRTHDAY. IT WAS JUST AN AMAZING COINCIDENCE THAT THE LAST DAY I WILL EVER SEE HER IS ON HER BIRTHDAY.NOT PLANNED AT ALL. SOME KIND OF AMAZING DESTENY.

AS I LEFT I WAS MAD BEING I WAS JUST THERE FOR 30 MINUTES THEN RUSHED OFF SO I WENT TO A NEAR PARK AND WROTE A LETTER TO HER. I CAME BACK AND SHE SAID "OH A DEAR JOHN GOODBYE LETTER. I WAS LIKE NO ITS JUST A LETTER- I BEGGED HER IF I COULD STAY THE NIGHT BECAUSE THERE WERE NO BUSSES TO GET BACK. HE FINALLY SAID RELUCTANTLEY OK. SHE TOLD ME I HAD TO SLEEP N THE FLOOR AND SHE DIDNT TALK TO ME AT ALL. I ASKED HER IF SHE IS GOING TO DRINK ANY OF THE TIQUILA I BOUGHT HER AND SHE DIDNT ANSWER AND DIDNT THAT WHOLE NIGHT. SHE WAS REALLY UNFRIENDLEY. I REMEMBER WHEN SHE SAID HER BED WAS BOTHERING HER SO WE TOOK UP THE TOP MATRESS AND THE OTHER AND THERE WAS A LITTLE PEBBLE AND I SAID WOW LIKE THE PRINCESS AND THE PEA AND SHE AGREED AND LAUGHED AND THAT WAS THE LAST LAUGH I EVER SAW JULIA DO. I STARTED WRITING A SONG CALLED "ONE TRUE FACE" ABOUT THIS NIGHT. THE NEXT MORNING SHE WAS UNFRIENDLEY COLD AND IMMEDIATELEY KICKED

ME OUT. I TOOK THE BUS AT ORANGE COUNTY THEN WENT HOME.

SOME OF THE LYRICS GO. " THE LADY SITS IN HER EMPTY ROOM BLINDED BY THE STARLIGHT
BLINDED BY THE PAIN AND THE FAME OF SHE. SHES TAKING OFF HER FACES. AKING THEM OFF ONE BY ONE. THE LIE IS NOT PART OF HER DESTENY NO THIS IS PART OF THE PLAN .

THE PLAN IS TO FIND THE TRUTH AND THEN SHE WILL UNDERSTAND HERSELF".

"ONE TRUE FACE"

"WHY DID I DESERVE THIS
YOU COMING INTO MY LIFE
DID I DO SOMETHING TO YOU
ALL THAT I ASKED FROM YOU WAS FOR YOU TO BE MY WIFE."

ONCE WE WERE WATCHING A MINSTER CHRISTIAN PROGRAM AND I ASKED JULIA THAT MAYBE WERE DESTINED TO HAVE KIDS AND SHE LOOKED AT ME WITH THIS LOOK LIKE "NO WAY NOT YOU". SHE DIDNT SAY IT BUT HER FACE EXPRESSED THIS SO MUCH. I WILL ALWAYS REMEMBER THAT MOMENT. IT SADLEY STICKS IN MY MIND EVEN TO TODAY IF I THINK ABOUT IT.

THE MINISTRY WAS ABOUT HOW COUPLES GET TWICE AS GOOD AND TWICE AS STRONG TOGETHER THEN APART AND SHE LOOKED AT ME LIKE THAT WAS NOT WHAT THAT WAS ABOUT WITH ME.

I REMEMBER HOW SHE SHOWED HOW I BASICALLY WASNT GOOD ENOUGH TO HAVE KIDS AND MARRY HER BUT AFTER KNOWING WHAT I KNOW ABOUT HER I WOULDNT WANT TO MARRY HER.

ONCE DANNY MODER CAME OVER FOR AUDITION FOR MUSIC OR A RADIO SHOW I WAS INVOLVED IN AND HE LOOKED AT THE PICTURE I HAD OF JULIA ON THE WALL AND SAID TO ME "YOU CAN HAVE HER BACK AWHILE IF YOU WANT" I SAID "NO THATS OK" AND DANNY HAS BEEN WITH HER EVER SINSE. GOOD LUCK TO DANNY. DANNY WAS HER CAMERA MAN ON MOVIES AND THAT WAS HOW THEY MET. WHEN I LOOK BACK AT IT ALL AFTER IT HAS ALL BEEN DONE WITH JULIA AND ME I REALIZE IWAS THE POSTER BOY OF BEING A GUY USED FOR THE "REBOUND".

IT IS SAD HOW JULIA USED ME AS A BOYFRIEND/ BODYGUARD AND/SERVENT.

JULIA WAS OF ALL THE WOMEN I EVEN BEEN OUT WITH WAS THE BIGGEST USER AND MANIPULATER I HAVE EVER KNOWN OF ALL GIRLFRIENDS.

I TALKED TO JULIA IN NOVEMBER OF 2002 ONCE AND FOR THE FINAL TALK ON THE PHONE. I TOLD HER I WAS ARRESTED FOR PLAYING GUITAR FOR MONEY ON THE STREET CORNER IN RANCHO CUCUMONGA AND SHE WAS INTRIGUED TO SAY THE LEAST. HE ASKED ME HOW LONG I WAS IN JAIL.

A COUPLE YEARS LATER MAYBE MORE YEARS THEN A COUPLE I SAW HER AT THE SAME BUS AREA I MET HER AT AND I ASKED HER IF I COULD DO A FILM AND SHE SAID YES BUT IF IT MADE MONEY SHE WOULD BE REACHING OUT TO ME. FROM THAT LAST MEET INSPIRED ONE MORE SONG I DID WITH A DUET WITH MY COUSIN CALLED "DIFFERENT LANDS". THIS SONG "DIFFERENT LANDS" IS ABOUT REALIZING WE, ME AND JULIA ARE BOTH FROM DIFFERENT LANDS FROM EACH OTHER YET WE DID MEET AND HAD A RELATIONSHIP AND SHE WAS MY FIANCEE.

I FINALLY DID THE FILM AND COMLETED IT CALLED "I WAS ENGAGED TO JULIA ROBERTS AND NO ONE BELEIVES ME".

ITS A COMEDY OF ALL THE SONGS I WROTE ABOUT HER THAT I DID IN MY 8 TRACK STUDEO ALONG WITH USING VARIOUS DRUMMERS AS I PLAYED ALL INSTRUMENTS BUT DRUMS AND WE USED THE MUSIC FOR THE SOUNDTRACK OF THE FILM.

AND THAT IS MY STORY OF JULIA ROBERTS AND ME.

QLL IN ALL I DONT REGRET BEING ENGAGED TO JULIA ROBERTS AND IN FACT IT WAS QUITE A LEARNING EXPERIENCE. I LEARNED FAMOUS PEOPLE LIKE JULIA ARE NOT TOO GOOD AT THINGS OTHER THEN WHAT SHE IS WHICH IS A MOVIE STAR/ACTOR. OTHER THEN BEING A MOVIE STAR/ACTOR SHE RELLY CANT DO AMYTHING ELSE THAT I CAN THINK OF. IT SEEMED HER HOBBY WAS TO BE OUT IN THE STREETS AS A BAG LADY AS WELL AS ANOTHER HOBBY SHE HAS IS SHE DRINKS ALCOHOL.

IN MY 2007-8 RADIO SHOW I HAD I DID A SEGMENT CALLED "SOUL OF A BAGLADY" WHICH IS WHAT I WROTE ABOUT WHICH WAS THE STORY OF ME AND JULIA ROBERTS 7 MONTH RELATIONSHIP FROM MARCH 26TH 2002 TO OCTOBER 28TH 2002 WHICH WAS COINCEDENTELLY HER BIRTHDAY WHICH WAS THE DAY I BROKE UP WITH HER, YES FATE WAS CALLING WHEN THE DAY WE BROKE UP WAS ON HER BIRTHDAY OCTOBER 28TH 2002. I NEVER KNEW HER AS SHE TURNED 35 THAT DAY.

52. TOMMIE DAVIS 53. HOWARD ROSEN OWNER OF CASABLANCA RECORDS.

I WAS AT BLACK ANGUS RESTRAUNT IN LATE SEPT 1983 AND I WOULD GO THERE FOR DANCING AND MEETING YOUNG LADIES. I WAS SINGLE AT THIS TIME AND THERE I SAW THIS VERY THIN BEAUTIFUL LONG HAIRED YOUNG

LADY. WE IMMEDIATELELY HIT IT OFF AND SHE GAVE ME HER NUMBER AND I CALLED HER. BEFORE I CALLED HER THOUGH WE TALKED AFTER THE NIGHT AT BLACK ANGUS IN THE PARKING LOT AFTER HOURS MEANING AFTER 2 AM SHE TOLD ME HER STEP FATHER WAS TOMMIE DAVIS OF THE LA DODGERS.I WAS REAL EXCITED BECAUSE NOT ONLY WAS SHE BEAUTIFUL BUT HAD AN OLD DODGER STAR FOR A STEPFATHER.

SHE LIVES WITH HIM AND HIS WIFE WHO IS HER REAL MOTHER. HER NAME IS KELI AND WE HIT IT OFF IMMEDIATELEY. WHEN I WENT ON OUR FIRST DATE I PICKED HER UP AT HER HOUSE ON WHIRLAWAY AVENUE ON THE TOP OF ARCHIBALD AVENUE. WHEN I CAME IN I MET TOMMIE. HE GAVE ME AN OAKLAND ATHLETICS HAT. TOMMIE I KNEW HAD PLAYED ON 10 TEAMS AND THOUGH HE WAS THE NATIONAL LEAGUE BATTING CHAMPION IN 1962 AND 1963 FOR THE DODGERS HE ALSO PLAYED FOR 9 OTHER TEAMS OTHER THEN THE DODGERS IN WHICH TOMMIE PLAYED WITH THE DIODGERS FROM 1959-1966.

ME AND TOMMIE HIT IT OFF SO WELL THAT HE INVITED ME TO GO TO THE PLAYOFFS. THE DODGERS ARE IN IN PHILEDELPHIA WITH BERT BLYLEVIN WHO LATER MADE THE HALL OF FAME.

I DIDNT MAKE IT BUT ME AND KELI HAD A QUICK RELATIONSHIP LASTING A LITTLE OVER A MONTH AND THIS IS WHY ME AND TOMMIE AND BERT BLYLEVIN DIDNT GO TOGETHER TO THE PLAYOFFS. HE ALSO INVITED ME TO WORK AT A BASEBALL CARD SHOW WHICH I DID GO WITH TIOMMIE.

AFTER THE BREAKUP WITH HIS STEP DAUGHTER KELI I STILL KEPT IN CONTACT WITH TOMMIE. HE WAS INTO MY MIUSIC SO I ONE TIME IN 1985 GAVE HIM WHAT HE ASKED, A DEMO TAPE. THE DEMO TAPE WAS IN 24 TRACK AND IS

WRITTEN BY ME AND ROLAND AKA NOW LIVING IN ENGLAND NAMED BILLY BRAGG.-

THIS MUSIC WAS OK BUT REALLY AT THIS TIME WAS ALL I HAD FROM WORLD CLASS LEVEL RECORDING SO I GAVE IT TO HIS WIFE BECAUSE TOMMIE WASNT THERE. LATER I FOUND OUT TOMMIE HEARD IT SO I TRIED TO GET THE TAPE BACK. UNFORTUNATELY THE WIFE OF TOMMIE HAD ME GO TO THE DOOR 4 TIMES AND SHE WOULDNT ANSWER TILL THE FORTH TIME. EACH TIME SHE SAID SHE WOULD EITHER HAND IT BACK TO ME OR PUT IT OUTSIDE I WAS COMING OFF OF ROCK COCAINE ADDICTION AND DIDNT LIKE THIS TREATMENT SO I GOT INTO AN ARGUMENT WITH TOMMIES WIFE. TOIMMIE WAS GOING TO GET THE MUSIC TO A GUY NAMED HOWARD ROSEN. HOWARD ROSEN IS THE OWNER OF THE OLD RECORD COMPANY CASABLANCA RECORDS. I HAVE BEEN TO HOWARDS MANY TIMES IN STUDEO CITY BURBANK AREA AND I SAW 25 GOLD AND PLATINUM RECORDS ON THE WALL WITH SUCH ARTISTS AS CHER AND THE VILLAGE PEOPLE AND KISS AMONG MANY OTHERS. BECAUSE OF THE ARGUMENT I HAD WITH HIS WIFE, TOMMIE RELUCTANTLEY AND FINALLY GAVE THE COPY OF THE TAPE AND ALLOWED ME TO FINALLY TALK TO HOWARD ROSEN IN 1986.

BUT THEY USED TO HAVE SUCH ARTISTS AS THE VILLAGE PEOPLE CHER AND KISS AMONG MANY OTHERS. I BEEN TO HOWARDS MANY TIMES AND THERE WAS LIKE 25 GOLD AND PLATINUM RECORDS ON THE WALL.

AFTER TOMMIE GAVE MY NAME TO HOWARD ROSENS RELUCTANTLEY THAT WAS THE LAST TIME I TALKED TO TOMMIE UNTIL WHEN I SAW HIM AT THE MARKET.

ALSO ONE TIME I WAS IN A BAND WITH A GUY NAMED RICHARD JACKSON.

RICHARD JACKSON AND TOMMIE DAVIS.

RICHARD USED TO WORK OUT AT THE HOLIDAY HEALTH SPA WITH ME AND OTHER FRIENDS. HE WAS A MUSICIAN. I FOUND THIS OUT. I WAS TALKING ABOUT TOMMIE WORKING AS AN A AND R MAN FOR CASABLANCA RECORDS AND TOLD RICHARD THAT TOMMIE TOLD ME HE DISCOVERED THE BAND CAMEO WITH THE HIT "WORD UP".

HE WAS IN AWE AND COULDNT BELEIVE I KNEW TOMMIE DAVIS WHO WAS THE CENTER FIELDER BEHIND SANDY KOUFAX IN SANDYS HALL OF FAME YEARS AND TOMMIE WAS BATTING CHAMPION TWO TIMES IN 1962 AND 63. HE KNEW THIS AND WANTED TO MEET TOMMIE. I TOLD HIM TO MEET TOMMIE WE NEED TO MAKE A DEMO WKTH HIS MUSIC AND MY SINGING AND LYRICS.

HE WAS OVERJOYED AND AGREED TO DO THIS. WE RECORDED TWO SONGS FROM HIS RECORDING STUDEO OF 8 TRACK, GOOD ENOUGH FOR A DEMO BUT NOT FOR RADIO BUT AGAIN IT WAS GOOD ENOUGH FOR A DEMO.

I TOLD HIM HE COULD GO WITH ME TO MEET TOMMIE DAVIS AND SO ME AND HIM WENT TO SEE TOMMIE. TOMMIE LIKED THE MUSIC AND TOMMIE IS A BIG FAN OF ANYHONE WHO CAN DO MUSIC BECAUSE HE CANT THOUGH OF COURSE WE ADMIRE HIS GREAT SKILL HE HAS. BASEBALL.

SO WE MEET TOMMIE AND RICHARD DIDNT BELEIVE I WAS TELLING THE TRUTH. MAN NOW THATS STARSTRUCK. ANYWAYS WHEN ME MET TOMMIE. TOMMIE WAS REAL COOL TO HIM AND RICHARD WAS AGAIN OVERJOYED.

WE GAVE THE MUSIC TO TOMMIE. MY MUSIC AND RICHARDS TOGETHER AND TOMMIE TOLD US HE LIKED IT AND THEN SAID HE WOULD SEND THE TAPE TO HOWARD ROSEN.

NOTHING CAME OF IT BUT WE HAD FUN. UNFORTUNATLELEY THE ARGUMENT I HAD A YEAR LATER IN 1985 WITH TOMMIE DAVIS WIFE, THIS SORT OF MESSED THE DESTENY OF US WITH HOWARD ROSEN.

FINALLY WITH HOWARD ROSEN. AFTER HOWARD SAID TO ME AND LAILAH AND OUR BAND WHO CAME THERE 50 MILES TO BURBANK AND STUDEO CITY AREA, HE SAID "WHEN ARE YOU GOING TO REALIZE WE ARE NOT GOING TO HELP YOU".

AFTER THAT I THREW A COUPLE OF HIS GOLD RECORDS ON THE GROUND WHERE THEY SHATTERED OR SOMETHING. I WAS KICKED OUT AND THAT WAS THE HISTORY I HAD WITH TOMMIE DAVIS AS WELL AS HOWARD ROSEN. I WAS MAD BECAUSE HE WASTED 30 VISITS AND 2 YEARS OF OUR LIVES JUST MESSING AROUND WITH US. NOT COOL, NOT COOL AT ALL.

WE WENT TO HOWARD ROSEN FOR HELP AT LEAST OVER 30 TIMES IN A 2 YEAR SPAN.

ONE OF HIS ASSISTANTS HEARD I WAS WRITING A SONG CALLED "HEY HOWARD" AND THE ASSISTANT SAID HE WOIULD LIKE THAT SO I WENT INTO THE 16 TRACK STUDEO AND DID THER SONG "HEY HOWARD" AND THAT DID NO GOOD. FINALLY WHEN I REALIZED HE WAS DONE WITH US I DECIDED TO PRANK CALL HIS OFFICE AND HIM SO I GOT ON THE PHONE AND SAID "ITS ME ELVIS"

HOWARD THEN SAID "ELVIS, YOU SHOULDNT BE CALLING, THERE COULD BE PEOPLE LISTENING ON THE LINE AND/OR RECORDING YOU" SO I GUESS TO HOWARD ELVIS WAS STILL ALIVE. THEN WHEN I YELLED JUST KIDDING. HOWARD GOT TO THE OPERATOR I OR YELLED AT THE OPERATOR "THERE IS A FRAUD ON THE PHONE THERE IS A FRAUD ON THE PHONE".

AND THAT WAS THE LAST TIME I EVER DEALT WITH HOWARD ROSEN. EVER.

54. HALLE BERRY 55. AND LEAH REMINI.

WHEN I FIRST SAW LEAH REMINI IT WAS ON T.V. ON A FAILED SIT COME SHE WAS ON THAT LASTED ABOUT 8 EPISODES OR 9. THE NAME OF THER SHOW WAS LIVING DOLLS. I THOUGHT SHE WAS THE MOST BEAUTIFUL GIRL I EVER SEEN. SHE HAD LONG CURLEY BLACK HAIR AND DARK FEATURES WITH THIS CUTE RUGGED VOICE FOR A FEMALE. SHE SOUNDED LIKE A TOMBOY. HE COMBONATION OF THE VOICE AND HER BEAUTY KNOCKED ME OVER THE TOP. IT WAS THE FALL OF 1989.

SO I DECIDED TO CALL THE SHOW AND I GOT THROUGH THE SHOW.

56. TONY DANZA

TONY DANZA ANSWERED BECAUSE HIS SHOW WAS NEXT DOOR TO THE LIVING DOLLS SHOW WHICH LEAH WAS ON. LEAH AT THIS TIME WAS AN UNKNOWN ACTRESS BUT I DIDNT CARE IF SHE WAS KNIOWN OR NOT. I WANTED TO GET TO KNOW HER. SHE SAID SHE DIDNT HAVE A BOYFRIEND WHEN I TALKJED TO HER.

BUT THAT COMES LATER.

BACK TO LEAH. I CALLED AND TONY DANZA TOOK A MESSAGE. HE ANSWERED WITH THE SHOW HE WAS ON. HE GAVE THE MESSAGE TO LEAH AND THEY WANTED TO KNOW WHAT I LOOKED LIKE. THAT IS LEAH AND THE GIRLS ON THE SHOW. THERE WAS A BLACK GIRL ON THE SHOW. HER NAME WAS HALLE BERRY. SHE TOO WAS AN UNKNOWN AT THE TIME AND AGAIN I DONT CARE IF YOUR KNOWN OR NOT. IM NOT INTERESTRED IN THOSE POLITIICS. I JUST WANT TO KNOW LEAH. SO LEAH AND

HER PEOPLE TOLD ME TO SENT A PICTURE-AND I DID. LEAH LOVED THAT PICTURE AND THEN ON THE NEXT CALL HALLE BERRY GOT ON THE PHONE.

THE NEXT CALL TO LEAH WHERE HALLE TALKS TO ME BUT NOT LEAH.

LIKE I SAID I CALLED AND THEY WERE REALLY EXCITED. THIS WAS FUN FOR THESE GIRLS BECAUSE THEY ARE ALL YOUNG AND SINGLE AND I AM ACTUALLY 26 YEARS OLD AND THATS REAL OLD FOR THEM WHOM THEY ARE IN BETWEEN 18 AND 22. LEAH WAS AROUND 18 AND HALLE WAS AROUND 22 BUT LOOKED MUCH YOUNGER.

AS I GOT ON THE PHONE HERE IS NOT LEAH BUT HALLE.

HALLE SAYS "LEAH IS NOT AVAILABLE RIGHT NOW SHES IN MAKEUP RIGHT NOW BUT YOU CAN GO OUT WITH ME." I HEARD YOU LIKE BLACK GIRLS AND I AM THE BLACK GIRL ON THE SHOW, WOULD YOU WANT TO GO OUT WITH ME?"

BEFORE I ANSWERED I REMEMBERED THE BLACK GIRL WAS PRETTY BUT DIDNT THINK MUCH ABOUT IT BECAUSE OF LEAH SO I SAID TO HALLE. "WELL, YOU KNOW IM IN THE PROCESS OF GOING OUT WITH LEAH AND SHE INVITED ME TO THE NEXT SHOW SO RIGHT NOW IT WOULD BE DISRESPECTFUL TO DO THAT". MEANING GOING OUT WITH HALLE BERRY SO YES, ITS CRAZY BUT I TURNED DOWN A DATE WITH HALLE BERRY AT THAT TIME AS A GENTLEMAN TO RESPECT LEAH SINSE I WAS TRYING TO GET TO KNOW AND GO OUT WITH LEAH WHICH NEVER HAPPENED.

THATS EVEN SADDER.

RIGHT? SO FOR YEARS I USED TO KICK MYSELF ALOT FOR REALIZING I TIURNED DOWN A DATE WITH HALLE BERRY AS SHE WAS THE PERSUER.

WELL THIS IS JUST THE START OF THE HALLE BERRY STORY BUT LET ME FINISH UP WITH AND ABLIT LEAH REMINI.

THE SHOW. NICK AUSTIN.

SOME STUFF HAPPENED THE NEXT WEEK. A GIRL NAMED REBECCA SHAEFFER WAS MURDERED BY A STALKER. THIS CHANGED THINGS FOR ME EVEN THOUGH I AM NOT A STALKER BUT NOW PARANOIA IS IN THE ACTING INDUSTRY ESPECIALLY THE SIT COM PART OF THE ACTING PROFESSION WHICH IS WHAT REBECCA SHAEFFER WHICH WAS A SHOW CALLED MY DAUGHTER SAM AND OF COURSE THIS PARELLELS WITH LEAH AND HALLE AND THE OTHERS ON THE SHOW WHICH THEY ARE TOO ON A SIT COM CALLED LIVING DOLLS.

SO THE SECURITY IS BEEFED UP.

KELLY KALLAN. LEAH WAS INTERESTED IN ME IN A ROUNDABOUT WAY. FIRST OF ALL SHE GOT HER MANAGER BOB RICH TO TALK FOR HER AND BOB RICH GOT KELLY KALLAN TO GET ME TICKETS TO THE SHOW. I TOLD HIM I WANTED TO SEE LEAH AS A PERSON NOT A FAN AND NOT THE SHOW AND HE SAID IT WOULD ALL FIT AND THAT I SHOULD JUST AFTER THE SHOW WALK TO THE BACKSTAGE AND JUST FIT IN AND I CAN TALK TO HALLE AND LEAH. I SAID I WAS INTERESTED IN LEAH NOT HALLE AND HE SAID HE UNDERSTOOD. I WAS WONDERING WHY BOB RICH MEANT HALLE WHEN I WAS TOTALLY TRYING TO GET TO KNOW LEAH.

BIUT IT THINK HE WAS PUTTING HALLE ON ME MORE THEN LEAH IN A ROUND ABOUT WAY AND IN THE LONG RUN I NEVER WENT OUT WITH LEAH BUT DID WITH HALLE YEARS LATER STARTING IN 2004.

SO THE TICKETS WERE MEANT FOR ME AT THE BOOTH AT THE FRONT OF GOWER STUDEOS.

LAILAH DROPPED ME OFF AT DENNYS ON GOWER AND SUNSET BLVD AND I HAD A 45 RECORD OF TWO SONGS WITH MY NAME AND PICTURE ON IT WITH MY NAME UNDERNEATH THE PICTURE. I DIDNT HAVE AN I.D. I DIDNT DRIVE SO BACK IN 1989 I DIDNT NEED AN ID TO WALK AROUND BUT NOWADAYS YOU CAN BE ARRESTED FOR VAGRENCY IF NO I.D. BECAUSE I DIDNT HAVE A DRIVERS LICENCE OR A CAR AT THAT TIME. I FELT OK WITH NO I.D. BUT THEY WILL BE THINKING DIFFERENT BECAUSE OF THE REBECCA SCHAEFFER INCIDENT.

AND THIS WOULD HAVE BEEN OK AT THE GOWER STUDEO A WEEK EARLIER BEFORE REBECCA SHAEFFER WAS MURDERED BY A PSYCHO DERANGED STALKER. NOW BECAUSE HE DID IT THEY ARE LOOKING AT ME AS BEING MORE LIKE HIM THAT WHAT I WAS LAST WEEK, A ROCKER IN A BAND WITH A COOL POSTER OF ME LOOKING ALL ROCKED OUT FROM A PHOTO SESSION I DID IN 1988. BECAUSE OF THE SCHAEFFER MURDER, ALL CHANGED IN HOLLYWOOD. IT IS NOW LESS INNOCENCE IN HOLLYWOOD. NOW OVER AT GOWER STUDEOS THERE I SEE LEAH AND SHE IS WITH A MUSTLE BOUND BLONDE GUY. I THOUGHT IT WAS HER WAY OF SAYING SHE HAD A BOYFRIEND BUT NO, HE WAS THERE FOR PROTECTING HER AS HER BODYGUARD SINSE THE SCHAEFFER THING. I HAD A TAPE TO GIVE HER OF A LOVE SONG I WROTE FOR HER. SHE WAS ASSIGNED A BODYGUARD JUST FOR ME. SAD.

I WALKED RIGHT THROUGH THE BODYGUARD AND GAVE IT TO HER. I SAID "HI I AM CHUCK", AND SHE SAID HI. SHE WAS BEHIND THE STAGE AREA OUTSIDE AND THIS IS HOW I SAW HER. NEXT THESE KEYSTONE COP CLOWNS CAME UP TO ME AND GAVE THE WHOLE TRIP ABOUT THAT I COULD BE A KILLER ETC AND THEY NEED MY I.D. I SAID I DIDNT

DRIVE AND DIDNT HAVE AN I.D. BUT I DO HAVE A 45 WITH MY NAME BELOW MY PICTURE AND OF COURSE THEY SAID THAT WASNT GOOD ENOUGH AND SO I NEVER GOT TO SEE THE SHOW OR MEET LEAH IN THE BACK STAGE AFTER THE SHOW AND I WAS PRETTY MAD AT THIS WASTE OF TIME AND LACK OF PROFESSIONALISM ON THEIR PART AND YELLED BITCH AS THE BODYGUARD TRIED TO ESCORT ME OUT. I WAS CALLING LEAH A BITCH BECAUSE I WAS MAD AT THIS WASTE OF THE DAY. THIS COULD HAVE BEEN TAKEN CARE OF MORE PROFESSIONALLY. INSTEAD I WAS THE ONE WHO LOST OUT.

THOUGH I WENT BACK TO DENNYS AND SAT THERE AND WAITED FOR LAILAH TO PICK ME UP AROUND LATER THAT NIGHT.

AND THEN WE WENT ON OUR FIRST OF THREE VACATIONS WE TOOK ONE A YEAR TO SOLVANG AND THIS WAS THE VACATION WE WOULD DO IN 1989.SO AFTER THIS DAY I NEVER MET LEAH BUT SHE DID CALL ME ON MY BIRTHDAY IN 1992.

I ALSO TALKED TO BOB RICH FOR THE NEXT FEW YEARS FROM 1989 TO 1992. HE SAID I CANT KNOW LEAH UNTIL I REACH HER SUCCESS LEVEL. I MADE FUN OF THIS STATEMENT HE MADE FOR YEARS AFTER THAT BECAUSE IT IS OBSERD AND PHONEY AND SNOOTY AND STUCK UP AND SHALLOW AND FOOLISH AND IGNORANT AND NOT COOL. I FOUND OUT LATER THIS ATTITUDE WHE WAS EXPRESSING WAS A SCIENTOLOGY ATTITUDE AND PHILOSOPHY WHEN I CHECKED OUT SCIENTOLOGY AND THIS WAS WHEN LEAH WAS INVOLVED WITH SCIENTOLOGY BEFORE SHE TURNED AGAINST SCIENTOLOGY.

LEAH CALLED ME IN 1992 ON MY BIRTHDAY AND IT WAS LIKE I WAS A FAN AND THUS SHE TREATED ME THIS WAY WHICH I DIDNT FEEL COMFORTABLE AS THIS FAN.. I

TALKED TO HER AND SHE ASKED ME IF I CALLED HER A BITCH THAT DAY AND I SAID NO BUT I REALLY DID. OUR CONVERSATION WAS GOOD AT FIRST AND THEN IT GOT A LITTLE WORSE AS IT WENT ON. THAT WAS THE LAST TIME I EVER DEALT WITH OR TALKED TO LEAH. THOUGH I KEPT TRYING TO GET TO KNOW HER THROIUGH HER NEW MANAGER WHOM I CANT REMEMBER THE NAME BUT FINALLY WHILE SHE WAS ON A SITCOM CALLED "FIRED UP" THE MANAGER SAID LEAH DOESNT WANT TO HAVE ME TRY TO CONTACT HER ANYMORE- AND THAT WAS IT FOR LEAH. I WROTE A COUPLE OTHER GOOD SONGS THAT WAS ABOUT HER LIKE "WHEN ITS GONE" AND "JUST ME" AND THE SONG "IF THERE WAS ONLY YOU IN MY LIFE".

ONE THING I DO REMEMBER ABOUT MY CONVERSATION ON THE PHONE WITH LEAH IN 1992 WAS SHE TOLD ME SHE WAS ABOUT READY TO QUIT AS AN ACTRESS AND I TOLD HER NOT TO THAT I BELEIVED SHE WAS DESTINED FOR A GREAT SIT COM IN THE FUTURE. THIS THAT I SAID BECAME TRUE IN 1999 WITH THE SIT COM SHE WAS ON CALLED KING OF QUEENS.

AND THAT WAS IT WITH LEAH AND NOW ON WITH THE REST OF THE HALLE BERRY STORY.

THROUGH MY LIFE I WROTE 2 ALBUMS ABOUT HALLE ENTITLED 20 SONGS AND EXPRESSIONS FOR HALLE 1 AND 20 SONGS AND EXPRESSIONS FOR HALLE 2.

2004. I KNEW A GIRL WHOS NICKNAME WAS PINEAPPLE AND THIS IS HOW I KNOW THIS LADY BY THE NAME PINEAPPLE.

SHE WAS AT MOMS HOUSE AND THERE I RENT A MUSIC STUDEO ROOM FROM MOM THERE. I AM LIVING IN FONTANA BUT 1/2 THE TIME TAKING CARE OF MOM WHO IS 88 YEARS OLD AT THIS TIME WHICH IS 2004. PINEAPPLE

LOOKS AT THE PICTURES I HAVE ON THE WALL OF
CELEBRATIES WHO AUTROGRAPHED PICTURES AND ALSO
THERE IS A PICTURE I TOOK OF JULIA WHO JULIA SIGNED
IT BUT DIDNT SAY JULIA SHE SAID ANTONETTE SO I ASKED
PINEAPPLE IF SHE KNOWS WHO THAT IS AND SHE SAYS
"SURE THATS JULIA ROBERTS". I SAID "MOST PEOPLE
DONT KNOW THAT BECAUSE THEY CANT SEE ITS JULIA
BECAUSE SHE ISNT WEARING ANY MAKEUP IN THIS
PICTURE AND DOESNT LOOK LIKE THE STEREOTYPE
JULIA".

PINEAPPLE SAYS "I CAN TELL BECAUSE I HAVE A COUSIN
WHO IS A FAMOUS MOVIE STAR AND SHE LOOKS EVEN
MORE UNLIKE HERSELF WITHOUT MAKE IN PICTURES AND
IN REALITY"'.

I SAID "OH WHO IS THAT?"

SHE SAYS "HALLE BERRY"

I SAID "REALLY"?

SHE TOLD ME SHE LOOKS NOTHING LIKE HERSELF WHEN
SHE HAS MAKEUP OFF AS WHEN SHE HAS MAKE UP ON
AND I WOULDNT RECOGNISE HER.

SHE SAID I PROBABLY SEEN HER IN POMONA AND DIDNT
KNOW IT WAS HER.

I SAID I ALWAYS LOVED HALLE BERRY AND TOLD HER THE
STORY ABOUT WHEN SHE TALKED TO ME ON THE BACK SET
OF THE SIT COM LIVING DOLLS AND I HAD TO TELL HER I
COULDNT GO OUT WITH HER DUE TO I WAS PERSUING AND
TRYING TO GO OUT WITH LEAH REMINI.

SHE SAID SHE COULD SET IT UP SO I CAN MEET HER. I
ASKED HOW AND SHE SAID "SHE WILL FIND YOU".

I SORT OF BELEIVED THIS STORY AND SORT OF DIDNT BECAUSE IT MADE NO SENSE THAT SHE COULD FIND ME OR AT LEAST SO I THOUGHT.

NEXT HALLE FINDS ME FOR REAL.

I AM DRIVING DOWN HOLT BLVD, MY OLD STOMPING GROUND AND AT THAT TIME STILL MY STOMPING GROUND. I ALWAYS CLAIM TO BE FROM POMONA THOUGH I LIVED IN CLAREMONT AND FONTANA FOR 56 YEARS. FONTANA 18 YEAR AND 38 YEARS CLAREMONT. I LIVED A STINT IN POMONA FOR REAL AT THE SUNRISA APARTMENTS OFF OF VALLEY BLVD ALSO KNOWN AS HOLT A LITTLE FURTHER DOWN VALLEY TURNS INTO HOLT BLVD.

I SPENT 1 YEAR AT SUNRISA SO I GUESS IT WOULD BE THEN 37 YEARS IN CLAREMONT.

I ALSO TRAVELED AND TOURED MUSICALLY FOR OVER 2 YEARS SO IT WOULD BE THEN 35 YEARS IN CLAREMONT.

ANYWAYS, AS I WAS TRAVELING DOWN CLAREMONT I STOPPED AT A LIQUOR STORE TO GET SOMETHING AND AS I WENT BACK IN THE CAR AFTER GOING INTO THE LIIQUOR STORE AND THEN COMING OUT HERE COMES THIS GIRL SQUINTING AND MOVING HER MOUTH TO THE LEFT. IT LOOKED LIKE A MEXICAN AND HALF BLACK GIRL. SHE SAID "HEY BABY LET ME GET INTO YOUR CAR WITH YOU. I SAID OK AND THEN SHE STARTED ACTING WEIIRD. I THEN KICKED HER OUT OF THE CAR. THAT WAS HALLE.

NXT I AM AT A HOTEL IN POMONA AND I SEE PINEAPPLE AND SHE SAYS "HEY MY COUSIN HALLE IS WITH ME IN THE HOTEL DO YOU WANT TO SEE HER?"

I SAID "OK".

AND OUT CAME A GIRL I DIDNT RECOGNISE AS HALLE BUT IT WAS HER.

NEXT I WAS KICKING IT AT A HOTEL IN ONTARIO AND I RAN INTO HALLE AND THIS TIME I KNEW IT WAS THE CHARACTOR SHE DID LAST TIME. SO I TOOK HER TO THE HOUSE AND WE HUNG OUT AND WORKED WITH DOING SOME FILM WORK AND AS SHE LEFT I SAW HER FOR THE FIRST TIME LOOKING LIKE HALLE BERRY. I SAID "'YOU LOOK LIKE HALLE BERRY. SHE SAID, "I AM HALLE BERRY"

I WAS EXCITED AND I FELT I WAS GOING TO FALL IN LOVE BUT SHE WOULDNT LET ME DO THAT. ITS HARD TO EXPLAIN BUT SHE AS WELL AS JULIA ROBERTS USED TO UPSET ME SO THAT I WOULD NOT BE IN LOVE.

NEXT TIME I RUN INTO ELSA. NOW THE GIRL I TOOK TO MY HOUSE THAT WAS HALLE WAS IN CHARACTOR OF A GIRL NAMED HAWAII. NEXT THIS CHARACTOR SHE IS IN IS CALLED ELSA. I MET HER AGAIN ON THE BLVD OF HOLT.

ELSA. I MET HALLE AS SHE WAS BEING THE CHARACTOR ELSA. I SAW HER AGAIN ON HOLT AND SHE PRETENDED SHE COULDNT SPEAK ENGLISH. I TOOK HER WHERE SHE WANTED TO GO AND LET HER DRIVE THE CAR A BIT. SHE WENT TO THIS BAR IN LOWER ONTARIO BELOW HOLT AVENUE ON EUCLID AVENUE. IT WAS A DIVE AND WAS ETHNIC. MOSTLEY 98 PERCENT SPANISH AND 2 PERCENT BLACK AND ME THE ONLY WHITE GUY BUT THERE WAS A WHITE GIRL. A TALL 6 FOOT 2 GIRL WHO PLAYED FOR THE L.A. SPARKS. IT WAS HALLES BASIC PERSON SHE WAS MEETING TO DANCE WITH ETC. I SAW THIS AND SO SHE SAID SHE WOULD HAVE DINNER WITH ME SO NEXT DOOR WE BOUGHT A COUPLE TORTAS.

SHE ATE IT FAST AND LIKE ALWAYS WAS ON A TIMELINE. VERY FAST SHE ATE AND I FELT RIPPED OFF AND THIS WAS

A 5 MINUTE DATE SO SHE COULD GET FOOD FROM ME. I WATCHED HER DANCE AND EVEN SLOW DANCE AND KISS THIS TALL WOMEN WHO I FOUND OUT WAS LIKE HER GIRLFRIEND. I RAN INTO THE TALL GIRL AT THE LIQUOR STORE NEXT DOOR AND SHE AGREED THAT HALLE IS ACTING STRANGE PLAYING CHARACTORS OUT IN RELAITY WHEN NOT ACTING.

JULIA ROBERTS DOES THIS TOO. LIKE I SAID IN MY STORY ABOUT JULIA ROBERTS.

SO AS ELSA WENT BACK TO HER GIRLFRIEND I WAITED OUTSIDE TO MAYBE TALK TO HER AGAIN. THE TALL GIRL WHO WAS GIRLFRIEND WITH ELSA SAID WE COULD HAVE A THREESOME BUT NOTHING WITHOUT HER, MEANING THE TALL GIRL.

I WASNT INTERESTED AND SO I LEFT AND THAT WAS THE END OF KNOWING HALLES CHARACTOR CALLED ELSA.

KIMBERLEY TORREZ.

I SENSED HALLE WAS AROUND AND SO I KEPT MY ONE EYE OPEN FOR HER AND THERE I SAW HER. SHE WAS AGAIN PRETENDING SHE WAS HOMELESS AND EVEN ON THE SHOW THE ACTORS STUDEO SHE SAID SHE WOULD PUT EGGS IN HER HAIR AND NOT BRUSH HER TEETH OR COMB HER HAIR OR WEAR GOOD CLOTS AND NOT TAKE A SHOWER TO PLAY A HOMELESS PERSON, AND THIS SHE DEFINATELEY DID.

THIS CHARACTER IS NAMED KIMBERLEY TORREZ AND AGAIN SHE SPEAKS SPANISH. I TAKE HER TO MOMS AND TELL HER HALLE BERRY IS THERE AND AT FIRST MOM IS OK WITH IT THEN IT BOTHERS MOM BECAUSE MOM IS REMEMBERING ALL THE TERMOIL THAT JULIA ROBERTS DID AT MOMS A FEW YEARS EARLIER.

I TOLD HER HALLE ISNT LIKE THAT AND SHE NEEDS TO BASICALLY SLEEP AT THIS TIME.

MOM SAYS OK. KIMBERLY STAYS THE NIGHT AND I I LET HER HAVE THE BED FOR HERSELF AS WELL AS I AM UP STAIRS. IN MY BEDROOM MOM KEEPS FOR ME WHEN I STAY IN CLAREMONT WITH MOM AT TIMES AND THIS IS ONE OF THE TIMES.

THE NEXT DAY I HANG OUT WITH HER AND FILM HER. I ALSO FIMED HALLES CHARACTOR AND AM DOING THIS FOR A FILM CALLED FINDING HALLE IN WHICH I FILMED KIMBERLY TORREZ AND HAWAII BUT NOT ELSA. I DIDNT HAVE A CAMERA AT THAT TIME UNFORTUNATELEY.

THIS PURPOSE OF FILMING HALLE IN DIFFERENT CHARACTORS WAS FOR A FILM I AM MAKING CALLED "FINDING HALLE" WHICH IS ABOUT FINDING THE REAL HALLE BERRY. REMEMBER, SHE WAS THE ONE WHO TALKED TO ME ON THE PHONE AT THE GOWER STUDEOS LOT FOR THE SHOW LIVING DOLLS IN 1989. NOW IT IS 2005 OR 6 AND I AM SAD THAT KIMBERLEY TORREZ IS GOING TO BE IN CHARACTOR AND NOT BE THE REAL HALLE BERRY PERSONALITY.

NEXT DAY AFTER GETTING HER A BURRITO FOR LETTING ME FILM HER AND ME JUST BEING SEMI ROMANTIC NOT REALLY EVEN HARDLEY KISSING AND NO SEX. JUST CUDDLING IN THE CAMERA. WELL AFTER THAT SHE MUST MOVE ON SO SHE IS GONE AND AS I SAY GOODBYE TO HER ON THE STREET SHE RIGHT IN FRONT OF ME CHANGES INTO ANOTHER CHARACTOR.

STRANGE DAYS INDEED.

AFTER I SEE KIM TORREZ LEAVE I SEE HER RIGHT THEN CHANGE INTO HER NEXT PERSONALITY AS SHE GOES DOWN TOWARDS HOLT BLVD.

BOTTOM LINE IS STREET PEOPLE ARE BEING GLORIFIED BY ACTORS. I BELEIVE SEEING MANY ACTORS DO THIS THAT THIS MUST BE A FORM OF ON THE JOB TRAINING GOING INTO THE STREET AND LEARNING TO BE LIKE A HOMELESS AND STREET PERSON.

I BELEIVE ACTORS FIND ALL CHARACTORS EVEN AND EQUAL SO THEY DONT JUDGE. I EVEN BELEIVE THAT THEY LIKE I SAID EARLIER GLORIFY THE STREET PEOPLE.

I ALSO BELEIVE THAT THE ACTORS WHO ARE OVER PAID AND RICH FEEL A BIT OF GUILT SO THIS IS THEIR WAY OF PUNISHING THEMSELVES OR TRYING TO PAY THEIR DUES BECAUSE THEY FEEL A BIT OF GUILT THEY ARE SO RICH AND OVERPAID FOR THEIR WORK AS ACTORS.

THEY FEEL THEY REALLY DONT DESERVE THE OVER PAYMENT AND THIS IS WHY IT IS CALLED JUST THAT OVER PAY.

MICKY.

MICKY WAS A DRUMMER AND BASICALLY WAS HALLES CLOSE TO WHITE LOOK. SHE REMINDED ME OF PINOCCHIO SORT OF NON SEXUAL AND WAS INTO HER DRUMS. SHE LOVES THE BAND "THE MONKEES" AND SHE DID DRUMS IN RECORDINGS FOR ME FOR JUST THE HALLE SONGS I WROTE ABOUT HER SO SHE IS IN CHARACTOR AS MICKY DOING DRUMS FOR THE SONGS I DID ON THE FIRST 20 SONGS AND EXPRESSIONS FOR HALLE ALBUM I DID, BUT NOT ON TJHE SECOND 20 SONGS AND EXPRRESSIONS FOR HALLE.

SHE AND ME AND A ORIENTEL GUY WHO PLAYS BASE NAMED HONG WERE A BAND AND THE BAND WAS UNDER THE NAME AUTRY ODAY.

AT THIS TIME I WAS ON A T.V. SHOW CALLED DARVYS SHOWCASE FOR BANDS, A CABLE SHOW ON CHANNNEL 56 ANAHEIM.

I AUDITIONED AND HAD TO PROVE I DID MUSIC FOR REAL SO I HAD TO RECORD ME DOING MUSIC ON KEYBOARDS AND VOCALS. I USED A SONG CALLED FREE AND IT WAS THE SONG PICKED ON THE SHOW. MICKY TOLD ME TO SAY THAT I CAN SAY HALLE BERRY IS MY DRUMMER AND SO I DID THAT IN THE INTERVIEW. MY DAUGHTER ALSO GOT A SPOT ON THE SHOW AS A SOLO TAP DANCER AND DID GREAT AS WELL AS HAD AN INTERVIEW ALSO.

THE MEETING ME AND MICKY DID ENDED BECAUSE ONCE I TOLD HER IF SHE ISNT GOING TO TO BE THE HALLE CHARACTOR THEN I CANT KNOW HER AND THIS GOT HER MAD AND I NEVER TALKED TO MICKY AGAIN AFTER THIS AND THUIS WAS SAD BECAUSE I REALIZED I REALLY MADE A BAD MISTAKE SAYING THIS.

I PUT IT IN MY FIILM ENTITLED FINDING HALLE AND I DID SOME VIDEOS WITH MICKY ON FILM AND FILMED THE RECORDING SESSIONS.

THE MOTHER OF MICKY TOLD ME NOT TO CALL HER ANYMORE AN THAT SHE IS TOO BUSY TO DEAL WITH ME ANYMORE AND SO I STOPPED CALLING HER THUS THUS WAS THE END OF THE MICKY AND AUTRY ODAY FRIENDSHIP, RECORDING SESSIONS AND BAND WITH HONG. HONG QUIT BECAUSE HE SAID HE DIDNT FEEL LIKE A FRIENDSHIP BOND IN THE BAND AND IT WAS NO FRIENDSHIP AND ALL BUSINESS AND I SAID "YEA THATS HOW IT IS."

WHAT IS AMAZING IS THAT ON ALL THE SONGS THAT NEEDED DRUMS ON THE ALBUM I MADE ENTITLED 20 SONGS AND EXPRESSIONS FOR HALLE BERRY, HALLE WAS

THE DRUMMER IN TWO DIFFERENT CHARACTORS WHICH WAS MICKY AS WELL AS ANOTHER.

FELICIA. MICKY WAS IN 2006 AND 2007 AND DIDNT SEE HALLE UNTIL 2013. IN A NEW CHARACTOR NAMED FELICIA AND THEN FINALLY 2 WEEKS AGO WITH THE LAST CHARACTOR OF HALLES NAMED GLORIA.

FELICIA. I MET FELICIA ON HOLT BLVD. HOLT IS WHERE SOME OF HALLES DISTANT FAMILY LIVES. SHE TOLD ME THIS. FELICIA AND ME LIVED TOGETHER FOR TWO WEEKS. WE WENT OUT ON DATES EVERY NIGHT AND WE TRIED TO HAVE A BABY. WE SUCCEEDED. YES , I GOT HALLE PREGNANT ANYONE WANT TO CONTEST IT LETS TAKE THE PATERNITY TEST. 9 MONTHS LATER THE FAMOUS CHARACTOR HALLE BERRY WAS HAVING A CHILD. I WAS TELLING PEOPLE THAT HALLE WOULD BNE PREGNANT AND SHE WAS JUST LIKE I SAID.

NEXT WE WENT OUT TO THE OLIVE GARDEN AND THE CHOCOLATE ELEPHANT AS WELL AS SAW A JASON BATEMAN MOVIE AND WENT OUT EVERY NIGHT. I WENT TO WORK DAILY PANHANDLING EVEN THOUGH I DIDNT HAVE TO. I DIDNT HAVE TO BECAUSE MOM DIED IN 2012 AND I GOT 80,000 FROM THE INHERITENCE. SHE WAS SAD I WAS GONE DURING THE DAY AND WAITED FOR ME FOR THE 14 DAYS. I TOLD HER I HAD TO WORK AND SHE UNDERSTOOD. ONCE WE WERE IN BED AND I WAS TALKING ALOT AND SHE ASKED ME NOT TO TALK SO MUCH.

AFTER 2 WEEKS FELICIA AKA HALLE WENT HER WAY AND I NEVER SAW HALLE UNTIL 2 WEEKS AGO. IT WAS LIKE SHE WAS WAITING FOR ME. I FOLLOWED HER AFTER TALKING TO HER AND TOLD HER I DID EVERYTHING TO HAVE A RELATIONSHIP WITH HER AND SHE SAID SHE DOESNT WANT TO TALK ABOUT IT. I TOLD HER I WROTE 40 SONGS FOR TWO 20 SONG ALBUMS ENTITLED "20 SONGS AND

EXPRESSIONS FOR HALLE" PART 1 AND 20 SONGS AND EXPRESSIONS FOR HALLE PART 2.

GLORIA SHE TOLD ME THIS TIME WAS HER NAME AND CHARACTOR. I TOLD HER WHAT I GOT TO DO TO HAVE A REAL RELATIONSHIP WITH HER AND MAKE IT BIG AND SHE SAID "PROBABLEY"-

I TOLD HER IT WAS WRONG TO PATRONIZE THE HOMELESS AND OVERDO THE STEROTYPE OF THE HOMELESS LIKE THE DAY LATER SHE SAID SHE FOUND CANDY IN A CRACKER JACK BOX. I TOLD HER HOMELESS PEOPLE DONT FIND CANDY IN A BOX AND EAT IT. SHE IS OVER DOING THE IGNORANT HOMELESS STEREOTYPE. SEE HALLE IS DOING THE ACTOR THING WHERE SHE DRESSES AND BECOMES A HIOMELESS PERSON LIKE JULIA AND ALL THE OTHERS. I VISITED HER TRAILOR SHE WAS LIVING IN SO SHE SAID. T WAS BOHEMIAN AND BROKE DOWN. 2 DAYS LATER IT WAS TOWED AWAY AND THE LAST DAY I SAW HER WHERE I SPENT TIME WITH HER. WE WENT TO CVS AND SHE BIOUGHT ROLLING PAPERS AND CIGERETTES.

THE LAST DAY I TALKED TO HER WAS ABOUT 12 DAYS OR 13 DAYS AGO. -I ASKED HER IF SHE NEEDED A RIDE AND SHE SAID "NO, IM FIGURING THINGS OUT AND IM ON A ROLL". SHE WAVED ME OFF IN DISRESPECT AND I NEVER SEEN HER SINSE. M OK WITH WITH NEVER SEEING HER AGAIN.

ACTORS ARE JUST

ACTORS

NO MORE NO LESS, MAYBE A LITTLE MORE SOMETIMES.

AND THIS IS THE STORY WITH ME AND HALLE BERRY.

HALLE IN MY OPINION WAS MY MUSE AS I WROTE MORE THEN 40 SONGS ABOUT HER AS WELL AS DID A MOVIE AND

A MOVIE SOUNDTRACK ABOUT HER ENTITLED "FINDING HALLE".

ALL IN ALL I CARE ABOUT HALLE AND I BELEIVE SHE LOVES GOD AND IS A GOOD PERSON. A LITTLE CONFUSED ABOUT HERSELF BEING FAMOUS AND ACTING WEIRD LIKE ALOT OF FAMOUS PEOPLE I HAVE KNOWN AND BEFRIENDED OR JUST MET AND/OR CAME ACROSS.

HALLE THOUGH HAS A HEART UNDERNEATH IT ALL.

I AM HONORED TO HAVE BEEN HALLES FRIEND AND DATING HER TOO AS WELL AS I HOPE WE MEET AGAIN AND I DONT CARE WHAT CHARACTOR SHE WANTS TO BE. HALLE IS HALLE , NO MATTER WHAT.

MY FRIEND.

57. BILLY BRAGG FOLK/PUNK SINGER FROM ENGLAND.

HISI REAL NAME IS ROLAND BURRITT OR AT LEAST THE NAME I KNEW HIM FROM IN THE START BEING THE HIGHS SCHOOL YEARS. FIRST MET ROLAND IN DECEMBER 1977. WE WERE IN WORLD HISTORY MR SLOVIKS CLASS TOGETHER. EITHER HE WAS IN FRONT OF ME ONE DESK OR I WAS IN FRONT OF HIM ONE DESK. ALL I KNOW IS WE GOT ALONG REALLY WELL AND WE HIT IT OFF IMMEDIATELEY. NOW AT THIS TIME ME AND ROLAND AKA BILLY BRAGG BOTH DIDNT DO MUSIC AT ALL. HE WAS 18 TURNING 18 DEC 20TH 1977 AND I WAS STILL ONLY 16 TURNING 17 COMING UP IN 1978 APRIL 16TH.

WE IMMEDIATELEY BECAME SUCH GOOD FRIENDS THAT DURING PERIODS WE WERE OFF WE USED TO GET HIGH AND PARTY TOGETHER. AFTER AWHILE WE STARTED GOING TO A PLACE WITH ANOTHER FRIEND OF MINE NAMED BILL SHORT. THE THREE OF US DID THIS EVERY TUESDAY BECAUSE THE THREE OF US HAD 3 AND

SOMETIMES WITH LUNCH FOUR PERIODS OF TIME OFF IN ERO SO WE HAD TIME TO PARTY AND THEN MAKE IT TO ART CLASS WHICH ME AND BILL BOTH HAD TOGETHER AND ROLAND I BELEIVE HAD COOKING CLASS.

SO IN THIS TIME TOGETHER WE HAD FOR FOUR PERIODS ME AND ROLAND AKA LATER ON BILLY BRAGG WOULD GO TO THIS PLACE CALLED THE FOUNDATION AND DRINK 4 OLD ENGLISH 800 BOTTLES BETWEEN THE THREE OF US AS WELL AND BRING AN OZ OR A HALF OZ OF WEED. BETWEEN THE POWERFUL OLD ENGLISH 800 ALCOHOL WHICH I BELEIVE HAD 10 PERCENT ALCOHOL AS OPPOSED TO 3 PERCENT BUDWEISER OR LOWENBRAU WELL, WE GOT PRETTY HIGH AND DRUNK. WE LAUGHED AND HAD GREAT TIMES BETWEEN THE THREE OF US. TALKING ABOUT GIRLS AND THE FUTURE ETC. ONCE I WAS CLIMBING ON THE FOUNDATION. THE FOUNDATION IS CALLED THAT BECAUSE WE WOULD GO TO A PLACE THERE WHERE THERE WAS ONLY THE BRICK OUTLINE AND ROCK OUTLINE OF A CABIN THUS CALLED THE FOUNDATION. THE FOUNDATION OF THIS CABIN.

ONCE I WAS CLIMBING UP THE FOUNDATION OF THE CHIMNEY AND AS I GOT TO THE TOP BILL AND ROLAND BET I WOULD DROP THE BEER AS I PUT IT THERE ON TOP WHEN I GOT TO THE TOP.

AS I GOT TO THE TOP CRASH IT CAME DOWN. THE OLD ENGLISH 800 HAD DROPPED AND BROKE AND THAT DAY WE ONLY DRANK 3 FOR THE THREE OF US. BUT LUCKILY HAD EXTRA WEED SO WE HAD FUN.

WE USED TO BE SO DRUNK AT TIMES THAT WHEN WE WENT BACK TO SCHOOL WE HAD LUNCH TICKETS AND BOUGHT 4 DAYS OF FOOD OFF THE 5 LUNCH TICKETS AND HAD ONE LEFT OVER FOR BILL LATER. WE HAD THE MUNCHIES BUT ONCE THE FOOD AND THE BEER DIDNT SETTLE TOO GOOD

FOR BILL SHORT. AS WE GO UNTO ART CLASS TOGETHER. HE IS SITTING THERE SPINNING IN HIS HEAD BY BEING SO DRUNK AND THEN BURPS AND IS ABOUT TO THROW UP. HE SLOWLEY GETS UP AND SLOWLEY WALKS OUT THE DOOR AS MRS GRAY THE TEACHER SAYS AND I WILL NEVER FORGET THIS WORD SHE SAYS, "PITIFUL". HE THEN PUKES OUTSIDE ON THE BIG ROCK IN FRONT OF THE ART CLASS.

1. THE HORSES LEG AND THE HELP GETTING BACK TO SCHOOL BY THE CLAREMONT COP.

ONCE AS WE WERE GETTING TOTALLY DRUNK AND AFTERWARDS BILL IS WALKING AHEAD OF US AS WE ARE GOING BACK TO CLAREMONT HIGH SCHOOL. BILL IS DOWN BELOW WHERE ME AND ROLAND AKA BILLY BRAGG IS IT. WE ARE ON THE HILL LOOKING DOWN AND WE SEE BILL STUMBLING AS HE STUMPLES HE FALLS AND PICKS UP A HORSES LEG OF ALL THINGS. HE LIFTS IT WITH PRIDE AND ME AND ROLAND ARE LAUGHING HAVING THE TIME OF OUR LIVES.

ALL OF A SUDDEN IS A COP COMING OUT OF NOWHERE AND HE HAS A BULLHORN AND SAYS "I KNOW YOU ARE UP THERE COME OUT WITH YOUR HANDS UP." WELL, BILL ALREADY IS STOPPED AND SORT OF DETAINED AND NOW IT IS OUR TURN TO BE SORT OF DETAINED. WE WALK DOWN THE HILL WE WERE OBVIOUSELY DRUNK BUT THE COP TOLD US TO GET IN OUR CAR AND DRIVE TO SCHOOL. I WAS SO DRUNK THAT WHEN I DROVE BACK I GOT LOST AND COULDNT FIND MY WAY BACK. FINALLY THE COP FOLLOWED US TO SCHOOL AND I SUPPOSE HE DINT KNOW WE WERE DRUNK. THAT SEEMS IMPOSSIBLE BUT IN THOSE DAYS THAT WAS HOW THINGS WERE.

WE WENT TO THE FOUNDATION EVERY WEEK FOR AT LEAST 4 MONTHS UNTIL THE SCHOOL ENDED OR WE

WOULD JUST GO TO THE BEACH ON 4 PERIODS OFF. (3 PERIODS INCLUDING 1 LUNCH PERIOD MAKING IT 45 MINUTE TIMES 4, 3 HOURS ALTOGETHER.)

ROLAND , I REALLY LOVED AS A BROTHER AT THIS TIME AND HE WAS A BIG PART OF MY JUNIOR YEAR IN HIGH SCHOOL WHICH TO ME WAS THE MOST MAGICAL TIME IN MY LIFE.

ANOTHER TIME ON A LUNCH BREAK AND 3 PERIODS OFF WHEN BILL WAS NOT AT HOME WE WENT TO THE BEACH TAKING ONE HOUR TO GET THERE AND EVEN LESS TIME THEN ONE HOUR AND THEN SOAKED IN THE SUN AND BODY SURFED AND I SURFED FOR AN HOUR OR A LITTLE MORE THEN WE JAM BACK BEFORE THE 330 TRAFFIC JAM.

AS WE WERE COMING BACK I GOT INTO A FENDER BENDER BASHING INTO THE BACK OF A BUMPER OF A MANS CAR. THE MAN DIDNT LET IT GO HE FOLLOWED US FOR AROUND 2-4 MILES UNTIL I WAS SORT OF FORCED TO PULL OVER BEHIND AN UPCOMING POLICE CAR. I KNEW IF I KEPT DOING HIT AND RUN THEY COPS WOULD GET US AND FIND US AND ARREST US SO WE FELT THE BEST THING TO DO WAS GIVE UP BEHIND THE COP CAR AND SAY WE WERE NOT HIT AND RUN AND THAT WE THOUGHT WE SAW A COP CAR UP AHEAD AND FELT IT BEST TO GO TO A COP. HE, THE COP BELEIVED US AND WE WERE ON OUR WAY. THE GUYS CAR WASNT DAMAGED AT ALL BUT MY CAMERO WAS. A 350 SS STICK SHIFT WITH A STRIP AND A HOOD SCOOP AS WELL AS A SPOILER AN 850 HOLY CARB AS WELL AS BIG 40 TIRES AND CENTERLINE WHEELS. I HAD ONE OF THE TWO BEST LOOKING CARS IN HIGH SCHOOL, THE OTHER CAR A CORVETTE 76 OWNED BY RICH BOY ALAN BARBISH, WHOM HE TOLD ME HIS DAD WAS IN ORGANISED CRIME.

SO AS WE WERE LEAVING HE SAW SOME WEED AKA MARIJUANA COMING OUT OF ROLANDS POCKET AND HE

TOOK IT AND GAVE ROLAND A TICKET BEING THERE WAS A LAW PASSED IN EARLY 1978 THAT SAID IF IT IS UNDER AN OUCE OF MARIJUANA THEN IT WILL BE JUST A MILD TICKET. ROLAND GAVE A FAKE NAME ROLAND SIGMUND WHEN HIS REAL NAME WAS BURRITT.

WE USED TO ALWAYS LAUGH ABOUT THAT AND REMIND EACH OTHER HOW CRAZY THOSE TIMES WERE.

LATER ON IN THE LATE SUMMER OF 1978 ME AND BILL SHORT THE OTHER TWO OF OUR THREESOME OF BUDDIES WENT OVER TO ROLANDS WHERE HE LIVES AND THERE I FOUND OUT HIS MOTHER LEFT HIM WHEN HE WAS 12 AND HE NEVER HAD A DAD.

HE WAS AT THIS TIME LIVING AT HIS UNCLES HOUSE AND HIS UNCLES WIFE WHO WASNT HIS AUNT JUST A AUNT BY THE UNCLE MARRYING HER.

SO AS ROLAND TOOK US TO THE POOL TO SWIM I NOTICED THEY THE AUNT AND UNCLE WERE BOTHERED BY ROLANDS PRESENCE AND THE FRIENDS HE BROUGHT WHICH WAS US.

WELL, MY WAY OF NOTICING WAS QUITE RIGHT. HE WAS SLEEPING IN THE FRONT ROOM OF THE HOUSE. THE HOUSE WAS A 6 BEDROOM HOUSE AND THE UNCLE I BELEIVE WAS IN HIS LATE 30S. MAKING HIM NOW IN HIS LATE 70S.

I NOTICED THE WIFE OF THE UNCLE OF ROLAND WAS MEAN TO HIM AND I KNEW HE WAS ON HIS WAY OUT. WE SWAM AND HAD BEERSAND HOT DOGS AND HAD A GREAT TIME EVEN THOUGH AT FIRST THEY WERE UPSET WE WERE DRINKING BEING I WAS ONLY 17 AND ROLAND WAS 18.

2 WEEKS LATER.

I GET A CALL FROM ROLAND ASKING ME IF I KNOW OF A PLACE HE CAN LIIVE. I WAS EXCITED BECAUSE I WANTED HIM TO LIVE WITH MOM AND DAD AND ME AND MY BROTHER JOHN.

I TOLD HIM I WOULD GET BACK TO HIM AND SEE IF I GOT A PLACE FOR HIM. AT THE TIME HE WAS HOMELESS FOR THE FIRST TIME IN HIS LIFE AND IN ROLANDS LIFE HE WILL HAVE A GREAT LIFE AND ALOT OF HIOMELESSNESS TOO.

THE CALL BACK TO ROLAND AKA BILLY BRAGG. I CALLED HIM AND I SAID "GUESS WHAT YOU CAN LIVE WITH US". HE WAS HAPPY AND I WENT TO PICK HIM UP AND TAKE HIM TO THE HOUSE.

ROLAND STAYED WITH US FROM SEPTEMBER TO DECEMBER 1978. WE WENT TO PARTIES TOGETHER AND WENT TO THE FOUNDATION WHICH IS THE PLACE WE USED TO PARTY AT BACK IN HIGH SCHOOL DAYS A YEAR EARLIER OR EVEN LESS THEN A YEAR BEING WE PARTIED IN HIGH SCHOOL AT THE FOUNDATION IN FEB TO JUNE 1978 AND NOW ITS ONLY 3 MONTHS LATER., SEPTEMBER AND ROLAND IS LIVING WITH US.

WE WENT TO THE BEACH AND HAD A GREAT TIME BECAUSE IN OCTOBER 27TH 1978. I QUIT LOVES BAR B QUE WHICH I WAS AT FOR 1 YEAR.

NOW I AM NOT WORKING AND ALL WE GOTTA DO NOW IS PARTY. ROLAND WASNT WORKING EITHER.

NOVEMBER 1978.

IN NOVEMBER 1978 DAD BOUGHT ROLAND A GUITAR.

ROLAND REALLY APPRECIATED IT SO HE LEARNED HIS FIRST SONG HE EVER LEARNED WHICH WAS HAPPY BIRTHDAY TO YOU. IT SOUNDED GREAT AND HE SANG AT

THE SAME TIME TOO. IT LOOKED COOL. I VE NEVER SEEN ANYONE PLAY GUITAR IN PERSON REALLY EXCEPT FOR AT DANCES AT OUR HIGH SCHOOL IN 1977-78.

NEXT ROLAND SANG IT TO MY DAD AND WHEN I GOT A JOB AT THE GAS STATION ON INDIAN HILL AND THE 10 FREEWAY.

ROLAND LEFT ON THE DAY I GOT THE JOB AT THE GAS STATION WHICH IS JANUARY 5TH 1979. IT WAS MY DADS BIRTHDAY ON JAN 5TH AS WELL AS I GOT THE JOB THAT DAY AND ROLAND LEFT THAT DAY-

1981. IN JUNE OF 1979, I ACTUALLY STARTED TO GET INTO A BAND CALLED ENVY AND FROM THAT TIME TO WHEN I NEXT SEE ROLAND IN NOVEMBER OF 1981. I HAD PERFORMED PROBABLEY 80 SHOWS IN AROUND TWO YEARS AND 4 MONTHS.

NOW IT IS NOVEMBER OF 1981 AND ROLAND IS WALKING DOWN WHERE ME AND TRISHA WERE AT. I WAS GOING TO WHERE ROLAND LIVED WITH HIS UNCLE AND STEP AUNT IN 1978.

AND LOW AND BEHOLD AS I WAS TALKING ABOUT MY FRIENDSHIP WITH ROLAND. HERE COMES ROLAND AND I SAY TO TRISHA WHO IS MY FIANCEE AND WITH ME ON THIS RIDE, "HERE COMES ROLAND". AND ROLAND GETS IN OUR CAR AND WE DRIVE OFF. ROLAND SAYS HES DOING MUSIC AND I TELL HIM I AM DOING MUSIC TOO. HE IS SO AMAZED TO HEAR THAT SO WE DECIDE TO GET TOGETHER ON THE MUSIC. I SING AND HE PLAYS GUITAR AND SONGS BACKGROUND VOCALS. LATER ON ROLAND WILL HAVE A STAGE NAME CALLED BILLY BRAGG AND HE WILL SING LEAD BY HIMSELF AS A SOLO ARTIST JUST HIM ON GUITAR AND VOCALS.

SHOWS. IN 2 MONTHS ME AND ROLAND WRITE 15 SONGS AND PERFORM EVERYWHERE FROM BACK YARD AND

HOUSE PARTIES TO THE MONTCLARE MALL TO GRISWALDS WHERE I GOT ROLAND A JOB TO A KINDERGARDEN TO A CRIPPLED CJHILDRENS HOME TO A REHAB IN POMONA CALLED THE POMONA A.T.S.UNIT.

WE PERFORMED ALOT AND THEN ONE PARTY WE GOT INTO A FIGHT IN THE CAR AFTER IT WAS DONE. AFTER THIS FIGHT OUR FRIENDSHIP WHICH WAS PERFECT UP TO NOW HAS STARTED TO CHANGE AND DEFINATELEY STARTED TO SOUR. ROLAND STAYED AT THE HOUSE FOR 1 YEAR OR MORE UNTIL I STARTED TO LIVE AT THE SUNRISA APARTMENTS IN JANUARY 1982 TO SEPTEMBER 1982 AND THEN I WOUND UP SMACK INTO THE ATS UNIT ALCOHOL TREATMENT CENTER IN OCT TO DEC 1982 SO I WAS AWAY FROM HOME AT MOM AND DADS ALL THROUGH 1982 AND ROLAND LIVED THERE WITH MY AUNT NAN WHO ALSO LIVED THERE-TOO. ROLAND LIVED IN MY OLD BEDROOM AND NAN IN THE FAMILY ROOM. IT WORKED GOOD BUT MY PARENTS WERE A LITTLE MAD I LEFT. MY PARENTS ARE DIFFERENT THEY DONT KICK ME OUT AT 18 LIKE THE AMERICAN WAY USUALLY IS.

ROLAND AGAIN WAS LIVING AT THE HOUSE AND I GOT HIM A JOB AT GRISWALDS, A HOTEL AND SMORGERSBORG AND THEN WE PLAYED 20 OR MORE SHOWS INCLUDING A PLACE CALLED WALTERS COFFEE SHOP AND PEPITAS AS WELL AS A PLACE CALLED THE WASH WHICH WAS A PLACE THAT I STARTED A BIG PARTY THERE EVERY FRYDAY SO ON FRYDAYS WE WOULD PLAY THE WASH AND SATURDAY TO TUESDAY PLAY PEPITAS FOR BEER AS WELL AS FOOD AND 20 A PIECE FOR FOUR HOURS. THEY GOT A BARGAIN.

1982 TO 1983.

ROLAND LIVED AT MOMS AS I LIVED AT THE SUNRISA. ROLAND SORT OF TOOK MY PLACE AS THEIR KID BUT NOT REALLY JUST A TEMPORARY SITUATION.

THROUGH 1982 ME AND ROLAND PLAY ALOT AND I AM ALSO IN A BAND CALLED LEF TOVERS IN 1982 FROM FEB 1982 TO SEPTEMBER 1982 WHEN I ENROLL IN CITRUS COLLEGE IN 1982.

WHILE I AM IN THE REHAB FROM OCT 1982 TO DECEMBER 1982.

I GET A DAY OFF TO GET AWAY FROM THE ALCOHOL TREATMENT CENTER AND IT IS A DESERVING DAY IF I DID GOOD FOR 1 MONTH. I FELT I DID AND THE UNIT FELT I DID WITH AND ALONG ALL THE NURSES THERE.

MY FUN DAY WITH ROLAND 1982 NOVEMBER AT MEMORIAL PARK THEN WALKING TO KAREN CASTS HOUSE ROLANDS GIRLFRIEND.

SO I GOT RELEASED FROM THE REHAB FOR THE FIRST DAY IN 1 MONTH. -IT WAS A REWARD FOR ME SINSE I DID SO WELL IN 1 MONTH. ME AND ROLAND HAD PERFORMED THERE AT THE EARLY 6 AM AA MEETING AND THEN AGAIN AT THE NOON MEETING.

SO OF COURSE I WANTED TO SPEND MY DAY WITH MY BEST FRIEND NAMED ROLAND BURRITT AND LATER HIS STAGE NAME BEING BILLY BRAGG.

WE FIRST GET A COUPLE SIX PACKS FOR HIM TO DRINK I AM NOT GOING TO DRINK AND TO MAKE SURE THERE IS NO TEMPTATION I TAKE A PILL THAT IF YOU DRINK ON THIS PILL YOU GET VERY VERY VERY SICK. OH YES IT IS CALLED ANTI-BUSE AND IS FOR PEOPLE WHO DONT WANT TO DRINK ALCOHOL. THE WAY IT WORKS IS THAT IF THE PERSON WHO TAKES THE PILL ANTI-BUSE DRINKS ALCOHOL THEN THEY WELL GET VERY VERY SICK AND I HEARD SOME STORIES WHERE THEY WERE DOUBLING OVER IN PAIN AND THIS IS LIKE THE SAME PAIN THAT MACE GIVES WHICH I MEAN THAT BOTH MACE AND ANTI-BUSEIS

GEARED TO GIVE YOU TOTAL PAIN BUT NO SCARRING AND NO BRUISES AND NO LONG TERM INJURIES JUST PAIN AND THEN IT GOES AWAY AND THEN IT SHOWS NOTHING THAT HAS BEEN THERE AND FOR EXAMPLE IF YOU GET STABBED IT LEAVES SCARRING AND INTERNAL DAMAGE AND IF YOU GET PUNCHED YOU GET A BRUISE OR A BLACK EYE OR YOU LOSE BLOOD BUT WITH ANTI-BUSE AND WITH MACE IT IS PAIN WORSE THEN BEING STABBED OR SHOT BUT THE THE MACE AND ANTI-BUSE LEAVES NO BRUISES OR INTERNAL OR EXTERNAL INJURIES OR SCARRING OR ANY LASTING EFFECTS, AGAIN JUST DESIGNED TO GIVE PAIN AND OH YES I HAVE BEEN MACED BUT NEVER TOOK ANTI-BUSE AND THEN DRANK ALCOHOL BUT WHEN I HEARD THE HORROR STORIES BELEIVE ME I DIDNT WANT TO DRINK OR EVEN HAVE ANY TEMPTATION TO DRINKK ALCOHOL.

OH YES ANTIBUSE.

MEANING YOU WILL NOT ABUSE THIS ALCOHOL ON THIS PILL. I ALWAYS WONDRED WHAT IF I ACTIDENTELLY TOOK SOME ALCOHOL IN COUGH SYRUP OR IN A CANDY FROM CHRISTMAS WOULD I GET SICK BUT NO NEED TO WORRY THIS WAS PRETTY MUCH THE LAST TIME I CAN REMEMBER THAT I TOOK THESE MEDS CALLED ANTIBUSE BECAUSE OF ACCIDENTELLY TAKING ALCOHOL IN A CHRISTMAS CANDY OR IN COUGH SYRUP OR IN BEER BATTER OR WHATEVER BUT THIS MEANS THAT I TOOK IIT INTO MY OWN HANDS AND STOPPED DRINKING OUT OF PURE SELF DICIPLIN.

WHEN WE HIT OUR FIRST DESTINATION WAS READY TO PARTY MEANING HE PARTY AND I ENJOY THE COMPANY OF HIS DRINKING AND HIS PERSONALITY.

WE GO TO MEMORIAL PARK FIRST AND SIT IN THE MIDDLE OF THE GRASS IN THE PARK WHERE I HAVE PERFORMED BEFORE ON STAGE THERE. ANYWAYS WE HAD A GREAT TIME UNTIL ROLAND FINISHED OFF HIS 11TH AND 12TH

BEER. I STARTED TO NOTICE A CHANGE IN HIS PERSONALITY AND HE SEEMED DISTANT AND WASNT CALLING ME CHUCK ANY MORE NOR DOES HE REALLY SEEM LIKE HE RECOGNISES ME. I AM REALIZING THROUGH MY EXPERIENCE THAT I KNOW AND BELEIVE HE IS BLACKING OUT FROM THE 2 SIX PACKS HE HAS JUST DRANK IN LESS THEN 1 HOUR.

I FEEL IF WE WALK TO THE NEXT DESTINATION THAT HE MIGHT GET BETTER AND WALK OFF HIS BLACKOUT, NOT TO BE.

I DONT KNOW WHERE THE NEXT DESTINATION IS SO I ASK ROLAND IS THERE ANYWHERE HE WOULD LIKE TO GO AND HE SAYS ""MY GIRLFRIEND KAREN". I HAVE HEARD ABOUT KAREN BUT NOT YET MET HER OR SEEN HER AS OF YET. SO WE WALK UP TO KARENS.

KARENS HOUSE IS ABOUT 3 MILES FROM MEMORIAL PARK WHICH IS ON INDIAN HILL BLVD IN BETWEEN BONITA AND FOOTHILL.

WE HAVE TO WALK TO MOUNTAIN AND BASELINE. ACTUALLY A LITTLE FURTHER NORTH ABOVE BASELINE ON MOUNTAIN AVENUE. THIS MOUNTAIN AVENUE IS LOCATED SOUTH OF CLARABOYA AND KARENS HOME IS IN BETWEEN MOUNTAIN AND BASELINE AND NORTH OF THIS AREA CALLED CLARABOYA.

AT THE TIME CLARABOYA WAS THE WEALTHIEST HOMES IN CLAREMONT. SINSE THEN THE MOST WEALTHIEST ARE NOW HOMES NEWLEY BUILT SINSE THEN ON MILLS AVENUE ABOVE BASELINE AND BELOW MT BALDY RANGE.

SO NOW WE ARE AT KAREN CASTS HOUSE WHO IS THE GIRLFRIEND OF ROLAND. WE GET IN THE FRONT ROOL AND THE 2 KIDS ARE SCREEMING AND ROLAND IS TRYING TO PLAY KAREN A SONG THAT ME AND ROLAND WROTE

RECENTLEY. THE KIDS WILL NOT STOP SCREAMING AND IT IS REALLY LOUD AND NO ONE IS PAYING ATTENTION TO ROLANDS GUITAR PLAYING AND MY SINGING BECAUSE KAREN HAS TO TEND TO THE SCREAMING KIDS. ALL OF A SUDDEN THE NOW BLACKED OUT AND OUT OF HIS MIND ON ALCOHOL ROLAND IS NOW ATTEMPTING TO THROW THE LITTLE LOVE SEAT THROUGH THE WINDOW AND HE DOES IT BREAKING THE BIG WINDOW IN THE FRONT ROOM THAT LOOKS OUTWARD. THE LITTLE LOVE SEAT IS NOW OUTSIDE AND THE WINDOW IS BROKEN COMPLETELEY.

ROLAND IS LOOKING FOR SOMETHING ELSE VIOLENT TO DO AND AT THIS MOMENT I REALIZE I NEED TO GET MYSELF PREPARED TO HAVE TO FIGHT HIM AND TAKE HIM DOWN FOR THE SAFTEY OF THE 2 KIDS AND KAREN AND OF COURSE MYSELF. THIS WAS SELF DEFENCE ME FIGHTING HIM AND SO I STARTED. I JUMPED ON HIM AND HE SLUGGED ME IN THE NOSE GIVING ME A LITTLE BLOOD IN MY NOSE. I USED MARSHALL ARTS AS A METHOD TO CONTOL ROLAND WITHOUT BEATING HIM UP OR HAVING TO RESORT OT REALLY HEAVY VIOLENCE AND HURTING. SO I PINCHED AND SLUGGED INTO THE MUSCLES AND NO NO AVAIL ROLAND WAS TWICE AS STONG AS I HAVE EVER SEEN HIM.

HE IS SWINGING WILDLEY AGAIN SO IHEAD BUTT HIM BUSTING THE BRIDGE OF HIS NOSE AND HE FALLS TO THE GROUND. I THEN JUMP ON TOP OF HIM AND HOLD HIM DOWN.

I SAY, "ARE YOU GONNA STOP IF I GET UP AND LET YOU GET UP"? HE SAYS "YEAH PUNK".

I SHOULD HAVE KNOWN HE WAS GOING TO LIE FROM THE PUNK STATEMENT BECAUSE THIS SHOWS HE DOESNT KNOW ME OR WHO I AM ANYMORE BECAUSE THIS IS WHAT ALCOHOL DOES WHEN YOU BLLACKOUT FROM DRINKING

WAY TOO MUCH. YOU START CALLING SOMEONE YOU KNOW A DISTANT NAME THATS NOT THEM LIKE PUNK BECAUSE HE CANT SEE OR RECOGNISE ME ANYMORE.

I WAS TIRED OF FIGHTING AND I MEAN PHYSICALLY TIRED SINSE I AM NOT A PRO WRESTLER AND WE HAVE BEEN FIGHTING/WRESTLING FOR 5 MINUTES IN ERO WHICH IS LIKE TWO ROUNDS IN A MATCH. AS I LET ROLAND UP HE RUNS INTO THE KITCHEN AND GRABS THE BIGGEST BUITCHER KNIFE HE CAN FIND AND THEN CHASES ME AROUND AND AROUND THE KITCHEN AND THEN THE LIVING ROOM AND VICA VERSA. THEN I DECIDE TO RUN INTO THE BATHROOM.

IN THE BATHROOM I HEAR ROLAND YELLING THAT HE WAS GOING TO KILL ME WHICH GIVES ME COMFORT TO KNOW HIS MIND IS NOT ON THE 2 KIDS AND KAREN TO KILL. THEY ARE SAFE AND AT THIS TIME I DECIDE TO CLIMB THROUGH THE SMALL AREA CALLED THE BATHROOM WINDOW LIKE THE BEATLES SOING. SHE CAME INTO THE BATHROOM WINDOW BUT INSTEAD I AM COMING OUT OF THE BATHROOM WINDOW AND NOT PROTECTED BY A SILVER SPOON BUT THERE WAS A SILVER BUTCHER KNIFE HELD BY ROLAND COMING AFTER ME IN A RAGE.

II DECIDE TO CLIMB THROUGH THE WINDOW BECAUSE ROLAND WAS BASHING DOWN THE DOOR AND I HEARD LATER THAT AFTER I LEFT THE BATHROOM THRI THE WINDOW THAT HE DID SUCCEED AT BANGING DOWN THE BATHROOM DOOR LIKE THE SHINING AND JACK NICKOLSON BUT INSTEAD OF HERES JOHNNY ITS HERES ROLAND AKA BILLY BRAGG. THIS WAS IN 1982 THE FALL AROUND NOVEMBER I BELEIVE.

THE NEXT DAY-THE NIGHT BEFORE I WAS LATE GETTING BACK TO THE ALCOHOL TREATMENT CENTER AND THEY

UNDERSTOOD SEEING I HAD BLOOD FROM MY NOSE AND A FEW SCRATCHES AND BRUISES.

THAT NIGHT I CALLED FROM A HOUSE DOWN THE STREET AND CALLED THE POLICE BECAUSE I WAS WORRIED ABOUT IF ROLAND TURNED HIS INSANE ANGER ON THE TWO KIDS AND KAREN CAST. HIS THEN GIRLFRIEND. AND I TRIED TO HELP AS HUMANLEY POSSIBLE THAT I COULD.

THE NEXT DAY HE CALLED ME FROM THE PAYPHONE THAT HE HAD THE NUMBER OF. I GAVE IT TO HIM A WHILE BACK HE CALLED ME AND LOUIS WHO IS ONE OF THE NURSES THERE TOLD ME ROLAND WAS ON THE PHONE HE TOLD ME HE COULDNT MOVE HE WAS SO SORE AND THAT HE WAS GOING TO ENROLL HIMSELF IN THE HOSTBITAL. I ASKED HIM IF HE WAS ARRESTED AND HE SAID NO THAT BY THE TIME THE COPS CAME HE WAS IN CONTROL OF HIMSELF. I WAS GLAD BECAUSE I DIDNT WANT TO REALLY PUT HIM IN JAIL. I ASKED HIM WHAT THE POLICE SAID ABOUT THE WINDOW AND HE SAID KAREN PUT UP DRAPES ON THE MISSING WINDOW AREA AND THAT SHE ALSO PICKED UP ALL THE GLASS AND ROLAND SAID HE HELPED PICK UP THE GLASS TOO SO ALL WAS THE BEST IT COULD BE. ROLAND HAD TO WORK EXTRA AT GRISWALDS TO PAY FOR THE WINDOW LATER ON AND I HELPED HIM A BIT TOO WITH THE MONEY TO COVER THE WINDOW. 300 DOLLORS WORTH OF DAMAGE AND THAT WAS IN THOSE DAYS 38 YEARS AGO.

AFTER ALL I WAS THE GUY THAT GAVE ROLAND A KNOWN ALCOHOLIC 2 SIX PACKS TO BLACK OUT ON.

WE REMAINED FRIENDS AND I TOLD HIM I UNDERSTOOD AND HAS HE EVER THOUGHT ABOUT JOINING AND ENROLLING IN THIS REHAB OR AT LEAST GO TO SOME AA MEETINGS.

HER SAID SURE. HE TRIED TO GET IN BUT DIDNT HAVE THE INSURANCE NEEDED BUT WE PLAYED THERE AGAIN AND WENT TO AA MEETINGS TOGETHER. I TOLD ROLAND HE NEEDS TO QUIT DRINKING. UNFORTUNATELELEY ROLAND DIDNT STOP DRINKING UNTIL AFTER I WAS HIS FRIEND ANYMORE IN THE YEAR 2001. AT LEAST I AM GUESSING 2001. I DIDNT SEE ROLAND FROM 2000 DECEMBER TO 2010. WHEN I SAW HIM SITTING ON THE BENCH SO I MAY BE WRONG WHEN HE QUIT ALCOHOL. HE COULD HAVE QUIT UP TO AS LATE AS 2010 BUT I AM BETTING THAT THAT ISNT TRUE CONSIDERING HIS SUCCESS STARTED EARLY 2000S. AT LEAST I AM GUESSING THAT TOO BECAUSE I SEEN HIM ON TV ON CONAN OBRIAN AND DAVID LETTERMAN AROUND THE EARLY 2000S.

AFTER THIS ME AND ROLAND HUNG OUT UNTIL 1983 JAN 1 IN WHICH HE WENT WITH ME TO AUDITION FOR A BAND CALLED OPPOSITE SIX. GET IT? INSTEAD OF OPPOSITE SEX.

WELL, ANYWAYS I GOT THE AUDITION AND THERE ROLAND LEFT FOR AROUND 6 MONTHS UP UNTIL 1983 SUMMER AND AT THIS TIME IT WAS A PERIOD OF HANGING WITH HIM LATE DECEMBER 1983 TO MID 1985 AND THEN HE WAS GONE AGAIN FOR AROUND A YEAR UNTIL 1986. WHERE HE LIVED WITH HIS BUSINESS AND MUSIC MANAGER TOM.

FROM 1983 JAN 1 TO JUNE I DIDNT SEE HIM AND WHEN I SEE HIM AGAIN HE IS STRUNG OUT ON METH.

1. BULLYING ME FOR MONEY FOR SONGS

2. HIPPY TOM TURNING ME ONTO A METH ADDICTION

3. CHUCK LIMOSPA

4. 77 , IT WAS HEAVEN 85, FULL OF JIVE--A SONG WRITTEN BY ME AND ROLAND IN 1985

5. ELF AND A STRIPPER AND SANTA

6, ROLAND PLAYING WITH MIKE AMBROSE.

7. WOOING GIRLS CARMELITA DEBBIE AND CARMILITAS FRIEND.

8. DAVE KNIGHT HIS FIRST MANAGER

9. WEED BULLY AND THEN THE MAGICAL MALL. DANCING ON CARS AND ASKING QUESTIONS IN THE MALL

10 FINDING A WHOLE BOTTLE FULL OF DALATTA AND CODENE VALIUME ETC

BULLYING ME FOR MONEY FOR SONGS AND TURNING ME ONTO HEROIN FOR THE 2ND TIME IN MY LIFE. 1983.

I FIRST SEE ROLAND IN JUNE OR EARLY JULY 1983 AND HERE IS IS COMING AT ME, RAGE IN HIS EYES LIKE THE BLACKOUT DRUNK BUT NOT THIS TIME HE IS ADDICTED TO A FAIRLEY NEW DRUG IN SOUTHERN CALIFORNIA CALLED CRYSTEL METH. AT THIS TIME IN MY LIFE I HAVE NEVER DONE CRYSTEL METH YET AS ROLAND IS FIRST STRUNG OUT ON IT AND I WILL BE TOO STARTING IN 1984. BUT AS OF THIS TIME IN 1983 I AM NOT STRUNG OUT ON CRYSTEL METH.

I REMEMBER HEARING THIS NAME CRYSRLE METH ONE TIME BEFORE AND IT WAS KENNY DUNNS BAND NAME AS HE CHANGED HIS NAME TO KENNY CRYSTEL AND THE BAND NAME WAS CRYSTEL METH. AT THAT TIME KENNY MADE UP THE NAME FOR HIS BAND I NEVER KNEW THE NAME CRYSTEL METH WAS A DRUG. THIS WAS 1979 WHEN KENNY DUNN NAMED HIMSELF KENNY CRYSTEL AND CALLED THE BAND CRYSTEL METH.

ROLAND TAKES A SWING AND I BLOCK IT AND I AM PRETTY MUSCULAR AND HAVE BEEN WORKING OUT AT THE SPA

OVER A YEAR NOW AND ROLAND HASNT JOINED AS OF YET BUT I WILL GET HIM TO JOIN LATER ON AS WE AGAIN TRY TO STOP OUR METH ADDICTIONS.

ROLAND HAS BEEN GONE AND SINSE HE WAS GONE I GOT 6 OF MINE AND HIS SONGS TOGETHER AND MY DAD EXECUTIVE PRODUCED THESE RECORDINGS AT WINETREE STUDEO. OWNED BY BOB DIRE, A STUDEO WHICH ROLAND HAS USED BEFORE ME AND SHOWED ME AND TURNED ME ON TO BOB DIRES STUDEO CALLED WINETREE STUDEOS. EVEN THOUGH IN THE END OF MY 24 TRACK RECORDING INCLIUDING A NEVE BOARD 500,000 BOARD I ONLY PAID 18 PER HOUR WHICH WAS BASICALLY FOR THE ENGENEERS TIME. BUT NOW IN 1983 BEING I DIDNT KNOW THE PRICES OR DEALS WE STARTED AT 45 PER HOUR FOR THIS 24 TRACK WHICH WAS GOING RATE IF NOT SIGNED TO THE LABEL OF THE OWNER OF THE STUDEO WHICH BOB DIRE HAD A CHRISTIAN LABEL CALLED DOVE RECORDS WE DIDNT KNOW ABOUT. AT THAT TIME IN 1983 WE WERE PAYING WHAT WE FELT WAS A DEAL AT 40 PER HOUR. SO I GOT SOME PLAYERS AROUND TOWN FROM AN AD AND DID SIX SONGS INCLUDING THE SONG ENTITLED :HEY YOU" AND THE SONGS "BEHIND THE ILLUSION" AND "BLUE MOON LADY". ROLAND HEARD THIS AND WAS MAD HE WASNT PART OF IT AND THOUGHT I AM STEALING HIS MUSIC WHICH WE BOTH WROTE THE MUSIC AND I WROTE THE LYRICS OF "HEY YOU", "BEHIND THE ILLUSION" AND ""BLUE MOON LADY" AS WELL AS ANOTHER SONG CALLED "INSPIRED".

WE FINALLY CAME TO AN AGREEMEMT OF 60 DOLLORS FOR THESE SONGS WE DID IN THE STUDEO. THE TRUTH OF IT IS I INVITED ROLAND TO PLAY ON THE RECORDINGS AND TO TAKE PART IN FULL OWNERSHIP OF SONGS WITH ME AND ROLAND AND MY DAD BEING HE GETS POINTS AKA

SPECS FOR PAYING FOR THE PRODUCTION OF THE 6 SONGS.

I FORGAVE ROLAND FOR HIS VIOLENT BEHAVIOR AGAIN.

THE NYLANDERS, AKA THE VIKINGS.

ROLAND WAS BLESSED TO BE HELPED BY A FAMILY NAMED THE NYLANDERS WHO WERE MORMANS AND THEY BOUGHT ROLAND A TRUCK AND GOT HIM A FULL TIME JOB AND WHEN ROLAND WAS INVOLVED WITH THEM HE SAW ME AND YELLED OUT A GRUNT AND KEPT GOING AS I WAS GETTING HIM TO GIVE ME A RIDE. THATS HOW ROLAND IS, WHEN HE IS SUCCESSFUL HE FORGETS ABOUT WHO HELPED HIM. AS NOW AS BILLY BRAGG HE WONT TALK TO ME UNLESS I PAY HIS MANAGEMENT 400 DOLLORS. CRAZY, BUT ROLAND IS ROLAND EVEN IF HE CHANGES HIS NAME HIS SELF IS STILL THE SAME.

BILLY BRAGG IS SUCCESSFUL NOW AS A FOLK SINGER AND GUITARIST AND WILL NOT DEAL WITH ME AT ALL. THAT HURTS BUT ILL GET OVER IT. MY OLDEST SON SHINED ME ON TOO. I USED TO THIS TREAMENT AND TORTURE,

MY OLDEST SON WILL BE 38 YEARS OLD ON SEPT 4TH OF THIS YEAR, THIS YEAR BEING 2020.

NEXT IT IS 1984-85 AND I SPEND ALOT OF TIME HANGING OUT WITH ROLAND DOING A THING CALLED WEED BULLY IN WHICH WE WALK AROUND CLAREMONT SORT OF BUGGING PEOPLE TO ASK IF THEY CAN SHARE SOME OF THEIR WEED WITH US AND IT ALWAYS WORKED.

ME AND ROLAND WERE REALLY GETTING INTO THE SPA AND AT THIS TIME IN 1984 ROLAND INTRODUCES ME TO HIS METH DEALER NAMED HIPPY TOM WHO ALSO SELLS A LITTLE WEED BUT METH IS HIS MOST IMPORTANT THING HE SELLS.

I MEET HIPPY TOM AND WE HIT IT OFF GREAT, ALOT OF THE TIME WE WOULD BUY THE METH THEN GET HIGH WITH HIPPY TOM WHO IS TOTALLY PARANOID. SO PARANOID THAT HE BRINGS KNIVES AND A HANDGUN WITH HIM FOR SELF DEFENCE TO GO ACROSS THE STREET TO 7-11 ON SAN BERNADINO AND INDIAN HILL.

WELl, BEING THAT WE DO METH AND WORK OUT, WELL OBVIOUSELEY WE WOULD BE ON METH WHILE WORKING OUT. METH MAKES YOU STRONG OR MAKES YOU THINK YOU ARE STRONGER WHEN IN REALITY YOU ARE STRAINING BEYIOND YOIUR LIMIT. WAS BENCHING 305 ON THE MACHINE WEIGHTS AND WAS ONLY DOING 235 NOT ON METH BUT ON METH 305. I THEN POPPED SOMETHING IN MY ARM AND THAT WAS IT FOR TRYING TO GO AND ADD ON MORE WEIGHT ABOVE 305 LBS.

ONE TIME MARK MCGWIRE THE BASEBALL LEGEND WAS THERE AND THIS WAS WHEN MARK WAS IN COLEGE. MARK WAS ABOUT 20 AND THIS IS 1984. I TOLD ROLAND THAT IF HE ASKS MARK MCGWIRE IF HIS NAME IS MOP MCGWIRE I WOULD GIVE HIM A JOINT AND SO HE DID THIS. THER REASON WHY I SAID MOP MCGWIRE WAS BACK IN THE EWRLY 70S MARK MCGWIRE WAS PLAYING SOCCER AGAINST MY BROTHERS TEAM THE JAGUIRES AND JOHN MY BROTHER WAS A GOALIE AND MARK WAS A FOREWARD AND HE HAD A MOP OF CURLEY CARROTT TOP RED HAIR SO WE CALLED HIM MOP THAT AT THIS TIME I NEVER THOUGHT MARK WOULD BE A SUPER STAR IN BASEBALL BREAKING ROGER MARIS HOME RUN RECORD.

ROLAND LOVED WEED AND ONCE TOOK APART A WHOLE DASHBOARD JUST TO FIND A JOINT HE THOUGHT HE LOST. HE NEVER FOUND THAT JOINT, FUNNY HUH?

TOM AND ME ON THE ROOF OF HIS HOUSE ARMED WITH RIFLES.

I WAS TWEAKING FOR 3 DAYS ON CRYSTEL METH AND THE CRYSTEL METH WAS GUIDING ME TO DO THIS. YES I AM GOING TO BLAME IT ON THE 3 DAYS HIGH WITHOUT SLEEP ON CRYSTEL METH. I WENT TO GET MORE FROM HIPPIE TOM AND HE GAVE ME SOME AND I GAVE HIM SOME FOR THE DEAL AND WE DID SOME TOGETHER. IT SMELLED LIKE RAT POISON AND I SAID TO TOM "MAN, THIS SMELLS AND TASTES LIKE RAT POISON", TOM IN THIS DEVIOUS SOUNDED DRUG ENHANCED VOICE AND LAUGH SAID "PROBABLY IS."

WE BOTH LAUGHED AND DIDNT REALLY CARE OR MIND IT AND SNORTED MORE. THIS IS THE EVILS OF ADDICTION. IT TAKES OVER YOUR MIND SLOWLEY BUT SURELEY.

SO ONCE TOM TOLD ME THIS STORY ABOUT HIS WIFE WHO LIVES THERE NAMED HIPPIE CAROL. HIPPIE CAROL WAS FRIENDS TOO BUT I NOTICED DIDNT GET ALONG WITH TOM. TOM TOLD ME THEY WERE STILL TOGETHER WHEN IN REALITY THEY WERE BROKEN UP. TOM WAS LIEING BECAUSE HE REALLY THOUGHT SINSE HE STILL WAS LIVING THERE THAT HE WAS WITH HIPPIE CAROL.

ONCE TOM TOLD ME THE GUY WITH HER IS STELAING HER FROM HIM WHICH IS A LIE. THE TRUTH IS THEY HAVE BEEN DIVORCED FOR A LONG WHILE BUT OOH THE DRUGS HOW THEY CHANGE AND LIE TO PEOPLE.

TOM ASKED ME IF I COULD HELP SHOOT THIS GUY FROM THE TOP OF HIS ROOF ON THE GARAGE. I FOR SOME INSANE REASON SAID OK AND HE HANDED ME A LOADED RIFLE. HE HAD ONE TOO.

WHEN THEY SHOWED UP.

CAROL AND HER NEW BOYFRIEND WERE COMING HOME TO HIPPIE TOMS AND HIPPIE CAROLS. WE WERE POINTING THE RIFLES AT HIS HEAD FROM THE TOP OF THE ROOF AND

TOM TOOK A SHOT BUT IT DIDNT WORK. I THEN REALIZED THAT I AM PART OF A KILLING IF HE WOULD HAVE SHOT HIM , BOYFRIEND OR STEALING TOMS WIFE, EITHER WAY I REALIZED IN MY TWEAKED OUT HEAD THIS IS WRONG. I THEN GAVE THE RIFLE AND JUMPED OFF THE ROOF. THANK GOD THEY HIPPIE TOMS WIFE CAROL AND THE NEW BOYFRIEND NEVER KNEW ABOUT THESE RIFLES POINTING AT THEM. I ONLY POINTED IT AT THE NEW BOYFRIEND AND DIDNT PULL THE TRIGGER. THANK GOD I DIDNT, ALSO TOM FELT BAD LATER ALSO.

ROLAND AND ME WERE TRYING TO QUIT METH AND AS TOM SAW US DOING SO HE DECIDED TO DO SO TOO.

BY 1986 ME AND ROLAND AND HIPPIE TOM WERE ALL OF METH AND BEAT IT BUT STILL METH HAS ALOT OF LONG TERM EFFECTS, ONE BEING LONG TERM DEPRESSION.

NEXT FOR ME AND ROLAND WAS WRITING MORE MUSIC TOGETHER IN 1985, ONE CALLED "77 IT WAS HEAVEN 85 FULL OF JIVE."

ROLAND THEN LEFT FOR AWHILE AS I TOOK CARE OF MY DAD FULL TO ME UNTIL DAD DIED ON SEPTEMBER 11TH 1985.

NOW SEEING ROLAND IN 1986 I HEARD HE LIVED AT THE WESTARM APARTMENTS SO I WENT TO THE ADDRESS AND THERE WAS ROLAND. HE HAD A NEW STAGE NAME CALLED JAY PARSONS AND HE HAD AN ALBUM ENTITLED "ON THE RUN". HE LIVED WITH A GAY MANAGER. I DONT THINK ROLAND WAS IN A RELATIONSHIP WITH THE MAN BECAUSE ROLAND IS TOTALLY NOT GAY.

THIS IS HIS SECOND MANAGER THAT IS GAY. THE FIRST ONE WAS A GUY I GOT HIM NAMED DAVE KNIGHT. DAVE COMMITTED SUICIDE IN THE LATE 80S, SAD TO HEAR IT . I ALWAYS LOVED DAVE KNIGHT. HE WAS A GOOD GUY.

ME AND ROLAND PLAYED MORE MUSIC TOGETHER AND THEN I DIDNT SEE HIM UNTIL 1991.

HE WAS SEEMINGLEY VERY HOMELESS AND LOOKED REAL THIN SO I OFFERED HIM FOOD AND SHOWER AND A BED AND HE TOOK IT. HE THEN LEFT VERY FAST.

I SEE HIM AGAIN IN 1992 AND HE IS GOING WITH ME TO THE FOUNDATION LIKE YEARS BEFORE BUT THIS TIME WE COULDNT MAKE IT BECAUSE THEY HAD IT BARB WIRE FENCED OFF.

IN 1992 AS I BOUGHT HIM A COUPLE SIX PACKS HE AGAIN BLACKED OUT AND GOT VIOLENT AND AGAIN STARTED CALLING ME PUNK.

I DITCHED HIM AND I DID FOLLOW HIM HOME FROM A DISTANCE TO MAKE SURE HE WAS OK AND NOT CAUSING TROUBLE WITH ANYONE BUT MADE SURE HE MADE IT TO THE GRAYHOUND BUS AND WHEN I SAW HE MADE IT TO THE GRAYHOUND BUS I THEN GAVE HIM 40 DOLLORS FOR THE PURPOSE OF HIM GOING TO HIS NEXT DESTINATION.

NOW I DONT SEE HIM UNTIL 2000.

AT THIS TIME HE CAME OVER PORTRAYING HE WAS HOMELESS BUT BEING BILLY BRAGG IN ENGLAND HE IS LIVING A QUITE DIFFERENT LIFE.

I HAVE A 240 SX NISSAN AND JUST BOUGHT IT AND DONT HAVE INSURANCE YET FOR IT BECAUSE I HAVE A SUSPENDED LICENCE BECAUSE I HAD 4 TICKETS IN 1 YEAR OF TIME.

ME AND ROLAND TAKE A CHANCE AND WE GO TO THE MOUNTAINS AND THIS IS WHERE I BUY ROLAND SOME BEER. I BUY HIM ONLY A QUART SO HE DOESNT GO CRAZY

LIKE HE ALWAYS DOES WHEN HE HAS ALL THE ALCOHOL HE CAN DRINK.

SO I AM LIMITING THIS AMOUNT OF ALCOHOL FOR HIM.

WE LISTEN TO MY MUSIC I DID IN THE 90S THAT HE HASNT HEARD YET-HE LOVED IT AND COMPLEMENTED ME VERY WELL.

I THOUGHT MAYBE NOW HE IS NOT GOING TO GET VIOLENT AND HE DOENST AND THAT NIGHT I SNEAK HIM INTO THE HOUSE AND HE STAYS A COULPE DAYS AND NIGHTS HE SAYS HE DOESNT HAVE A GUITAR AND ASKS IF HE CAN HAVE ONE OF MINE AND I TOLD HIM THAT EACH ONE OF MY GUITARS I NEED, ONE ACOUSTIC FOR PRACTICE AND ONE ACOUSTIC FOR SHOWS AND ONE ELECTRIC FOR PRACTICE AND ONE ELECTRIC FOR SHOWS AND SO HE REALLY WANTED TO GET A GUITAR FROM ME AND I AM SORRY I COULDNT GIVE HIM ONE.

SO NEXT HE SET AN APPOINTMENT TO PLAY SOME MUSIC WITH ME FOR THE FIRST TIME IN OVER 10 YERS WITH ME.

COMING OVER THE NEXT DAY.

THE NEXT DAY HE CAME OVER SO DRUNK HE WAS FALLING OVER HIMSELF SO I TOOK HIM IN AND GAVE HIM THE DIRECTION TO THE SHOWER. HE LEFT AFTERWARD BECAUSE I TOLD HIM HE CANT COME OVER DRUNK AND I WILL SEE HIM THE NEXT DAY SOBER.

THE NEXT DAY.

HE WAS NOT SOBER BUT NOT YET DRUNK. HE HAD A QUART OF BUDWEISER IN HIS HAND SO I SAID "DUDE TURN AROUND" HE WASNT COMING IN WITH ANY AMOUNT OF ALCOHOL IN HIS BODY OR IN HIS HAND AND IN THIS CASE I DIDNT KNOW HOW MUCH HE HAD DRANK BUT HE TOLD ME

HE ONLY IS GOING TO HAVE 1 QUART AND THAT IS THE SAME QUART IN HIS HAND.

"I JUST DONT BELEIVE YOU ANYMORE AND I THINK YOU MAY KILL ME WHILE IM SLEEPING WHEN YOU ARE BLACKED OUT DRINK AND THEN YOU WAKE UP AND NOT KNOW WHAT HAPPENED".

HE TURNED AROUND AND I SAID "SEE YOU IN 10 YEARS".

HE SAID "OK I CAN DO THAT".

10 YEARS LATER IT WAS AROUND THE YEAR 2010 AND I AM WALKING TO THE LIQUOR STORE AND AS I AM WALKING THERE I SEE A GUY WEARING A BIG BEARD AND I LOOK CLOSER AND IT IS ROLAND. I SAY "HEY ROLAND" HE SAID "IM NOT ROLAND MY NAME IS BILL". I THEN SAY "OH YEAH BILLY BRAGG". HE SAYS NOTHING AND I SAY "IM SORRY FOR KICKING YOU OUT 10 YEARS AGO", HE SAYS "THATS ALRIGHT".

I NEVER SEE HIM IN PERSON AGAIN.

LATER ON I LOOK UP BILLY BRAGG IN THE COMPUTER AND I AM OVERWHELMED WITH WHAT I SEE. I SEE HIM HAVING MADE 11 ESTABLISHED ALBUMS AND PERFORMING ARENAS AND GIANT CONCERTS. I SEE HIM WITH A PROFESSIONAL MANAGEMENT AS WELL AS A PROFESSIONAL RECORD COMPANY. I SEE HIM DOING MANY VIDEOS AND ALL THIS AFTER I LAST SAW HIM.

IF HE WOULD HAVE JUST BEEN HONEST I WOULD HAVE GONE TO EUROPE WITH HIM AND PLAYED GIGS AND BEEN IN A BAND WITH HIM AS I HAVE BEEN BEFORE WITH THE BANDS WE WERE IN TOGETHER. BURRITT AND CONNOR AND THE BAND ONE. I PLAYED OVER 50 SHOWS WITH HIM AND HE HAS DONE OVER 1000 OTHER SHOWS MAYBE EVEN 2000 SHOWS.

AT THIS WRITING HE IS OUT OF MY LEAGUE PROFESSIONALWISE. HE IS MORE SUCCESSFUL THEN ME BUT I AM NOT JEALOUS, IN FACT IM HAPPY FOR HIM. HE HAD A HARD LIFE BEING HOMELESS MOST OF HIS EARLY LIFE.

I SAW ROLAND ON THE BUS A COUPLE TIMES BUT DIDNT FEEL I SHOULD TALK TO HIM. ONE TIME IN 2002 HE GOT ON THE BUS AFTER ME AND MY GIRLFRIEND JULIA GOT ON AND HE SAID HI CHUCK AND HI JULIA, YES HE KNEW JULIA. I GUESS JULIA ROBERT IS FRIENDS WITH BILLY BRAGG.

COMING FROM MEETING HIM IN DECEMBER OR NOVEMBER 1977 TO 2010, I KNEW ROLAND AND THEN AFTER THAT HE WAS BILLY BRAGG TO ME.

ME AND WHEN ROLAND WAS BILLY BRAGG NEVER WERE FRIENDS THOUGH I TRIED BUT I TRIED ON FACEBOOK AND DID IT THROUGH HIS FAN PAGE. AT FIRST I FELT HE WAS GOING TO GRAB ME FROM AMERICA SO WE COULD PLAY TOGETHER BUT THAT WAS NOT TO BE. HE SAID I NEED A SECURITY NUMBER WHICH I GOT AND THEN A MEMBERSHIP CARD WHICH THE NEXT TIME I TRIED TO GET THE CARD HIS DEAL WAS I NEEDED TO PAY 450 DOLLORS AND THOSE WERE AMERICAN DOLLORS TO HIS MANAGEMENT. THIS REMINDED ME OF HOW STUCK UP LEAH REMINI SENT ME TO HER MANAGER OR SHALL I SAW THREW ME UNDER THE BUS TO HIS MANAGER. THIS I KNOW IS THE SAME. ROLAND AKA BILLY BRAGG NOW THINKS HES TOO GOOD TO TALK WITH ME ONE ON ONE.

I WAS WONDERING IF IT WAS BECAUSE I KICKED HIM OUT OF OUR LAST MUSIC PRACTICE APPOINTMENT SO HE IS NOW SETTING AN APPOINTMENT AND TO HUMILIATE ME BY CHARGING ME 400 JUST TO TALK WITH HIM ON A COMPUTER. THROUGH VIDEO CHAT.

I DID NOT PAY IT BECAUSE I DONT TRUST THE SITUATION-

I ALSO TOLD HIM I NEVER SCREWED HIM OVER EVER AND THE ONLY TIME I KICKED HIM OUT OR HAD TO FIGHT HIM WAS BECAUSE HE WAS TRYING TO KILL 2 KIDS AND A WOMAN BLACKED OUT DRUNK AND AGAIN KICKING HIM OUT LAST TIME BECAUSE HE WAS ALWAYS DRUNK AND IMPOSSIBLE TO DEAL WITH WHEN DRUNK.

HE STILL OBVIOUSELEY HOLDS A GRUDGE AND USES HIS EUROPEAN FAME TO SHUN ME AND TO BELEIVE HE IS BETTER THEN ME.

SAD BUT TRUE.

AND THAT IS THE STORY OF BILLY BRAGG AKA ROLAND BURRITT OR YOU CAN SAY THAT IS THE WONDERFUL STORY OF ROLAND BURRITT AKA NOW BILLY BRAGG .

HIS MANAGEMENT AND HIM TELLS ME THAT ITS THE LAW THAT I HAVE TO GIVE 400 DOLLORS TO TALK TO HIM.

THATS SOME B.S. IF I EVER HEARD TRUE B.S. ALL IN ALL I WAS OFFENDED.

58. JANET JACKSON

I MET JANET JACKSON IN 2013 WHILE HANGING OUT IN THE HOOD OF SAN BERNADINO. WE BECAME FRIENDS. I DATED HER A COUPLE TIMES AND TALKED TO HER ON ONE OF HER 8 PHONES. I ASKED WHY SHE HAD SO MANY PHONES AND SHE SAID BECAUSE SHE HAS A PHONE FOR EACH SEPERATE LIFE SHE LEADS.

SO WE TALK AND TEXT AWHILE AND THE I ASK HER IF SHE WANTS TO DO SOME STUDEO WORK ON AN ALBUM AND SHE SAYS OK SO I MEET HER AT A HOTEL IN BERDOO AND SHE DOES TWO SONGS. 1. A SONG NATALEE COLE DID AND 2 . AMAZING GRACE. SHE DID IT ACAPELLA AND SHE

REALLY KNEW HOW TO HOLD THAT MIKE MOVING IT BACK AND FORTH DEPENDING ON HER DYNAMICS OF HER VOICE AT THE TIME.

IT MADE IT EASIER FOR ME NOT TO HAVE TO RE-ENGENEER HER VOICE. T WAS PERFECT THEY WAY SHE DID IT.

LATER WE TALKED AND HUNG OUT AND GOT FOOD. SHE TALKED ABOUT HER BROTHER AND SAYS SHE FEELS DESTINED TO DIE AT 50. AT THIS TIME I BELEIVE SHE WAS IN BETWEEN 45-47 YEARS OLD AND AS YOU SEE SHE IS WRONG FOR SHE IS NOT DEAD AND NOW SHE IS OVER 50.

I TOLD HER THAT HER BROTHER MICHEAL SHOULD HAVE TRIED SARAQUIL LIKE I DO TO GO TO SLEEP AND JANET SAYS "MY BROTHER ATE SARAQUIL LIKE IT WAS CANDY". OH I SAID.

WE GOT INTO AN ARGUMENT LATER THAT DAY BUT STILL REMAINED FRIENDS. ONE TIME SHE ASKED ME IF I WANTED TO GAMBLE WITH HER IN AN UNDERGROUND BERDOO GAMBLING PLACE. I HAD TO GO SOMEWHERE ELSE AND COULDNT ACCOMPANY HER AT THAT TIME. WHEN SHE DRINKS SHE IS A BIT ARGUEMENTATIVE.

AND THE NEXT TIME I TALKED TO HER WE WENT TO A PLACE CALLED CORKYS AND EVERYONE SEEMED TO KNOW HER THERE. SHE ASKED ME "ARE YOU IN REALITY? I ASKED WHAT SHE MEANT. SHE SAID "DONT YOU KNOW WHO YOUR WITH". I SAID YES AND KEPT EATING. EVERYONE THERE WAS STARSTRUCK OF HER AND THIS WAS WHERE SHE FELT MORE COMFORTABLE, AT A MIDDLE CLASS RESTRAUNT. SHE ALSO FELT GOOD IN THE SAN BERNADINO HOOD.

THE LAST TIME I SEE HER.

I GIVE HER A LIFT NEAR WHERE SHE SAYS A RELATIVE IS CONVELESING.

I TOLD HER I ADDED LEAD GUITAR TO HER ACAPELLA AND SHE WAS REALLY INTERESTED IN HEARING IT. I WAS ABOUT TO PUT IT IN MY C.D. PLAYER IN MY CAR AND I TELL HER ONE MORE THING BEFORE I PUT THE SONG IN. I TELL HER I WROTE A SONG CALLED BURN IT DOWN. THIS SONG IS ABOUT THE MICHEAL BROWN CASE OF HIM BEING MURDERED AND I WAS MEANING BURN IT DOWN LIKE BURN DOWN THE POLICE STATION OR THE CITY IN MISSOURI.

JANET TOOK IT TOTALLY THE WRONG WAY. SHE SAID IT WAS RACIST AND STARTED SCREAMING AT ME. II DROPPED HER OFF AND TOLD HER SHE IS SO WRONG THAT I AM ON HER SIDE AND I AM ON THE SIDE OF THE OPPRESEED WHO WAS MURDERED NAMED MICHEAL BROWN.

AND THIS WAS THE LAST TIME I EVER SAW HER IN PERSON.

59. jUAN CROCIER, BASE PLAYER FOR THE ROCK N ROLL 80S BAND RATT.

THERE WAS AN AD IN SCREAMER MAGAZINE WHICH SCREAMER MAGAZINE WAS A LOCAL ROCK N ROLL MAGAZINE ABOUT THE ROCKERS THAT ARE BASICALLY IN THE MINOR LEAUGES. THE MINOR LEAGUES ARE WHEN YOU ARE A BAND THAT HAS SHIOWS AND IS KNOWN THROUGHOUT THE LOS ANGELES CIRCUIT AS WELL AS THE HOLLYWOOD CIRCUIT THAT DOESNT YET HAVE A MAJOR RECORD DEAL. INDY LABELS ARE INVOLVED WITH THE MINOR LEAGUES BUT ITS NOT THE MAJOR LEAGUES UNITL YOU GET A TOUR TO OPEN FOR A MAJOR ACT OR MORE THEN ONE MAJOR ACT AS WELL AS A RECORD DEAL AND THAT IS A MAJOR RECORD DEAL.

JUAN WHEN ME AND LAILAH MET HIM WAS A VERY NICE DOWN TO EARTH PERSON. HIS STUDEO IS LIKE IN A BOTTOM AREA LIKE A BASEMENT OR A LOWER LEVEL OF THE HOUSE.

HE TOLD US HE LIKES THE OLD 456 2 INCH REEL TO REEL TAPES TO RECORD ON. AGREED AND I TOLD HIM RELUCTUNTLEY WE RECORDED ON 3 SEPERATE 8 TRACK DAT MACHINES. I DIDNT LIKE IT AND ME AND JUAN BOTH AGREED WE LIKE THE OPEN AND AIREY QUALITY THAT THE 456 REELS HAVE. THE 456 REELS HAVE ALOT OF SPACE ON THE TWO INCH REELS AND THE 8 TO 24 TRACK COMPUTER DAT MACHINES DONT HAVE THAT VIBE AND SOUND AND FEEL.

WE THEN AUDITIONED HIM AND HE LIKED OUR TAPE AND THEN OFFERED US A PRICE 500 PER DAY AND 500 MORE PER DAY TO USE AND WORK WITH JAKE E LEE.

JUAN SAID HE WOULD ENGENEER AND CO PRODUCE AND WE WANTED TO DO IT BUT DIDNT HAVE 500 DOLLORS.

OR 1000 DOLLORS BUT SURE WANTED JAKE E LEE TO BE ON MY ALBUM,

HE TOLD US HE DIDNT GET ALONG WITH THE GUYS IN RATT AND DOESNT LIKE TO PERFORM THAT MUCH AS WELL AS THE LAST THING I REMEMBER HIM SAYING WAS HE WOULD NEVER PLAY WITH RATT AGAIN.

A LIE

I JUST SAW JUAN ON A COMMERCIAL WITH THE BAND RATT PLAYING IN A LIVING ROOM WITH THE JOKE THAT THERE ARE RATS IN THE HOUSE.

I GUESS JUAN IS BACK WITH THEM.

WE DO A COUPLE SONGS BY RATT ENTITLED "ROUND AND ROUND" AS WELL AS THE SONG
"BACK FOR MORE" IN OUR BAND RELICX.

AND SO THAT WAS THE STORY OF MY DEALINGS WITH JUAN CROCIER THE BASSIST OF RATT.

60. STEVEN PIERCY LEAD VOCALIST OF RATT 61. KIRBY PUCKETT 62 . TED TEMPLEMAN PRODUCER FOR DOOBIE BROTHERS AND VAN HALEN AND HEAD CEO WARNER BROS RECORDS.

STEVEN PIERCY. I WAS OUTSIDE OF THE HOLLYWOOD NIGHTCLUB GAZZARIS AND I WAS IN THERE FOR A SECOND BUT THEY WERE DOING A VIDEO FOR THE BAND RATT. IT WAS PACKED AND IN WENT OUTSIDE AND THERE WAS STEVEN PIERCY OUTSIDE. I SAID HI AND HE SAID HELLO BACK AND I WISHED HIM LUCK ON THE VIDEO. HE ASKED IF I WAS IN A BAND AND WHAT I DO IN THE BAND I TOLD HIM AUTRY ODAY AND WAS LEAD VOCALIST TOO. HE WENT BACK IN AND THAT WAS THE LAST TIME AND ONLY TIME I TALKED TO STEVEN PIERCY.

61. KIRBY PUCKETT.

I WAS EATING A SANDWICH AT THE RESTRAUNT CALLED THE HAT IN UPLAND AND THERE WITH A YOIUNG LADY WAS KIRBY PUCKETT. ASKED HIM IF HE WAS KIRBY PUCKETT AND HE SAID YES. I ASKED HIM IF I COULD GO BACK HOME TO GET SOMETHING HE COULD AUTOGRAPH AND HE SAID YES. IT TOOK MY 30 TO GET BACK TO HIM AND WHEN I GOT BACK HE WAS STILL THERE LIKE HE SAID HE WOULD. HE WAS WAITING JUST FOR ME. HE AUTOGRAPHED A NOLAN RYAN BOOK I HAD THAT WHAT I HAD AT THE TIME LIEING AROUND. HE WAS TOTALLY FRIENDLEY COOL AND HE TOLD ME "I CANT BELEIVE YOU RECOGNISED ME". I SAID "YEAH YOU LOOK LIKE YOURSELF TOTALLY". HE LAUGHED

AND I LAUGHED AND THAT WAS THE LAST TIME I EVER SAW THE HALL OF FAMER KIRBY PUCKETT. HE DIED A COUPLE YEARS LATER UNFORTUNATELEY.

62. TED TEMPLEMAN

I WAS GOING INTO WARNER BROS RECORDS AND THERE WAS TED TEMPLEMAN. HE RECIEVED MY REELS.AND LATER GAVE IT TO HIS SECRATERY TO GIVE TO ME. HE DIDNT CHOOSE ME TO PRODUCE ME. THOUGH I TRIED MANY TIMES THROUGH A LETTER MY ENTERTAINMENT LAWYER HARRY WEISS GOT ME. THE LETTER ASKS TED TEMPLEMAN FOR A CONSIDERATION OF THIS MATERIAL.

HE NEVER GOT BACK TO US BUT I DID MEET HIM ONCE. HE WAS COMING OUT OF WARNER BROS RECORDS AND I WAS GOING IN THROUGH THE BACK WAY AND HE SAID "YA GOT A CUTE SON KID, HE LOOKS LIKE MY GRANDKID". SAID "THANKS".

AND THAT WAS THE LAST TIME AND THE ONLY TIME I EVER TALKED TO TED TEMPLEMAN.

63. DIANA ROSS

I MET DIANA ROSS IN 1991 WHEN I BELEIVE 47 SHE WHEN I MET HER I DIDNT BELEIVE AT FIRST IT WAS HER. AT THIS TIME IN MY LIFE I HAVE NOT MET AN ALREADY FAMOUS PERSON. YES I DID GO OUT AND DATE COURTNEY LOVE AKA MICHELLE HARRISON BEFORE THIS BUT SHE WASNT FAMOUS AS OF THE YEAR 1991 SO DIANA ROSS WAS THE FIRST PERSON I HAD MET WHO WAS FAMOUS AND THAT I DATED. SHE WAS OUT ON INDIAN HILL AND PRACTICING HER ACTING. SHE WAS GOING TO BE IN A MOVIE ABOUT A GIRL WHO LIVES OUT HERE ON INDIAN HILL WHO WAS QUITE FAMOUS HERSELF NAMED JACKEE. I ONCE TALKED TO JACKEE FOR A LONG TIME BECAUSE I JUST GAVE HER TEN TO HELP HER OUT AND SHE TOLD ME SHE IS

COMFORTABLE OUTSIDE BECAUSE SHE WAS GANG RAPED WHEN SHE HAD APARTMENT. JACKEE ALWAYS STAYED OUTSIDE AND I HAVE SEEN PEOPLE INVITE HER TO LIVE WITH THEM AND SHE TURNED THEM DOWN BEING COMFORTABLE ONLY OUTSIDE BECAUSE OF THE TRAUMA OF THE GANG RAPE THAT HAPPENED TO HER BEFORE.

JACKEE BECAME A FRIEND AND DIANA ROSS IS PORTRAYING HER IN A MOVIE ABOUT A GIRL NAMED JACKEE WHO IS SKITZOPHRENIC.

SO I SEE HER SITTING ON THE BUS STOP WHERE JACKEE IS USUALLY AROUND AND I SAY TO HER "YOU LOOK EXACTRLELY LIKE DIANA ROSS AND SHE SMILES. SHE ASKS ME "ARE YOU A SPECIAL AGENT?. II DIDNT KNOW WHAT SHE WAS TALKING ABOUT BUT FOUND OUT LATER WHAT SHE MEANT.

SHE MEANT AM I A BODY GUARD FROM A FAR WATCHING OUT FOR HER SAFETY.

I DONT REMEMBER WHAT I SAID WHEN SHE ASKED ME THAT BUT I DO REMEMBER I DIDNT SAY I WAS.

I THEN TRY TO KISS HER AND SHE SORT OF LETS ME. I DID THIS BECAUSE I THOUGHT SHE WAS A DIANA ROSS LOOKALIKE-AND THOUGHT THIS UNTIL I SAW THE MOVIE SHE MADE AND I SAID THAT IS HER CHARACTER SHE WAS PLAYING OUT THERE.

A COUPLE DAYS LATER I SEE HER AGAIN AND THIS TIME ON MISSION BLVD RIGHT BY THE DONUT SHOP IN THE HOOD AND THIS TIME SHE IS SORT OF WILD AND FREE. IT WAS AMAZING.

SHE JUMPS IN MY CAR AND WE HAVE ROMANCE AND THAT IS AS FAR AS I WILL SAY.

I WAS LIKE EVERYONE ELSE. I THOUGHT WHY WOULD DIANA ROSS BE OUT HERE IN POMONA.

ANSWER, ITS CALLED METHOD ACTING AND SHE HAD TO FEEL THE AREA AND FEEL THE JACKEE SITUATION AND SINSE THEN MANY OTHERS THAT ARE ACTORS I HAVE SEEN OUT IN THE HOOD AND IN THE STREET.

AND ALL THE WOMEN I AM TALKING ABOUT WILL BE WRITTEN ABOUT IN THIS BOOK. THE TRUTH AND NOTHING BUT THE TRUTH.

64, 65 AND 66.

JESSICA ALBA AND MICKY ALBA AND STEVE ALBA.

LETS START WITH JESSICA ALBA. A LONG TIME AGO AND I DONT REMEMBER WHEN BUT I HEARD A GIRL TALKING TO ME IN MY CAR ABOUT A FUTURE MOVIE STAR NAM ED JESSICA ALBA AND I KEPT HEARING THE NAME OVER AND OVER FROM THE STREETS OF POMONA. JESSICA USED TO LIVE IN POMONA AND SHE WENT TO CLAREMONT HIGH SCHOOL AND BEFRIENDED MR. MARTINEZ WHO IS A PHOTOGRAPHY TEACHER. I HAVE JESSICA ON MY FACEBOOK PAGE ON MY COMPUTER.

I MET HER IN AND AROUND 2005. WE HUNG OUT AND SHE WAS HANGING OUT IN POMONA. HER RELATIVES TOLD ME SHE TAKES A BREAK AND VISITS FAMILY IN THE WINTER. I LET HER DRIVE MY CAR WHIICH SHE FOUND FUN. ANOTHER TIME I SAW HER IN FRONT OF THE LIQUOR STORE IN POMONA AND REALIZED I DIDNT HAVE TIME TO TALK TO HER SO I MISSED THAT OPPORTUNITY TO TALK AND HANG OUT WITH HER.

I THEN HUNG OUT WITH JESSICA A COUPLE TIMES MORE AND THEN THE LAST TIME I SAW HER WAS AT STARBUCKS

IN CLAREMONT WHERE SHE WAS LOOKING DISAPPOINTED AT ME AND I DONT KNOW WHY.

MICKY AND STEVE ALBA.

I SKATEBOARDED WITH BOTH OF THEM AT THE PIPELINE SKATEPARK BACK IN THE LATE 70S. I SKATED POOLS WITH THEM AND WAS IN COMPETITIONS WITH THEM IN SKATEBOARD CONTESTS AND I DONT REALLY REMEMBER CONVERSATING WITH THEM BUT I DID SKATE WITH THEM AND TALKED SMALL TALK. OF COURSE IT IS HARD TO REMEMEBR BEING THIS WAS OVER 42 YEARS AGO.

I REMEMBERED THEY WERE QUITE TALENTED SKATEBOARDERS ESPECIALLY IN THE ART OF SKATING POOLS.

67. SAUNDRA BULLICK

I MET SAUNDRA THE SAME WAY I MET ALOT OF THESE ACTRESSES WHO GO OUT PRACTICING THEIR METHOD ACTING LIKE DIANA ROSS AS WELL AS KATE HUDSON, BRIDGETTE FONDA AMONG MANY OTHERS I HAVE MET LIKE HALLE BERRY AND JULIA ROBERTS. THEY ARE ALL INFACTUATED WITH SOMETHING I HATE, THE STREETS. AND BELEIVE ME IF YOU EVER REALLY BEEN IN AND SUFFERED IN THE STREETS YOU WOULD NOT GLORIFY THE STREETS BUT THEY DO BECAUSE IT IS A CHANGE FROM PAPARAAZZI AND STAR STRUCK PEIOPLE ARE NOT AROUND THIS AREA CALLED THE INLAND EMPIRE.

OH YEAH I USED TO FIND THE STREET LIFE COOL UNTIL I WAS JUMPED IN AN ALLEY AND ALSO RIPPED OFF 938 DOLLORS AT 7-11 PARKING LOT GYPSY STYLE A S WELL AS JUMPED ON A BUS, MACED IN A PARKING LOT IN THE STREETS AND JUMPED AT SUPERIOR MARKET IN AN ETHNIC AREA.

NO I HATE THE STREETS NOW BUT THESE ACTORS LKE THE STREET BECAUSE AND SO THEY CAN REMAIN AWAY FROM THE SPOTLIGHT AND THEIR SOCIETY FAME. STREET PEOPLE ARE NOT LIKE THE AVERAGE STARSTRUCK CITIZEN. THEY DONT WATCH T.V, THE HOMELESS THAT IS AND BECAUSE THEY ARE HOMELESS SO THEY WONT BE ABLE TO IDENTIFY THESE PEOPLE AND ONE CALLED SAUNDRA BULLICK.

I FIRST MET SAUNDRA THE DAY AFTER I CAME BACK FROM SEATTLE FOR 2 WEEKS. I SAW HER AND WE HUNG OUT. SHE WAS COOL AND DOWN TO EARTH AND WE WERE FRIENDS.

YEARS LATER I THEN SEE HER AGAIN AT WOLFS MARKERT WHICH IS A RICH PERSONS AREA AND A SNOOTY MARKET. AN INDY AND MOM AND POP BASIC STORE. I BUMP RIGHT INTO SAUNDRA BULLICK AND SHE IS LIKING THE WAY WE BUMPED INTO EACH OTHER UNTIL SHE KNEW I KNEW WHO SHE WAS. SHE THEN FREAKED OUT AND LEFT AND ALSO SHE HAD BLONDE HAIR SO NO ONE BELEIVED ME BECAUSE SAUNDRA DIDNT HAVE BLONDE HAIR BUT THEN THEY FOUND OUT SHE WAS DOING A MOVIE CALLED "THE BLINDE SIDE" AND SHE HAD BLONDE HAIR. THIS IS WHY SHE HAD BLONDE HAIR. THE WAY WE BUMPED INTO EACH OTHER WAS LIKE THE MOVIES AND WE ALMOST KNOCKED EACH OTHER DOWN WE BUMPED SO HARD AND SHE SMILED AND LIKE IT. I BELEIVE SHE DID THIS ON PURPOSE. SHE LIKED THE WAY WE BUMPED INTO EACH OTHER BECAUSE IT IS LIKE HOW THEY BUMP INTO EACH OTHER IN A MOVIE.

AND THEN IVE SEEN HER AT A GAS STATION AND A MALL.

AND THIS IS MY STORY OF SUNDRA BULLICK. SHE WAS MELLOW AND PRETTY DOWN TO EARTH EXCEPT WHEN

SHE ACTED WEIRD WHEN I RECOGNISED HER AT WOLFS MARKET.

68. NIKKI SIXX AND 69. TOMMIE LEE BOTH IN THE BAND MOTLEY CRUE, TOMMIE IS THE DRUMMER AND NIKKI SIZXX THE BASSIST.

I FIRST MET TOMMY LEE AT CHARTER OAK HIGH SCHOOL. WE WERE PLAYING A SHOW IN 1980 FOR 3 HIGH SCHOOLS. AFTER THE SHOW TOMMIE TOLD ME HE REALLY LIKED THE SOUND AND HOW I LOOKED THE PART OF RONNIE VAN ZANT, THE SINGER OF LYNYRD SKYNYRD.I WAS IN THIS BAND CALLED "NOTHIN FANCY. NOTHIN" FANCY WAS THE NAME OF LYNYRD SKYNYRDS FIRST ALBUM AND WE DID 90 PERCENT LYNYRD SKYNYRD AS WELL AS 10 PERCENT OTHER SOUTHERN ROCK LIKE THE EAGLES AND NEIL YOUNG, MOLLY HATCHET AND THE OUTLAWS SONG ENTITLED "GREEN GRASS AND HIGH TIDES". VERY TALENTED KIDS AND ONE THER BASSIST WAS 15 THE DRUMMER 16 THE GUITARIST NUMBER 1 WAS 17 AND THE SECOND GUITARIST 18 AND I WAS 19. THE OLDEST. THIS WAS 1980 IN THE BEGENNING OF SUMMER IN JUNE OR LATE MAY.

TOMMIE EVEN TOLD ME HE LIKED HOW I WAS BAREFOOT LIKE RONNIE VAN ZANT DOES. I TOLD TOMMIE I DID IT TO RESPECT THE LATE GREAT FANTASTIC VOCALS AND PERSONNA OF RONNIE VAN ZANT. THIS WAS IN 1980,

I MET TOMMIE A SECOND TIME AND HE WAS WITH NIKKI SIXX WHICH ISNT HIS REAL NAME BUT TOMMIES NAME IS REAL. THEY HAD A HOUSE THEY WERE AT ON RAMONA AVENUE IN   MONTCLARE AND THEY WERE AUDITIONING VOCALISTS. WE DID STAIRWAY TO HEAVEN AND THE AUDITION DIDNT GO TO WELL BUT ME AND TOMMIE HAD ALREADY KNEW EACH OTHER. I DIDNT WORK OUT WITH THEM. THAT WAS THE ONLY TIME I MET NIKKI

SIXX., I REMEMBER THEY HAD TONS OF BEER CANS STACKED UP IN A PYRIMID TO THE CEALING. THIS WAS IN 1981 OR LATER 1980. DONT REALLY KNOW FOR SURE.

THE NEXT TIME I MET TOMMIE WAS AT BANDS WEST STUDEOS. WE WERE PRACTICING THAT NIGHT AND IN THE NEXT ROOM TOMMIE WAS SIGNING AUTOGRAPHS AND I WENT IN THERE AND TALKED TO HIM AFTER HE WAS DONE SIGNING AUTOGRAPHS FOR THE FANS OF HIM AND HIS BAND MOTLEY CRUE. THIS WAS IN 1988. AFTER HE WAS DODNE SIGNING AUTOGRAPHS WE TALKED WHILE.

THE NEXT TIME I SEE TOMMIE IS IN JAIL. I AM IN THERE FOR A FALSE ARREST OF ARMED ROBBERY AND TERRORIST THREATS WHICH ALL I DID WAS ASK FOR MONEY AND WHEN SHE CALLED ME A BUM I GAVE HER THE MIDDLE FINGER WHICH TECHINCALLY IS A TERRORIST THREAT. AND THE LADY WHO GAVE ME A DOLLOR, LIED AND SAIDS I GRABBED IT BACK WHICH WAS THE CASE OF ARMED ROBBERY. ACCORDING TO A PSYCHO COP FROM UPLAND WHO IS 21 YEARS OLD AND OVER ZEALOUS AND WANTS TO GET SOMEONE FOR A FELONY. CRAZY. I TALKED TO TOMMIE WHO WAS BEING TRANSFERED FROM TENNESSEE I BELEIVE, NOT SURE. THIS WAS IN 2000 OR 2001.

THE NEXT TIME I SEE TOMMIE WAS IN SAN DIMAS. ON THE BORDER OF SAN DIMAS AND GLENDORA WHICH WAS HIS YOUTH STOMPING GROUNDS.. HE WAS ON A MOTOR CYCLE AND DRIVING SLOW NEXT TO ME AND LAILAH. THIS WAS IN 2019.

AND THE LAST TIME I SAW TOMMIE LEE WAS WHEN I WAS IN SAN DIMAS AND HE WAS BEHIND ME ON HIS MOTORCYCLE AGAIN. HE PASSED ME AND I WAVED AND NODDED AND HE WAVED AND NODDED BACK. THIS WAS IN 2020.

ALSO IN 1990 I WAS WORKING ON THE SET OF THE DOORS MOVIE WHICH T THAT TIME WAS THE

ALL IN ALL TOMMIE IS A COOL NICE PERSON AND A DOWN TO EARTH DUDE.

I HOPE TO SEE HIM AGAIN AND BE FRIENDS WITH HIM FOR ALWAYS.

COOL TO SAY HI OR BECOMING FRIENDS TOO EVEN DO DRUMMING FOR ME HOPEFULLY ONE DAY.

OH YES I FORGOT I SAW TOMMIE LEE AT THE MAKING OF THE DOORS MOVIE AT THE OLYMPIC AUDITORIUM. HE ASKED ME IF I WANTED TO SMOKE A JOINT AND I SAID NO BECAUSE I WAS AN ADDICT THAT HAS QUIT ALL FORMS OF ALCOHOL, CIGERETTES AND DRUGS. HE WAS NOTICEBLEY UPSET AND I THINK IT IS BECAUSE HE DIDNT BELEIVE ME AND THOUGHT I WAS USING IT AS AN EXCUSE BUT THE TRUTH WAS IS THAT I WAS QUITTING AT THE TIME AND WAS IN SOBRIETY.

RECENTLEY A COUPLE TIMES I HAVE SEEN TOMMIE ON HIS MOTORCYCLE DRIVING THROUGH SAN DIMAS AND GLENDORA. I WAVED TO HIM AND HE WAVED BACK.

70. BORIS MIDNEY AND 71. POP ROCK AKA RON BRADY.

BORIS MIDNEY WAS A PRODUCER AND OWNED A MASTERING LAB IN THE SAN FERNANDO VALLEY DOWN THE STREET FROM HOWARD ROSEN THE OLD OWNER OF CASABLANCA RECORDS. BORIS TOLD ME FIRST HE WAS GAY ANDI DIDNT CARE. ALL I CARED WAS IS IF HE CAN MASTER THIS MUSIC OF MINE FOR THE ALBUJM BADDCLOWN 2 WHICH WAS 15 SONGS IN ALL.

WE WORKED TOGETHER FIVE DAYS IN ERO AND HE GAVE ME A GOOD DEAL OF 500 FOR THE WHOLE THING WHICH

WAS 100 PER DAY WHICH WAS A GREAT BARGAIN PRICE..
HE LIKED MY MUSIC AND SAID HE WOULD GO TO BAT FOR
ME AT WARNER BROS RECORDS AND BE MY PRODUCER
ON MY NEXT MUSIC AND ATTEMPT TO GET ME A GOOD
RECORD DEAL.

HE ALSO BOUGHT SOME LYRICS OFF ME THAT I HAD
WRITTEN 100 DOLLORS FOR 10 LYRICS. I GAVE HIM A DEAL
AND ALSO WHEN HE WENT HE SAID HE WAS WITH 13
PEOPLE AND THE DEAL WAS IS THAT 6 PEOPLE VOTED YES
FOR ME TO HAVE A RECORD DEAL AND 7 AGAINST. YES,, I
LOST A RECORDING CONTRACT FROM WARNER BROS BY 1
VOTE 7 TO 6. AFTER BORIS FINISHED MY ALBUM AND EQ
MASTERING IT, HE LEFT QUICKELY TO EUROPE AND I
NEVER HEARD FROM HIM AGAIN.

BORIS WAS THE PRODUCER OF THE EVIDA SOUNDTRACK.
HE TOLD ME AND I SAW MANY OF HIS GOLD AND PLATINUM
RECORDS.

71. RON BRADY, A.K.A. POP ROCK.

RON WAS IN A BAND CALLED THE BUMBLE BEES OR KILLER
BEES OR SOMETHING TO DO WITH BEES IN THE MID 1960S.
AS RON BECAME IN HIS 50S HE STARTED A TV SHOW ON
CABLE CALLED POP ROCKS HOLLYWOOD SHOWCASE FOR
BANDS.

I WANTED TO GET ON THE SHOW. THE SHOW WAS FOR
BASICALLY BANDS ANYWHERE THAT WANTS TO GET
FILMED. THE SHOWS WERE AT THE GREEN DOOR, A
NIGHTCLUB IN MONTCLARE THAT SADLEY ISNT THERE
ANYMORE AND HAS BEEN TORN DOWN FOR REPLACEMENT
STORES LIKE CLOTHING STORES ETC.

THIS WAS A LEGENDARY SPOT AND IS PART OF THE TOUR
OF THE CHITLIN CIRCUIT. THE CHITLIN CIRCIUT IS A
LEGENDARY OLD TOUR ROUTE THAT ALL THE GREAT

BLACK PEOPLE AS WELL AS JOHNNY CASH AND ELVIS PRESLEY USED TO TAKE. AS WELL AS WILLIE NELSON TOO.

POP WOULD SET UP 4 CAMERAS AND I GOT ALONG GREAT WITH POP ALMOST ALL THE TIME. HE IS REAL DOWN TO EARTH AND HIS SHOW FOR BANDS THAT HAVENT YET MADE IT BIG WAS THE ONLY SHOW OUT THERE AT THAT TIME AND WAS ON CHANNELL 56 KDOC.

RON AKA POP ROCK WAS A GREAT GUY AND A SHOW BUSINESS GUY. I REMEMBER FIRST SEEING HIM HE WAS HAPPILY SETTING UP CAMERAS FOR DIFFERENT PARTS OF THE STAGE SCENES.

THE FIRST SHOW WE DID WAS GREAT AND WE WERE DRESSED TO OUR BEST. WE WERE ROCKED OUT AND THIS WAS THE END OF THE HOLLYWOOD SCENE.

BUT RON WAS TRYING TO KEEP IT GOING.

BILL GAZZARI DIED, THE OWNER OF THE NIGHT CLUB GAZZARIS. RON TOOK OVER THE PART AND WAS OUTSIDE OF THE CLUB BRINGING PEOPLE IN. EARLIER THAT DAY WE DID A VIDEO SESSION WITH RON.

THERE WAS A CONTEST FOR THIS SHOW ENTITLED HOLLYWOOD SHOWCASE FOR BANDS WITH POP ROCK AND WE GOT SECOND PLACE. THE BAND NO DOUBT WAS THERE AND WE ACTUALLY BEAT THEM. I DONT REMEMBER WHO WON FIRST PLACE BUT WE GOT 2ND AT A SHOW AT A PLACE CALLED FENDERS BALLROOM IN LONG BEACH- BASICALLY A PUNK ROCK SCENE THERE BUT WE PLAYED THERE AND WAS FILMED THERE ALSO.

AS WE GOT SECOND PLACE WE WON A VIDEO AS WELL AS 50 DOLLORS. THE 500 CAME QUICKER THEN THE VIDEO. THIS WAS PREFORMED AT FENDERS BALLROOM IN LONG BEACH CALIFORNIA.

WE SHOT THE VIDEO AT THE MT BALDY PIPELINE AND IT WAS GREAT AS WE HAD A CAST OF ABOUT 12 PEOPLE INCLUDING THE 4 BAND MEMBERS WHICH AT THE TIME WAS AUTRY ODAY.

WE FILMED ON THE SPILLWAY WHICH WAS REAL STEEP AND FILMED AT THE PIPE WHICH WAS RANKED GREATEST NATURAL SKATEBOARD SPOT EVER IN SKATEBOARDER MAGAZINE.

WE SPRAY PAINTED VARIOUS WORDS THAT RELATED TO THE VIDEO WHICH WE MADE WHICH WAS A VIDEO CALLED AS SAMMY SAID.

PHRASES LIKE "RAP WAKE UP TO ROCK" AND "REALIZE WARS A FIGHT" AND "LONG TIME COMING"

RON LIKED OUR VIDEO IDEAS.

BY THE END OF THE FINISHING OF THIS VIDEO IT WAS 1992.

RON UNFORTUNATELEY HAD TO CANCEL THE SHOW. HE SAID IT WOULD ONLY BE TEMPORARY BUT HE NEVER HAD THE SHOW AGAIN.

WE WENT TO PARAMONT AND TRIED TO EDIT THE VIDEO WITH ME AND LAILAH PRODUCING IT AND RON GIVING IDEAS TOO. THIS WAS THE LAST TIME I WILL EVER SEE RON. RON NEVER FINISHED THE VIDEO AND I HAD TO BEG HIM FOR THE FOOTAGE. WE STARTED THE VIDEO FROM A GUY NAMED MIKE MANDAVILLLE AND HIS WIFE BEING CHARGED 20 DOLLORS AN HOUR AT THE RECORDING STUDEO OF BEACH RECORDING WHICH WAS WHERE WE SIGNED AN INDY LABLEL RECORD CONTRACT. I BEGGED RON TO GET IT TO ME AND SO HE FINALLY DID AND KEVIN DEREK FINISHED THE VIDEO IN 1996 SO THE VIDEO STARTED IN 1988 AND FINISHED IN 1996. IT WAS EXCITING

SEEING US ON KDOC ON TV FOR THE FIRST TIME IN MY LIFE.

AND THAT IS THE STORY OF POP ROCK AKA RON BRADY, MY GOOD OL FRIEND.

72, 73 ,74, 75-DARVEY OF DARVEY SHOWCASE FOR BAND , PAUL RODGERS AND BOZ BURRELL AND THE BAND CALLED THE KNACK.

72. DARVEY SHOWCASE FOR BAND.

DARVEY WAS A GREAT GUY AND I DID AN INTERVIEW WITH HIM AND WAS BLESSED TO BE ON HIS SHOW ON KDOC 56. I USED TO WATCH THE SHOW EVERY WEEK AND IT WAS FROM ANAHEIM.

I WANTED TO GET ON THE SHOWS. WHEN I WATCHED THE SHOWS I SAW ALOT OF TALENTED UNKNOWN ARTISTS THAT WERE SEEKING A RECORDING CONTRACT.

I CALLED UP ANED THEY WANTED PROOF THAT I WAS A MUSICIAN SO I PUT CAMERA ON THE EDGE OF MY KEYBOARD AND I MADE TJHE AUDITION, PRAISE THE LORD THE FATHER, SON AND HOLY SPIRIT.

THE SHOW.

ME AND LAILAH AND MY DAUGHTER AND ME WENT TO IN N OUT BURGER DOWN THE STREET AND MY DAUGHTER CHEYENNE ALSO GOT ON THE SHOW,

MOM WENT AND IT WAS A GREAT TIME FOR ALL-VERY PROFESSIONAL AND A BEAUTIFUL STUDEO. MY DAUGHTER DID HER DANCE FIRST AND THEN I DID MY SONG FREE. THIS SONG FREE I ALSO DID A DUET WITH A KID NAMED MISHON RATLIFF WHO WAS ON A SHOW CALLED LINCOLN HEIGHTS.

FREE IS A FAVORITE BY EVERYONE WHO HAS LISTENED TO IT-AND THIS WAS THE SONG IN WHICH I HAVE IN MY SET IN MY NEW CHRISTIAN BAND ENTITLED "LAST RIDE". EVEN A POTENTIAL MANAGER WHO HEARD MY LAST ALBUM ON THE BAND "LAST RIDE' PICKED OUT OF 15 SONGS TO PICK FROM THE SONG FREE AS THE ONE HE WANTED TO WORK ON FIRST AS THE FIRST SINGLE AND FOR THE FIRST VIDEO.

LAILAH MY MANAGER WENT AND THE FOUR OF US AFTERWARDS WENT TO A CHINEESE RESTRAIUNT THAT WAS A FAVORITE AND WE HAD A DELICIOUS MEAL.

MOM LATER WENT A WEEK LATER WITH ME AND WE CELEBRATED HER 90TH BIRTHDAY AND REALLY SHE WAS 91 BUT WE CELEBRATED HER BIRTHDAY LATE.

DARVEY THEN DID AN INTERVIEW WITH US AS WE HAD TO COME BACK FOR THIS INTERVIEW BUT WHAT WAS FUNNY WAS THE INTERVIEW WENT ON FIRST BEFORE THE PIANO SONG AND THE DANCE MY DAUGHTER DID. CHEYENNE ALSO DID AN INTERVIEW TOO AND WAS SORT OF SHY BUT IT WAS CUTE . SHE WAS AROUND 10 OR 11. CHEYENNE HAD BEEN IN DANCE CLASS SINSE SHE WAS 4 YEARS OLD SINSE 1999 AND NOW IT IS AROUND 2006 OR 2007. CHEYENNE DID THE DANCE PERFECT ON THE FIRST TAKE AND I TOO DID THE SONG FREE ON THE FIRST TAKE.

SO I BELEIVE SHE WAS AROUND 12 OR 11.

WE WATCHED IT ASND CHEYENNE HAD NEVER SEEN HERSELF ON TV BEFORE. IT WAS REAL FUN.

I BELEIVE THE SHOW ENDED THE NEXT YEAR AND IT WAS TOO BAD BECAUSE THERE WASNT ANYTHING LIKE THAT BEING INTERVIEW BY DARVY WHO ALSO IS A GOOD SINGER AND SINGS AS A REGULAR AT A BAR FEATURED DARVY IN ANAHEIM. I BELEIVE IT WAS IN ANAHEIM WHERE DARVY

WORKED AT AS A LOUNGE SINGER AND HE REALLY WAS QUITE A CROONER.

74. AND 75. PAUL RODGERS AND BOZ BURRELL BOTH OF THE BAND BAD COMPANY.

THIS WAS IN JEAN NEVADA AT THE GOLDSTRIKE HOTEL AND CASINO.

IT WAS THE GREAT SINGER PAUL RODGERS AND THE BASSIST OF THR BAND BOZ BURRELL. I WAS IN FRONT OF THE EATING AREA AND THEY COME UP TO ME AND TALKED SMALL TALK. THEY ASKED ME IF I WANT TO SIT AT THE RESTRAUNT WITH THEM AND HAVE A CIGERETTE AND I TOLD THEM I DONT SMOKE AND THAT WAS IT. WE TALKED A BIT MORE AND THAT WAS IT.

76. THE KNACK.

ME AND MY OLD FRIEND ROBERT MORENO WENT TO SEE THE BAND THE KNACK IN SUMMER OF 1979. I REMEMBER HOW MUCH I LOVED THE SONG MY SHARONA AND ALOT OF OTHERS DID TOO. THE KNACK WAS ESPECIALLY LOVED IN CALIFORNIA AND THE PLACE WHERE WE SAW THE BAND AT WAS ROYCE HALL AT UCLA. ME AND ROBERT REALLY ENJOYED THE CONCERT AND REMEMBER THE BAND BEFORE THE KNACK CAME ON CALLED THE RUBBLE CITY REBELS. THEY WERE BOOED NOT BECAUSE THEY WERE BAD BUT BECAUSE THE AUDIENCE WANTED AND CAME TO SEE THE KNACK.

AFTER THE SHOW WAS OVER WE JUST CASUALY HOPPED UP ON THE STAGE AND WENT TO THE BACKSTAGE AREA WHERE WE MET AND CHATTED WITH THE SINGER OF THE KNACK AND THE OTHER PLAYERS IN THE BAND TOO.

LATER ON IN MY LIFE WE OPENED FOR THE KNACK AT TOPPERS CAFE IN LA VERNE SAN DIMAS AREA IN

SOUTHERN CALIFORNIA.. I REMEMBER THE SINGER BEING REAL NICE AND FRIENDLEY AND DOWN TO EARTH AND GAVE US ALL THE TIME WE NEEDED TO TALK TO HIM AND THEM.

GOOD FOLKS THE GUYS IN THE KNACK WERE.

77. PAT TRAVERS-- GUITARIST

WE OPENED UP FOR PAT TRAVERS AT MONOPOLIES NIGHTCLUB IN RIVERSIDE. THE CLUB IS NOT THERE ANYMORE BUT THIS WAS 1989 AND WE FIRST PLAYED AND THEN AFTERWARDS I TALKED TO PAT IN THE BACKSTAGE. HE WAS SNORTING COCAINE AND HE HAD A SONG CALLED "SNORTING WHISKY AND DRINKING COCAINE" AND HAD A SONG CALLED "BOOM BOOM OUT GOES THE LIGHTS-". I REMEMBER HEARING THAT SONG PLAY REGULARLEY IN 1979 IN SOUTHERN CALIFORNIA AND IT WAS A GREAT SONG AND PAT WAS NAMED BEST NEW ARTIST OF 1979 FOR ROCK N ROLL AND NOW 10 YEARS LATER IN 1989 WE ARE OPENEING UP FOR HIM. OUR GUITARIST SHOWED UP PAT AND SO THE SOUND MAN WHO WAS RUNNING THE BOARD FOR BOTH BANDS SABATOSHED OUR BAND TRYING TO MAKE RAUEL WHO WAS OUR GUITARIST LOOK NOT AS GOOD TO MAKE PAT LOOK BETTER. IT DIDNT WORK PAT WAS STILL BEATEN BY OUR GUITARIST RAUEL "CHINA" RANOA.

I HAD A GUY IN THE BAND NAMED PAT AND I REMEMBER THE TWO PATS TALKING BACKSTAGE. SAYING HELLO IM PAT AND MY PAT SAYING HELLO IM PAT, IT WAS FUNNY.

IN THE SHOW PAT TRAVERS KNOCKED OUT ALL THE LIGHTS ON STAGE TO MAKE THE SONG BE COOLER WHEN HE PERFORMED THE SONG BOOM BOOM OUT GOES THE LIGHTS.

THAT WAS THE ONE AND ONLY TIME I EVER MET AND OPENED UP FOR PAT TRAVERS.

78. DAVID BOWIE

I MET DAVID BOWIE ON MANY DIFFERENT OCCASIONS.

1. I WAS AT A CLUB/RESTRAUNT NAMED DON JOSES AND IT WAS IN MONTCLARE CALIFORNIA AND WHEN I WENT IN I SEE AN OLD FRIEND AND A GUY WHO I WORKED WITH IN HIS 24 TRACK RECORDING STUDEO. HIS NAME IS BOB DIRE AND HE OWNED THE RECORDING STUDEO ENTITLED WINETREE RECORDING STUDEOS.

I USED HIS STUDEO IN 1983 WHICH WAS THE FIRST TIME I USED 24 TRACK THOUGH I HAVE DONE STUDEO WORK IN A HOME STUDEO BEFORE ENTITLED A 4 TRACK BY MIKE CORRIERE BACK IN 1982. THAT WAS MY FIRST PROFESSIONAL RECORDING STUDEO I HAD WORKED IN.

I SEE A GUY WHO LOOKS EXACTELEY LIKE DAVID BOWIE AND EVERYONE IS TELLING ME THERE IS A GUY WHO LOOKS EXACTELEY LIKE DAVID BOWIE. BEING AT THIS TIME IN 1987 I HADNT RAN ACROSS A WHOLE LOT OF FAMOUS PEOPLE OR MUSICIANS AT THAT TIME BEING THIS WAS IN 1987 BEFORE I MET COURTNEY LOVE AKA MICHELLE HARRISON AND BEFORE DIANA ROSS IN 1991 AND JULIA ROBERTS IN LATE 1991. SO BOWIE WAS ONE FO THE FIRST OTHER THEN ONES LIKE SOUPIE SALES WHO WERE THERE TO PROMOTE THEIR SELVES.

SO I LIKE MOST PEOPLE WHO NEVER RUN ACROSS FAMOUS PEOPLE ASSUMED HE WAS A LOOK ALIKE.

HE WASNT A LOOK ALIKE, IT WAS DAVID BOWIE.

HE WAS WITH BOB DIRE AND WAS THERE TO WORK IN HIS STUDEO.

I REMEMBER THEN WHAT BOB DIRE USED TO DO. HE WOULD GIVE FAMOUS MUSICIANS HIS STUDEO AND ENGENEERING FOR FREE TO FAMOUS PEOPLE AND BOWIE TOOK THAT DEAL. IT WAS A WORLD CLASS 24 TRACK STUDEO AND YES BOWIE COULD USE SOME FREE STUDEO TIME.

BACK WHEN I WAS WORKING WITH BOB HE WAS WORKING FOR FREE WITH LINDA RONDSTADT AS WELL AS THE BAND BERLIN WHO I BELEIVED HE CHARGED BECAUSE THEY DID THE HIT SONG IN HIS STUDEO BEFORE THEY HAD MADE IT TO THAT DEGREE OF SUCCESS.

SO HERE I AM AND BOWIE AND BOB DIRE AND SOME BLONDE GIRL WHO WAS THERE FOR I DONT KNOW WHAT REASON BUT SHE WAS REALLY DRINKING ALOT AND I NOTICED SHE DID SOME COCAINE THERE TOO AS WELL AS A PILL.

THE NEXT THING I REMEMBER AT THIS TIME IN 2020 33 YEARS LATER IS THAT WE ARE ALL OUTSIDE AND THE BLONDE GIRL HAS OVERDOSED AND I START GIVING HER MOUTH TO MOUTH UNTIL THE AMBULANCE GETS THERE AND AS I DO THIS IT SAVES HER LIFE AND THE AMBULANCE COMES AND THE PARAMEDICS TAKE OVER. AFTER ALL THIS I NOTICE DAVID BOWIE LOOKING AT ME WITH AN ATTITUDE OF BEING IMPRESSED AND IN AWE. I GUESS IM A REGULAR JOE SAVING A LIFE AND HE HASNT DONE THAT YET. I DONT KNOW BUT THIS IS WHAT I BELEIVE AND ASSUME.

AS HE DRIVES OFF IN HIS SPORTS CAR I SAY TO HIM , "YOU ARE DAVID BOWIE RIGHT?" HE SAYS "IM BILL". THIS IS ONE OF DAVID BOWIES ALTER EGOS. I KNOW THIS BECAUSE OF THE SONG 'BILL DRIVES A SPORTS CAR UNTIL ITS TOO LATE BUT WE WILL HAVE A HOT TIME ON THE TOWN TONIGHT . AND BANG BANG I GOT MINE ETC"

1. ALWAYS THOUGHT THAT WAS ABOUT ME BUT IT WASNT.

2. AT SPEARMINT RHINO

I SAW DAVID BOWIE A FEW TIMES HERE AND AT THIS I ALSO SAW DAVID CROSBY AND GRAHAM NASH NEAR AND AROUND THIS TIME.

I REMEMBER SEEING DAVID BOWIE AND EVEN SAT WITH HIM AND KICKED IT WITH HIM A COUPLE TIMES WHEN SEEING HIM THERE.

I REMEMBER ASKING A FEMALE BAERTENDER AND STRIPPER THERE "DO YOU KNOW WHO THAT IS? SHE SAYS "BILL". I SAY ITS DAVID BOWIE BUT DONT SAY ANYTHING. SHE SAYS "I ALWAYS THOUGHT HE LOOKED JUST LIKE DAVID BOWIE". I SAY ""BECAUSE IT IS DAVID BOWIE"

SHE CANT BELEIVE IT. BUT DOES AND SHE KEEPS IT A SECRET.

3. I SEEN BOWIE IN THE BLACK AREA FOR PROSTITUTES AS WELL AS A COOL POMONA HANG OUT.

4. SAW HIM BUYING BEER AT A 7-11 IN POMONA THE WORLD CLASS HO STROLL AT THAT TIME.

5. LAST TIME I SAW HIM WE WERE IN A SOUL FOOD RESTRAUNT AND ME AND HIM WERE THE ONLY 2 WHITE GUYS. I WAS WEARING A LEATHER JACKET AND HAD A PONYTAIL AND SO DID HE. I ALWAYS THOUGHT HE WAS USING MY IMAGE FOR ANOTHER ONE OF HIS PERSONALITIES.

I REALLY DONT KNOW .

HE WAS A TRIPPY DUDE AND I WOULD SAY FRIENDLEY BUT A LITTLE SHY.

5. OH YEAH ONE MORE TIME. RIGHT BEFORE HE DIED LIKE WITHIN A YEAR I SAW HIM AT STARBUCKS IN CLAREMONT/ POMONA BORDER. HE WAS ATTEMPTING TO LOOK BOHEMIAN AND HAD A BACKPACK THAT WAS A DESIGNER BACKPACK JUST LIKE ONCE WHEN I SAW NATALEE COLE WITH A BACKPACK TOO.

ALL IN ALL I FEEL LUCKY AND BLESSED TO HAVE CAME ACROSS AND WAS ACQUANTANCES AND/OR FRIENDS WITH DAVID BOWIE.

ITS THE THREE WHO LIKE BLACK WOMEN, -ME AND BOWIE AND ROBEET DENERO.

AND THAT WAS THE STORY OF ME AND DAVID BOWIE.

I FIRST MET CCH POUNDER IN THE HOOD AREA OF POMONA. I FIRST SAW HER AND I DIDNT KNOW HER NAME BUT I HAVE SEEN HER ALOT ON T.V. AND ON VARIOUS MOVIES ETC. SHE IS A GOOD ACTOR. WE BECAME FRIENDS AND I REMEMBER HER ASKING ME WHY I HAVENT MADE IT BIG IN MUSIC AND I SAID I DIDNT KNOW. I GUESS IT ISNT THE TIME OR MAYBE IT NEVER WILL BE THE TIME WAS MY ANSWER.

I HUNG OUT WITH HER ALOT AND SHE CAME OVER TO THE HOUSE AND WE DATED. SHE WAS A FAN OF MY MUSIC AND I WAS A FAN OF HER ACTING ON TV SHOWS AND MOVIES.

I SAW HER THROUGHOUT THE YEARS AND WHENEVER I SEE HER I SAY HI AND ASK WHAT HAS BEEN HAPPENEING. SHE TOLD ME THE TRICKS OF MOVIES AND TV SHOWS ON HOW THEY MAKE SOME PEOPLES EARS BIGGER FOR A MORE GLAMOUROUS LOOK AND THAT SOME PEOPLE ACTUALLY LOOK BETTER WITH BIG EARS THEN WITH LITTLE EARS.

ONE TIME ON THE PARKING LOT OF GAREY AND FOOTHILL WHERE LOVES BBQ USED TO BE AT WHICH LATER TURNED INTO A MEXICAN RESTRAUNT WE ALMOST GOT INTO AN AUTO ACCIDENT AND THERE I REMEMBER TO THIS DAY HOW WORRIED AND ANGRY SHE WAS THAT WE ALMOST CRASHED. I SAID SORRY AND KNEW SHE WAS AN ACTOR BUT DIDNT KNOW HER NAME AT THAT TIME SO I LOOKED IT UP IN FILMS SHE WAS IN AND FOUND POUT HER NAME WAS CC POUNDER THEN CHANGED IT TO CCH AND I ASKED HER WHAT THE H AS IN CCH AND SHE LAUJGHED AND SAID SHE DIDNT KNOW.

ALL IN ALL SHE WAS A COOL PERSON.

80. JACK NICHOLSON

I MET JACK IN HIS OLDER DAYS, OVER 60 STARTING AROUND THE EARLY 2000S.

HE WOULD ALWAYS NOT WEAR HIS TEETH SO HIS JAW LOOKED DIFFERENT AND IT LOOKED LIKE A PARTIAL JACK NICHOLSON. WE ONCE SAID TO HIM ME AND THE MOTHER OF MY 2ND KID ANNIE THAT HE LOOKED LIKE JACK AND HE SAID JACK IS IN THE SOUTH OF FRANCE.

MANY TIMES LATER I SAW JACK. ONCE WHEN HE WAS DRESSED TO LOOK YOUNGER. THESE ACTORS LIKE TO DO THIS EVEN WHEN THEY ARE NOT ACTING.

THE LIKE TO DRESS UP AND LOOK IN VARIOUS WAYS.

AS THE YEARS WENT BY I SEE HE LIKES TO JUST KICK IT AND CHECK THINGS OUT. ONCE I SEE HIM IN MCDONALDS. I TURN AROUND AND FELT HIM LOOKING AT ME. HE HAD SHADES ON AND I COULD SEE HIM ACROSS THE STREET IN MCDONALDS.

THEN I SEEN HIM ON HOLD BLVD AND YELLED JACK AND SMILED. FINALLY I FILMED HIM ON VARIOUS DAYS FOR A VIDEO CALLED "MR SMITH".

IT WAS COOL AND WHAT WAS STRANGE WAS AFTER I FILMED HIM AND HAD ENOUGH CLIPS OF HIM I NEVER SAW HIM AGAIN.

STRANGE

BUT TRUE

IVE ALSO SEEN HIM ON THE BUS ANOTHER PLACES TOO. REMEMBER HOLLYWOOD IS ONLY 40 MILES FROM WHERE HE HANGS HERE IN THE INLAND EMPIRE AND REMEMBER THERE ARE NO STALKERAZZA A.K.A. PAPARAZZI IN THE INLAND EMPIRE. ONLY IN LOS ANGELES AND BEVERLEY HILLS AND HOLLYWEIRD. A.K.A. HOLLYWOOD.

81. DENNIS HOPPER

I FIRST MET DENNIS HOPPER AT A GAS STATION IN UPLAND- I SAID TO HIM "DO YOU KNOW WHO YOU LOOK LKE?" HE SAID 'DENNIS HOPPER" I SAID "RIGHT. HEY YOU ARE DENNIS HOPPER"

HE SAID 'YEAHHHHH I AM".

I LEFT HIM ALONE AFTER THAT AND THEN WHEN HE WAS LEAVING AFTER BUYING A SUBWAY SANDWICH CONNECTED TO THE GAS STATION I FELT I HAD TO TALK TO HIM AGAIN AND ASK HIM A QUESTION.

I SAID "MR HOPPER I REALLY WISH WE COULD BE FRIENDS". HE LIKED THAT. I SAID TO HIM "MAN YOU WERE IN REBEL WITHOUT A CAUSE". HE SAID "I LIKED IT BEST IN THE DAYS OF EASY RIDER-"

WE TALKED AND LAUGHED. HE ASKED ME WHAT I WAS ABOUT. I SAID "IM GOING AROUND THE U.S.A. PLAYING GUITAR TO MAKE A LIVING AND PAY FOR IT." HE SAID "LIKE EASY RIDER". I SAID-"YEAH". HE SIAD "ILL SEE YOU IN ARIZONA". I THOUGHT HE WAS JUST TALKING TO BE FRIENDLEY BUT GUESS WHAT?

I SAW HIM IN KINGMAN ARIZONA.

THE FIRST NIGHT I LEFT I MADE IT TO KINGMAN ARIZONA AND I SLEPT IN THE HOSTBITAL PAERKING LOT. AS I WOKE UP I FELT REFRESHED AND FREE.

I REALLY NEEDED TO GET AWAY. SO I WALK TO THE UNDERPASS AND I PLAY SOME STREET SHOWS AND I MAKE ONLY 10 DOLLORS. I FELT ABOUT READY TO LEAVE FROM KINGMAN AND GO TO FLAGSTAFF.

THEN ALL OF A SUDDEN I SEE A GUY WHO WALKS UP TO ME AND ITS DENNIS HOPPER. I CAN TELL BY HIS VOICE AT FIRST AND I WAS THINKING WHERE HAVE I HEARD THIS VOICE BEFORE AND THEN IT HIT ME. DENNIS AND I SAID "DENNIS?" AND HE LAUGHED. HE DID HIS CHARACTOR NAMED GALEN WHICH IS HIS DAUGHTERS NAME.

WE IMMEDIATLEY HIT IT OFF AND IM EXCITED TO BE HANGING OUT WITH GUY I ALWAYS WISHED AND PRAYED TO MEET. NOW WERE BUDDIES AND WERE FLAGGING SIGNS. I WOULD MAKE A FIVE DOLLOR BILL THEN GIVE HIM 2. HE WOULD GET A LITTLE "NIPPY POO" OF ALCOHOL AS DENNIS CALLED IT.

HE WAS A COOL GUY AND TOLD ME STORIES BUT AS OF THIS TIME WE WERE MAKING MONEY TILL THE EVENING. AS WE DROVE FROM PLACE TO PLACE IN KINGMAN ARIZONA I ASKED HIM IF I COULD FILM THIS AND HE LAUGHS AND SAYS. "A SECOND EASY RIDER EXCEPT WERE NOT ON BIKES BUT IN A CAR. STILL IN THE STREET".

HE GAVE ME POINTERS ON HOW TO FILM AND HE ASKED ME WHAT THE FILM NAME WAS AND I SAID "BEING WHITE IN 2009. IT WAS ONLY EARLY DECEMBER OF 2008 WHEN I WAS IN KINGMAN WITH DENNIS BUT I KNEW I WOULD BE HEADING INTO 2009 IN THE NEXT 28 DAYS AND I WAS ON THIS TOUR FOR AND UNTIL FEB 15TH 2009.

BY THE END OF THE DAY WE HAD MADE ALMOST ENOUGH TO SHARE A HOTEL ROOM WITH 2 BEDS BUT I HAD TO MAKE A LITTLE MORE SO WE WENT TO A TRUCK STOP IN KINGMAN ARIZONA AND I WAITED IN THE CAR WHILE FILMING STORIES WITH DENNIS II FOUND OUT ALOT ABOUT DENNIS ONE WAS HE SUPPORTED THE RUBY RIDGE WITH THE WEAVERS IN IDAHO WHERE THE FBI AND ATF KILLED FAMILY MEMBERS OF THE WEAVERS. ALSO I LEARNED BUT DIDNT FILM THE RACIST SIDE TO DENNIS. THIS TURNED ME OFF AND I WAS THINKING IF I SHOULD STILL HANG OUT WITH HIM OR PUNCH HIM RIGHT THERE BECAUSE I HAVE A MIXED DAUGHTER AND SON AND THIS WAS VERY AGGRIVATING HEARING HOW DENNIS DOESNT LIKE BLACK PEOPLE AND EVEN MORE HARSH WORDS ABOUT BLACK PEOPLE WHICH IS WEIRD BECAUSE WHEN I SAW DENNIS AT THE UPLAND SHELL STATION .

IT WAS WEIRD THAT HE WAS RACIST BECAUSE HE WAS VOLUNTARELY SIGNING AUTOGRAPHS TO BLACK PEOPLE IN A LINE TO GET HIS AUTOGRAPH AND SEEMED VERY NICE. THATS AN ACTOR HUH? I PANHANDLED ANOTHER 20 FOR THE HOTEL AS WELL AS TOMORROWS GAS IN WHICH I PROMICED HIM I WOULD TAKE HIM TO BULLHEAD CITY TO COURT TO PAY FOR A TICKET FOR HIM DRINKING IN PUBLIC IN BULLHEAD CITY.

WE GOT A HOTEL AND IT WAS RIGHT NEXT TO THE 93 FREEWAY. IT WAS CONVIENENT SO WE COULD IMMEDIATELEY TAKE OFF IN THE MORNIG TO GO TO THE COURTHOUSE IN BULLHEAD CITY.

THAT NIGHT WE TALKED ALOT AND HE ASKED ME HOW I FELT ABOUT GAYNESS AND I SAID I DIDNT LIKE IT OR BELEIVE IN IT AND THAT IT WAS A SIN AND I ALSO BORROWED HIS PHONE BEING IN THOSE DAYS I HADNT YET DEVELOPED TO GET MY OWN PHONE YET.

HE ASKED ME IF I EVER LAUGH AND I SAID NOT REALLY BUT SOMETIMES AND I APOLOGISED. I WAS THINKING ABOUT HIS RACIST COMMENTS HE MADE EARLIER THIS DAY.

I WENT TO USE THE PHONE TO CALL MY WIFE AND CALL LAILAH MY MANAGER AT THAT TIME.

SHE DIDNT BELEIVE I WAS WITH DENNIS HOOPER THE ACTOR.

I TOLD LAILAH THE STORY AND THE STORY MADE SENSE MEETING HIM IN UPLAND AT THE SHELL GAS STATION ON CORNER OF MOUNTAIN AND FOOTHILL AKA THE ROUTE 66. SHE STILL DIDNT BELEIVE IT BECAUSE LAILAH IS SORT OF STAR STRUCK OF ACTORS. I GUESS SHE DOESNT THINK ACTORS WALK THE SAME EARTH AS US.

BEFORE THE END OF THE NIGHT DENNIS SAID ALWAYS ITS GREAT TO PRAY TO GOD AT THE END OF THE NIGHT AND AT THE END OF A WORKING DAY TO HAVE A PLACE TO SLEEP AND LAY YOUR HEAD. DENNIS WAS A BELEIVER IN JESUS CHRIST THE LORD GOD AND THE FATHER SON AND HOLY SPIRIT. WHEN HE WAS SLEEPING I FILMED HIM WITH HIS PEACE SIGN AROUND HIS NECK AND HE LOOKED TOTALLY LIKE DENNIS ASLEEP AND IT WAS SOME GOOD SHOTS.

HE ALSO ASKED ME "WHAT WOULD YOU DO IF I GAVE YOU A MILLION DOLLORS" AND "DO YOU THINK I SHOUKLD FAKE MY DEATH" ? AND "WHAT DO YOU THINK ABOUT FAKING MY DEATH"?

I TOLD HIM HE SHOULD FAKE HIS DEATH AND HE TOLD ME HE WANTED TO TO GET OUT OF WORKING IN MOVIE AFTER MOVIE. ALSO I SAID I DIDNT KNOW WHAT I WOULD DO WITH A MILLION DOLLORS. THIS WAS NOT A GOOD ANSWER AND HE NEVER GAVE IT TO ME.

ON WAKING UP THE NEXT DAY.

DENNIS WAKES ME WITH "CHUCK GOOD MORNING". HE TAPS ME ON THE SHOULDER AS I WAS ASLEEP. HE MUST BE AN EARLY MORNING PERSON AND I WASNT. I THEN DROVE HIM ON THE 93 TO GO TO BULLHEAD CITY OR IT COULD HAVE BEEN THE OTHER FREEWAY. THE 40.

WHILE DRIVING THERRE WE CHATTED AND THEN I DROPPED HIM OFF AT THE COURTHOUSE AND THAT WAS THE LAST TIME I EVER SAW DENNIS. AT FIRST I WAS GOING TO WAIT FOR HIM BECAUSE HE WANTED TO NEXT HANG OUT IN VEGAS THEN GALLUP NEW MEXICO THEN TAOS NEW MEXICO BUT I WAITED FOR COUPLE HOURS AND HE DIDNT COME OUT SO I WENT TO A HEALTH FOOD PLACE AND BOUGHT A HEALTH FOOD SANDWICH AND THEN DECIDED TO LEAVE.

NEXT ONTO FLAGSTAFF ARIZONA.

82. GARY BUSCHI

83. GEORGE HAMILTON

82. GARY BUSCI

I HAD PICTURES OF JJULIA ROBERTS I WANTED TO SELL AND I WOULDNT HAVE TRIED TO SELL THEM IF JULIA WAS A DECENT PERSON TO ME BUT SHE WASNT.

SO I CALLED FOR CELEBRATY LAWYERS AND I MEANT LAWYERS THAT DEAL WITH CELEBRATIES. WELL, THEY THOUGHT I MEANT A LAWYER WHO IS A CELEBRATY SO THE

LAWYER REFFEREAL SERVACE SAID "OH WE GOT A LAWYER FOR YOU" AND THEN HE LAUGHED. THE GUY FROM THE LAWYER REFFEREAL SERVACE.

AND HE GAVE ME A CELEBRATY WHO IS A LAWYER, IT IS GARY BUSCI. HE TOLD ME HIS MOTHER WAS ESTHER WILLIAMS AND HIS FATHER WAS THE DAD OF THE GUY ON RENEGADE THE SHOW. I DIDNT BELEIVE HIM BUT I LOOKED IT UP AND IT WAS TRUE. HE WAS A HYPER DUDE ON THE PHONE AND SAID HE WAS INTERESTED IN SELLING THE PICTURES OF JULIA.

SO I DROVE THE NEXT DAY TO SAN DIEGO. WHEN I GOT THERE I GOT AN ENERGY DRINK THEN WENT INTO THIS PLACE WHERE BEN GAGE WORKED AT.

I WAITED ABOUT 1/2 AN HOUR IN HIS OFFICE AND THEN HE CAME IN-IT LOOKED LIKE EXACTELEY LIKE GARY BUSCI. SMILE TEETH AND ALL.

HE SAID THE PICTURES WERE JULIA AND HE WANTED 1000 DOLLORS TO START WITH. I TOLD HIM ID GET BACK TO HIM AND I DIDNT. I AINT GONNA PAY UP FRONT 1000 DOLLLORS FOR SELLING PICTURES. I THOUGHT HE WOULD DO IT ON A CONTINGENT BASIS BUT WHEN I LEFT I REMEMEBR IN MY MIND EVEN UP TO NOW HIS SMILE FROM A 10 FOOT DISTANCE AS I LEFT AND NEVER CQME BACK AND DIDNT EVEN THINK ABOUT GIVING HIM 1000 UP FRONT. LAST TIME I GAVE MONEY UP FRONT TO A LAWYER HE SWINDLED ME, THREE DIFFERENT TIMES SO I LEARNED MY LESSON ABOUT LAWYERS ESPECIALLY ACTOR CELEBRATY LAWYERS.

83. GEORGE HAMILTON

I WAS DOING A JOB BEING AN AUDIENCE PARTICAPIENT AT A SHOW CALLED THE GEORGE HAMILTON SHOW. WE HAD TO APPLAUD WHEN THE LIGHT SAID APPLAUD AND WE HAD

TO LAUGH WHEN THE SIGN SAID LAUGH. THAT WAS THE JOB AND SO I DID THAT. THIS DAY I WENT TO WHERE STAR SEARCH USED TO BE HELD. YOU REMEMBER THE STAR SEARCH TALENT SHOW FOR SINGERS?

WELL FIRST I OPENED THE DOOR FOR JANET LEIGH WHO WAD TO BE A GUEST ON THE SHOW THAT DAY. I DIDNT KNOW WHO SHE WAS AND DIDNT FIND OUT UNTIL I SAW HER ON THE SHOW AND I SAID, "HEY THATS THE LADY I OPENED THE DOOR FOR" SHE TURNED OUT TO BE JANET LEIGH THE ACTOR ON THE MOVIE PSYCHO IN THE SHOWER SCENE AS WELL AS SHE IS JAMIE LEE CURTIS MOTHER AND TONY CURTIS EX WIFE.

NEXT I SEE THE SHOW WHICH HAD LL COOL J ON IT AND ELANA STEWERT WHO WAS THE EX OF GEORGE HAMILTON AS WELL AS THE EX OF ROD STEWERT.

AT THE END OF THE SHOW I SEE MY OLD VIDEO PRODUCER AND FILMER DAVID COHEN WHO NOW IS WORKING FOR GEORGE HAMILTON AS HIS ASSISTANT. AS I APPROACH DAVID TO SAY HI GEORGE GETS SCARED OF ME AND RUNS OFF. I WASNT EVEN INTERESTED IN TALKING OR DEALING WITH GEORGE HAMILTON. MY PURPOSE THERE WALKING UP WAS TO SAY HI TO DAVID WHO WAS THE EDITOR AND FILM MAKER OF THE FIRST VIDEO I EVER DID IN 1990 ENTITLED HER GAME.

THOSE CELEBRATY PEOPLE SURE ARE PARANOD.

84. BRIAN JOHNSON, THE SINGER FOR AC/DC

I WAS AT A HARDWARE STORE AND HERE IN A BRAND NEW CAMERO OR SOMETHING IS A GUY WHO LOOKS JUST LIKE BRIAN JOHNSON AND IS EVEN WEARING THE HAT HE AND EVERYONE KNOWS.

I SAID "HEY, YOUR THE SINGER FOR AC/DC? HE SAYS IN AN IRISH/ENGLISH ACCENT" IM WITH ANGUS".

I GIVE HIM ONE OF MY ALBUMS ENTITLED BADDCLOWN 1 AND MODERN DAY OUTLAWS, NEW AMERICAN BLUES. HE LOOKS AT IT AND SAYS THE NAME OF THE ALBUM NEW AMERICAN BLUES AND THANKS ME AND LEAVES. I GO TO HIS CAR WITH A NOTE AND MORE ALBUMS ASKING HIM IF HE CAN HELP ME OuT, THAT I AM A STARVING MUSICIAN AND NEVER GOT A SHOT.

HE NEVER HELPED OR REPLYED.

AND THAT WAS WHAT I KNOW AND SEEN FROM BRIAN JOHNSON THE LEAD SINGER OF AC.DC. HE DID TELL ME HE WAS QUITTING THE BAND IN WHCIH HE DID 6 MONTHS LATER LIKE HE TOLD ME.

85. KATE HUDSON

I WAS COMING BACK FROM THE SOUTHERN TOUR I DID THAT TOOK PLACE FIRST IN ALBERQUERQUE THEN AMERILLO TEXAS THEN SHRIEVPORT LOUSIANA THEN BIRMINGHAM ALABAMA THEN TALAHASEE FLORIDA THEN BACK TO SHRIEVEPORT THEN TO AMERILLO THEN BACK TO LAS VEGS NEVADA. FOR THE FIRST TIME I CAME FROM THE FREEWAY 93 , THE BACKSIDE OF VEGAS. IT WAS LIKE GOING DOWN A SLOPE AND SEEING ALL OF VEGAS FROM THE OTHER SIDE I USUALLY SEE COMING FROM THE EAST THIS TIME AND NOT FROM THE WEST.

AS I GOT IN I PAID ONE DAY FOR A HOTEL. I ONLY HAD ENOUGH MONEY FOR 1 DAY BECAUSE OUT IN MEMPHIS TEXAS , NOT TENNESSEE BUT TEXAS IS A LITTLE TOWN WITH ONE JUDGE ONE BAILIFF AND ONE OFFICER OF THE COURTS ALL THE SAME ONE GUY. WELL, I MADE A DEAL TO HAVE IT OFF MY RECORD FOR 125 ALTOGETHER. I PAID THIS TOURIST TRAP AND WENT ON THEN THAT SAME DAY I

WENT TO FLAGSTAFF AND MADE 75 AND THEN BY THE TIME I GOT TO LAS VEGAS I HAD 100 DOLLORS LEFT AND THIS PAID FOR A HOTEL FOR ONE DAY AT 50 THEN I HAD 50 LEFT OVER.

I DECIDED TO CRUISE AROUND THIS NIGHT AND RAN INTO A YOUNG BLONDE GIRL, PRETTY WEARING A HOOD AND COVERING HER FACE.

IT WAS KATE HUDSON.

WE WENT BACK TO THE HOTEL AND I LET HER SLEEP ON THE BED AS I SLEPT ON THE FLOOR. EARLIER THE NEXT DAY SHE TOOK A SHOWER. AND THEN WE HUNG OUT THE NEXT DAY. OUR GOAL WAS TO GET A HOTEL FOR A WEEK AND IT WAS OCT 1ST SO I WAS TO GET A CHECK THAT DAY SO WE WENT TO THE BANK AND SHE STAYED IN THE CAR WHILE I GOT 900 DOLLORS OUT FROM MY BANK AND THEN WE CRUISED AROUND GOT HER SOME PARTY MATERIAL AND THEN WE WENT TO THE RAILROAD PASS WHICH IS A CASINO NOT IN VEGAS BUT ON THE BORDER OF THE CITY OF BOULDER AND ARIZONA.

AS WE GOT THERE I GAVE HER 10 TO GAMBLE WITH AND SHE WON 50. SHE GAVE ME BACK THE TEN DOLLARS AND WE WENT AND ATE AT AN ALL YOU CAN EAT THERE THAT WAS ON SALE FOR 5 PER PERSON IF THERE ARE TWO PEOPLE AND THERE WAS ME AND KATE. THERE AT THE ALL YOU CAN EAT TABLE SHE PUT ON HER FULL MAKE UP AND LOOKED GREAT.

SHE WAS PUTTING ON MAKEUP AND WE ATE. AFTERWARDS I GOT INTO IT WITH ONE OF THE PIT BOSSES AND WE WERE KICKED OUT. AFTER THIS WE DROVE AROUND AND I TOLD HER STORIES OF THE FAMOUS PEOPLE I MET AND SHE SAID SHE LOVED THE STORIES. WE WENT TO HOMES SHE SAID SHE OWNED AND THERE

WERE SQWATTERS THERE IN EACH PLACE. SHE THEN WENT TO BUY SOMETHING WHERE I DROPPED HER AND SHE TOOK AN HOUR. I WAITED AND WONDERED WAS SHE TRYING TO DITCH ME. AS I SAW HER WALKING AWAY I GAVE HER ANOTHER RIDE TO WHERE WE WENT TO A HOME SHE SAID SHE OWNED. THERE WERE MORE SQWATTERS THERE AND THERE I WAITED FOR 2 HOURS THEN LEFT. I NOTICED IN THE BACK OF THE CAR SHE LEFT ALOT OF JEWLERY SO I LEFT THAT JEWLERY AND STUFF IN THE FRONTYARD.

AND I NEVER SAW HER AGAIN. I STAYED THAT NIGHT AT THE CAR PORT OF CIRCUS CIRCUS CASINOS ON THE 4TH FLOOR. I THEN LEFT THE NEXT DAY AND WENT BACK TO HOME IN FONTANA WITH MY WIFE AND KIDS..

SHE SEEMED LIKE A NICE PERSON EXCEPT IT IS TRUE SHE IN THE END WAS TRYING TO DITCH ME. I THINKED SHE TRIPPED OUT WHEN I GOT MAD AT SOMEOMNE AT THE CASINO AT RAILROAD PASS WITH THE PIT BOSS.

86. KEVIN DEREK

KEVIK DEREK IS THAT FAMOUS BUT HE IS TALENTED AND I IFELT I SHOULD ADD HIM BECAUSE HE HAS BEEN A VIDEO PRODUCER FOR MY MUSIC IN VIDEOS

1. POOR ROCKENROLLER.

2. AS SAMMY SAID -PARTIAL PRODUCE ALONG WITH RON BRADY AKA POP ROCK A.K.A. RON HAD ALREADY STARTED ON THIS BUT QUIT EVEN THOUGH RON OWED US A VDIEO BEING WE WON IT AND GOT 2ND PLACE IN A BATTLE F BANDS AT HOLLYWOOD SHOWCASE FOR BANDS CONTEST FROM KDOC STATION AND IT WAS DONE AT THE GREEN DOOR AND THEN FENDERS BALLROOM. 1988-89.

3. BOOBS ALONG WITH AN ACTING SKIT.

4.- BADDCLOWN.

5, LOST IN HOLLYWOOD.

I WORKED WITH KEVIN FROM 1994 TO 2002. HE QUIT BECAUSE HE FELT HE WAS GETTING MORE SUCCESSFUL THEN ME AND WE ALSO HAD A FALLING OUT ABOUT HIM GIVING ME A ROLL OF FILM THAT I SHOT WITH MY KIDS THAT WAS BLANK.

WHEN I WAS GOING OUT WITH JULIA ROBERTS IN 2002 I CALLED KEVIN AND SAID THAT JULIA IS WILLING TO BE FILMED FOR A FUTURE VIDEO I AM DOING ON A FUTURE SONG. HE SAID "I DONT HAVE A GOOD ENOUGH CAMERA TO FILM HER". JULIA SIAD SHE DIDNT CARE ABOUT CAMERA TYPE AND THAT WE SHOULD DO THIS VIDEO TODAY. KEVIN BASICLLY CHICKENED OUT WITH THAT LAME EXCUSE. I BELEIVE IT WAS BECAUSE HE HAD A CASE OF BEING STAR STRUCK.

KEVIN WAS A MUSLLIM AND I WAS A CHRISTIAN AND KEVIN WAS BORN RICH WITH HIS PARENTS BEING RICH ETC, I USED TO SAY
"KEVIN, YOU THE POOREST RICH PERSON I EVER KNOWN". HE SAID "CHUCK, YOU ARE THE RICHEST POOR PERSON I EVER KNOWN:. I CONSIDERED KEVIN A FRIEND THOUGH I FELT DIFFERENT WHEN HE DIDNT INVITE ME TO HIS WEDDING BUT I DIDNT CARE AS LONG AS HE WOULD STILL DO VIDEOS. I ALSO CONTRIBUTED 3 SONGS ON HIS FILM ENTITLED "THE ULTIMATE GAME" WHICH IS A KARATE FIGHTING PICTURE-ANDI DID ALOT OF THE SOUNDTRACK ALSO BEHIND THE FIGHTING SCENES. HE PAID ME 175 FOR THE DAY. I ALSO PAINTED HIS FENCE FOR 100 DOLLORS GOING ALL THE WAY TO EL TORO JUST TO DO THAT AND ALSO HE WAS HELPING ME TO FILM A FILM ABOUT THE MUSIC LIFE. HE QUIT BEFORE IT WAS FINISHED BUT HE GAVE ME ALL THE FOOTAGE AND I EDITED IT AND FINALLY

MADE THE FILMS. THIS INCLUDED FOOTAGE FOR THE SONGS "ABORTION KILLS BABIES "AS WELL AS THE SONG "GOD HELP THE STARVING CHILDREN" AND "MY SWEET SON" IN WHICH I EDITED ALL THE FOOTAGE AND THOUGH KEVIN FILMED IT I EDITED THOSE VIDEOS WASNT AS GOOD AS KEVIN COULD DO BUT I TRIED, I WOULD SEE KEVINS VIDEO THE ULTIMATE GAME IN HOLLYWOOD VIDEO STORES ALL OVER THE AREA AND I ACTUALLY RENTED ONE FROM HOLLYWOOD VIDEO AND AT THAT TIME FOUND IT COOL THAT I RENTED A VIDEO AND MY MUSIC WAS IN IT. PRAISE GOD.

ALSO WE DID THE MASTERPIECE "LOST IN HOLLYWOOD".

WE SHOT THE TRUTH OF HOLLYWOOD IN JUST 2 DIFFERENT DAYS AND IT WAS GREAT. IT SHOWED PURE HOLLYWOOD AND NOT THE HYPED UP MOVIE STAR VERSION. WE FILMED HOMELESS PEOPLE ACTING OUT GANGSTER PARTS AS WELL AS THE CELEBRARTY LOOK ALIKES ON THE STRIP AND RUNNING INTO THE DAILY REALITY OF HOLLYWOOD IN THE AFTERNOON OF A WEEKDAY. WE DID TWO WEEKDAYS AND NOT ANY WEEKENDS BECAUSE IT WOULD BE WAY MORE TOURISTY ON THE WEEKENDS.

AS SAMMY SAID WAS ANOTHER VIDEO AND SONG AND THE SONG WAS THE FIRST ROCK N RAP VIDEO OF ITS KIND THAT IS FULLY ORIGIONAL THOUGH AEROSMITH AND RUN DMC DID IT WITH WALK THIS WAY, IT WASNT ORIGIONAL BECAUSE IT WAS OFF A COVER FROM AEROSMITH ENTITLED WALK THIS WAY. IN THE SAMMY SAID VIDEO WE WENT TO THE NUMBER ONE LEFGENDARY SKAEBOARD SPOT OF ALL TIME ENTITLED THE MT BALDY PIPELINE AND WE WROTE OUR IMPORTANT QUOTES IN THE SONG ON THE WALL IN A GRAFETTI TYPE SCNENERO.

IN SAMMY SAID AND LOST IN HOLLYWOOD AND BADDCLOWN AS WELL AS POOR ROCKENROLER THERE WERE CAMEO APPEARENCES BY MY SON IN EACH OF THOSE VIDEOS AS WELL AS LAILAH AND ANNIE THE MOTHER OF MY SECOND CHILD AS WELL AS LAILAH IS AND WAS MY MANAGER THEN. APPEARENCES BY PERRIS WHO IS MY SON CHARLIES SISTER AND ALL IN ALL THE VIDEOS WERE GREAT AND GOOD QUALITY. THE OTHER VIDEO BOOBS WE WENT OUT ONE DAY IN SANTA MONICA AND FILMED BEAUTIFUL WOMEN WHO WOULD POSE WITH ME WITH BIG BOOBS AND DID SCENES WITH THREE WOMEN WITH BIG BOOBS ONE BEING LAULAH MY MANAGER AND THE OTHER BEING GAIL MY NOW WIFE AND ALSO TWO GIRLS FROM THE HOOD OF POMONA THE ISLANDS AND LOWER POMONA NAMED ALLENE AND JOSEA.

THE FIRST VIDEO WE DID WITH KEVIN WE GOT A FAKE BAND TO PORTRAY A BACKYARD SHOW AND WENT AROUND TOWN WITH A SIGN SAYING I WANT TO FIND MY FIRST BORN SON JASON AND THAT VIDEO WAS THE LEAST PROFESSIONAL BUT IT WAS MY SECOND BEING DAVID COHEN DID THE FIRST ONE IN 1990 BUT THIS WAS THE FIRST WITH ME AND KEVIN DOING THE VIDEOS AND THIS ONE BADDCLOWN WAS DONE IN 1994 AND I HAD THE FULL CLOWN MAKEUP FOR THIS.

KEVIN STARTED DOING SIDE MOVIES AND WAS NOT INTERESTED THAT MUCH IN WORKING WITH ME AS THE 2000S CAME BUT I TRIED TO REACH HIM AND WE STILL DID EDITING AND OTHER THINGS.

ME AND KEVIN PROBABLEY WORKED TOGETHER 50 TIMES,MEANING 60 DIFFERENT DAYS FROM 1994 TO 2000. I BOUGHT HIS FIRST 8 MILLIMENTER CAMERRA OFF HIM FOR 600 DOLLORS AND DID ALOT OF FILMING WITH IT MYSELF.

HE NOW WORKS AT THE LAGOONA BECAH FILM F ESTIVAL. I TRIED TO REACH HIM ON FACEBOOK BUT HE WILL NOT RESPOND BACK.

WE ALSO DID FOOTAGE OF MY DAUGHTERS FIRST BIRHTDAY PARTY. SHE TURNED ONE AND WE HAD IT AT KEVINS HOUSE. I REALLY THOUGHT AT THIS TIME ME AND KEVIN WERE NOT JUST CAMERAMAN AND MUSICIAN BUT ALSO FRIENDS . I WAS WRONG.

THE BOOBS VIDEO FEATURED A LITTLE SKIT AT THE BEGENNING OF THE VIDEO BEING I AM LOOKING FOR GIRLS AND HERE COMES SOME DOWN THE STREET. I ASK THEM AND FOLLOW THEM TO THE STORE WHERE AT FIRST THEY WOULDNT WORK WITH ME BUT LATER WOULD BEING THEY SAW AND BOUGHT MY ALBUM IN THE STORE IUP THE STREET CALLED MUSIC PLUS.

ALL IN ALL I DONE 27 VIDEOS AND KEVIN DID SOME GREAT ONES OUT OF THAT. KEVIN WORKED ON AND DID 5 VIDEOS .

I ALWAYS WONDERED HOW MUCH MORE WORK WE WOULD HAVE IF KEVIN WOULD HAVE FILMED JULIA ROBERTS IN 2002 AND WOULD HAVE FILMED MORE MUSIC VIDEOS FOR ME AND THE PROJECT AUTRY ODAY AND BADDCLOWN.

WE DID GREAT SHOTS LIKE BUSTING A GUITAR OVER A POLE AND ALL THE BEAUTIUL GIRLS THAT WOULD PARTICIPATE IN THE BEACH AREAS AND IT WAS GREAT HOW THE PEOPLE REALLY LOVED MY CLOWN CHARACTOR. THOUGH SOME DIDNT LIKE THEM MOST DID LIKE THE MAKEUP I WORE AND THE CHARACTOR OF THE CRAZY CLOWN THAT I PLAYED AND PARTICIPATED TO BE.

ALOT OF FILMING LIKE I SAID WAS MY SON WHO PLAYED A ROLE AND STARRING ROLE IN THE SONG "MY SWEET SON. "THOUGH I DIDNT EDIT aND FINISHED PUTTING THIS VIDEO

TOGETHER UNTIL 2010 WHEN MY SON WAS 18 I HAD SOME GREAT FOOTAGE.

THE SONG IS ABOUT MY SON GOING THROUGH THE DAY DRIVING AND GETTING GAS AND GETTING COFFEE AND SMOKING A CIGAR, FIRST WAKING TO AN ALARM CLOCK AND COOKING EGGS AND BACON. OF COURSE IR WAS ALL AT AGE 5 LIKE HES DOING ALL THIS ADULT STUFF BUT AS A KID.

IT WAS A GREAT CONCEPT AND FUNNY STORY.

ALL IN ALL I WAS GLAD TO HAVE MET KEVIN AND BEEN ACQUANTINCES WITH HIM THOUGH I WAS SAD HE DIDNT INVITE ME TO HIS WEDDING, I TOOK IT OK.

I GUESS ITS HARD TO MAKE REAL FRIENDS IN THIS BUSINESS.

87. GARY RICHRATH GUITARIST FOR REO SPEEDWAGON 88.CHRSPIN GLOVER AND 89. CHRISTIAN SLATER.

87. GARY RICHRATH. WE WERE OFFERED TO PLAY THE PICO RIVER SPORTS ARENA OPENING UP FOR GARY RICHRATH OF THE BAND REO SPEEDWAGON. I GUESS HE WAS THE LEAD GUITARIST FOR THAT BAND BUT IS DOING SOMETHING SOLO HERE. WE PLAYED IT AND HE WAS PRETTY GOOD. MANY PEOPLE AFTER THE SHOW SAID WE BLEW HIM AWAY WITH RAUEL AS MY LEAD GUITARIST YES RAUEL WAS FASTER BUT GARY WAS MORE MUSICAL AND MELODIC SO I REALLY DIDNT BELEIVE WE BLEW HIM AWAY MUSICALLY AND BAND AGAINST BAND. I BELEIVE ITS THE OPINION OF PEOPLE WHO FIND IT BETTER FASTER.

GARY WAS A COOL GUY AND I REMEMBER BEFORE THE SHOW THE COUSIN OF MY THEN GIRLFRIEND LAILAH WASS MAKING PASSES AT ME ASKING ME TO HELP HER TO PEE. IT WAS WEIRD BUT SOMETIMES PEOPLE LOSE

THEMSELVES IN AN ARENA SETTING I SUPPOSE-SHE WAS JUST 18 SO I IUNDERSTOOD AND DIDNT GO THERE TO HELP HER PEE. I WENT TO MY GIRLFRIEND LAILAH AND ASKED FOR HELP AND LAILAH HELPED ME BY GETTING ME AWAY FROM HER COUSIN.

I HEARD THERE WAS 5000 THERE AND I THOUHGT MAYBE 3000 BUT THE COUNT WAS 5 THOUSAND AND OUR BAND GOT A WHOLE 300 DOLLORS. WOW.

88. CRISPIN GLOVER.

IT WAS BLACK ANGUS RESTRAUNT IN 1986 IN WEST COVINA.

I USED TO GO THERE ON THE WEEKENDS ON FRYDAY AND SATURDAY AND SUNDAY. EVERY WEEK I WOULD SEE THIS HIGH STRUNG GUY DRESSED IN A GARDNERS OUTFIT. WHAT A WEIRD THING TO WEAR AT BLACK ANGUS DANCING AND DINNER, A RESTRAUNT.

I WOULD SEE HIM EVERY SINGLE WEEK AND I ONCE SPOKE TO HIM AND HE WAS DISTANT BUT SAID HELLO.

ONE NIGHT I GOT KICKED OUT AND SO DID HE. HE WOULD GET KICKED OUT FOR HIS ATTITUDE AND THE WAY HE WAS DRESSED, IN A GARDNER OUTFIT.

I SEE HIM OUTSIDE OF THE RESTRAUNT.

WE TALK FOR AWHILE AND BOTH ARE UPSET AT THE BLACK ANGUS RESTRAUNT FOR KICKING US OUT. WE DECIDE TO GO IN MY CAR TO THE MOUNTAINS AND HE WILL GET A SIX PACK AND I WILL GET NEAR BEAR BEING I AM TRYING TO STAY SOBER. THIS IS 1986 AND AT THIS TIME I WAS LIVING AT KAREN HARLENS HOUSE AND THROWING PARTIES FOR A LIVING.

WE DIDNT KNOW HOW GOOD WE HAD IT. AS I DROVE TO THE MOUNTAINS I TOOK HIM TO A PLACE IN FRONT OF THE AREA IN THE MOUNTAINS ME AND BILL SHORT USED TO PARTY BEFORE WORKING AT LOVES BAR B QUE IN POMONA BACK I 1977.

AS WE ARE THERE WE ARE GOING TO A STREAM AND WE GO ON THE SIDE OF THE STREAM. HE SAYS HIS NAME IS LYNDSAY BUT HE HAS A STAGE NAME CHRISPIN GLOVER AND HE SAYS HE IS DOING A MOVIE FOR A COLLEGE THAT HAS DENNIS HOPPER IN IT AND IT IS CALLED RIVERS EDGE AND HE IS ONE OF THE STARS OF THE MOVIE CALLED LAYNE.

HE SAID HE WAS AN ACTOR AND AS WE TALKED HE BECAME ALOT DIFFERENT PERSONNA AND ALOT FRIENDIER AND NICER.

IT WAS A FUN NIGHT AND WE PARTIED UNTIL THE SUN CAME UP HE DRANK BEER AND ME PARTYING ON NEAR BEER IF THAT IS POSSIBLE.

I SEE HIM AGAIN 2 MORE TIMES BUT NEVER AT BLACK ANGUS AGAIN BUT HE PULLS UP IN A TAXI AS ME AND ROLAND ARE UP ON AN ALL NIGHTER DECIDING TO GO TO CITRUS COLLEGE AND DRESSED IN HEAVY METEL OUTFITS. CRISPIN PICKS US UP AND RAVES ABOUT HOW TAXI DRIVERS DESERVE MORE AND THEY ARE SUCH GREAT PEOPLE.

HE TOOK US TO THE HOUSE AND THEN HE LEFT.

THE OTHER TIME WAS WHEN I WAS WITH MY THEN GIRLFRIEND LAILAH WHO WAS AROUND 22 OR 23. THIS WAS IN LATE 1986 OR EARLY 1987 AND WE ALL HANG OUT AT MICHEAL J-S RESTRAUNT WHICH ME AND LYNDSAY AKA CRISPIN AND LAILAH HANG OUT AND HE IS FLIRTING WITH

LAILAH AND THEY HAVE A GOOD LONG TALK AT THE TABLE AS I GO OUTSIDE.

I WAS IMPRESSED WITH CRISPINS DRIVE TO BE AN ACTOR AND TO THIS DAY HE IS STILL WORKING AS AN ACTOR ALOT.

89. CHRISTIAN SLATER. CHRISTIAN SLATER WAS ARRESTED IN SAN DIMAS FOR ASSAULTING HIS GIRLFRIEND AND HE I GUESS LOVED THE AREA AFTER DOING HIS TIME BECAUSE I SAW HIM IN POMONA AT A 99 CENT STORE AS A CO OWNER OR OWNER OR A WORKER FOR THE EXPERIENCE.

WHAT HAPPENED IS THAT I LOCKED MY KEYS IN MY CAR.

I WENT INTO THE 99 CENT STORE WHICH WAS WHERE I LOCKED MY KEYS AT AND WAKED IN THERE TO USE THE PHONE. WELL, CHRISTIAN SLATER SAID NO SO I GOT REAL MAD AND WENT TO A GAS STATION TO GET A COAT HANGER TO GET THE WINDOW OPEN OR SOMEHOW UNLOCK THE DOOR.

WHEN I CAME BACK I HAD TO CALL A TOW TRUCK GUY FROM MY INSURANCE THAT TOOK CARE OF IT AND HE WASNT ABLE TO DO IT SO I CALLED THE POLICE AND THEY DROVE ME THERE BUT I HAD TO WALK BACK. I WAS ABOUT 2 MILES FROM THERE BEING THIS WAS TOWNE AVENUE AND AAROW HIGHWAY AND I WAS AT INDIAN HILL BLVD AND AAROW .

THE COP LADY TALKED TO CHRSTIAN SLATER AND SAID HE WAS SORRY. SHE SAID SHE DONT LIKE THOSE HOLLYWOOD PEOPLE AND AS I WANTED TO SAY THE LAST WORD CHRISTIAN CAME UP TO ME AND SAID "I AM CHRISTIAN". THOUGHT HE MEANT HE WAS A CHRISTIAN SO I SAID "THEN ACT LIKE IT" BUT WHAT HE MEANT WAS HIS NAME WAS CHRISTIAN.

THE SKATEBOARD YEARS 1975-1978.
90. MIKE WEED

91. WALDO AUTRY

92. KEVIN THE WORM ANDERSON

93. RUSS HOWELL

AH YES SKATEBOARDS.

IT ALL STARTED BEFORE THE SUMMER OF 1975. I HAD BEEN A TENNIS FANATIC AND WAS GOOD ENOUGH AS A FRESHMAN TO MAKE THE VARSITY TEAM AS WELL AS THE CLAREMONT TENNIS LEAGUE I WAS SECOND PLACE LOSING ONLY IN THE FINALS.

AS I WAS DOING THIS TENNIS THING I WAS SMOKNG MARIJUANA WHICH STARTED LATE 1974 OR EARLY 1975.

IT WAS AROUND MAY OR JUNE 1975 AND MY BROTHER JOHN HAD A SKATEBOARD. IT LOOKED QUITE BEAUTIFUL THERE WITH A KICKTAIL THAT WAS CURVED BY SOME KIND OF FIRE OR SOMETHING. IT WAS A NATURAL KICKTAIL AND I NEVER SEEN A SKATEBOARD THAT HAD A KICKTAIL IN MY LIFE AND HE HAD THESE NEW WHEELS. YES THAT STILL HAD BALLBEARINGS IN THEM BUT HAD A NEW TYPE OF WHEEL REPLACING THE CLAY WHEEL CALLED A EURATHANE WHEEL INVENTED BY FRANK NASWORTHY.

I WAS REALLY IMPRSSED WITH THIS WAYNE BROWN HOBIE SKATEBOARD THAT WAS FIBREGLASS WITH EURATHANE WHEELS AND AFTER THAT I WAS HOOKED.

I THEN BOUGHT A HOBIE WAYNE BROWN SKATEBOARD AT THE BEACH. AT THIS TIME I HAD NO INTEREST IN SKATEBOARDING OR SURFING UNTIL THIS MOMENT AND RIGHT THEN I STARTED TO ALSO ADMIRE SURFING

BECAUSE SURFING IS LIKE THE SAME AS SKATBOARDING BEING THE SAME MOVEMENTS ETC.

AND FROM THEN ON I WAS IN LOVE WITH SKATEBOARDING.

AND NEVER LOOKED BACK, ONLY FOREWARD.

EARLIER IN THE YEAR I WAS SMOKING MARIJUANA AND THEN IN MAY OF 1975 RIGHT BEFORE GOT INTO SKATEBOARDS I HAD A BAD TRIP ON MARIJUANA. I HAD WHAT WAS CALLED A MARIJUANA FLASHBACK.

SO AS I STARTED SKATEBOARDING I WAS SOBER AS THEY GET. I DIDNT WANT TO HAVE ANYTHING TO DO WITH ALCOHOL OR MARIJUANA.

SKATEBOARDING WAS MY DRUG. AT THE TIME I STARTED SKATEBOARDING I HAD KNOWN ABOUT ONE TRICK CALLED TICK TACKS WHICH WAS MOVING THE BOARD BACK AND FORTH WITH THE BACK FOOT GUIDING AS THE FRONT FOOT WAS TICK TACKING BACK AND FORTH AND THE REASON WHY IT WAS CALLED THAT WAS BECAUSE THE SOUND WHEN THE WHEELS IN THE FRONT WERE HITTING THE GROUND WAS "TICK TACK TICK TACK."

THE TIMES WERE AMAZING BECAUSE THE SKATEBOARD DAYS WERE JUST STARTING ITS SECOND GENERATION AND WE WERE STARTING AT THE SAME TIME AS EVERYONE ELSE DID INCLUDING GUYS WE SKATED WITH AT THE PIPELINE LIKE MIKE WEED AND KEVIN ANDERSON AND TONY ALVA AND GREGG WEAVER AS WELL AS JAY ADAMS AND STACY PERALTA AMONG MANY OTHERS.

ONE I LEARNED THE SKATEBOARD TO RIDE IT I IMMEDIATELY HAD A SPECIAL TALENT FOR THIS SPORT OTHERS AND MANY CALL A FAD BUT I KNEW AND FELT IT WAS A SPORT.

WITHIN THE WEEK I WAS ABLE TO DO TICK TACKS AND ANOTHER TRICK CALLED A 180 OR A 360 IN WHICH A 180 IS HALF A FULL SPIN AND A 360 OF COURSE WAS A FULL SPIN, ONE FULL SPIN.

BY JUNE 1975 I WAS OBSESSED WITH SKATBOARDING AND WAS IN LOVE WITH IT BEING GIRLS DIDNT LIKE ME YET SO MY LOVE OF MY LIFE AT THIS AGE OF 14 AND 2 MONTHS WAS SKATEBOARDING.

ONCE IN THE FALL OF 1975 I WAS LOOKING AT THE NEWSPAPER AND THERE WAS A GUY SKATEBOARDING A PIPE. THE PIPE WAS CALLED THE MT BALDY PIPELINE. WHAT THIS PIPE WAS FOR WAS IT WAS WHAT CONNECTED ONE SIDE OF THE MT BALDY DAM TO THE OTHER SIDE AND THE PIPE ITSELF WAS UNDER THE DAM ITSELF.

THE PIPE WAS CALLED THE GREATEST NATUJRAL SKJATEBOARD SPOT EVER IN THE WORLD. NOW EVEN THOUGH IT WAS MADE FROM AND BY MAN IT WAS STILL NATURAL. WHAT THIS MEANT IS THAT IT IS NATURAL IF THE PIPE WASNT MADE FOR SKATBOARDING BUT FOR ANOTHER REASON. LIKE A SKATEPARK ISNT NATURAL BUT THIS PIPE WAS BECAUSE THE SKATEPARK WAS INVENTED AND MADE FR SKATEBOARDING AND THE MAIN PURPOSE WHICH IS FOR SKATEBOARDING.

THAT PICTURE CHANGED MY LIFE AND ALL THROUGHOUT THE WINTER OF 1975 AND THROUGH 1976 WE WOULD HITCH HIKE DAILY AFTER SCHOOL TO THE MT BALDY PIPELINE WHICH WAS 5 MILES FROM CLAREMONT HGH SCHOOL NORTH OF CLAREMONT HIGH SCHOOL.

AS I WENT TO THIS PIPE DAILY THERE WOULD BE THE BEST SKATERS IN THE WORLD THERE AT THAT TIME AND BY US SKATING WITH THEM WE STARTED TO GET THAT GOOD TOO.

THE FRIENDS THAT WENT TO THE PIPE WITH ME WAS PHIL WOOTTON AS WELL AS ANGELO CORBIN, A BLACK FRIEND AS WELL AS MY BROTHER JOHN AND BRIAN HOFFMAN AND JOHN "SQWEEK"HENDERSON.

ALL WE TALKED ABOUT WAS SKATEBOARDING.

THIS IS WHERE ON ANY GIVEN DAY WE WOULD SKATE WITH GIUYS WHO WERE SKATING THE PIPE AS HIGH AS 3/4 UP THE SIDE WHICH WOULD BE ABOVE VERTICAL. MIKE WEED WAS ONE THERE EVERY DAY AND WOULD COME FROM THE BEACH AREAS. YES THE BEST SKATEBOARD SPOT IN THE WORLD WAS IN OUR BACKYARD LITERELLY.

PEOPLE FROM ALL OVER THE USA AND THE WORLD AS WELL AS THE BEACH AREAS WOULD GO INTO OUR AREAS AND SKATE HERE.

90. MIKE WEED. WE WOULD SEE THIS HUMBLE GUY WHO WAS THE BEST AT THE PIPE AND SO GOOD WAS MIKE WEED THAT HE MADE THE COVER OF TWO SKATEBOARDER MAGAZINES.

MIKE WAS THE NICEST GUY WHO TAUGHT US HOW TO SKATE THE PIPE. HE DIDNT ACT LIKE A STAR GUY AND HE WAS HUMBLE AND TOOK TIME OUT TO TEACH US LESS TALENTED. BY THE END OF MIKE TEACHING US WE WERE ABLE TO GET 5 FEET ON THE WALL AND WE WERE NOT SATASFIED.

MIKE TOLD US TO CARVE ON THE WALL FIRST SINSE WE NEVER HAD ANY VERTICLE EXPERIENCE OF RIDING THE WALL.

I HAD NEVER SKATED A POOL YET BUT THE PIPE WAS THE NEXT BEST THING TO LEARNING TO RIDE THE VERTICLE WALLS. THIS WAS THE SUMMER AND WINTER OF 1975. I WAS 14 YEARS AND A HALF OLD.

94. GREGG "DREAM WEAVER" WEAVER

THE FIRST SKATEBOARDER MAGAZINE I EVER SAW I BELEIVE WAS IN JUNE OF 1975. IT WAS THE FIRST SKATEBOARDER MAGAZINE AND IT HAD THIS BLONDE TAN SURFER LOOKING GUY NAMED GREGG WEAVER. HE WAS ABOUT 6 FEET HIGH UNDER THE LIGHT RIDING A SWIMMING POOL WALL. HE WAS COMPLETELEY VERTICLE AND WE THOUGHT AT LEAST OUR FIRST IMPRESSION WAS IT WAS A FAKE TRICK PHOTOGRAPHY PICUTRE.

OF COURSE IT WASNT AND BY THE END OF 1976 I WAS SKATING 12 FOOT HIGH VERTICLE WALLS TWICE AS HIGH AS GREGGS PHOTO SHOT IN THE JUNE 1975 FIRST SKATEBOARDER MAGAZINE.

ONCE WE SAW GREGG WEAVER AT THE PIPELINE AND EVERYONE HAD THE ROCK SONG DREAM WEAVER THEY WERE PLAYING AND SINGING ALONG TO AS GREGG SKATED THIS PIPE. HE WAS A COOL FRIENDLEY GUY TOO WHO ALSO HELPED US NEW SKATERS. GREGG WAS ONE YEAR OLDER THEN ME AS MIKE WEED WAS A FEW YEARS OLDER.

AND 93. KEVIN ANDERSON AND 92. RUSS HOWELL.

RUSS WAS ONE OF THE FIRST GENERSTION SKATERS WHO WAS AROUND 27 WHEN WE WERE 14 SO HE SKATED WITH TY PAGE AND RUSS WASNT INTO WALL OR POOL SKATING. NO, THIS WAS THE 2ND GENERATION BUT RUSS WAS IN CHARGE OF THE ANAHEIM WAVE SKATEPARK IN ANAHEIM. HE WAS THE HEAD GUY CONTROLLING IT AND WE GOT TO TALK WITH AND ASK QUESTONS TO THE GREATEST TALENTED FLATLAND SKATER IN THE WORLD. RUSS WAS KIND OF GRUMPY BUT WAS REAL AND DOWN TO EARTH. I ONCE SAW HIM BELOW THE HUNTINGTON BEACH PIER DOING 22 360S IN ERO SPINNING LIKE A TOP. I ASKED HIM

IF HE COULD GIVE ME ANY POINTERS AND HE GAVE ME SOME AND BY THE END OF THE DAY I WAS GOING FROM DOING 4 360S TO 10 360S. RUSS AND MIKE WEED AND KEVIN ANDERSON WHO USED TO SKATE A 3 FOOT BOARD ON THE PIPE. HE WAS ON A COVER TOO. I DONT KNOW WHY HIS NICKNAME WAS "THE WORM".

ALL THESE GUYS NOT ONLY WERE COOL AND FRIENDLEY AND TOOK TIME OUT TO TEACH US LOCALS BUT THEY ALSO SHARED WEEK WITH US AND AT TIMES THE MT BALDY PIPELINE WAS LIKE A GIANT MARIJUANA PIPE AND YOU COULD SMELL THE MARIJUANA ALL THE WAY BACK 150 YARDS INTO THE PIPE WHICH WAS THE LENGTH OF THE MT BALDY PIPELINE. I TO THIS DAY HAVE DREAMS THAT THE PIPE WE WERE IN BUT IT HAD BLOCKS THERE TO KEEP US FROM SKATING IT.

BY THE END OF 1976 I WAS SKATING OVER 1/2 ON THE PIPELINE.

91. WALDO AUTRY.

WALDO WAS THE GUY THAT OVER TOOK MIKE WEED ON THE BEST PIPE SKATER. WALDO WASNT KNOWN TO SKATE POOLS LIKE HE SKATED THE MT BALDY PIPE. WALDO SKATED THE HIGHEST AND THE PROOF WAS IS WHEN YOU GET AS HIGH AS YOU CAN GO YOU PUT A STICKER UP THERE AND PLACE IT THERE AND THE HIGEST STICKER WAS THE ONE WHO GOT THE HIGHEST AND WALDO WAS SO HIGH HE ALMOST PUT THE STICKER ON THE TOP OF THE 18 FOOT HIGH PIPE.

WALDO AGAIN WAS ANOTHER NICE GUY. IN FACT THE ONLY SNOOTY ONES WERE STACY PERTALTA AND JAY ADAMS.

95. STACY PERALTA. I NEVER SAW STACY AT THE PIPE BUT I SAW 96. TONY ALVA COMING UP THE WALKWAY UP THE CLIFF TO COME FROM THE PIPE UP TO THE STREET. THE

PIPE WAS IN A VALLY AT THE END OF A WASH. THE WASH WAS 50 FEET OR 75 FEET BELOW THE STREET WHICH WAS AT THE TOP OF THER LAST HILL CALLED THE MT BALDY RANGE SO AS TONY AND JIIM MUIR WERE COMING UP THE PATH ON THE HILL TONY SAID TO ME AND BRIAN. MAINLEY TO ME TONY SAID "THE PIPE IS OUT FOR BLOOD TODAY". I SAID TO MYSELF "NOT FOR THE LOCALS". TONY WAS COMING FROM DOGTOWN AKA SANTA MONICA AND VENICE BEACH.

I DID SEE STACY PERALTA AT THE OCEANSIDE SKATEPARK IN 1976. HE WAS IN LINE NEXT TO ME AND MUCH TALLER BEING HE WAS AROUND 5 FEET 10 NCHES AND I AROUND THEN WAS 5 FOOT 1 THOUGH LATER I TURNED OUT TO BE 5 10 ALSO. I REMEMBER TO THIS DAY HOW STUCK UP STACY PERALTA WAS AND REMEMBER WHEN HE SKATED WE WERE MUCH BETTER THEN HIM AND THAT WAS WHEN WE FIRST LEARNED ABOUT HYPE AND KNOWING THAT FAME AND THE PHOTOGRAPHERS FOLLWING THE DOG TOWN BOYS WAS WHY THEY WERE KNOWN AND NOT BY HIS TALENT.

JIM MUR WAS ONE OF THE GUYS ON THE ZEPHYR TEAM AND JIMS HEAD WAS CRACKED OPEN WITH LOTS OF BLOOD AND THIS GOT THEM TO QUIT THAT DAY. THE PIPE RIDING WAS WHAT MADE JIMS HEAD BE ALL BLOODY. THEY WERE SUPERSTICIOUS BUT ME AND BRIAN WERENT AND WE WENT DOWN THERE AND SKATED ALL DAY NO PROBLEMS.

96. JAY ADAMS. AT ANOTHER POOL BEHIND THE MAGIC LAMP INN IN RANCHO CUCUMONGA AND BACK THEN WAS CALLED CUCUMONGA. THERE WAS AN L SHAPED POOL AND THE BEST POOL EVER CALLED THE GROVE POOL. JAY WAS TRYHING AND ATTEMPTIING TO SKATE THE SHALLOW WALLS BY THE STEPS WHERE NO ONE TRIED. I DO BELEIVE JAY WAS THE FOUNDER OF THE RADICAL IDEAS IN

A POOL THOUGH ME AND MY FRIEND BOBBY VALENTINE WERE TWO OF THE OTHERS FROM THE BADLANDS WHO WERE SKATING OUT OF THE POOL ALSO AROUND THE SAME TIME IN LATE 1976. EARLY 1977 TO MID 1977. AT THE FOX PARK POOL IN POMONA THEY WERE CALLING JAY J-BIRD AND HE WAS EXTREMELY SNOOTY AND UNFIRNDLEY AND IMMATURE. IM JUST TELLING YOU THE TRUTH.

THIS IS WHY THE GROVE POOL WAS THE BEST POOL EVER. IT WORKED FOR ALL LEVELS OF SKATERS FROM BEGENNERS NEVER RIDING A POOL OR EVEN A PERSON WHO NEVER RODE ANY TYOE OF SLOPE TO THE BEST SKATERS IN THE WORLD HAVING THEIR OWN WALL THAT ONLY THE BEST COULD RIDE.

THERE WAS THE BOTTOM OF THIS LARGE L POOL WHICH WAS A SLOPE AND BEGENNERS COULD START THERE. NO ONE MADE FUN OF NO ONE AND EVERYONE WITHOUT PRESSURE ENCOURAGED THE BEGENNERS AND WE WERE ALL AT A DIFFEERENT GROWTH IN OUR SKATEBOARD LIFESTYLE AND I AND ALL REMEMBER WHEN THEY WERE BEGENNERS TOO AND THATS WHY THERE WAS SO MUCH SYMPATHY FOR THE BEGENNER. THEN ON THE BOTTOM OF THE L YOU COULD SKATE A 9 FOOT POOL AND 3 FOOT VERTICLE AND THAT WAS NEXT THEN THERE WAS THE ONES WHO COULD SKATE ALL FOUR WALLS. THAT WAS BUDDY AND TAY HUNT WHOSE REAL NAME WAS TAYLOR HUNT. HIS SISTER JOANNA WAS GIRLFRIEND OF THE GUITARIST BLANE IN THE BAND I WAS IN CALLED ROULETTE IN 1981. I WAS GOOD FRIENDS WITH JO ANNA AT THAT TIME AND ALWAYS WANTED TO KNOW TAY MORE TOO BECAUSE HE WAS SUCH A GREAT SKATER GETTING ON THE COVER OF SKATEBORDER MAGAZINE.

OF JAY ADAMS AND STACY PERALTA AND TONY ALVA, TONY WAS THE MOST DOWN TO EARTH.

JAY AND STACY THOUGHT THEY WERE BETTER THEN US WHOSE TERRITORY WAS OURS AND THEY WERE SKATING ON OUR TERRITORY WITH NO RESPECT.

ANOTHER STORY ABOUT WALDO WAS ONCE THE BOARD OF HIS LOST CONTROL ON THE WALL AND CAME BARRELLING DOWN THE WALL HITTING MY RBOTHER JOHN.

IT HURT MY BROTHER VERY MUCH, ENOUGH TO MAKE HIM CRY.

SO WHAT DOES WALDO DO? HE GAVE MY BROTHER THE SKATEBOARD THAT HIT HIM AS WELL AS A JOINT FOR THE PAIN. WALDO WAS THE BEST PIPE SKATER OF THOSE DAYS AND HE WAS ALSO A VERY DOWN TO EARTH PERSON

97. THE LOGAN BROTHERS.

THEY WERE BRIAN LOGAN AND BRUCE LOGAN AMONG OTHER BROTHERS I CANT REMEMBER THEIR NAMES BUT BUILT A GREAT SKATEBOARD CALLED THE LOGAN EARTH SKI. OH YES THE OTHER BROTHER WAS NAMED BRAD.

I SAW THEM AT THE PIPE AND THEY WERE LIKE BEGENNERS IN THE PIPE BECAUSE THEY TOO WERE FROM THE FIRST GENERATION OF SKATERS LIKE TY PAGE AND RUSS HOWELL AND THEY WERE NOT ABOUT RIDING VERTICLE OR BOWLS OR SLOPES, ONLY ON FLAT LAND.

BUT LIKE EVERYONE WE WERE PATIENT WITH THEM AND WISHED THEM THE BEST AS WE TRIED TO HELP THEM.

IT MADE ME REALIZE WE HAVE MORE TALENT ON THE SKATEBOARD WALLS AND SLOPE AND POOLS THEN THE LEGENDERY LOGAN BROTHERS THOUGH NO ONE COULD BEAT THEM ON THE FLAT LAND SKATING WHICH MEANS THE TRICKS ARE NOT ABOUT WALLS BUT TRICKS DONE ON FLATLAND. AGAIN THEY CAME FROM A DIFFERNET ERA OF

TRICKS AND HOW TO RIDE A SKATEBOARD. THEY WERE THE GENERATION BEFORE US 1966 TO 1975 WE WERE 1975 TO 1980.

ME AND MY FRIEND BRIAN HOFFMAN WERE INTERESTED AND LOVED EVERYTHING YOU COULD POSSIBLEY DO ON A SKATEBOARD.

WE DID

1. SLOLEM.

2. HIGH JUMP. WE WOULD MAKE TWO STANDS AND PUT HORIZONTELLY A BAR MADE OF WOOD. WE WOULD PLACE IT IN FRONT OF US AND TRY TO JUMP OVER THE BAR. I SARTED AT ONE FOOT ALL THE WAY UNTIL IT WAS FOUR FEET AND I DID IT. I HIT FOUR FEET WHICH AT THAT TIME TIED TOM SIMS FOR THE UNOFFICIAL WORLD RECORD. SEE WHAT YOU DO IS JUMP OVER THE BAR ON YOUR SKATEBOARD AND THEN LAND BACK ON THE BOARD, THE SAME BOARD ON THE OTHER SIDE OF THE BAR YOU JUST JUMPED.

TOM SIMS WAS THE OWNER OF THE SIMS TEAM.

3. DOWNHILL

OH YES I DID DOWNHILL SKATING FROM 1975 TO 1979.

HOW I STARTED DOWNHILL.

WE STARTED GOING DOWN VIRGINIA ROAD IN 1975 THEN WE WENT TO A PRETTY LOCAL SPOT AROUND 12 MILES AWAY CALLED ARCHIBALD AVENUJE WHICH WAS SO LONG AND STEEP ALL THE SKATERS THEN USED TO GO SIDEWAYS BACK AND FORTH AND NON ONE TRIED GOING STRAIGHT. IT WOULD BUILD UP TOO MUCH IN SPEED CAUSING SPEED WOBBLES ON THE BOARD BECAUSE OFN HOW LONG THIS STREET WAS.

ME AND BIRAN HOFFMAN AND "SQWEEK" HENDERSON USED TO SKATE UP THERE BEING DROPPED OFF BY SQWEEKS DAD.

WE WOULD BE IN THE BACK OF THE TRUCK BEING DRIVEN THERE WITH NO SHELL ON. WE WERE IN THE WIND AND LOVING IT.

THEN WE MET THIS GUY NAMED ROBERT REEVES WHO TOLD US THE ULTIMATE SKATE DOWNHILL AREA WAS CLARABOYA IN UPPER SNOOTY CLAREMONT. ROBERT CLAIMS HE IS THE KING OF THIS HILL AND THAT NO ONE BUT HIM HAS BEEN A SUCCESS WHICH MADE ME WANT TO TRY IT OR AT LEAST CHECK IT OUT. EARLIER THAT YEAR IN 1976 I MADE A RUN CALLED THE CROSS IN SANTA BARBARA WHICH WAS A ROAD THAT CURVES TO A 180 DEGREE SLOW ANGLE AND AT THE END OF THE RUN WAS A CROSS OF JESUS.

I TRIED IT AND REALIZE WHY NO ONE CAN DO IT, BECAUSE AT THE END IS A CLIFF.

SO AT THE END I MADE IT BUT HAD TO SLIDE OUT OTHERWISE I WOUND FALL OFF THE CLIFF.

SO I FELT CONFIDENT AND I HAD BOUGHT THIS 3 FOOT BOARD OFF ONE OF MY BROTHERS FRIENDS.

A COUPLE YEARS AGO I GAVE IT TO SOME YOUNG SKATER KIDS.

BUT AT THIS TIME I TRIED CLARABOYA AND WHO DO I SEE THAT IS THERE BUT ROBERT REEVES. ROBERT HAS BEEN FEATURED IN VARIOUS SKATEBOARD MAGAZINES AS WELL AS SKATEBOARDER MAGAZINE. THE TOP MAGAZINE IN THE WORLD FOR SKATEBOARDERS.

I MET MY BEST FRIEND FOR MANY YEARS MARK AKA "MR SMITH" FERGERSON. WE WERE IN THE BOOK STORE AND WE WERE BOTH lOOKING AT SKATEBOARDER MAGAZINE AND HAVING THIS IN COMMON I BECAME BEST FRIENDS WITH MARK.

SO AS I WAS ON TOP OF THE LAST HILL ON CLARABOYA. I SEE ROBERT REEVES THERE. HE SAID "YOU KNOW WHO I AM KID"? I SAID "YES I DO YOUR ROBERT REEVES". HE WAS PRETTY COOL AND HE WAS THE INVENTOR OF THE GORILLA GRIP WHICH WAS BACK BEFORE WHAT THE KIDS ARE DOING NOW ON A SKATEBOARD YOU HAD TO GRAB THE SKATEBOARD FROM YOUR TOES CURLING OVER AND UNDER THE BOARD ON BOTH FEET FROM BACK TO FORTH.

I RACED ROBERT REEVE AND BEAT HIM AND HE COULDNT BELEIVE THAT I I BEAT HIM BUT I DID AND I COULDNT BELEIVE TOO THAT I BEAT HIM BUT I DID. PRAISE THE LORD. WE WERE AROUND 40 MPH. HE TOLD ME I SHOULD TRY FROM HIGHER UP SO I SLOWLEY TRIED HIGHER EACH DAY I WENT THERE UNTIL FINALLY I STARTED HIGHER THEN ANY ONE HAS EVER GONE BEFORE OR AFTER TO THIS DAY. I STARTED ABOVE THE 2ND STREET IN BETWEEN THE 2ND AND 3RD STREETS.

I WAS UP SO HIGH I NEEDED LOOKOUTS AT THE CURVES TO LET ME KNOW WHEN THE COAST WAS CLEAR TO GO BECAUSE CARS COMING UP COULD HIT ME WHEN I GO AROUND THE TURNS BECAUSE I NEED THAT OTHER SIDE TOO TO MAKE THESE RUNS.

I WAS TIMED AT OVER 52 MPH BY A COP WHO GAVE ME A TICKET FOR WRECKELESS AND SPEEDING. THATS SPEEDING AS A MOTOR VEHICLE LIKE A CAR. I WENT TO COURT AND THE NEWSPAPER WERE THERE TO MAKE IT A STORY AND THE JUDGE FELT IT WRONG TO GIVE ME A TICKET FOR BREAKING THE WORLD SPEED RECORD ON A

SKATEBOARD-SO HE DROPPED THE CHARGE. PRAISE JESUS

4. FLAT LAND TRICKS

WE INVENTED A THING CALLED THE TWO AND THREE BOARD FLANGE WHICH TO DO THIS TRICK YOU GOT TO START WITH A HANDSTAND AND THEN LOWER YOURSELF TO WHERE YOUR BODY IS HORIZONTAL TO THE SKATEBOARD AND DOING THIS THREE BOARDS ON TOP OF EACH OTHER THEREFOR ME AND BOBBY VALENTINE INVENTED THIS TRICK.

WE DID EVERY TRICK FROM 360S IN WHICH I HAVE DONE UP TO 12 360S WHICH IS SPINNING ON YOUR SKATEBOARD AS THE BOARD GOES AROUND TOO.

NOSE WHEELEYS WHICH IS BALENCING YOURSELF ON THE NOSE OF THE BOARD LIKE A HANG TEN ON A SURFOBOARD AND BALENCING ON THE FRONT TWO WHEELS AS WELL AS OTHER WHELLEIES AND CATAMORANS.

WE WERE BLESSED TO GET TO DO A DEMONSTRATION SHOW FOR THE LA VERNE COLLEGE AND THIS WAS IN 1976 AND AT THIS TIME THE HIPPYS WERE STILL AROUND IN COLLEGES. THIS WAS PRETTY MUCH THE LAST CONNECTION TO THE TRUE HIPPIES OF 1967-69.

I ALSO DID SHOWS FOR PRE SCHOOL AND KINDERGARDEN AS WELL AS CLAREMONT HIGH SCHIOOL.

WE USED TO JUMP OVER SHOPPING CARTS ME AND BRIAN HOFFMAN AND LAND BACK ON THE BOARD.

I FORGOT TO SAY THAT DURING LUNCH BREAKS ON SUNDAY AT ,LOVES BAR B QUE WHEN I WORKED AT THERE AS A BUSBOY I WOULD ON MY LUNCH BREAK GO TO CLARABOYA AND DO A DOWNHILL RUN.

I NEVER CRASHED ON CLARABOYA AND NUST HAVE DONE OVER 100 RUNS THERE ALL AT LEAST OVER 45 MPH.. IF I WOULD HAVE CRASHED I COLD HAVE DIED BUT GOD DID NOT WANT THAT DID HE?

I SKATED HILLS IN ANAHEIM IN 1979 AND I WAS CONFIDENT AS A DOWNHILLER UP UNTIL 1982 WHEN I CRASHED BECAUDSE OF IGNORANCE AND OVERCONFIDENCE AND NEW EQUITMENT OF WHEELS ON THE BOARD WHICH IS MUCH MORE FASTER THEN IT WAS BACK IN 1975-79.

THE CRASH ON MY BOARD IN 1982.

I WAS OVERCONFIDENT AND WEARING ONLY SHORTS AND NO SHOES AND NO SHIRT AND I DECIDED TO DO THE RUN AT THE END OF MT BALDY RIGHT UNDERNEATH THE PLACE THAT LED TO THE TRAIL THAT LEADS TO THE MT BALDY PIPELINE.

THE BOARD I HAD WAS DAVE ENKES AND HE BOUGHT IT THAT YEAR IN 1982. I DIDNT KNOW THAT THE WHEELS ARE ALOT FASTER THEN THEY WERE IN 1975-79 BUT THEY ARE TWICE AS FAST AND ALSO I AM ONLY GOOD ON THE LONG BOARD WHEN IT COMES TO SKATING DOWN HILL.

SO AS I START I AM SHOCKED TO SEE HOW SMOOTH IT IS RIDING ON THIS GRAVEL THE CONCRETE AROUND 1/2 WAY DOWN I AM GOING TWICE AS FAST AS I THOUGHT I WOUND HITTING 30 ALREADY AND THIRTY WAS HOW FAST IT WOULD BE IN THE END.

SO AS I HIT THE MIDDLE OF THE RUN I AM GETTING SPEED WOBBLES MEANING ITS MORE THEN 30 MPH SO I HAVE TO DECIDE TO RIDE IT OUT AND CRASH OR JUMP NOW AND SLIDE AND IF I TRY TO RIDE IT OUT UNTIL THE BOARD THROWS ME I WOULD NOT BE IN CONTROL OF THE CRASH BUT IF I JUMP NOW IN THE MIDDLE OF THE RUN AS THE BOARD IS WOBBLING I, AT LEAST KNOW I WILL LIVE-AND

KNOW I HAVE TO JUMP AND SLIDE ON ONE SIDE OF MY BODY SO I CHOSE THE LEFT SIDE TO JUMP RATHER THEN THE RIGHT SIDE WHICH WOULD BE THE MIDDLE OF THE STREET AND THERE MY DAD COULD POSSIBLY HIT ME AND RUN ME OVER BEING HE IS TIMING ME AND IS 35 FEET BEHIND ME.

SO I SLIDE AND WIPE OUT 1/2 MY BODY. GRAVEL AND LOTS OF STUFF HAS BEEN EMBEDDED IN MY SKIN. I AM IN SUCH PAIN THAT MY DAD OFFERS TO GIVE ME A RIDE HOME BUT I DECIDE TO RIDE HOME BEING I AM IN SUCH PAIN. I GO STRAIGHT TO WALTERS COFFEE SHOP AND WHAT DO I FIRST DO? I GET 2 PITCHERS OF BEER AND THAT DOESNT HEAL MY PAIN SO I FINALLY GO HOME AND RECOOPERATE AND SO THIS IS THE LAST TIE I WILL EVER GO DOWNHILL ON A SKATEBOARD.

5. BOWL AND BANK RIDING

THERE WAS A BOWL ON THE TOP OF ARCHIBALD NEAR THE SKATE RUN OF ARCHIBALD AVENUE. NOW HOUSES ARE BUILT THERE BUT 44 YEARS AGO IN 1976 THERE WAS A FIELD WITH A BOWL AND ONCE RUNNING FROM THE BOWL WHICH IS PRIVATE PROPERTY A GUY WITH ROCK SALT IN HIS SHOTGUN SHOT AT US AND HIT US. IT HIT ME IN MY HAND AND STILL TO THIS DAY IS A SCAR FROM THAT ROCK SALT. THANK GOD IT ISNT A SHOT GUN SHELL OR I WOULDNT BE ABLE TO PLAY GUITAR AND KEYBOARD AND PIANO NOW.

THERE WERE MANY BOWLS ME AND BRIAN SKATED AND EMBANKMENTS. ONE WAS CALLED THE WAVE. IT WAS IN ONTARIO ON 6TH STREET I BELEIVE AND IS STILL THERE UNDER LOCK AND KEY. IT WAS GREAT-ALSO HAD A LITTLE SPOT IN CORONA ME AND BOBBY VALENTINE AND CRAIG REED ONCE TOOK MY DADS CAR WHILE THE CAR WAS PARKED FOR CAR POOL AND WE DROVE TO CORONA FOR

BANKS TO SKATE AND ALSO WENT TO THE WAVE AS WELL AS THE ACID DROP WHICH WAS ANY EMBANKMENT CRAIG REED DISCOVERED BACK IN 1976.

6. THE SKATEPARKS. I SKATED THE UPLAND SKATEPARK WHICH HAD THE FIRST PIPE AND SKATED THE MONTELBELLO SKATEPARK WHICH WAS THE WORST ONE. THE CEMENT WASNT AS SMOOTH AS THE ANAHEIM WAVE AND THEN WILLOW SKATEPARK ON POMONA AS WELL AS OCENSIDE WHICH WAS THE FIRST SKATEPARK I EVER SKATED.

7. POOLS. I SKATED THE GROVE POOL AND LEARNED THERE FIRST, THEN THE FOXPARK POOL. THE SAN DIMAS POOL., HE EUCLID POOL, THE INDIAN HILL IN N OUT BURGER POOL WHICH WAS WHERE I FIRST WROTE THE BADLANDS ON CEMENT THERE. ME AND BOBBY INVENTED THAT NAME THE BADDLANDS. ONE DAY BOBBY ASKED ME WHAT WE SHOULD CALL THIS AREA OF SKATERS BEING THERE WAS A PLACE CALLED DOGTOWN THAT WAS IN SANTA MONICA. WELL, WE DECIDED TO BE CALLED THE BADLANDS.

ALL IN ALLL I SKATED 50 POOLS INCLUDING ONE OUR FRIEND JAMES HILL OWNED CALLED THE CLAREMONT LOCAL POOL BUT AT THIS TIME IN LATE 1978 I WAS LOSING INTEREST IN SKATEBOARDING. ALSO THIS GUY NAMED SIMON HILL WAS SO GOOD HE BLEW US AWAY DOING AIRBORNS. I FELT THE NEW GENRATION WAS COMING AND IS HERE AND I DIDNT FIT ANYMORE. WE WERE THE 2ND GENERATION OF SKATERS IN WHICH THE FIRST GENERATION OF SKATERS WERE THE FLAT LAND SKATERS AND MADE A MOVIE CALLED SKATER DATER AS WELL AS THIS WAS IN THE LATE 50S AND EARLY TO MID 60S. THE NEXT GENERATION 1979 TO 85.

OUR TIME WAS 1975, 77. T WAS A WONDERFUL TIME AND PRE GIRLS. A TIME MY GIRLFRIEND WAS SKATEBOARDING IN A METAPHORE.

AT ONE TIME IN MY LIFE I USED TO LISTEN TO BEACH BOYS AND LED ZEPPELIN AND LOOK AT SURF AND SKATEBOARDER MAGAZINE WATCHING ALL THE SKATERS I KNEW AND RODE WITH GET IN THE MAGAZINE AND WILL ALWAYS CHERISH THOSE TIMES.

THEY WERE THE FUNNEST TIMES IN MY LIFE, FUNNER THEN ANYTHING EVER.

BECAUSE OUR ONLY RESPONSIBILITY WAS TO RIDE YOUR BOARD AND THAT WASNT A RSPONSIBILITY THAT WAS A GIFT AND THAT WAS FUN. TRUE FUN THAT GIVES YOU THE MOST ENERGY IN ANYHING I EVER DONE. I WAS VERY VERY HAPPY AND SATASFIED WITH MY LIFE AND LIFE ITSELF.

NOW THAT I DID SKATEBOARDING SERIUOUS FOR THREE YEARS 1975-76-77 TO THE BEGENNING OF1978 AND THEN DOING MUSIC FROM 1979 TO 2020. I AM REALIZING I AM AT THE END OF IT ALL. I DONT KNOW HOW LONG I WILL LIVE BUT I AM SLOWING DOWN.

I AM JUST GREATFUL TO HAVE 3 YEARS AS A SERIOUS A SDKATEBOARDER AND 41 YEARS AS A MUSICIAN/SINGER, 45YEARS IN THE LAST 45 YEARS OCCUPIED BY SKATEBOARDING AND MUSIC AND BANDS AND ALBUM MAKING IS QUITE A BLESSING.

98. ALICE COOPER

I HAVE SEEN ALICE COOPER TWICE, ONCE WAS IN THE MID 80S IN HOLLYWOOD AND HE WAS WALKING LOOKING ALL SKETCHEY AND WEIRD LIKE HE DINT WANT TO BE NOTICED

AND I SAID "OOOH ALICE COOPER MAN COOL". HE TRIPPED OUT.

THE OTHER TIME I SAW HIM WAS AT A LAS VEGAS CASINO. IiT WAS ACTUALLY JEAN NEVADA ON THE OUTSKIRTS OF LAS VEGAS. THIS IS A CASiINO YOU GO TO BEFORE YOU HIT VEGAS. ITS ABOUT 10 MILES FROM THE BORDER AND 40 MILES FROM VEGAS AS VEGAS IS 50 MILES FROM THE BORDER.

AS I SEE ALICE I SEE HIM AGAIN ACTING LIKE HE DOESNT WANT TO BE NOITICED AND I NOTICE HIM. I GO UP TO HIM AFTER HE EATS AT THE ALL YOU CAN EAT AND AS E IS ON A SLOT MACHINE. I INTODUCE MYSELF TO HIM AND HES PRETTY COOL UNTIL I ASK HIM IF HE NEEDS A GUITRIST AND HIS EGO THINKS HES BETTER. IT UPSET ME AND HIS ATTITUDE WAS BAD AFTER THAT. I CANT REMEMBER WHAT HE SAID BUT I REMEMBER IT WASNT NICE OR COMPLEMENTERY.

99. TAY HUNT 100. LEE GAHEIMER 101. GREGG AYERS. 102 . BOBBY VALENTINE

99.TAY HUNT WAS THE BEST POOL RIDER IEVER SEEN AT THE TIME I SAW HI IT WAS IN 1976 AND HE WAS THE BEST AT THE GROVE POOL IN WHICH I LEANRED TO SKATE POOLS THERE.

TAY COULD RIDE A WALL WITHOUT ANY SPEED,JUST CRAWL UP THE WALL TO THE TOP NO MATTER HOW HIGH JUST ON WILL ALONE WITH-NO SPEED.

I USED TO NEED SPEED AND LOT OF IT- SPEED NOT THE DRUG BUT THE SPEED OF THE SKATEBOARD WHILE GOING UP THE POOL WALL. NOT TAY. HE WAS THE ONLY GUY TO SKATE ALL THE WALLS TO THE TOP AT GROVE POOL.

TAY MADE THE FRONT COVER OF SKATEBOADER MAGAZINE. HE WAS ONE OF THE GUYS IN THE NAME I INVENTED FOR THIS AREA ENTITLED THE BADLANDS.

ALSO TAYS SISTER USED TO BE A BIG HELPER AND PART OF ROULETTE THE BAND FOR HE WAS THE GIRLFRIEND OF MY GUITARIST NAMED BLANE HAMMOCK.

BY THE WAY JUST FOR THE RECORD WHEN I SAW TONY ALVA AND JAY ADAMS AT THE GROVE POOL TAY BLEW THEM AWAY. AT THE TIME OF 1976 THE UNKNOWN TO THE SKATEBOARD WORLD NAMED THE BADLANDS WAS BETTER THEN DOGTOWN AND THAT IS A FACT.

100. LEE GAHEIMER LEE MADE IT TO THE PEPSI TEAM AND I USED TO SEE HIM ALL THE TIME AT A PLACE CALLED THE MCDONALDS POOL. BEHIND MCDONALDS ON GAREY AVENUE.

LEE WAS ONE OF THE BEST SKATEBOARDERS EVER ON A BOARD IN A POOL.

101. GREGG AYERS

GREG AYERS WAS THE FIRST GUY WHO I EVER SEEN DO A THING IN THE PIPE CALLED A FAKEY. THIS WAS THE MT BALDY PIPELINE AND HE WOULD START AT THE END OF THE PIPE WITH NO SPEED WHEN BEFORE I SEEN HIM DO THIS I NEVER SEEN ANYONE SKATE A PIPE BUT FROM THE 150 YARD LENGTH IT IS TO CATCH SPEED TO GET HIGHER. NOW GREGG JUST GOES TO THE END OF TJHE PIPE AS HE ROCKS BACK AND FORTH WITHOUT KICK TURNING. KICK TURNING MEANS YOU LIFT THE FRONT OF THE BOARD UP AND BACK TOWARDS DOWN TO CHANGE YOUR DIRECTION.

GREGG DIDNT DO THIS HE ROCKED BACK AND FORTH WITHOUT KICK TURNING WHICH WAS NAMED FAKEY

INVENTED THE NAME BY GREGG AYERS. I KNOW I SAW HIM DO IT.

HE WOULD ALSO TRY THIS AT THE WAVE IN ONTARIO. THE BEST SPOTS IN THE WORLD WAS ALL IN THE BADLANDS AT THIS TIME WHICH IS THE SAME GEOGRAPHY AS THE INLAND EMPIRE. WHICH IS WHAT THE AREA IS CALLED NOW EXCEPT IT IS NOT SKATBOARD GEOGRAPHY ITS REGULAR CITY GEOGRAPHY ENTITLED THE INLAND EMPIRE AND THEN UNDERGROUND IT IS CALLED "THE BADLANDS."

102. BOBBY VALENTINE

SOME OF THESE GUYS ARE NOT FWORLD FAMOUS BUT THE NAME IS FAMOIUS NOT WORLD FAMOUS AND ALL THESE SKATERS IN THE WORLD OF THE UNDERGROUND CALLED THE SKATEBOARD WORLD IT IS CALLED "BADLANDS".

BOBBY WAS THE BEST POOL SKATER IN THE BADLANDS, AT LEAST THE WEST SIDE OF THE BADLANDS. THERE WAS A GUY NAMED CHOCHO AND HE WAS THE BEST IN SAN DIMAS AND BOBBY WAS THE BEST POOL RIDER IN THE BADLANDS IN THE POMONA CLAREMONT AREA. I TAUGHT BOBBY TO SKATE POOLS AND I WAS THE 2ND BEST POOL RIDER IN THE BADLANDS.AT THAT TIME. ROBEERT REEVES GOT INTO THE MAGAZINE SKATING THE EASIEST POOL IN THE WORLD ENTITLED THE EUCLID POOL BUT ROBERT WAS NOT AS GOOD AS ME OR BOBBY SKATING POOLS. I HIT COPING AT THE MONTCLARE HOLT TRAILOR PARK POOL WHICH IS STILL THERE BUT ITS FILLED WITH WATER AND ME AND BRIAN AND BOBBY WERE THE BEST UNTIL LITTLE SIMON HILL TOOK OVER OWNING HIS OWN POOL, HE COULD SKATE EVERY DAY SINSE HE LIVED AT THE HOUSE WHERE THE POOL WAS AT.

BUT IN LATE 1977 I SAW BOBBY FLY OUT OF A POOL AND STAY ON HIS BOARD IN THE FOX PARK POOL. THEN BY THE END OF THAT DAY WAS SO PRESSURED TO DO IT, TO FLY OUT OF THE POOL THAT I ACCOMLISHED IT ON MY 20TH OR 25TH TRY, THEREFORE ME AND BOBBY WERE THE FIRST TO EVER FLY OUT OF THE POOL AT THE POMONA FOX PARK POOL. BEFORE JAY ADAMS AND TONY ALVA. BECAUSE JAY ONLY TRIED AND DID IT UNTIL HE CRASHED AT THE END OF HIS RUN. I KNOW THIS BECAUSE I SEEN JAY DO THIS IN THE SHALLOW END OF THE GROVE POOL. IT IS TRUE JAY WAS THE FIRST TO TRY THESE THINGS BUT NOT THE FIRST TO ACCOMPLISH THESE THINGS. ME AND BOBBY WERE THE FIRST TO ACCOMPLISH FLYING OUT OF THE POOL AND COMING BACK IN THE POOL COMPLETING THE POOL RUN.

IT WAS ME AND BOBBY. BOBBY FIRST AND ME SECOND TO GO AIRBORN AND TO STAY ON THE BOARD IN A POOL. SIMON HILL WAS ALSO IN THE TOP TEN DOING IT AT HIS POOL AT THE JAMES HILL CLAREMONT POOL IN EARLY 1978.

I KNOW I SAW IT. I WAS THERE SKATING.

I WAS FRIENDS WITH JAMES HILL WHO I WANT TO SAY WAS NOTHING BUT A FRIEND AND A GREAT GUY AND TOTALLY COOL AND FRIENDLEY AND HOSTBITIBLE.

BOBBY WAS MY SKATER BRO SINSE 1976 EARLY. ME AND BOBBY AND BRIAN WERE INTO IT. WE ALSO SKATED THE LINCOLN AVENUE POMONA POOL AND WAS ONCE RAIDED BY COPS WHERE WE HAD TO DITCH EM AND WE SUCCEEDED. ME AND BOBBY AND BRIAN ALSO CLEANED OUT HALF A POOL HALF FULL OF WATER AND BOUGHT A POOL PUMP THAT TOOK WATER OUT. HE DEAL WAS IF WE CLEANED THE POOL WE COULD SKATE IT.

SO WE DID JUST THAT.

BOBBY ALSO WAS THE ONE WHERE I USED TO TAKE MY DADS CAR BEFORE I HAD A LICENCE AND WHILE MY DAD WAS AT WORK COMING FROM A CAR POOL HE LEFT THE CAR THERE SO I DUPLICATED IT FOR 15 CENTS ACROSS THE STREET AT T G AND Y STORE AND WE TOOK THE CAR SKATING EMBANKMENTS WE SAW IN CORONA CALIFORNIA..

BOBBY WAS THE GUY WHO GAVE ME A BONG WITH MARIUJUANA IN IT AT THE GROVE POOL IN 1976 AND I DIDNT KNOW WHAT IT WAS FOR I NEVER SEEN A BONG SO AS HE GAVE IT TO ME I TURNED IT UPSIDE DOWN BEING I DIDNT KNOW WHAT TO DO WITH IT.

EVERYONE THERE LAUGHED INCLUDING ALVA AND ADAMS. I WONDER IF TONY ALVA REMEMBERS THAT OR JAY. OF COURSE JAY DIED IN 2014. I WONDER IF JAY IS REMEMBERING ME WITH THAT BONG IN HEAVEN.

IT WAS GREAT TO KNOW IN JAYS EARLY LIFE THAT HE IN THE END BECAME A JESUS LOVING CHRISTIAN. HE TALKED AT SCHOOLS ETC. ABOUT THE BADS OF DRUGS AND THAT LIFE.

BOBBY ME AND BRIAN WERE THE BEST SKATERS IN CLAREMONT. BOBBYS MOM WORKED AT A RESTRAUNT CALLED FREDRICKS. SHE WAS A GREESEY SPOON WAITRESS AND I KNOW THIS BECAUSE FREDRICKS WAS GREESEY SPOON PLACE. BOBBY AND HIS MOM DIDNT GET ALONG AND SHE TRIED TO KICK BOBBY OUT AND BOBBY LIVED WITH US FOR AWHILE.

ME AND BOBBY USED TO SKATE SO MUCH WHEH HE WOULD LEAVE ME FOR THAT DAY HE WOULD SAY "LATER DATES SKATER MATES". THIS IS WHAT HE SAID TO BRAN AND SQWEEK HENDERSON AND ME.

WE STARTED THE BADLANDS IN POMONA BUT WE WERE LIVING IN CLAREMONT AT THE TIME. THE NAME BADLANDS AND THE COMPETITION DOGTOWN HAD WITH US SHOWED IN WHICH JIM MUIR IN THE MOVIE WAS BITING LIKE A DOG A LICENCE PLATE THAT SAID BADLANDS.

LATER ON JAKE E LEE HAD A BAND NAMED BADLANDS.

IT WAS A GREAT BAND FEATURING RAY GILLIAN ON LEAD VOCALS AND RAY LATER DIED OF AIDES IN THE EARLY 1990S.

ONCE ME AND BOBBY IN SUMMER OF 1978 WE HAD A PONY KEG SO ME AND BOBBY DRANK IT ALL AND I BELEIVE IT WAS HALF WHEN WE STARTED FROM THE KEG LAST BEING AT A SMALL PARTY THE DAY BEFORE-WE DID THIS IN THE MOUNTAINS AND BOBBBY WAS SO DRUNK HE TRIED TO FIGHT ME IN WHICH I PUNCHED HIM ENOIUGH FOR HIM TO STOP.

I FORGAVE HIM AND KNEW IT WAS THE DRINKING THAT MADE HIM LIKE THRT FOR HE HAD NEVER DONE THAT BEFORE.

BOBBY LATER BECAME ONE OF THE FIRST PUNK ROCKERS IN THE HISTORY OF THE AREA IN WHCIH HE INVITED ME TO A CLUB CALLED THE RITZ IN RIVERSIDE WHERE EVERY PUNKER THERE WAS AROUND THEN WERE ALL THERE, ME AND BOBBY AND HIS BLACK FRIEND DEE LEFT WITH ME AS I WAS SUPPOSED TO TAKE THEM HOME AND THEY PURPOSELEY MADE ME DRIVE TO DEVORE THE WRONG WAY BEFORE I FIGURED OUT THEY WERE LEING ABOUT DIRECTIONS AND IN REALITY BOBBY AND DEE WERE HOMELESS.

THAT WAS THE END OF ME AND BOBBY AS FRIENDS

LATER I HEARD BOBBY GOT HIS TEETH KNOCJED OUT AT THE BOTTOM OF A SWIMMING POOL RIDING HIGH.

THEN I SAW HIM WITH A FAMILY LIVING IN POMONA. I LOOKED AT HIM AND HIS ATTITUDE WAS SO BAD I DIDNT WANT TO APPROACH HIM. I DONT REMEMBER WHEN THAT WAS. I BELEIVE I THE LATE 80S OR EARLY 1990S.

103. AMERICA FERRERA

AMERICA IS ANOTHER ONE THAT AT THAT TIME LIKED TO PARTY. AT THIS TIME I WAS HANGING OUT WITH GARY OLDMAN AND AFTER I BROUGHT AMERICA FERRERA TO HELP HER TO TRY TO GET HER IN REHAB GARY THEN KNEW I KNOW FAMOUS PEOPLE AND NOW HE ACCEPTED ME MORE THEN A GUY WHO JUST SAYS HE KNOWS ALL THESE FAMOUS PEOPLE.

REMEMBER I AM NOT FAMOUS BUT I KNOW HUNDEREDS OF FAMOUS PEOPLE AND MY CONCLUSION TO THIS IS THAT PEOPLE CALLED AND PUT IN THE SPOT OF A CELEBRATY NEED TO KNOW PEOPLE WHO ARE NOT CALLED CELEBRATIES. I AM THE ONE WHO RELATES TO CELEBRATIES MORE THEN ANY OTHER PERSON WHO IS NOT FAMOUS. THIS I BELEIVE.

BECAUSE OF MY GOD GIVEN TALENT IN MUJSIC TO WRITE OVER 2000 SONGS AND PLAY OVER 920 SHOWS AS WELL AS MAKING 50 ALBUMS IN 8-16 AND 24 TRACK AND THEM KNOWING THIS THEY ALWAYS ASK ME WHY I AM NOT FAMOUS AND I COJLDNT ANSWER THEM BECAUSE I SAY MY SKILLS LIE IN MUSIC NOT BEING A CELEBRATY.

WHEN I MET AMERICA I HUNG OUT WITH HER FOR THE DAY AND SHE JUST WANTED TO CRUISE THEN SHE SPENT THE NIGHT. NO SEX AND THEN THE NEXT DAY I TOOK HER TO GARY OLDMAN AND I BELEIVE GARY GUIIDED HER TO THE RIGHT DIRECTION.

AND THAT WAS THE LAST TIME I SAW AMERICA WHEN SHE WAS BE TOOK TO GARY OLDMANS APARTMENTS.

104. MICHEAL SWEET-OF THE BAND STRYPER.

105. TIM GAINES OF THE BAND STRYPER.

106. OZ FOX OF THE BAND STRYPER.

104. LEAD GUITARIST AND LEAD SINGER MICHEAL SWEET OF THE BAND STRYPER

I MEET MICHEAL SWEET AT A PIZZA MEET AND GREET. I WENT UP TO HIM AND ASKED HIM IF HE NEEDS A BASE PLAYER AND HE LOOKED AT ME LIKE I WAS NOTHING AND JUDGED ME AS NOT GOOD ENOUGH ALREADY.

I LEFT MAD AND I WAS WITH MY THEN GIRLFRIEND AND FUTURE WIFE GAIL. WE WERE ABOUT READY TO LEAVE WHEN MIKE CAME OUT AND OVER TO ME.

HE WAS IN IS OWN TRYING TO MAKE UP FOR THE SNOOTY ATTITUDE HE HAD WITH ME IN THE PIZZA PLACE WHEN I WAS TALKING TO HIM ABOUT ME TRYING TO BE HIS BASSIST.

HE WAS ALOT FRIENDLIER OUTSIDE TO ME AND MY GIRLFRIEND AND FUTURE WIFE GAIL.

WE TALKED AWHILE AND THEN I LEFT AND I ALSO MET HIS GIRLFRIEND OR WIFE. I REALLY CANT REMEMBER WHICH. I NOTICED HIM LUSTING AFTER MY WIFE AND I DONT GET UPSET BECAUSE I HAVE DONE IT TO. THE BOTTOM LINE IS YOU CAN LOOK BUT NOT TOUCH LIKE ONE TIME WHEN PAT BASICH BROTHER OF OINGO BOINGO KEYBOARDIST AND PROMOTER AT THE GREEN DOOR ACTUALLY TOUCHED LAILAHS "WHO IS MY MANAGERS:" BREASTS AND THERE WAS WHEN I PHYSICALLY WENT AFTER PAT. THIS WAS AROUND 1989 OR 1990.

NOW IT IS 1993 WHEN WE GO SEE MICHEAL SWEET AND THAT WAS IT WITH MICHEAL SWEET AND THAT WAS REAL COOL.

105. TIM GAINES BASSIST FOR THE BAND STRYPER.

TIM HAD THIS ATTITUDE LIKE HE WAS MAD IF YOU DIDNT KNOW HE WAS TIM GAINES OF STRYPER. HE WORKED AT THE ALTA LOMA MUSIC CENTER AND MUSIC STORE AND I SEEN HIM AROUND.

WE DIDNT REALLY GET ALONG AND ACTUALLY GOT INTO A LITTLE ARGUMENT ABOUT HIM BEING MAD AND WONDERING IF HE WAS STILL FAMOUS OR NOT.

I DIDNT CARE AND MY ARTITUDE DID NOT MESH WITH TIM GAINES THE BASSIST OF THE 80S CHRISTIAN BAND STRYPER.

106. OZ FOX. 2ND LEAD GUJITARIST OF THE BAND STRYPER.

WHEN I MET OZ HE WAS PERFORMING AT RED HILL PARK IN ALTA LOMA. I MET HIM AFTER HE TOOK A BREAK AND WAS SITTING IN THE PARK. I CAME UP TO HIM AND TOLD HIM I ADMIRED HIS PLAYING AND HE ASKED ME TO SIT WITH HIM AND PRAY AND I DID. I WILL ALWAYS REMEMBER WHAT A GOOD CHRISTIAN AND DOWN TO EARTH GUY OZ FOX WAS WHEN I SAW WITH HIM FOR A 1/2 JHOUR AND PRAYED AND TALKED WITH HIM ABOUT GOD AND MUSIC.

107. SANDY WEST THE DRUMMER OF THE RUNAWAYS.

108. KIM FOWLEY PRODUCER OF BANDS AND FOUNDER OF THE BAND THE RUNAWAYS.

SANDY WEST. DRUMMER AND ONE OFTHE FOUNDERS OF FIRST ALL GIRL ROCK GROUP THAT MADE IT BIG THE RUNAWAYS.

I WAS AT AN AUDITION AT THE SAME TIME THE BAND WAS TO ALSO AUDITION A DRUMMER. I WAS AUDITIONING AS A KEYBOARDIST AND THE GUYS IN THE BAND TOLD ME THAT THE DRUMMER WAS SANDY WEST OF THE RUNAWAYS. I HAD NEVER HEARD OF SANDY WEST BUT I HAD HEARD OF THE RUNAWAYS BECAUSE KIM FOWLEY TOLD ME HER DISCOVERED THEM BACK WHEN I WAS FRIENDS WITH KIM IN 1983.

WHEN SANDY GOT THERE SHE WAS WITH A LESBAN GIRLFRIEND WHO I ALWAYS WILL REMEMBER WAS QUITE A BEAUTY. AS SHE SET UP THE DRUMS I ASKED HER "SO YOU PLAYED WITH JOAN JETT"? AND HER ANSWER IN AN ANGRY WAY WAS "NO JOAN PLAYED WITH ME."

I SANG AND I REMEMBER WE DID STAIRWAY TO HEAVEN WHICH SHE WAS BAD. SHE BARLEY COULD PAY DRUM. IM JUST BEING HONEST. i DONT KNOW IF SHE GOT INTO THE BAND BUT I KNOW I DIDNT.

AND I REMEMBER SHE WAS PRETTY COOL AND I REMEMBER HER LOOKING LIKE A FEMALE JOE WALSH IF YOU COULD PICTURE THAT. ALL I KNOW IS SHE HAD A BEAUTIFUL GIRLFRIEND-AND SHE WALKED IN LIKE SHE WAS A STAR.

I JUST FOUND OUT TODAY THAT I AM WRITING THIS THAT SHE DIED IN 2006. I BELEIVE THE YEAR OF THIS AUDDITION WAS LATE 90S.

108 KIM FOWLEY.

I MET KIM IN THE MOST OBSCURE PLACE-AT ALPHA BETA IN CLAREMONT AND HE GAVE ME SOME VALIUM.

WE IMMEDIATELELY HIT IT OFF AND HE TOLD ME HE DISCOVERED THE RUNAWAYS WHICH AT THAT TIME I HAD

NEVER HEARD OF THE RUNAWAYS UNTIL KIM TOLD ME HE DISCOVERED THEM.

AS I WAS HANGING OUT AT ALPHA BETA IN 1983 FOR SOME UNKNOWN REASON.

AND HERE COMES THIS GUY WALKING UP OT ME AND TALKING TO ME.

HE IS A THIN TALL GUY, 6 FOUR OR SIX 5 IN HEIGHT..

I AM 5 10 IN HEIGHT.

WE HIT IT OFF AS FRIENDS AND HE IS A FUNNY GUY MEANING HE HAS A GREAT SENSE OF HUMOR. HE GIVES ME VALIUM AND CODENE AND HE SAYS HES IS LOADED WITH DRUGS HE GETS FOR FREE FOR PERSCRIPTION.

HE SAYS HE IS BEING SENT TO THE RAMADA INN OR HOWARD JOHNSON HOTEL IN GLENDALE I CANT REALLY REMEMEBR THE NAME OF THE HOTEL BUT I BELEIVE IT WAS HOWARD JOHNSON OR RAMADA, MAYBE NOT BUT HE LATER WAS STATIONED THERE. HE SAID HE WAS ARRESTED AND SENT TO PRISON AND THAT HE GETS TAKEN CARE OF BY THE GOVERNMENT. LATER I BELEIVE ITS BECAUSE HE IS IN THE MUSIC BUSINESS . KIM LATER TOLD ME AT A TIFFINY ALBUM SESSION THAT HE WAS IN THE MUSIC BUSINESS AND I SAID COOL. HE WAS IN TROUBLE EARLIER AND HE WAS IN PRISON AND WAS WORKING OFR ORGANISED CRIME. HE SAID EITHER WAY HE WAS DEALING WITH ORGANISED CRIME INCLUDING THE MUSIC BUSINESS ACCORDING TO KIM WAS IN ORGANASIZED CRIME IN THE MUSIC BUSINESS BECAUSE THE MUSIC BUSINESS IS RUN BY ORGANISED CRIME AND THATS WHAT KIM TOLD ME. I DONT KNOW IF IT IS TRUE BUT IT IS WHAT HE SAID IS THAT HE GOT A FREE HOTEL ROOM AND FREE LIQUID SARAQUIL ALONG WITH CODENE VALIUM AND HE HAD A LITTLE COCAINE TOO.

BEFORE WE WENT OT HIS HOTEL ROOM ON THE HIGH FLOOR AT THE HOTEL KIM STILL WAS AROUND CLAREMONT AND THE 4TH OF JULY PARADE IN WHICH ME AND KIM WENT TO AND GOT INTO AN ARGUMENT WITH SOME PEOPLE WHO WERE STILL SUING ME FROM A MINOR CAR ACCIDENT IN 1979 LATE IN DECEMBER.

ANYWAYS KIM REALLY GAVE THEM THE BUSINESS AND CUSSED THEM OUT AND TOLD THEM TO LEAVE US ALONE AND TO F---K OFF.

I SORT OF BONDED WITH HIM THERE AND RESPECTED HIM LIKE AN OLDER BROTHER BEING KIM WAS ALOT OLDER THEN ME, I THINK 15 YEARS OR MORE.

WE PARTIED AND HE MET MY MOM AND DAD AS WE WENT THERE AND HAD DINNER THERE AND HIM BEING OUR GUESTS ON MOMS LEGENDARY SPAGHETTI.

NEXT I FOUND OUT WHERE KIM WAS AT AND HE SAIDS HE WOULD DO A DEAL WITH ME AND THAT IS IF I BRING WOMEN HE WILL PROVIDE THE DRUGS.

SO I WAS WITH THAT AND AT THAT TIME I DIDNT HAVE A CAR SO I WOULD GET THESE WOMEN WHO SAID THEY WOULD GO AND WORK WITH THEIR CAR TOO.

I BROUGHT WOMEN THERE AND SOMETIMES THEY WERE NOT HIS TASTE AND HE WOULD YELL OUT CRAZY INSULTS RIGHT TO THEIR FACES IN FRONT OF ME AND I THOUGHT IT WAS REALLY FUNNY BUT AT THE SAME TIME I WAS EMBARRASSED.

I WOULD FIND THE GIRLS AT THE MONTCLARE PLAZA AND IN THAT PLAZA I WOULD GET THEM FROM THE MALL OR IN THE PARKING LOT WHICH HAD A RESTRAUNT NAMED BLACK ANGUS RESTRAUNT WHICH WE FOUND MORE THERE BECAUSE IT WOULD ALRLEADY BE 9 OCLOCK AND

IN THE EVENING AND I COULD ASK ONE OR TWO OR EVEN THREE GIRLS IF THEY WANNA HAVE ALL THE DRUGS AND ALCOHOL AND GO TO THIS GUYS HOTELM ROOM WHO WAS THE GUY WHO FOUNDED THE BAND THE RUNAWAYS.

YES KIM TOLD ME OVER AND OVER HE FOUNDED THE BAND THE RUNAWAYS.

I BROUGHT ABOUT 15 GIRLS THERE ALMOST ALL FROM BLACK ANGUS BECAUSE WHEN I ASKED THEM TO GO IT WAS FOR RIGHT THEN AT 9 AND BE THERE BY 10. YES I WOULD TELL THEM ITS IN GLENDALE AND ONLY 1 HOUR AWAY FROM CLAREMONT AND/OR MONTCLARE CALIFORNIA.

THEY WOULD GO BECAUSE IN THOSE DAYS THE ODDS OF A PRETTY GOOD LOOKING BLONDE GUY WITH MUSCLES AND A NICE PERSONALITY WHICH WAS ME USUALLY DOESNT GET LOOKED AT AS A PERVERT, A RAPIST OR A KILLER.

THEY TRUSTED ME BUT ONE TIME I BROUHGT I GIRL NAMED LAURIE AND SHE WORKED AT A EXCERSIZE PLACE CALLED SPA LADY AND SHE WAS IN GREAT SHAPE DOING AROBIC CLASSES ALL DAY ETC. I BROUGHT HER AND HER FRIEND GEE GEE AND WE TOOK LSD. LSD NEVER DID MUCH FOR ME. MY FRIEND ROLAND AKA BILLY BRAGG ONCE TOOK 90 TO 100 HITS OF LSD IN ONE NIGHT AND HIS FRIEND AND MY FRIEND TIM HALL TOOK AROUND 50 AND LOST HIS MIND. VERY SAD AND WRONG OF ROLAND TO DO THAT TO HIS GOOD FRIEND AT THAT TIME TIME.

BACK TO KIM.

I BRING GIGI AND LAURI TO KIMS HOTEL ROOM IN SUMMER OF 1983 GOING TO CRUISE THE STRIP WHEN CROKUS THE BAND WAS PLAYING AT THE WHISKY A GO GO.

IT WAS A GREAT TIME IN LIFE. IT WAS THE BEST SUMMER. YES 1983. I WAS 22 AND I BELEIVE KIM WAS IN HIS 30S. HE LOOOKED YOUNG THOUGH.

KIM ALSO MANAGED ME AS A MUSICIAN AND HE WAS ABLE TO GET ME A GREAT POWER AMP. HE WAS A COOL GUY AND AT THAT TIME I WASNT AS SERIOUS AS HIM.

I HEARD HE DIED AND I WAS VERY SAD ABOUT THAT. I HEARD HE DIED A COUPLE YEARS AGO.

FROM THIS WRITE OF THIS BOOK

GIGI AND LAURIE MEET KIM AND IT WAS MUTUEL THEY DIDNT FIND HIM ATTRACTIVE AND HE DIDNT FIND THEM AT ALL ATTRACTIVE. LAURI WAS BLACK AND HE SAID DONT BRING ME NO N-------- WOMEN. I FOUND OUT KIM MAY BE A LITTLE RACIST.

HE SAYS HE LIKES BLACK PEOPLE BUT NOT ATTRACTED TO BLACK WOMEN. I WAS LIKE OK. HE DID LIKE GEE GEE THOUGH AND HE WAS TRYING TO GO FOR IT SORT OF LIKE HARVEY WEINSTEIN GOT CAUGHT DOING EXCEPT KIM USED DRUGS FOR HIS CLOUT AND THAT HE WAS FOUNDER OF FIRST ALL GIRL BAND THAT MADE TJHE BIG TIME CALLED THE RUNAWAYS. HE GAVE THEM AND ME COCAINE THEN LIQUID SARAQUIL AND THE COMBO OF A SPEED LIKE COCAINE AND A DOWNER LIKE LIQUID SARAQUIL IF DONE RIGHT IS LIKE SMOKING A PRIMO. NOW A PRIMO IS MARIJUANA WITH COCAINE SPRINKLED ALL OVER THE JOINT OF MARIJUANA.

IT MADE ME MELLOW YET WIRED AND HIGH IN A SPEED TYPE WAY TOO.

THEY WERE FEELING IT TOO AND GEE GEE WAS SORT OF REJECTNG KIMS ADVANCES SO SHE SAYS "LETS ALL CRUISE THE SUNSET STRIP IN HOLLYWOOD."

SO WE DID.

GEEI GEE HAD THE CAR SO LAURI AND GEE GEE WERE IN THE FRONT SEAT AS LAURIE WAS THE PASSENGER IN THE FRONT.

ME AND KIM WERE IN THE BACK AND KIM WAS INSLUTING THE GIRLS IN A WAY I CANT REMEMBER WHAT HE SAID BUT BEING SO HIGH AND BEING ON THE STRIP WITH TWO BEAUTIFUL GIRLS AND WITH KIM FOWLEY MADE ME REALIZE THIS IS GREAT. KIM WAS MAKING ME LAUGH SO MUCH IO ALMOST PEED MY PANTS.

I REALLY LOVED KIM AND WAS GLAD HE GOT THE RECOGNITION FROM THE RUNAWAYS MOVIE AND GETTING INTO THE ROCK N ROLL HALL OF FAME.

KIM WAS MAKING ME LAUGH SO HARD I COULDNT CONTROL MYSELF.

HE HAD A TALENT, HE HAD ALOT OF TALENTS AND HE WAS SMART.

GOING TO BAXTERS RESTRAUNT AND THEN BEING DROPPED OFF LITERELLY AT HOME AT THE END OF THE NIGHT.

I MADE FRIENDS WITH LORRENA AT THE RESTRAUNT CALLED SEASONS.. A COUPLE YEARS EARLIER SEASONS USED TO BE CALLED SAMBOS UNTIL THEY BOYCOTTED AND WAS ABLE TO CHANGE THE WAY SAMBO WAS BEING. SEE SAMBO WAS A LITTLE DARK KID FROM INDIA BUT THEY CALLED HIM LITTLE BLACK SAMBO AND THE BLACK CULTURE WAS AGAINST THAT AND I WAS TOO AGAINST IT SO I WAS COOL THAT THEY CHANGED THE NAME OF THE RESTRAUNT FROM SAMBOS TO SEASONS.

WELL I MET LORRENA AS SHE WAS WORKING AT THE RESTRAUNT AS A WAITRESS. WE WENT TO VISIT KIM AND THEY GOT ALONG GREAT. WE ALSO BROUGHT ANOTHER WAITRESS FOR KIM TO DATE. YOU KNOW THAT WAS THE DEAL. I GET HIM A WOMEN OR TWO OR THREE OR EVEN FOUR AND HE GIVES ME AND THE GIRLS AND HIM ALL THE DRUGS WE WANT TO DO INCLUDING GREAT COCAINE.

THE DATE AT BAXTERS.

IT WAS ME AND LORRAINE AND KIM AND A GIRL I CANT REMEMBER HER NAME BUT BEFORE THE DATE WE WENT TO KIMS HOTEL ROOM AND THERE I DRANK SOME LUQUID SARAQUEL AND THEN WHILE KIM WASNT LOOKING I DRANK ALOT MORE, THE RESULTS WERE THIS.

I PASSED OUT ON THE DATE AT BAXTERS. AT THE TABLE I PASSED OUT AND THEN KIM THEN DROPPED ME OFF AT MOMS FRONT LAWN WITH ALL MY MONEY AND MY WALLET. NOTHING WAS STOLEN BECAUSE KIM ISNT LIKE THAT. KIM WAS A FRIEND AND WAS MY MANAGER FOR A FEW MONTHS AS WELL AS A DRUG BUDDY AND ONE OF THE FUNNIEST GUYS I EVER MET.

TIFFINYS.

THIS ISNT BREAKFAST AT TIFFINYS, NO THIS IS TIFFINY THE RECORDING ARTIST AND I WAS GIVEN THIS JOB BY KIM. KIM WAS THE PRODUCER OF THIS ALBUM TIFFINY WAS MAKING AND IT WAS I BEELIVE AN ATTEMPT TO DO A WESTERN. IM NOT QUITE SURE BECAUSE THIS WAS A LONG TIME AGO.

KIMS PASSING AND HIS MONEY HE GOT TO HAVE BY THE RECORD COMPANY.

AS KIM WAS PRODUCING THIS ALBUM HE WASNT HANDING OUT 100S AND TWENTYS TO PEOPLE WHO DID GOOD ON

ONE SPOT OF THE SALBUM OR ANOTHER. THIS WAS THE BACK GROUND SINGERS AND I WAS ONE OF THOSE, A BACKING SINGER. I AM A LEAD VOCALIST BY TRADE BUT DONT MIND DOING BACK UP FOR MONEY.

AND THERE I DID IT AND KIM WOULD GIVE ME A HUNDERED AND 60 EXTRA AND EVEN ABOVE THE UNION PAYMENT.

KIMS PHRASING WAS WHEN HE EXPLAINED HOW HE WANTED THE PASSION FROM THE BACKING SINGERS HE USED SEX PRASING LIKE "WHEN YOU SING THIS WORD SING LIE YOU ARE C---------ING AND REACH ORGASIM. AMONG MANY OTHER PHRASING THAT WAS EVEN MORE PERVERTED BUT I KNEW KIM AND KNEW THIS IS HOW HE TALKED AND HE WASNT BEING A PERVERT HE WAS JUST SAYING THINGS PEOPLE IN THE BUSINESS OR OUT OF THE BUSINESS DONT SAY.

ALL IN ALL KIM WAS A FRIEND AND HE SENT ME SOME HOME MADE FAKE COCAINE FROM LIMO OHIO. IT WASNT ILLEGAL AND IN FACT HE TOLD ME HE BOUGHT ALL THE INDGREDIENTS FROM A HEAD SHOP. A HEAD SHOP IF YOU DONT KNOW IS A SHOP FOR YOUR HEAD. IT SELLS DRUG PARAPHANALIA.

SO HE WANTED MONEY BACK BUT I LOST TOUCH WITH HIM AND HE MOVED TO A NEXT ADDRESS. AND BY THE TIME I FINALLY GOT THE MONEY I OWED HIM TO GIVE HIM HE MOVED TO ANOTHER RESIDENCE.

I NEVER SAW KIM SINSE THEN AND THEN A COUPLE YEARS AGO OR EVEN LESS I HEARD THAT HE DIED AND I THOUGHT FOR A SECOND. THAT THE LAST TIME I SAW HIM WAS THE LAST TIME EVER.

HOPE WE MEET AGAIN IN HEAVEN ONE DAY.

109. PENNY CASH

110. ROLAONDA WATTS

111.. MICHEAL MOORER

PENNY CASH WASNT THAT FAMOUS BUT I PUT HER IN THIS BOOK BECAUSE SHE WAS A CHARACTOR. I MET HER AS SHE WAS DOING HEROIN IN FRONT OF STEPS AT A RUN DOWN UPLAND MOTEL ON MORENO AVENUE ON THE BORDER OF UPLAND AND MONTCLARE.

SHE WAS HARD AND TOUGH BUT JUST A TINY 5"3 90 POUND LADY. SHE TOLD ME SHE WAS IN SWANK MAGAZINE AS A PIN UP FOR A CERTAIN MONTH AND I REALLY DIDNT BELEIVE HER BUT SHE SHOWED IT TO ME AS WELL AS SHE SHOWED ME SHE WAS IN A FILM CALLED GIRLS OF HOLYWOOD HIGH. A SOFT CORE PORNO FLICK DONE IN THE LATE 70S OR EARLY 80S AND SHE SHOWED THAT TO ME TOO. SHE TOLD ME SHE WAS AN ILLEGITIMATE DAUGHTER OF JOHNNY CASH AND THOUGH SHE DIDNT HAVE PROOF. I BELEIVED HER BECAUSE SHE HASNT LIED TO ME SO FAR. THE GIRLS OF HOLLYWOOD HIGH SOFT PORN WAS ONE OF THE FIRST OF ITS KIND AND I HEARD WAS A CULT FAVORITE. I WAS ABLE TO RENT IT AT THE CLAREMONT MUISIC PLUS AND THERE WAS THE STAR OF THE MOVIE PENNY DOING SOME SOFT CORE STUFF BUT DOING ACTING TOO.

IT WAS ABOUT A COUPLE DAYS AT THE BEACH AND THEN MAKING A MOVIE OF IT WITH SOFT PORN IN IT.

NOT HARD PORN LIKE TODAY JUST SHOWING NOT THE WHOLE THING JUST ENOUGH TO KNOW ITS SOFT CORE PORN.

I HEARD MORE ABOUT PENNY AS I WAS IN JAIL AND HE TOLD ME SHE WAS IN OTHER FILMS TOO. I BELEIVE THEM BECAUSE SO FAR NO ONE HAS LIED.

PENNY CAME TO SOME OF MY BIG SHOWS I THREW WITH INBETWEN 8 AND 15 BANDS PER SHOW. I TOOK HER HOME AFTER A SHOW AND THAT WAS THE LAST TIME I EVER SAW HER.

BUT I DID FIND OUT SHE DID EVERYTHING SHE SAID SHE DID WHICH WAS 1. THE STAR OF THE CULT CLASSIC SOFT CORE PORN FILM ENTITLED "THE GIRLS OF HOLLYWOOD HIGH. 2. SHE WAS DAUGHTER OF JOHNNY CASH AND OWNED A GREAT HOUSE IN UPLAND. 3 WENT OUT WITH JOE PERRY OF AEROSMITH AND JOE IS LEAD GUITARIST AND FIRST RHYTHEM GUITAR IN THE BAND AEROSMITH, 4. WAS A PIN UP IN SWANK MAGAZINE. SHE WOULD RAHRTER HANG OUT IN THE STREETS THEN BE IN THIS 6 BEDROOM HOUSE. CRAZY. I LOVE HER THOUGH AS A LONG TIME FRIEND. I HAVENT SEEN HER SINSE THE LATE 1980S AROUND LATE 1989. I HOPE SHE IS STILL ALIVE.

110. ROLONDA WATTS

THE ROLONDA SHOW IS A TALK SHOW IN THE MID TO EARLY 1990S. I GOT ON THE SHOW FOR SOMETHING THAT WASNT TRUE. I WAS ON THE SHOW FOR CHEATING ON MY THEN GIRLFRIEND AND NOW WIFE GAIL. WHEN I GOT THERE ALL WAS COOL. THE AIRPLANE FLIGHT WAS FUN AND I HAD NEVER BEEN TO NEW YORK BEFORE-ME AND GAIL WERE REALLY ENJOYING IT.

WHEN WE GOT TO THE STUDEO WE WERE MET BY HELPERS WHO TOLD US WHAT TO DO AND THE FIRST THING WAS THE MAKEUP DEPARTMENT.

WE FINALLY GOT ON THE SHOW ITSELF AND RIGHT AS WE GOT ON STAGE WE WERE THEN TO BE GREETED BY

ROLONDA WATTS WHO IS THE STAR AND THE ANNOUNCER OF THE SHOW OR AS YOU WOULD SAY THE HOST.

WHEN WE MET HER IT WAS QUICK AND SORT OF SNOBBISH.

SHE ALSO ASKED ME TO SAY I CHEATED ON GAIL WITH 40 DIFFERENT WOMEN WHICH WAS A LIE.

BUT I DID IT BECAUSE SHE PROMICED TO GIVE ME 250 MORE DOLLORS..

SO I DID IT AND I WAS CRUCIFIED BY THE AUDIENCE.

I WAS INSULTED OVER AND OVER AND IT ACTUALLY HURT MY FEELINGS. SOME PEOPLE CALLED ME A FAT SLOB AND OTHERS UGLY AND UGLY BODY.

I PUT UP WITH IT FOR THE MONEY BUT DIDNT REALIZE AND FORGOT TO REALIZE THIS WAS GOING TO BE SHOWN ALL OVER THE UNITED STATES.

THIS WAS TERRIBLE.

AND ON THE SHOW THERE WAS A SURPRISE. MY SON CHARLIE AND THE MOTHER OF MY SON CAME AS A SUPRRISE. I WASNT READY NOR DID I KNOW THEY WERE COMING ON THE SHOW. I THOUGHT IT WAS JUST ME AND GAIL.

SO IT LOOKED BAD.

AFTER THE SHOW I STARTED REALLY GETTING MAD AT THE BACK STAGE WHERE ROLONDA AND HE THEN BOYFRIEND MICHEAL MOORER. HE WAS THE CHAMPION BOXER OR ONE OF THEM AT THAT TIME I REALLY ENJOYED COMING BACK TO L.A FROM NEW YORK ON A PLANE WITH MY SON CHARLIE NEXRT TO ME THE WHOLE TRIP.

111. MICHEAL MOORER.

AS I WAS YELLING BACK AT ROLONDA I TOLD THIS ONE GUY TO SHUT UP AND EVERYONE JUST HUSHED WHEN I DID THAT. I FOUND OUT WHY.

IT WAS BOXING CHAMP MICHEAL MOORER.

ANYWAYS THEY SAID TO ME-"BETTER WATCH OUT TALKING TO HIM LIKE THAT". I ASKED WHY AND THEY TOLD ME BECAUSE IT IS MICHEAL MOORER BOXING CHAMP. SO I GOT OUT OF THERE AFTER APOLOGISING SINCERELY TO HIM AND HE WAS COOL WITH THAT.

AFTER THE SHOW WE GOT TO STAY ANOTHER DAY AFTER AND WE ENJOYED GOING AROUND NEW YORK. IT WAS QUITE FUN.

WE FLEW BACK AND UNFORTUNATELEY GAILS FATHER WATCHED THE SHOW AND HE THOUGHT IT WAS TERRIBLE OF WHAT I SUPPOSIDELEY DID. THOUGH I DIDNT. REMEMBER I SAID 40 WOMEN ONLY TO GET THE 250 DOLLORS. THE THINGS PEOPLE DO FOR MONEY HUH?

SO AS WE WERE ON THE SHOW I FELT IT WAS A SET UP. I TRIED TO TALK AFTER I SAID I CHEATED 40 TIMES WHICH I DIDNT. AND I SAID THAT BECAUSE ROLONDA TOLD ME SHE WANED TO SHOW TO BE MORE EDGEYER.

THIS WAS A LIE. ROLONDA WANTED TO PERSECUTE SOMEONE AND THAT SOMEONE WAS ME.

ALL ROLONDA DID WAS INSULT ME AND ASK ME QUESTIONS SHE WAS READY FORM BUT NO QUESTIONS THAT I WAS READY FOR.

ROLONDA WAS RUDE TO ME AND ACTED LIKE SHE HATED ME.

ON THE BREAK I TOLD HER I HEARD SHE WAS FOR ABPORTION AND I SAID SHE IS TERRIBLE. SHE SAID "THATS GOOD TELEVISION".

WHEN WE GOT BACK TO THE SHOW ON AIR SHE SAID TO ME "TELL ME CHUCK WHAT YOU TOLD ME ON BREAK". I STARTED TO TRY AND TRY BUT THEY PERSCUTED ME NOT LETTING ME SAY MORE THEN 3 WORDS OR LESS.

I FELT RAILROADED AND MY FEELING WERE HURT BY THEM SAYING I WAS UGLY AND NOT POSSIBLY A STRIPPER. IN THE TIMES I COULD TALK I WAS GOING TO START TO TALK ABOUT BEING A STRIPPER AND THAT IS WHY I AM PERMISCUOUS BECAUSE I WAS SPOILED BY LADIES WHEN I WAS A STRIPPER.

BUT I COULDNT GET THAT OUT BECAUSE ROLONDA LET THE AUDIENCE RESPOND AFTER I SAID THE WORDS "I WAS A STRIPPER". SOME GUY IN THE AUDIENCE SAID "NO ONE WOULD EVER WANT TO LOOK AT YOUR UGLY BODY".

I WAS UPSET AND FINALLY AFTER MORE PERSECUTION BECAUSE OF THE LIE THAT I WAS WITH AND CHEATED WITH MY GIRLFRIEND WITH 40 WOMEN, WELL I DECIDED TO WALK OFF THE SHOW AND WHEN I DID THAT I THREW A TAPE OF MY BAND AND THE ALBUM I MADE EARLIER IN 1994 ENTITLED BADDCLOWN 1.

AFTER THE SHOW ALL THE INSULTERS AND HATERS SAID GOODBEY AND ACTED DIFFERENT. THEY WERE NICE TO ME AND I JJST DIDNT GET THEIR PHILOSOPHY OF BEING HATERS TOWARDS ME WHILE I AM ON STAGE AND THEN WHEN I AM OFF STAGE AFTER THE SHOW THE PEOPLE WHO WERE DOING ALL THE CALLS AND INSULTS AND HECKLERS WERE NOW BEING FRIENDLEY AND ASKING ME IF THERE IS ANYTHING I NEED. IT WAS LIKE THEY WERE ALL

PHONEY JUST FOR THE SHOW WHEN INVOLVED WITH THE SHOW.

THATS WHY I DONT LIKE SHOW BIZ AS IT IS NOW. ITS TOO FAKE.

112 CARNEY WILSON

ANOTHER SHOW I WAS ON AND AGAIN IT WAS IN 1995. THE WAY I GOT ON THESE SHOWS WAS WRITE A STORY TO THEM ABOUT A TOPIC THEY MIGHT PICK ME TO BE ON AND THEY DID.

THIS ONE UNLIKE THE OTHER TALK SHOW CALLED ROLONDA WAS THAT I LIKED WOMEN ONLY FOR THEIR BODIES AND THE OTHER GUY AGAINST ME LIKED WOMEN FOR THEIR BRAINS AND IT WAS AGAIN A LIE AND JUST AN ACT.

IN FACT THE GUY LIKING WOMEN FOR THEIR BRAINS TOLD ME AFTER THE SHOW HE LIKED WOMEN FOR THEIR BODIES.

ANYWAYS IT WA ANOTHER SILLY TALK SHOW THAT I TOOK THE JOB FOR THE AIRPLANE FLIGHT AS WELL AS FOR THE MONEY IN WHICH I GOT 400 DOLLORS WHICH WAS MORE THEN WHAT THE ROLONDA SHOW GAVE ME.

BEFORE THE SHOW WE WERE TO MEET CARNEY WILSON AT THE GREEN ROOM. THE GREEN ROOM IS WHAT THE CALL THE WAITING ROOM FOR THE PEOPLE TO BE ON THE SHOW BEFORE THEY ARE ON THE SHOW.

I TOLD CARNEY I HAD BEEN WITH 1000 WOMEN AND I HAVENT BUT THAT WAS THE ACT SO I KEPT UP THE ACT WITH CARNEY TOO AND ANYONE ELSE INVOLVED IN THE CARNEY WILSON SHOW.

BEFORE THE SHOW THE CONTESTENTS WERE REALLY FUNNY AND INTERESTING AND ONE I WOULD SEE LATER PLAY IN DIFFERENT SHOWS LIKE L.A. LAW AND LAW AND ORDER.

THIS GUY IN THE GREEN ROOM WITH ME WAS FLIIRTACIIOUS WITH THE LADIES THERE BUT THE AUDIENCE THOUGHT HE WAS DEEP DOWN GAY AND WHEN THEY CONFRONTED HIM ON THAT IT WAS LIKE HE AGREED,

OTHER PEOPLE ON THE SHOW WERE ONES AGAINST ME AND THERE WERE 10 PEOPLE OR SO ON THE SHOW AND 1/2 WERE TO BE FOR WOMENS BRAINS OR MENS BRAINS AND 1/2 FOR WOMEN AND MENS BODIES. THE GIRLS WHO WERE ON MY SIDE WERE QUITE BEAUTIFUL AND THEY WERE SUPPOSED TO BE LIKING GUYS JUST FOR THE BODY AND IT WAS LIKE A FUN LITTLE COMPETITION AND OF COURSE THE AUDIENCE INSULTED ME AGAIN AND ONE ORIENTEL GIRL SAID TO ME "I HEAR IF YOU HAVE SEX 2-3 TIMES A DAY YOU WILL LOSE WEIGHT AND WELL IF THAT IS TRUE THEN WHY ARE YOU SO OVERWEIGHT?"

AND MORE INSULTS CAME ABOUT. HEY EVEN HAD A CHART ABOUT WHY CERTAIN MEN LIKE WOMEN FOR BODIES AND SOME FOR BRAINS. GOT UP THERE AND TOOK THE CHART AWAY AND AFTER THE SHOW WE WERE ALL INVITED TO HANG OUT AT A BAR JUST LIKE THE ROLONDA SHOW WHEN ME AND GAIL MY WIFE NOW AND GIRLFRIEND THEN WAS TAKEN OUT TO A BAR BY ONE OF THE CONTESTANTS THEN TOO AND THE GUY WAS TRYING TO HAVE A THREESOME ORGY.

THAT DIDNT HAPPEN.

SO ON THE CARNEY WILSON SHOW AFTER THE SHOW WAS OVER I DANCED WITH CARNEY ARM AND ARM AT THE END OF THE THE SONG FOR THE SHOW.

ALL IN ALL THIS WAS MORE FUN AND LESS INSIULTS AND ON ROLONDA I WAS OVER AND OVER INSULTED AND THIS ONE ONLY A FEW INSULTS.

AFTER GETTING MAD AT THE ORIENTEL GIRL FOR INSULTING ME BRIAN WILSON DAD OF CARNEY CAME OUT TO STOP ME FROM GETTING MAD. GUESS BRIAN WAS A SORT OF BODYGUARD AND SECURITY FOR THE SHOW JUST AN UNOFFICIAL ONE. THERE WAS TALK ON THE SHOW THAT BRIAN FELT HE OWED CARNEY BY BEING A BAD DAD IN THE PAST SO NOW HE WAS MAKING UP FOR LOST TIME.

BEFORE I GOT ON THE SHOW I WAS TALKING TO BRIAN WILSON FOR LIKE AN HOUR AND WE TALKED ABOUT EVERYTHING BUT MUSIC BECAUSE I DIDNT KNOW AT THE TIME I WAS TALKING TO BRIAN THAT HE WAS BRIAN WILSON. I THOUGHT HE WAS JUST A STAGE HAND OR SOMETHING BEING I DIDNT RECOGNISE HIM.

113. BRIAN WILSON. SONGWRITER FOR THE BEACH BOYS, MAIN SONGRWRITER AND FOUNDER OF THE BAND THE BEACH BOYS.

WHEN I WAS BACK HOME FROM NEW YORK I ASKED FOR AN AUTOGRAPHED PICTURE OF CARNEY AND ONE OF BRIAN AND THE GUY IN CHARGE TOLD ME YES TO CARNEY BUT NO TO BRIAN WILSON. AS I SAID EARLIER IN THE BOOK, ME AND BRIAN TALKED BACKSTAGE FOR AROUND 3 HOURS AND I DIDNT EVEN KNOW IT WAS HIM. OF COURSE I SHOULD HAVE KNOWN BEING HIS DAUGHTER CANREY IS THE HOST OF THIS SHOW I AM ON AT THIS TIME, ME AND BRIAN TALKED ABOUT MOTORCYLES TO THE WAR TO LIFE BUT NOTHING ABOUT MUSIC. REAL IRONIC. AFTERWARDS PEOPLE WERE EVEN STAR STRUCK OF ME TREATING ME BETTER BECAUSE THEY WERE AMAZED I TALKED TO BRIAN FOR 3 HOURS THOUGH THEY ASKED ME IF I KNEW WHO I

WAS TALKING TOO AND I SAID NO AND THEY TOLD ME. IT WAS A TRIP. THEN AS IS SAID BEFORE THE ONLY TIME I DEALT WITH HIM AS I KNEW HIM I WAS REJECTED BY HIM AND HIS PEOPLE TELLING ME I CANNOT HAVE AN AUTTOGRPHED COPY OF A BRIAN WILSON GLOSSY. THOUGH CARNEY SENT TIME ONE WITH SOME NICE INFO ON IT.

114. JENNY JONES. THE JENNY JONES SHOW WAS IN CHICAGO AND I LIKE CHICAGO ALOT MORE THEN NEW YORK. NO ONE INSULTED ME IN THIS ONE IN FACT WHEN WE DID THE USHER MAKE OVER PEOPLE TREATED US LIKE STARS

CHICAGO WAS A FUN TIME. LET ME PLEASE EXPLAIN.

WHEN I GOT THERE I GOT A DAY TO KICK IT AND THEN THE NEXT DAY ALSO I GOT TO HANG OUT UNTIL THE NEXT DAY WHICH WAS THE SHOW AND THEN SPEND THE NIGHT A THIRD NIGHT. THEN WE LEFT ON THE 4TH DAY.

IT STARTED WHEN I ORDERED A GRANDS SLAM WITH STEAK BEING 22 DOLLORS BUT OF COURSE WE ARE GIVEN 100 DOLLORS CREDIT TO BUY FOOD ON THE TAB OF THE OWNERS OF THE SHOW JENNY JONES. SAME AS THE CARNEY WILSON SHOW AS WELL AS THE ROLONDA SHOW. IN EACH SHOW WE GOT TO SPEND UP TO 100 DOLLORS ON FOOD FOR CREDIT AT THE HOTEL WE WERE STAYING IN AND BOTH TIMES IN NEW YORK I WAS STAYING AT THE ST MORITZ HOTEL WHICH IS RIGHT ACROSS THE STREET FROM CENTRAL PARK AND I FORGOT TO SAY HOW I LOVED JUST STARING AT THE WHOLE PARK OUT THE WINDOW ON THE 24TH FLOOR.

AND THE 16TH FLOOR I BELEIVE AT CARNEY WILSON AND 24TH AT ROLONDA SHOW.

BUT NOW I AM IN CHICAGO AND FOR THE FIRST TIME IN MY LIFE I AM SEEING IT SNOW IN THE CITY-

SO ON THE SECOND DAY I HUNG OUT WITH A GIRL NAMED LISA AND THEN DID A MALE STRIP FOR 6 GIRLS AND THEY WERE EXCITED I DID THAT. ALSO MADE ALOT OF FRIENDS IN THE 3 DAYS WE WERE THERE.

NOW THE SHOW.

RMEMEBER THAT 22 DOLLORS IN NEW YORK IS LIKE 6 DOLLOR IN CALIFORNIA AND SAME AS CHICAGO WAS PRETTY DARN EXPENSIVE THOUGH BOTH IN CHICAGO AND NEW YORK I TRIED THE NEW YORK HOT DOG IN NEW YORK AS WELL AS THE CHICAGO DOG IN CHICAGO AND THAT WAS A TIE. THEY BOTH WERE AMAZING.

AND THE PRICE WASNT BAD 2 DOLLORS FOR A DOG IN BOTH PLACES.

I BROUGHT MY KEYBOARD SO I COULD SING ON THE SHOW, THEY DIDNT USE IT, THEY CALLED MY MUSIC "YOUR LITTLE MUSIC".

WHILE I WAS AT THE CHICAGO HOTEL WHICH IS THE BEST WESTERN IN DOWNTOWN ON MICHIGAN AVENUE, I I REALLY LOVED IT. IT WAS SNOWING AND I WALKED ON THE STREETS IT WAS RIGHT NEXT TO THE TALLEST BUILDING IN CHICAGO AND ONE OF THE TALLEST IN THE WORLD.

I WAS CHATTING WITH THE OTHER GUESTS AT THE BAR DOWNSTAIRS AND PLAYED 2 SHOWS ON BOTH DAYS ON THE PIANO IN THE PIANO BAR. THEY OFFERED ME A PAYING GIG THERE BUT I HAD TO GO BACK TO MY FAMILY IN CALIFORNIA OTHERWISE I WOULD HAVE.

ON THE THIRD DAY WE GOT TO GO TO THE STUDEO AND I FORGOT TO SAY WHEN I GOT A TAXI TO THE HOTEL I WAS

WITH THE OTHER TWO GUYS I WAS TO BE ON THE SHOW WITH ON A CONTEST OF ALL THREE OF US LIKING FAT BLACK WOMEN. I JUST SAID THAT TO GET ON TV AND MAKE MONEY AND GET A FREE TRIP TO CHICAGO. THE TAXI DRIVER WAS A BLACK RACIST GUY AND ASKED THE TWO BLACK GUYS WITH ME ON THE AND IN THE TAXI WHAT I WAS WHAT THEY WERE DOING WITH THE ME, SOME WHITE GUY. I AS OFFENDED AND TOLD THE TAXI DRIVER THAT AS I GOT OUT.

THE DAY OF THE SHOW. WE WERE ALL WAITING TO DO OUR PARTS ON THE SHOW AND WAITED IN ONE BIG ROOM. WE DID PREVIEWS ON WHAT THE THREE OF US WERE DOING WHICH WE WERE TO BE DRESSED LIKE THREE NURDS AND THEN HAVING AN USHER MAKEOVER WHICH MEANS DRESS LIKE USHER RAYMOND THE CHICOGO NATIVE DANCER AND SINGER. AT THAT TIME HE WAS JUST BREAKING OUT AS A CELEBRATY. I NEVER HEARD OF HIM BUT SAW HIM DANCE SO I DECIDED TO IMITATE HIM. SO FIRST THEY DID A SHOT OF THE THREE OF IUST BEING NURDS AND THEN A SHOT LATER OF US COMING OUT LIVE SO THE AUDINCE SEES THE DIFFEENCE AND WE WERE TREATED LIKE STARS. THE CROWD REALLY MOBBED US AND GREETED US WITH GREAT ANTICIPATION AND RESPECT. IT WAS FUNNY AND FUN.

BEFORE THIS JENNY JONES MET US BEFORE THE SHOW AND SAID TO ME. "OH YOUR DRESSED LIKE THAT AND AM GOING ON T.V.". JENNY WAS THE NICEST ONE OF ALL THE 5 TALK SHOWS I WAS ON.

ON THE SHOW

WHEN I GOT ON WE FIRST WERE SHOWN WE WERE ALL NURDS IN A PRE-RECORDED FILMING OF THE THREE OF US AS NURDS AND DRESSED IN NURD CLOTHING THAT WE

GOT FROM THE JENNY JONES COLECTION OF CLOTHS THEY HAD IN "WARDROBE".

WE THEN WERE ON AGAIN COMING IN DRESSED IN A NEW MAKEOVER. IT IS CALLED AN USGHER MAKEOVER.

AND I DIDNT LIKE THE DRESS BUT IT WAS THE STYLE FOR CHICAGO PEOPLE AND IN THE CITY.

IT WAS LIKE FULL SWEAT CLOTHS IN ONE JUMPER AND IT WAS NEAT AND TIDY BUT I DIDNT LIKE IT BUT THE CROWD WENT CRAZY AFTER SEEING US AS NURDS THEN BEING THESE 3 COOL LOOKING GUYS WHO LOOK LIKE WE ARE ALL IN THE SAME BAND OR SOMETJHING CONNECTED LIKE THAT.

NEXT WE SAT DOWN AND WE WERE SUPPOSED TO BE INTERVIEWED BY A BLACK FAT GIRL AND THE WINNER GETS HER ON A DATE. SHE ASKS US QUESTIONS LIKE ON THE DATING GAME EXCEPT SHE CAN SEE US UNLIKE THE DATING GAME WHICH ON THAT SHIOW THEY ARE BEHIND A WALL WHEN BEING ASKED QUESTIONS BY THE FEMALE DATE.

THEN THEY TOLD US TO GET UP AND DANCE AND THERE I WENT AS WELL AS THE TWO BLACK GUYS. IT WAS ONLY 3 CONTESTENTS, ME AND THE OTHER TWO BLACK GUYS. I WAS IN THE MIDDLE OF THE DANCE WITH ONE BLACK GUY ON EACH SIDE. AS WE DANCED JENNY JONES SAID "I THINK WE KNOW THE WINNER, NUMBER 2 " WHICH WAS ME.

BUT I DIDNT WIN AND THANK GOODNESS. FIRST OF ALL I DIDNT WANT TO GO ON A DATE WITH THIS LADY BUT SHE DEFINATELY WASNT MY TYPE AND ANYWAYS BACK IN CALIFORNIA I HAD A WIFE.

SO THANK GOD THEY PICKED NUMBER ONE AND AS WE LEFT I WAS ASKING FOR 500 INCLUDING PAYING FOR THE TIME I PARKED MY CAR IN L,A, EX. I GOT 600 DOLLORS AND ONE OF THE OTHER GIRLS SAID "HEY, I ONLY GOT 100 DOLLORS". HE SAID " YEAH BUT CHUCK MADE THE SHOW."

AS I TOOK THE AIRPLANE HOME I MET SOME REAL NICE ELDERELY PEOPLE WHO SAID THEY TRAVEL ALOT AND-ON THE PLANE WHEN IT WAS GOING DOWN TO LA EX. MY EARS GOT SO CLOGGED I WAS 75 PERCENT DEAF FOR FOUR DAYS AFTER I GOT BACK.

JENNY JONES WAS A NICE PERSON AND COOL TO ME. SHE FELT THAT I WON THE CONTEST BEING I STARTED DANCING LIKE I WAS A MALE EXOTIC DANCER MEETS USHER.

115. MARYLYN KEGEN

I GOT ON THE MARYLYN KEGEN SHOW AND OUT OF THE FIVE SHOWS I WAS ON IN BETWEEN 1995-2000, THIS WAS THE ONLY ONE THAT WAS NOT IN NEW YORK OR CHICAGO. THIS ONE IS CALLED THE MARYLYN KEGEN SHOW WAS ACTUALLY IN LOS ANGELES I BELEIVE IN THE PARAMONT STUDEO. IM NOT SURE THOUGH. I CANT REMEMBER TO BE HOMNEST WITH YOU.

WE WERE PICKED UP AT MOMS HOUSE, ME AND GAIL MY WIFE THAT IS AND THIS IS THE SECOND SHOW GAIL GOT ON WITH ME. THE OTHER SHOW GAIL WAS ON WITH ME WAS THE ROLONDA SHOW AND NOW THE MARYLYN KEGEN SHOW. THE LIMO DRIVER WHO PICKED US UP TOLD ME HE WAS DAVID CROSBYS CHEUFFER. I HOPE HE WAS TELLING THE TRUTH.

IIT WAS QUITE COINCIDENTEL BECAUSE I HAD MET DAVID CROSBY AT THE STRIP BAR 2 WEEKS EARLIER.

WHY WAS ME AND GAIL ON THIS SHOW?

THE TOPIC.

AGAIN I WROTE A LETTER TO THEM WITH A STRANGE STORY THAT WAS MOSTELY TRUE WITH A LITTLE BIT OF EXAGGERATION. THE LETTER I WROTE TO THEM AGAIN WAS THAT I HAD BEEN WITH 1000 WOMEN WHICH I WASNT REALLY BUT THEY BELEIVED ME OR AT LEAST BELEIVED I COULD PLAY THE PART OF A GUY WHOM SLEEPS WITH 1000 WOMEN SO I WROTE THE SAME LETTER AS I XROXED A COPY AND SENT ONE TO MARYLYN KEGEN.

I WAS ALSO OFFERED TO GO ON GORDEN ELLIOT AND ANOTHER SHOW MAURY POVICH. THOSE WERE FOR ME AND MY FIRST CHILD TO REUNITE BUT I COULDNT DO IT BECAUSE THE MOTHER OF MY FIRST CHILD WOULDNT GO ALONG WITH IT SO I DIDNT GET ON MY 6TH AND 7TH SHOW. NO 6TH OR 7TH SHOW. THE MOTHER OF MY FIRST CHILD NAMED TRISHA CUSSED OUT THE PEOPLE WHO CALLED HER FROM MAURY POVICH. IT WAS SAD AND A WASTE OF A GOOD NEW YORK TRIP IF ALL WOULD HAVE AGREED.

SAD,

THEY DIDNT PICK ME TO BE ON THIS SHOW FOR THE TOPIC OF THE LETTER I DID.

THEY CHANGED IT AND ASKED IF I COULD PLAY THE PART. THEY KNEW IT WAS FAKE AND I HAD TO DO A FAKE TOPIC AND THAT TOPIC WAS .

BEIUNG OBSESSED WITH SEX TOYS.

BEFORE THE SHOW WE WERE PUT IN SEPERATE DREESSING BOOTHS ABOUT THE SIZE OF A RETROOM STALL. WHILE I WAS DRESSING THE GUY NEXT TO ME STARTED TALKING TO ME. AT THIS TIME HE WAS REAL FRIENDLEY AND HE SAID HE WAS FROM HUNTINGTON BEACH WHICH I KNOW THERE THEY ARE AGAINST MXING

RACES LIKE ME AND GAIL WHO IS WHITE. ME AND BLACK-GAIL.

BUT HE HASNT YET SEEN GAIL SO HE TOLD ME HE WAS ON THE SHOW TOO AND I DIDNT ASK HIM WHAT WAS HE ON FOR BECAUSE I THOUGHT HE WAS INTO SEX TOYS TOO.

BUT HE WASNT .

AS WE GOT ON THE SHOW I FOUND OUT HE WAS INTO WEARING DIAPERS AND HIS GIRLFRIEND TO BABY HIM AS THEY HAVE SEX. I THOUGHT THE SHOW WAS ABOUT SEX TOYS AND IT TURNS OUT THERE WAS A LITTLE TWIST. FREAKY SEX AND WEIRD SEX FETISHES IS NOW WHAT IS WHAT CHANGED TO AND NOW WHAT IT WAS CALLED.

SO ME AND GAIL PRETENDED ON THE SHOW. GAIL SAYS SHE LIKES TO TIE ME UP WITH NYLONS WHICH SHE HAS NEVER DONE AND ME AND GAIL ARE NOT INTO THIS TOPIC OF SEX TOYS AND SEX FETISHES. ME AND GAIL IN REALITY HAS NO SEX FETISHES OR SEX TOYS. WE ARE JUST INTO EACH OTHERS BODIES. GAIL AT THIS TIME IS PREGNANT ON THE SHOW SO I SAID I WAS INTO   PREGNANT WOMEN TOO WHICH I MADE UP BUT I AM NOT TURNED OFF BY PREGNANT WOMEN.

THE GUY WHO I TALKED TO IN THE DRESSING ROOM WAS INTO WEARING DIAPERS WHILE HIS GIRLFRIEND FEEDS HIM ETC SO I SAID "FORGET THE SEX TOYS I WANNA WEAR A DIAPER". EVERYONE LAUGHED AND I THINK THE GUY WAS EMBARRASSED AND HUMILIATED.

AFTER THE SHOW I SAID WE SHOULD HANGOUT SOMETIME AND HE SAID NO IN A MAD WAY SO I GUESS I GOT HIM UPSET AND HE THOLUGHT I WAS MAKIING FUN OF HIM WHEN IN REALITY I REALLY LIKED THE DIAPER IDEA MORE THEN THE FAKE IDEA THAT I LIKED SEX TOYS.

THE CROWD WASNT TREATING ME SO BAD LIKE THEY DID ON THE ROLONDA SHOW AND THE CARNEY WILSON SHOW.

MARYLYN KEGEN WAS A NICER PERSON AND DIDNT INSULT ME LIKE ROLONDA DID AND CARNEY DID. JENNY JONES WAS NICE TOO AS WAS MARYLYN KEGEN.

I ALWAYS WONDER WHAT MARYLYN IS UP TO AT THIS MOMENT.

GAIL WAS A GOOD ACTRESS ON THE SHOW ANDS WAS A GOOD SPORT AND WENT WITH ME. SHE WAS OFFERED TO GO ON THE FORGIVE AND FORGET SHOW WITH ROBIN GIBBONS.

BUT SHE TURNED THAT OPPORTUNITY DOWN.

SO GAIL HAD BEEN ON 2 OF 5 SHOWS I WAS ON FOR TALK SHOWS.

ALL IN ALL MARYYN KEGEN WAS A PRETTY COOL NICE PERSON TO ME.

116-118

MOLLY RINGWALD, JOE NAMETH AND BRIGETTE FONDA.

116. MOLLY RINGWALD.

I RAN INTO MOLLY RINGWALD TWO TIMES IN MY LIFE AND IT WAS ALL BEFORE 1992.

I BELEIVE THE FIRST TIME WAS IN THE LATE 1980S. I WAS AT WALTERS COFFEE SHOP IN CLAREMONT AND HERE IS MOLLY RINGWALD WITH A BABY THAT I BELEIVE IS NOT HER.

I BELEIVE THAT LATER BECAUSE I SEE HER IN A MOVIE REAL SOON AFTER THIS ABOUT HER WITH A BABY.

WHEN I LOOK AT HER SHE MAKES THE WELL KNOWN MOLLY RINGWALD SNARL AND THAT WAS IT FOR THE FIRST TIME.

THE SECOND TIME I AM AT RALPHS MARKET IN CLAREMONT ON THE BORDER OF POMONA AND CLAREMONT ON INDIAN HILL BLVD. I SEE HER AND MY FRIEND ANNIE IS WITH US AND SHE IS TO BE THE MOTHER OF MY SECOND SON SAYS "THERES MOLLY RINGWALD". WHEN I PASS MOLLY SHE TURNS AROUND WHILE STILL WALKING FOREWARD AND I DO THE SAME AND ANNIE DOESNT MIND THE FRUSTRATION BEING ANNIE IS STAR STRUCK AND FOUND IT IMPRESSIVE THAT MOLLY SEEMED TO LIKE ME. IF ANNIE WASNT THERE I WOULD HAVE GONE TO TALK TO HER TO GO OUT WITH HER BUT THAT DIDNT HAPPEN. THIS REMINDS ME OF ANOTHER PERSON NAMED TATIA WHO I MET THE SAME WAS. TATIA TURNING AROUND WHILE STILL WALKING FOREWARD AND ME DOING THE SAME. LATER TATIA HARRIS BECAME MY GIRLFRIEND AND THEN FIANCEE.

117.. JOE NAMETH.

ME AND A GIRLFRIEND IN 1981 NAMED VICKI AND MY FRIEND JERRY THOMPSON WENT TO THE BEACH TOGETHER AT LAGOONA. THERE I WAS ROMANTIC AND INTIMATE WITH VICKI IN A CAVE.

AS ME AND JERRY AND VICKI WERE DRIVING HOME ON THE 5 FREEWAY WE SEE JOE NAMETH IN A PORSCHE CAR AND WE KNEW IT WAS HIM BY SIGHT BUT ALSO KNEW BECAUSE JOES CAR SAID NAMETH ON THE BACK OF THE CAR. I WAVED TO JOE AND HE NODDED. JOE SEEMED LIKE A REAL COOL GUY.

I TO THIS DAY REMEMBER THIS ALMOST 40 YEARS LATER AND ITIS GOOD TO KNOW JOE IS STILL ALIVE EVEN NOW AT THIS WRITE.

118. BRIGETTE FONDA.

LIKE ALOT OF THESE METHOD ACTRESSED I MET BRIGETTE IN THE STREETS OF POMONA. WHEN I MET HER SHE SAID HER DAD WAS PRACTICING METHOD ACTING AT A PLACE HE IS STAYING AT. A HOTEL IN ONTARIO ON HOLT BLVD.

WHEN I FIRST MET HER I DIDNT RECOGNISE HER. I MADE A PASS AT HER AND SHE REJECTED IT NICELEY.

I THEN SEE HER THE NEXT TIME AND SHE ASKS ME HOW I FEEL ABOUT THE LAST TIME I SAW HER AND I SAID YES, I WAS STILL INTERESTED.

I HELP HER PAY A TICKET AT THE HAVEN COURTHOUSE AND GO WITH HER AND SHOW HER EXACTELEY WHAT TO DO. AFTER THIS WE RUN INTO NICK NOLTE WHO IS PICKTING A PETITIONING A CHILD MOLESTER GAY JUDGE NAMED, WELL, I WONT SAY THE NAME BUT NICK WAS REALLY LIVELEY AND TALKATIVE TO ME UNTIL HE KNOWS I RECOGNISE HIM AND THEN GETS SNOOTY.

THERE WAS A GUY FILMING NICK FROM A HIDING PLACE AND I RUN INTO HIM AND LATER WE TRY TO DO A DOCUUMENTERY WITH THIS GUY WHO LIVES WITH HIS FAMILY IN SAN BERNADINO HI NAME WAS LADRUM I BELEIVE.

BUT THIS DAY HE IS FILMING NICK NOLTE ON THIS PROTEST NICK IS DOING. IF YOU ARE WONDERING WHY NICK NOLTE IS THERE. ITS BECAUSE WHEN HE GOT HIS DUI IN THE MAILIBU LA AREA HE WAS SECRETELEY MOVED TO GO TO COURT AT HAVEN COURTHOUSE 50 MILES FOR SO EAST OF LOS ANGELES.

119. NICK NOLTE

I EVEN SAW NICK NOLTE A TIME BEFORE AT THE COLURTHOUSE. HE WAS BEING ARRANGED OR SOMETHING THE SAME TIME I WAS IN COURT AND THE SAME COURTROOM ALSO.

BACK TO BRIGETTE.

AFTER I HELPED HER AT COURT SHE TOLD ME IF SHE IS BROKE THAT SHE IS ROYALTY AND WARNER BROS WILL ALWAYS FINANCIALLY HELP HER.

I TOOK HER TO THE FAIR ONCE AND DROPPED HER OFF BECAUSE SHE WAS DOING SOME KIND OF WORK THERE. THATS THE LOS ANGELES COUNTY FAIR.

I THEN PICKED HER UP AND SHE SPENT THE NIGHT ON THE COUCH DOWN IN MY MUSIC ROOM. IT WAS PLUTONIC THOUGH I FIND HER ATTRATIVE IT JUST DIDNT HAPPEN. NO SPARKS UNFORTUNATELELY.

ALL IN ALL BRIGRTTE FONDA WAS A DOWN TO EARTH REAL NICE PERSON. THE LAST TIME I SAW HER WAS AT A POINT IN TIME WHERE IT WAS MEANT TO CHANGE SOON. HERE IS WHAT I MEAN. SHE WAS SITTING TALKING TO A FRIEND. A FRIEND WHO WAS A GIRL AT THE OLD BURRITO PLACE RIGHT BY THE OLD ROULETTE BAND PLACE AND HOUSE WE PRACTICED AT. SINSE THEN THE OLD ROULETTE HOUSE WAS GONE AND ABOUT A WEEK LATER THE LEGENDARY OLD BURRITO PLACE I USED TO BUY BURRITOS AT 25 YEARS EARLIER IN 1981 WAS TO BE DEMOLISHED AND MOVED TO A NEW AREA IN ONTARIO. THE LAST WEEK THAT BURRITO PLACE WAS THERE WAS WHEN BRIGETTE WAS SITTING THERE WITH A FRIEND AND TO THNIK IT WAS ALL TO CHANGE IN 1 WEEK. A NEW WHOLE TIME VIBE IS TO CHANGE. I LOVED THE OLD AREA IN POMONA WHERE THE BAND ROULETTE USED TO PRACTICE AT.

BRITETTE WAS ALOT OF FUN.

120. EDDIE MURPHY. 122. RICHARD PRYIOR AND 122. MARIE OSMOND

120. EDDIE MURPHY

WE WERE HEADING TOWARDS THE RECORDING STUDEO IN STUDEO CITY AND HERE NEXT TO US IN THE CAR IN A GREEN MERCEDES IS EDDIE MURPHY. HE WAS FRIENDLEY AND APPRECIATED THAT I WASNT STAR STRUCK AND WANTED TO SAY HI TO ME AS MUCH AS I WANTED TO SAY HI TO HIM. HE LIKED MY VIBE AND I LIKED HIS VIBE. HE WAS COOL.

YEARS LATER I TALKED TO A PERSON NAMED MARGERETTE WHO SAYS SHE IS RELATIVES WITH EDDIE MURPHY AND SHE SAID HE IS GAY AND WAS PROBABLEY TRYING TO PICK UP ON ME. I NEVER GOT ANY PROOF OF WHAT SHE IS SAYING.

THIS IS A LIE. I DONT BELEIVE THAT AT ALL. I BELEIVE HE WAS JUST IN A GOOD MOOD AND WAS HAPPY I WAS A NORMAL PERSON WHO WASNT STAR STRUCK.

121. RICHARD PRYOR

AGAIN IT WAS IN CARS. RICHARD WAS IN LIKE A ROLLS ROYCE AND HE SEEMED VERY AGGITATED. I DIDNT EVEN WANT TO WAVE HI AS HE PASSED BY AGGITATED AND QUICKLEY LOOKED OVER AT US.

122. MARIE OSMOND

I USED TO HAVE A JOB BEING AN AUDIENCE MEMBER. IT WAS THE LOWEST JOB IN THE TOTOM POLL FOR ENTERTAINMENT BUT WE HAD TO APPLAUD WHEN THE LIGHT SAID APPLAUD AND LAUGH WHEN THE LIIGHT SAID LAUGH.

ONCE WE WERE WATCHING MARIE OSMOND AND BETTY WHITE IN A FUTURE SOON TO BE FAILED SIT COM.

MARIE WAS ALWAYS FORGETTING HER LINES AND THOUGHT IT WAS FUNNY WHEN SHE DIDNT AND WE DIDNT FIND IT FUNNY BEING WE WANTED TO GO HOME.

ONCE DURING A BREAK MARIE HAD A BOX OF DONUT HOLES AND DONUTS SHE WAS THROWING TO THE AUDIENCE. WHEN SHE THREW ONE OVER MY HEAD I CAUGHT IT AND ATE IT. SHE LOOOKED UPSET BECAUSE SHE WASNT THROWING IT TO ME BUT OVER MY HEAD AND I SURPRISD HER BY RAISING MY ARM UP AND CATCHING IT.

LATER ON SHE SMILED TO ME WHILE SHE WAS ON THE SIDE OF THE STAGE. I SMILED BACK AND THAT WAS IT.

123- BEN HARPER ANDS 124. BUCKETHEAD.

123. BEN HARPER

I USED TO SEE BEN AT THE PLACE THAT HIS DAD OWNED. THE CLAREMONT MUSIC STORE.

ALOT OF TIMES I WOULD SEE BEN HARPER AROUND CLAREMONT WHEN HE WAS PRETTY YOUNG. MANY TIMES I SEEN BEN AT THE PAY PHONES WHERE ME AND HIM WERE CALLING MUSIC RECORD COMPANIES. I REMEMBER US BOTH DOING IT AND ASKING HOW HIS LUCK WAS. I REMEMBER WHEN HE GOT A STARTER RECORD DEAL WHICH IS A SMALL RECORD DEAL WITHOUT GAMBLING TOO MUCH. I KNOW HE NOW HAS WON GRAMMYS AND IS PRETTY LOVED IN EUROPE AND HE PERFORMS IN RINGO STARRS ALL STAR BAND

HE STILL IS ABOUT POMONA AND CLAREMONT. HE WAS A NICE DOWN TO EARTH GUY.

I ALSO SAW HIM WITH HIS WIFE AT THAT TIME LAURA DERN AT DISNEYLAND AND SAW HIM AT A PLACE CALLED PIZZA AND SUCH. SINSE THEN I HAVENT SEEN HIM BUT FOLLOWED HIM ON T.V. WHERE HE WAS TOTALLY SUPPORTING AND BEHIND A GUY WHO WAS ON AMERICAN IDOL WHO WAS AND IS FROM POMONA

124. BUCKETHEAD

HIS REAL NAME IS BRIAN CARROLL. MY FRIEND BURL USED TO TELL ME HE IS A BIG FAN OF MY BAND AND MY STYLE BADDCLOWN. BURL TOLD ME AND I BELEIVE THIS IS WHERE HE GOT THE IDEA TO WEAR A BUCKET ON HIS HEAD. I DONT KNOW FOR SURE BUT I BELEIVE IT TO BE TRUE BECAUSE HE LIKED THE BADDCLOWN IDEA WHICH WAS ME BEING A CLOWN, NOT A BOZO CLOWN BUT A WILD AND CRAZY LOOKING CLOWN, A BAD CLOWN.

RIGHT AFTER THIS BAND OF MINE CAME TO BE BRIAN THEN DOES THE BUCKET IDEA FOR HIS HEAD AND WEARS A CRAZY MASK ON HIS FACE.

I FINALLY MET HIM IN PERSON AT A SHOW HE DID IN AND AT THE POMONA MALL. UNFORTUNATELEY HE WAS SNOTTY AND HAD AN ATTITUDE AGAINST ME AND I JUST DONT KNOW WHY. MAYBE BURL SAID A LIE ABOUT THAT I MAY HAVE SAID SOMETHING BAD ABOUT BUCKETHEAD.

I LATER FOLLOWED BUCKETHEAD AND HEARD HE WAS IN GUNS AND ROSES AND THEN QUIT BECAUSE IT BOTHERED HIM THAT AXL WAS ALWAYS ON DRUGS.

I DONT BELEIVE HE SHOULD JUDGE UNLESS TGHE DRUG CONSUMPTION BY AXL HURT THE BAND AND THE ONLY THING THAT HURT THE BAND WAS BIUCKETHEAD QUITTING.

THE LAST TIME I SAW BUCKETHEAD HE WAS RIDING DOWN THE STREET ON ROLLER SKATES PLAYING HIS GUITAR LISTENING TO HIS GUITAR ON A ROCKMAN WHICH IS A LITTLE AMP COINNECTED TO HEAD PHONES SO HE CAN HEAR THAT WHICH THIS WAS CONNECTED ON HIS WASTE BELT.

WE TALKED AND HE WAS COOL THEN. HES A TALL GUY ABOUT 6 FOOT 6.

125. LINDA RONDSTADT. 126. PIA ZADORA. 127. GENE SIMMONS OF THE BAND KISS.

WE RAN INTO LINDA RONDSTADT AT BOB DIRES 24 TRACK RECORDING STUDEO CALLED WINETREE RECORDING STUDEO.

LATER BOB MOVED AND HAD HIS STUDEO BE AT HIS HOUSE I GUESS SO HE DOESNT HAVE TO PAY RENT ON A SEPERATE PLACE FOR THE RECORDING STUDEO BUT AT THIS TIME WE WERE COMING IN TO DO STUDEO WORK AND HERE COMES LINDA RONDSTADT IN A LIMOUSINE AND AS SHE SEES US AFTER WE SAY HI TO HER SHE ROLLS THE WINDOW UP. LINDA RONDSTADT WAS A SNOB , BOTTOM LINE.

126. PIA ZADORA.

ME AND ROLAND AKA BILLY BRAGG WERE PLAYING STREET MUSIC IN WESTWOOD AND A MUSLEM WANTED US TO REPRESENT THEM AND THEN A CHRISTIAN WANTED US TO REPRESENT HIM AND WE PICKED THE CHRISTIAN AND AS WE WE WERE PLAYING PIA ZADORA IN CLASSY CAR LIKE A MERCEDES. I REALLY CANT REMEMBER BECAUSE THIS WAS IN 1985 BUT PIA ZADORA STOPS AT THE LIGHT AS WE ARE PLAYING FOR HER AND SHE TURNS HER NOSE UP LITERELLY AND ROLLS THE WINDOW UP. I WILL ALWAYS REMEMBER THAT.

127. GENE SIMMONS THE BASSIST OF KISS.

GENE SIMMONS WAS GOING I GUESS TO PARAMONT STUDEOS BECAUSE WE WERE HEADING THERE. IT WAS ME AND PATRICK HICOX WHO SAW HIM AND SAID HI AND HE WAS REAL FRIENDLEY SAID HI AND THEN DID THE TONGUE LOOK HE DOES. I APPRECIATE THAT HE GAVE US HIS TRADEMARK FOR FREE. IT WAS COOL AND I WILL ALWAYS LIKE GENE SIMMONS.

128. SAMMY DAVIS JR 129. TODD RUNDGRIN 130. FRANK SINATRA.

128. SAMMY DAVIS JR.

ME AND ROLAND BURRITT AKA BILLY BRAGG WAS OFFERED TO OPEN FOR SAMMY DAVIS JR AT A CABLE STATION BACK IN 1984. WE HAD THE GIG SEWED UP AND I GOT IT THROUGH A FRIEND OF MINE NAMED THOMAS TAYLOR AND HE WAS A GUY WHO WORKED AT THE HEALTH SPA AND THOMAS FOUND ME AND ROLANDS MUSIC AS A DIET GREAT SO HE ASKED HIS MOTHER WHO WAS OWNER OF A CABLE STATION AND SHE GOT US TO BE ABLE TO OPEN FOR SAMMY DAVIS JR.

WELL IT DIDNT HAPPEN BECAUSE ROLAND CHICKENED OUT.

ANYWAYS, I GOT A CHANCE TO FINALLY MEET SAMMY DAVIS JR AND IT WASNT IMPRESSIVE. IN FACT IT MADE ME THINK HE WAS STIUCK UP.

LET ME EXPLAIN.

I WAS DOING A LIMO JOB OUT AT LION COUNTRY SAFARI ARENA AND I WAS TALKING TO ANOTHER LIMO DRIVER WHO WAS SAMMY DAVIS LIMOUSINE DRIVER AND HE WAS TELLING ME I CAN MEET HIM.

SEE, WE WERE WAITING FOR THE SHOW TO END AS LINO DRIVERS DO WE WAIT OUT IN THE PARKING LOT WITH ALL THE OTHER LIMOS.

MY LIMO WAS NOT A STRETCH LIMOUSINE BUT THE BEST THEY MADE IN 1971. I HAD A 71 FLEETWOOD LIMOUSINE AND THE DRIVER OF SAMMY DAVIS JR WAS A STRETCH AND THIS WAS A BRAND NEW 1984 IMOUSINE BEING THIS WAS 1984 IT WAS BRAND NEW.

I WAITED AND WANTED AND IN FACT MY PEOPLE CAME FIRST SO I ASKED THEM IF THEY CAN WAIT ABOUT AN HOUR AT THE MOST AS I MEET SAMMY AND I WOULD TAKE OFF THE TIME MONEY WISE AND GIVE THEM THE HOUR FREE AND THEY MY CUSTOMERS OF THE LIMOUSINE OF MINE WERE GOOD WITH THAT.

FINALLY HERE COMES SAMMY WITH A BIG BODYGUARD.

THE LIMOUSINE DRIVER OF SAMMYS TALKS TO THE BODYGUARD AND THEN THE BODYGUARD TALKS TO SAMMY DAVIS JR.

HE MOTIONS FOR ME TO COME OVER.

I COME OVER AND SIT IN THE FRONT SEAT AS SAMMY IS IN THE BACK AND THEN THE DRIVER ROLLS DOWN THR LIMOUSINE AND THE BODY GUARD SAYS TO ME AS SAMMY EXTENDS HIS HAND TO ME BUT DOESNT SAY ANYTHING.

WHAT THE BODYGUARD SAID WAS SOMETHING TO THIS DAY I FELT PHONEY.

THE BODYGUARD OF SAMMY DAVIS JR TOLD ME "MR. DAVIS IS EXTREMELY EXHAUSTED AND WANT TO SHAKE YOUR HAND BUT CANT SPEAK AT THIS MOMENT BECAUSE HE IS EXHAUSTED.

I SHOOK HIS HAND AND THAT WAS IT.

I THANKED THE LIMOUJSINE DRIVER THE BODYGUARD AND SAMMY AND OFF I WENT TO DO THE REST OF THE NIGHT WITH MY LIMOUSINE CUSTOMERS.

129. TODD RUNDGRIN.

I WAS AT THE GUITAR STORE IN HOLLYWOOD FOR ANOTHER REASON THEN TO SEE TODD RUNDGRIN BUT JUST COICIDENTELEY TODD WAS GETTING A STAR ON THE HOLLYWOOD GUITAR CENTER HALL OF FAME.

WE WATCHED HIM TALK AND HE WAS SINNICLE AND BORING AND ACTED LIKE ITS NO BIG DEAL.

HE SEEMED LIKE A MIUSICIAN WITH AN ATTITUDE.

THAT WAS IT FOR TODD RUNDGRIN.

130. FRANK SINATRA.

I WAS IN PALM SPRINGS HAVING FUN KICKING IT THERE FOR 5 DAYS LAYING OUT IN THE SUN AND HANGING OUT AT MY FAVORITE POOL IN PALM SPRINGS. I KNOW ABOUT THIS PLACE BECASUE MERRILL IN 1981 WAS MY GIRLFRIEND AND SHE FIRST TOK ME THERE TO HER APARTMENT SHE HAD THERE AND I ALWAYS LOVED THAT SPOT.

ONE DAY AS I WAS WAKING UP OUTSIDE I SEE THIS SORT OF PARADE OF CARS AND THEN THE LAST CAR HAD FRANK SINATRA IN A CONVERTABLE I BELEIVE IT WAS A MECEDES OR SOMETHING LIKE A ROLLS OR SOMETHING AND THIS GUY FRANK SINATRA LOOKED SO STAND OFFISH AND SO HATEFUL IT TURNED ME OFF. I COULDNT BELEIVE HOW FRANK WAS SO MEAN LOOKING BUT HE WAS AND THAT WAS THE FIRST AND LAST TIME I EVER SAW FRANK SINATRA FROM LIKE 10 YARDS AWAY.

IT WAS LIKE HE WAS CREATING THE OBVIOUS ATTENTION AND AT THE SAME TIME TAKING IT AWAY AND HATING IT AND ACTING LIKE HE HATES IT ALL.

FRANK WAS AN UNHAPPY GUY THEN WHEN I SAW HIM AND THT WAS IT FOR AND WITH FRANK.

131. VAL KILMER 132 . ANNA NICOLE SMITH. 133. GARRET MORRIS

131. VAL KILMER

I WAS IN THE DOORS MOVIE AS A MOVIE EXTRA AND ONE TIME THEY WERE PUTTING L.S.D. IN THE TEA. AT LEAST THAT IS WHAT I HEARD SO LIKE A FOOL I DRANK A WHOLE LOT OF THAT TEA.

SO NEXT THING THAT HAPPENED I OVERDOSED ON THIS TEA AND IT DID TRULY HAVE L.S.D. IN IT BUT YOU ARE NOT SUPPOSED TO DRINK 25 CUPS OF IT, JUST ONE CUP.

BUT ME, I DIDNT DRINK ONE CUP. LIKE A DRUG ADDICT I DRANK 25-30 CUPS.

NEXT THING I STARTED GETTING CHEST PAINS AND I ALMOST PASSED OUT.

ANYWAYS TO MAKE A LONG STORY SHORT THE PEOPLE KNEW I WAS OVERDOSING ON THIS TEA SO THEY TRIED EVERYTHING TO KISS MY ASS SO I WOULDNT SUE.

I DIDNT SUE AND I WASNT GOING TO SUE. I WOUDNT SUE WHEN IT IS MY FAULT AND THIS WAS TRULY MY FAULT.

SO HERE COMES BILLY IDOL AND OLIVER STONE AND THEN THE GUY WHO IS PLAYING JIM MORRISON NAMED VAL KILMER. THEY ALL TREAT ME REAL NICE AND TALK TO ME AND BILLY IDOL GAVE AN AUTOGRAPH FOR MY FRIEND LAILAH WHO REALLY LIKES BILLY IDOL.

VAL TALKS TO ME AS DOES OLIVER STONE AND VAL IS FRIENDLEY AND SO WAS OLIVER STONE AND BILLY IDOL.

IT WAS QUITE AN INTERESTING DAY.

134. OLIVER STONE AND 135. BILLY IDOL.

ANOTHER TIME I MET OLIVER STONE WHEN I I WAS IN CHAIR AND AS LOOKING AT HIM AND WONDERING IF HE SEES ME AND HE WAS NICE TO ACKNOLEDGE ME. I THEN TALKED TO OLIVER STONE AGAIN AND WAS ALLOWED TO AUDITION FOR A FUTURE MOVIE CALLED ZEBRAHEAD WHICH ME AND MICHEAL RAPPAPORT AUDITIONED .

136. MICHEAL RAPPAPORT. HE WAS COMPETITIVE AND GOT THE PART BECAUSE HE ACTED MORE LIKE A WHITE BLACK GUY WHO LOVES THIS BLACK GIRL AND MY ACT WAS I WAS ACTING LIKE A WHITE GUY WHO LIKES BLACK WOMEN. OLIVER STONE PICKS MICHEAL RAPPAPORT.

ALSO WHEN I WAS IN SEATTLE IN 2004 I MET MICHEAL RAPPAPORT AND AKSED TO USE HIS PHONE AND HE WAS REAL COOL AND TOLD ME TO TAKE MY TIME. HE REMEMBERED ME AS I DID HIM AND MICHEAL RAPPAPORT IS A NICE GUY AND SO IS BILLY IDOL AND OLIVER STONE AND VAL KILMER.

THE OTHER TIME I MET VAL KILMER WAS I WAS IN THE BACK BEHIND THE OLYMPIC AUDITORIUM AND HE VAL IS TAKING A BREAK. I WAS IN HIPPY CHARACTOR AND I SAW PEACE TO VAL AND VAL WANTED TO GET OUT OF CHARACTOR AND HE WAS ANNOYED WITH ME.

I THEN SAID TAKE IT EASY BRO AND HE WAS MORE INTO THAT MENTALITY.

BILLY IDOL. I HAD A DRINK WITH AT A BAR ACROSS FROM THE OLYMPIC AUDITORIUM AND HE IS COOL AS OLIVER

STONE WAS FAIR AND KIND AT THE AUDITION FOR ZEBRAHEAD.

ANOTHER TIME I MET VAL KILMER WAS WHEN HE WAS SPOKES PERSON FOR AMERICAN RADIO NETWORK AND A COUPLE TIMES I TALKED TO HIM IN HIS OFFICE AS WELL AS ASKED QUESTIONED WHEN I AUDITIONED AND GOT TO BE ON THE AMERICAN RADIO NETWORK.

ONE TIME THIS GUY WHO WORKED THERE WAS BEING RUDE TO ME AND COMPETITIVE AND SO I COMPLAINED TO VAL AND WE TALKED ABOUT IT AND SOLVED THE PROBLEM. I WAS IN THE RADIO SHOW TILL I GOT TO DO IT LIVE ON THE STATION THAT HAD A BIG FOLOWING AND WAS PLAYED IN IOWA.

ANNA NICOLE SMITH.

I WAS DOING MOVIE EXTRA AND IN THIS JOB ALL I HAD TO DO WAS BE IN THE AUDIENCE AND WHEN THE LIGHT SAID LAUGH WE LAUGHED AND WHEN THE LIGHT SAID APPLAUD WE APPLAUDED.

IT WAS EASY AND WE GOT 35 DOLLORS TAX FREE FOR EACH SHOW AND SOMETIMES WE WATCHED AND PARTICIPATED IN THE AUDIENCE FOR 3 TO 4 SHOWS EVEN IN AN 8 HOUR PERIOD BEING SHIPPED FROM ONE STUDEO TO ANOTHER.

ONE SHOW IN PARTICULAR THERE WAS ANNA NICOLE SMITH WOULD BE ON THE SHOW AS A GUEST APPEARENCE.

SO ONE SHOW SHE WAS ON IT FOR SOME BIT PART AND WE WERE YELLING HI TO ANNA AND SHE SAID "SHUT THE FUCK JP YOU ASSHOLES". SHE WAS REAL MEAN AND UN FRIENDLEY AND SEEMED LIKE SHE WAS ON DRUGS. I REMEMBER THIS WAS IN 1995 OR 96.

OF COURSE LATER SHE DIED IN 2007.

GARRET MORRIS.

ON ONE OF THE SIT COMS WE WERE IN THE AIUDINCE AFTER ONE SHOW GARRET MORRIS JUST STOOD OUT IN FRONT OF THE AUDIENCE AND SO SINSE I KNEW HE WAS THERE TO TALK TO THE AUDEINCE OR ANYONE WHO WANTED TO TALK. I DECIDED TO TALK TO GARRET MORRIS. I TOLD HIM HE DID A GREAT SHOW WHICH HE TRULY DID AND TOLD HIM I LOVED HIM A CHICO ESQUALA ON SATURDAY NIGHT LIVE AND HE APPRECIATED THAT AND ACTUALLY DID A LITTLE IMITATION OF HIS SELF BACK IN THOSE DAYS SAYIING "BASEDBALL BEEN BEDDY BEDDY GOOD TO ME". WE LAUGHED AND I SHOOK HIS HAND AND IT WAS QUITE AN HONOR MEETING HIM.

136. TED TURNER.

THIS WAS AT A BASEBALL CARD SHOW IN WEST COVINA OF ALL PLACES.

HIS TEAM WAS AT THE BASEBALL AND FOOTBALL CARD SHOW AND TED WAS THERE. HE PASSED ME AND NODDED TO ME AND THAT WAS IT. WHEN HE PASSED HE WA COOL AS HE NODDED IN A HUMBLE ACKNOLEDGE TYPE WAY.

137. SMOKEY ROBINSON 138. UMA THURMAN 139. AL BELL OF BELLMARK R4CORDS.

137 . SMOKEY ROBINSON.

I MET SMOKEY ROBINSON OF ALL PLACES AT A CLUB IN WEST COVINA. HE HAD A ROLLS ROYCE OR A BENTLEY OR SOMETHING LIKE THAT AND HE WAS THERE FOR JETSET RECORDS.

I WAS TALKNG TO A GIRL WHO HAD ME BE A CELEBRATY JUDGE IN A CONTEST AND I WAS BEING SARCASTIC SAYING

WHATS THIS JETSET THING AND COINCIDENTELY THEY THE MOTHER OF THE GIRL WHO GOT ME A GIG AS A CELEBRATY JUDGE HAD A MOTHER WHO ACTUALLY HAD A RECORD COMPANY CALLED JETSET RECORDS AND THERE WERE ALOT OF NEW ARTISTS THERE AND I GUESS SMOKEY ROBINSON WAS A JUDGE. I STOOD RIGHT NEXT TO HIM ON THE SIDELINES AND HE DIDNT SMILE DO I DIDNT REALLY RECOGNISE HIM UNTIL HE SMILED WHEN THERE WAS A SONG BY A NEW ARTIIST CALLED WHEN SMOKEY SINGS AND THEY WERE TREATING HIM NICELELY.

I TALKED TO HIM SMALL TALK AND WE HUNG OUT TALKING FOR ABOUT 45 MINUTES TO AN HOUR.

138. UMA THURMAN. ONCE IN RANCHO CUCUMONGA THERE WAS A GIRL I THOUGHT LOOKED AN AWFUL LOT LIKE JULIA ROBERTS WHO I HAD GONE OUT WITH AND I TOLD HER SHE LOOKED LIKE JULIA ROBERTS AND SHE SAID UMA IM A THURMAN. AT LEAST I THOUGHT SHE SAID THAT. SO I SAID YOUR A THURMAN AND SHE SAID "NO I AM UMA THURMAN" AND I SAID OH AND THEN LEFT. I REALLY WASNT A FAN OF HER MOVIES BUT I HEARD ABOUT HER THAT SHE WAS MARRIED TO ETHAN HAWK AT ONE TIME OR ANOTHER.

139. AL BELL OF BELLMARK RECORDS,

I USED TO JUST GO TO HOLLYWOOD AND EXPLORE ALL THE BIG SKY SCRAPERS AND BIG BUILDINGS. I WOULD FIND EVERYTHING FROM CENTRAL CASTING TO QUINCY JONES OFFICE TO JOE JACKSON, MICHEALS DADS OFFICE TO ATLANTIC RECORDS AND CAPITOL RECORDS OF COURSE HAVING THEIR OWN BUILDING AND THEN WARNER BROS AS WELL AS LEAH REMINIS MANAGEMENT WHERE I FOUND WHEN I WAS TRYING TO GET TO KNOW HER. THAT FAILED BUT I TRIED AT LEAST. I HAD FOUND THE DISNEY CHANNEL AND THERE I MET-----

140. JOE MORTON. JOE WAS TELLING ME HE HAD JUST DONE STUFF AT THE X FILES AND TO OTHER THINGS AND I WAS HAPPY TO HEAR IT. I GOT A TALKING PART THERE BUT DIDNT GET IT BECAUSE I WASNT WITH THE SCREEN ACTORS GUILD.

ONCE I FOUND A PLACE CALLED BELL MARK RECORDS AND IT HAD ONE LITTLE DOOR. WHEN I WENT IN IT I WAS TREATED PRETTY ISOLATED BUT WE GOT TO SOMEHOW ASSOSSIATE OURSELVES WITH DEBORAH WALKER WHO WORKED THERE AS I BELEIVE AN A AND R PERSON. DEBORAH MET WITH US AND ONCE EVEN HAD SENT PEOPLE TO SCOUT OUR BAND WHILE WE WERE PLAYING THE RUEBENS CIRCUIT IN ORANGE COUNTY.

UNFORTUNATELELY WE WERE SINGING A SONG CALLED MONKEE JIVE WHICH HAD NOTHING TO DO WITH MONKEES OR BLACK PEOPLE BUT INSTEAD WAS A THING MY OL GUITARIST KENNY MEOLI SAID THAT MUSICIANS ARE FLAKEY AND IN OTHER WORDS MONKEE JIVE AROUND. SO THE GUYS AT BELL MARK RECORDS ARE ALL BLACK AND IT IS A BLACK ORGANASATION WHEN THEY HEARD THAT SONG THEY WALKED OUT AS IF THEY WERE INSULTED. THIS WAS A MISUNDERSTANDING AND WE TRIED TO TELL DEBORAH BUT SHE GOT OFFENDED TOO AND IT HAD NOTHING TO DO WITH BLACK PEOPLE OR RACISIM ONLY A COMMENT ON HOW MUSICIANS MONKEE AROUND. KENNY CALLED IT MONKEE JIVING AROUND SO WE WROTE A SONG CALLED MONKEY JIVE WHICH IS ONLY ABOUT FLAKEY MUSICIANS. WHITE ONES BASICALLY.

SO WE LOST OUT ON BELLMARK RECORDS AND THEY FINALLY MADE IT BIG THROUGH THE SONG OOPS THERE IT IS.. AND OTHERS. WE ALMOST GOT SIGNED THERE BUT NOT QUITE.

I LEARNED ALOT WATCHING THEM IN ONE BIG ROOM AND ACTUALLY DOING ALL THE PACKAGING THEMSELVES AND THEY WERE REALLY GRUMPY AND UNFRIENDLEY PEOPLE TO US. AL BELL WAS A TOTAL MEAN SNOB IN MY OPINION. IF I DIDNT KNOW BETTER I WOULD THINK HE WS RACIST AGAINST WHITE PEOPLE.

AND THAT WAS IT WITH AL BELL THE OWNER OF BELLMARK RECORDS,

141. JOE BENSON KLOS 95.5 DISC JOCKY.

JOE REALLY LIKED AUTRY ODAYS MUSIC AND PUT OUR MUSIC ON HIS RADIO SHOW 95.5 KLOS AND JOE WAS ONE OF THE GUYS WHO HAD BEEN THERE THE LONGEST. JOE PUT US ON THE RADIO 5-10 TIMES AND WAS VERY APPRECIATIVE OF OUR MUSIC. ME AND LAILAH TALKED TO HIM AND ATTEMPTED TO GET AN INTERVIEW BUT HE DIDNT GIVE US THAT BUT WAS VERY GENEROUS WHEN IT COMES TO PUTTING US ON THE RADIO SHOW KLOS 95.5 LOCAL LICKS.

ALL IN ALL JOE WAS A RESPECTFUL AND FAIR PERSON. I LIKED HIM ALOT AND FELT HE HAD ALOT OF CHARISMA AND REPECT HIM AS A LEGENDARY DISC JOCKY IN LOS ANGELES.

142. BOBBY BLOTZER 143, BING CROSBY, 144 SONNY BARGER

142. BOBBY BLOTZER. DRUMMER FOR THE BAND RATT.

ANNIE, THE MOTHER OF MY SECOND SON HAD A JOB AND HER JOB WAS TO HAVE SOMEONE BUY A HOME IN WHICH THE PERSON LIVING THERE WAS LOSING THEIR HOME. IN THIS CASE THE HOME WAS OWNED BY BOBBY BLOTZER AND HE WAS LOSING THE HOME SO ANNIE AND A WORKER THAT GOT HER INTO THIS BUSINESS IS WANTIKNG ME TO

BUY HOMES AND AS I BUY THE HOME I DONT PAY ANYTHING. THE PURPOSE OF THIS PURCHASE IS TO LET BOBBY BLOTZER STAY LONGER IN THE HOME.

SO I WOULD BUY IT AND IN 8 MONTHS GET TERRIBLE CREDIT BECAUSE I AM NOT PAYING ON THE HOME. AS I SAID THE SOLE PURPOSE IS TO LET BOBBY STAY THERE LONGER.

I WAS TO GET PAID 300 PER HOME WHICH IS NOT WORTH IT. I WAS GOING TO DO IT UNTIL I MET BOBBY AND I SORT OF MADE A DEAL THAT IF HE DOES STUDEO WORK FOR A DECENT PRICE AS A DRUMMER TYHEN I WILL DO THIS. BUY A HOUSE TO KEEP BOBBY TO STAY THERE LONGER AND THEN I WILL LOSE IT AND GET BAD CREDIT.

WELL BOBBY GOT HIGH AND MIGHTY ASKING FOR THE PRICE OF 500 TO DO STUDEO WORK. I HAVE HAD AIUDIE DESBROW DO STUDEO WORK BEFORE AND HE ONLY CHARGED ME 35 A SONG WHICH WAS 1-5 FOR THE DAY BEING WE HAD DONE THREE SONGS. 1. GET HIGH AND 2. FLY WITH GOD AND 3. -EZ AZ 1-2-3.

BOBBY WITH HIS HIGH AND MIGHTY PRICE TURNED ME OFF AND I DIDNT BUY THE HOUSE TO HELP HIM BECAUSE HE WAS WAY TOO EXPENSICVE FOR THE DEAL.

I WOULD BE PAYING BOBBY THE 300 I GOT FOR LOSING MY CREDIT AND BUYING THIS HOME TO HELP HIM OUT AND STILL 200 MORE SO SORRY AND THAT WAS THE END OF KNOWING BOBBY BLOTZER THE DRUMMER FOR THE BAND RATT.

143 BING CROSBY.

THIS IS A QUICK BUT TRUE STORY. WHEN I WAS AROUND 12-13 YEARS OLD WE SAW HIM. HERE IS THE STORY.

DAD AND MOM USED TO TAKE US TO SANTA BARBARA EVERY OTHER WEEK FOR MANY YEARS IN THER 1970S FROM LIKE 1971 TO 1978. WE WENT THERE FOR THE P[URPOSE OF VISITNG MOMS SISTER NAN WHO IS MY AUNT.

THESE WERE SOME OF THE FUNNEST TIMES OF MY LIFE AND WE USED TO GO TO PATRINIS PIZZA AND ITALIAN FOOD AND GO TO DIFFERENT GREAT PLACES TO GO TO EAT AND WE WOULD PLAY SPORTS OUTSIDE IN FRONT OF NANS FROM CATCH WITH A TENNIS BALL TO A BASEBALL TO LATER ON SKATEBOARDING VISITS. IT WAS ONLY GREAT MEMORIES AND VERY WONDERFUL.

MY AUNT WAS A GREAT LADY AND A GREAT GENEROUS AUNT.

SHE PASSED IN 2010 AT AGE 93.

AFTER 1981 SHE MOVED CLOSER TO HER SISTER WHO IS MY MOM CHARLOTTE CONNOR. SHE LIVED IN CLAREMONT JUST UP THE STREET ON BONITA AVENUE.

ONE DAY WE WERE DRIVING ON THE 101 FREEWAY OR THE 5, WHATEVER FREEWAY IS NEAR AND VISIBLE TO SEE THE OCEAN AND AS WE WERE DRIVING HERE COMES THIS ROLLS ROYCE WITH A GUY SMOKING A PIPE AND MY DAD SAYS "WOW, THERE IS BING CROSBY". AND THERE HE WAS. I SAW HIM AND HE WAS SMOKING HIS PIPE JUST LIKE HIS IMAGE WHEN HE IS ON THE ORNGE JUICE COMMERCIALS ETC THAT WE SEE AT THAT AGE THAT I WAS..

I SAW HIS LICENCE AND DAD MENTIONED IT TOO AND IT WAS BNG 222. I ALWAYS WONDERED WHAT THE 222 MEANT. WE WAVED TO HIM AND HE HAPPILY WAVED BACK AND WAS A REAL NICE GUY. THIS WAS IN THE EARLY TO MID 70S.

144. SONNY BARGER THE FOUNDER OF THE BIKE CLUB THE HELLS ANGELS.

ME AND MY BROTHER JOHN DONT GET ALONG. HE USED TO HANG OUT ALOT WITH THE HELLS ANGELS AND HE USED TO BE THE MECHANIC FOR ALOT OF THE HELLS ANGELS. MY BROTHER WAS A WANNABEE BIKER AND A WANNABEE HELLS ANGEL. HE NEVER MADE IT BUT HE WANTED TO. HE HAD A FRIEND WHO WAS IN THE HELLS ANGELS NAMED PHILLIP. AND PHILLIP WOUND UP RIPPING MY MOM OFF AND TRICKING HER IN HER ELDERLEY STATE. I TRUSTED IT BECAUSE PHILLIPS WAS A SUPPOSID "BROTHER" TO MY BROTHER JOHN. SOME BROTHER HUH?

ONE DAY I WAS AT MC DONALDS AND I SEE THIS GUY SITTING IN THE GRASS RELAXING NEAR MC DONALDS. IT WAS A GUY WITH SOMETHING IN HIS THROAT TO MAKE HIM TALK BETTER LIKE A TUBE OR SOMETHING. THIS TURNED OUT TO BE SUNNY BARGER. HE WAS WITH A YOUNG LADY WHO WAS EITHER HIS DAUGHTER OR A GIRLFRIEND . I DONT KNOW I DONT FOLLOW SONNY BARGER. I NEEDED ABOUT A DOLLOR TO COMPLETE MY ORDER FOR MC DONALDS AND ASKED SONNY AND HE CUSSED ME OUT AND WAS VERY UNFRIENDLEY TO ME AND THAT IS MY MEETING WITH SONNY BARGER. THIS WAS IN 1995.

145. WHITNEY HOUSTON

THIS WAS IN THE MID 1990S AT THE START USED TO TELL PEOPLE I SAW WHITNEY HOUSTON IN THE POMONA HOOD. I TOLD PEOPLE SHE WAS IN A VAN AND HANGING OUT WITH OTHER PEOPLE THAT WERE DOING DRUGS AND THIS WAS WHEN PEOPLE DIDNT KNOW OR BELEIVE THAT WHITNEY HOUSTON HAD A DRUG PROBLEM OR EVEN DID DRUGS.

SO AS I TOLD PEOPLE THAT I FOR SURE SAW WHITNEY HOUSTON DOING AND ON DRUGS.

PEOPLE WERE OUTRAGED THAT THE "SACRED" WHITNEY HOUSTON TO EVER BE ACCUSED OF DOING DRUGS. PEOPLE WERE ABOUT READY TO FIGHT ME OVER THE ACCUSATION THAT THEIR FAVORITE SINGER DOES ROCK COCAINE AND METH AND WEED.

NO ONE BELEIVED IT BECAUSE IT WASNT YET KNOWN IN THE TABLOIDS. I SAID I SEE WHITNEY ALWAYS IN THE POMONA HOOD. PEOPLE ASKED ME IN A RAGE "WHAT WOULD WHITNEY BE DOING IN THE POMONA HOOD?"

I TOLD THEM THAT POMONA IS THE BEST SPOT AT THIS TIME IN THE 1990S IN THE STATE AND NEAR LOS ANGELES WHERE WHITNEY LIVES. THIS IS THE PLACE TO GET DRUGS IF YOU WANT TO NOT BE SEEN AS A FAMOUS PERSON BUT AS AN ANNONOMOUS PERSON AND THAT THE INLAND EMPIRE WHICH INCLUDES POMONA DOESNT HAVE PAPPARAZZI AND DOESNT HAVE PEOPLE FOLLOWING HER LIKE SHE IS IN A MAGNAFYING GLASS.

LATER ON I HUNGOUT WITH WHITNEY BUT SHE DIDNT TALK ABOUT HER CAREER OR MUSIC AT ALL. THE SAME WAY HALLE BERRY IS AND THE SAME WAY JANET JACKSON IS. THEY WANT TO BE NORMAL WITHOUT THE FAMOUS THING.

SO I UNDERSTAND AND DONT TALK TO HER ABOUT HER CAREER OR ANYTHING BUT WHAT SHE WANTS TO TALK ABOUT.

I KNEW WHITNEY UNTIL THE WORLD THEN FOUND OUT WHAT I FOUND OUT. THAT WHITNEY HOUSTION HAS A SERIOUS DRUG PROBLEM WHICH IN THE LONG RUN AND IN THE END KILLED HER.

146. MICKY DOLENZ, DRUMMER AND SINGER FOR THE MONKEES .

I WAS AT ONE OF THER BORDER CASINOS IN NEVADA AND THERE NEXT TO AND AT THE BAR WAS MICKY DOLENZ. HE LOOKED LIKE HE WAS HAVING A GOOD TIME AND I SAID HELLO AND TOLD HIM I THINK HE IS A GREAT SINGER AND DRUMMER IN THE MONKEES AND HE WAS VERY APPRECIATIVE AND NICE.

147. JIM BELUSCHI.

I WAS INVOLVED WITH MOVIE EXTRAS BACK FROM 1989 TO 1995. FROM THE DOORS MOVIE IN 1990 TO THE FAN WITH ROBERT DENERO IN 1995 TO MR DESTENY WITH JIM BELUSCHI IN 1989.

THIS WAS THE FIRST ,MOVIE EXTRA I EVER DONE AND IT WAS AT ANGEL STADIUM AS WAS THE MOVIE THE FAN WAS ALSO IN ANAHEIM STADIUUM BEING THAT THE MOVIE THE FAN WAS ABOUT A STALKER STALKING A BASEBALL PLAYER ON A TEAM.

AS I WAS INVOLVED IN THE MOVIE MR DESTENY. I WAS INVOLVED IN A CLOSE TO JIM BELUSCHI SCENE. I WAS PART OF THE SCENE WHEN BELUSCHI WAS DOING SOME KIND OF ARGUMENT WHILE WALKING AND I BUMP INTO HIM AND KEEP WALKING.

AS I KEEP WALKING I DISAPPEAR INTO THE OUTER CORRIDOR TO THE FIELD.

THERE A GIRL MEET ME THERE WHO IS I GUESS MY GIRLFRIEND OR MY WIFE IN THE ACT. EVEN THOUGH I AM OUT OF THE CAMERAS EYE AND NOW ON THE OTHER SIDE OF THE CORRIDOR GOING INTO THE STANDS TO MEET THIS PRETEND ACTOR WIFE AND WE STILL ACT AS SHE FRENCH KISSES ME 5 TIMES AND ON THE FIFTH TIME I KNEW IT WAS A TAKE.

I HAD HEARD THAT SOMEONE EARLIER ACTUALLY CALLED JIM BELUSCHI JOHN WHICH WAS HIS BROTHER JOHN BELUSCHI. IT WAS A SIMPLE MISTAKE AND JIM STARTS YELLING AT HIM AND CUSSING THIS POOR GUY OUT WHO ACTUALLY UNINTENTIONALLY CALLED JIM JOHN.

JIM SAID "JOHN IS DEAD YOU PIECE OF SH---" AMONG OTHER THINGS, SO WHEN I DID A MOVIE SCENE WITH HIM I DIDNT WANT TO TALK TO HIM. OR KNOW HIM OR SAY ANYTHING TO HIM BECAUSE I WAS AFRAID HE WOULD BE STUCK UP OR CUSS ME OUT.

SO AS WE WERE ABOUT TO DO THE SCENE WE WERE OUTSIDE OF THE SCENE AND I WAS 3-5 FEET CLOSE TO HIM AND HE DIDNT SPEAK NOR DID I BUT HE WAS AND SEEMED SURPRISED I DIDNT SAY HELLO TO HIM OR ADDRESS HIM IN SOME WAY. AGAIN I DIDNT LIKE HIM BECAUSE OF WHAT I HEARD ABOUT HOW HE TREATED PEOPLE WHO WERE NOT ACTORS WITH TALKING PARTS.

JIM SEEMED LIKE AN ANGRY UPTIGHT DUDE AND I NEVER SPOKE TO HIM THOUGH I WAS IN A SCENE WITH HIM AS WELL AS BEFORE THE SCENES WE WERE CLOSE PHYSICALLY TO EACH OTHER WITHIN 3-5 FEET CLOSE, DIDNT LIKE IT BUT THE DIRECTOR TOLD ME TO STAND IN A CERTAIN PLACE. ACTORS ARENT ALL THAT BIG OF A DEAL. BELEIEVE ME AS YOU SEE IVE KNOWN OR MET OR CAME ACROSS OVER 100 ACTORS.

148. LYNDSAY LOHEN

I WAS IN RENO NEVADA IN 2018. I LOVED RENO BECAUSE ONE THING I WAS IN A HOTEL CALLED THE CASTAWAY HOTEL WHICH WAS WALKING DISTANCE TO A RIVER OR A LAKE. I DONT KNOW IF IT WAS A RIVER OR A LAKE BUT IT WAS BEAUTIFUL AND WAS GOING THROUGH THE CITY.

ONE DAY AS I WAS CRUISING THE BIGGEST LITTLE CITY IN THE WIORLD I SEE THIS GIRL WHO LOOKS LIKE LYNDSAY LOHEN AND IT ACTUALLY WAS HER DOING THE SAME DEAL NATALEE COLE AND JANET JACKSON AND HALLE BERRY AND WHITNEY HOUSTON DOES , TRYING TO LIVE THE STREET LIFE FOR A LITTLE BIT AND TO THEM I BELEIVE ITS A FUN ADVENTURE FOR THEM AND SOMETHIG DIFFERENT THEN EWHAT THEY NORMALLY GO THROUGH ON A DAILY BASIS.

I BELEIVE THESE ACTRESSES AND MUSICIANS THAT ARE FEMALE ARE INFACTUATED WITH THE STREET LIFE AND WHY IS THIS?

THEY LIKE THE ANNOMONOUS TREATMENT THEY GET. SEE, THE PEOPLE IN THE STREETS WHO ARE THE HOMELESS AND WHO ARE DRUG DEALERS AS WELL AS PEDISTRIANS WHO LIVE AT THE POVERTY LEVEL. THESE ACTRESSES AND ACTORS LIKE THESE PEOPLE BECAUSE THEY DONT ACT LIKE THE MIDDLE CLASS AND UPPER RICH CLASS WHO GLORIFY AND LOOK UP TO THEIR FAVORITE ACTOR OR MUSICIAN WHERE THE STREET PEOPLE , HOMELESS, DRUG DEALERS AND CRIMINALS AND PEDESTRIANS WHO VENTURE AND LIVE AT THE LEVEL OF STREET LIFE ARE NOT STAR STRUCK AND DONT USUALLY KNOW THE ACTOR OR MUSICIAN OR ACTRESS DUE TO THE REASON THAT THEY HAVE NO TELEVISION OR MEDIA OUTLET TO CHECK OUT THE MOST FAMOUS PEOPLE WHERE THE MIDDLE AND RICH PEOPLE DO OBSESS OVER THEIR FAVORITE ACTOR OR MUSICIAN THEREFORE THESE ACTORS AND ACTRESSES AND MUSICIANS FEEL IT AN ESCAPE AND CERTAIN FREEDOM TO LIVE IN THE STREET FOR A UNDISCLOSED AMOUNT OF TIME.

IN THIS CASE IT IS LYNDSAY LOHEN WHO I NOTICE IS UNDERWEIGHT. AND VERY SMALL AND SKINNY AND SORT OF DIRTY. SHES DRESSED IN A TANK TOP TYPE OUTFIT

AND LOOKS SORT OF SLEEZY BUT SEXY. SHE IS PRETTY AND I ALWAYS FELT LYNDSAY LOHEN AS SEXY. I MADE A PASS AT HER AND SHE WASNT INTERESTED THOIUGH WE WENT ON A DATE. WE GOT PIZZA WHICH I PAID FOR THEN I PAID FOR HER TO GET ALCOHOL AND AS I DID THIS SHE SAID "I THINK YOU HAVE A GOOD HEART AND THIS IS WHY YOU ARE GIVING ME 10 DOLLORS FOR ALCOHOL" IT SOUNDED LIKE A CON JOB BUT I DID IT AND AT THE TIME BEFORE THINKING ABOUT IT FELT THAT I BOUGHT THE IDEA THAT I HAD A GOOD HEART TO FOR GIVING HER 10. AFTER I BOUGHT HER THE PIZZA I HAD A SLICE AND THEN WE WENT INTO A CASINO ON THE SOUTH SIDE OF THE CITY, SHE GAMBLED WITH A LITTLE MONEY SHE HAD AND I WAITED FOR HER THEN AS SHE LEFT THE CASINO SHE SAW AS WELL AS I TOO SAW THIS GUY DOING STREET MUSIC AND LYNDSAY DIDNT EVEN KNOW THAT THE SAME DAY THAT I MEET HER I TOO HAVE ALSO DONE STREET MUSIC- THOUGH THIS GUY WASNT TOO GOOD AND NO ONE WAS WATCHING HIM SO SHE WENT THERE AND HUGGED THE GUY AND GAVE HMI SOME COIN CHANGE AND LET HER BUTT COME OUT A LITTLE FOR HIM TO SEE. I FELT SHE WAS SORT OF PERMISCUOUS.

AFTER I GAVE HER THE 10 SHE ASKED ME IF I COULD WAIT FOR HER WHICH I WAITED 20 MINUTES AS SHE TALKED TO A BUNCH OF GUYS AT AND IN THE LIQUOR STORE.

FINALLY AS SHE GOT INTO THE CAR WITH HER ALCOHOL I DROPPED HER OFF AT HER HOTEL IN WHICH SHE LEFT WITH THE BOX OF PIZZA AND AS WELL THE ALCOHOL AND TOOK AN ELEVATOR TO THE SECOND OR THIRD FLOOR IN THIS RENO HOTEL.

AND THIS WAS THE LAST TIME I EVER SAW LYNDSAY LOHEN. SHE SEEMED LIKE A PRETTY COOL PERSON. I JUST DONT KNOW IF HER TELLING ME I HAD A GOOD

HEART WAS A CON JOB AND WAS SHE BLOWING SMOKE UP MY ASS.

149. ROBERT DENERO.

I MET ROBERT DENERO ONE NIGHT AT ANAHEIM STADIUM WHILE THE MOVIE THE FAN WAS BEING FILMED. THAT NIGHT I WENT UP TO HIM AND SAID "HI MR DENERO I AM A FAN OF YOUR WORK. " HE SAID THANK YOU AND HE THEN SAID HE WANT ROBERT DENERO AND THAT HE WAS HIS DOUBLE. I SAID "OH WELL, HERE IS AN ALBUM OF MUSIC I PRODUCED AND WROTE AND SANG ON AND DID ALL LYRICS TOO". ONCE HE SEES THIS HE CHANGES HIS LIE TO THE TRUTH WHICH IS "OH YEAH I AM ROBERT DENERO. SAY WHEN DID YOU MAKE THIS AND I REALLY LIKE SOME OF THE TITLES LIKE "LETS GET NECKED". I WAS HAPPY TO HEAR THIS AND WE TALKED A LITLE MORE. THEN HIS ASSISTANT SAID HE HAS TO DO ANOTHER SCENE SOON AND COULD I LET HIM GO AND I SAID SURE. AFTER THIS EVERYONE WHO WAS MOVIE EXTRAS THOUGHT I WAS SPECIAL BECAUSE I WAS ABLE TO TALK TO ROBERT DENERO THAT NIGHT.

THE NEXT NIGHT HE WAS IN THE STAND AND WAS DOING A SCENE AND I DIDNT KNOW THIS BUT HE HAS HIS OWN MOVIE EXTRAS THAT ARE IN ALL HIS MOVIES SO I WAS THERE TOO AND WASNT SUPPOSED TO BECAUSE I WAS IN WITH ANOTHER CASTING COMPANY THAT CASTED ME AS A MOVIE EXTRA IN ANOTHER SITUATION AND NOT IN MR DENEROS SPECIAL MOVIE EXTRAS. I HEARD RUMERS THAT HE WOULD GO TO LUNCH WITH THEM EVERY DAY WHEN LUNCH TIME CAME WITH HE AND THEM.

AS I SAW HIM THAT SECOND NIGHT I INTERRUPED HIM WITHOUT KNOWING IT BECAUSE IN BETWEEN SCENES IT SEEMS LIKE AROUND OVER AND HOUR SO AFTER I SCENE THAT SECOND NIGHT I THOUGHT I WOULD TALK TO HIM

BECAUSE I THOUGHT THERE WAS TIME BEFORE THE NEXT SCENE I ASKED HIM HOW HE LIKED THE ALBUM AND HE SAID HE DID. BUT THEN HIS ASSISTANT TOOK ME AWAY AND SAID "MR DENERO APPRECIATES ALL YOU GAVE HIM AND WILL TALK TO YOU LATER ON IT" I SAID OK AND NEVER TALKED TO ROBERT DENERO AGAIN.

IM GLAD HE LIKED MY MUSIC THOUGH.

150. WESLEY SNIPES. THE SAME NIGHT I MET ROBERT DENERO.

THE NIGHT MET WESLEY WE HAD TO DO 3 SCENES AND I WAS IN THE FRONT OF THE AUDIENCE AND LOOKING LIKE I HATE WESLEY SNIPES THOUGH I DONT HATE HIM. IT IS ALL AN ACT. WESLEY PLAYS A BASEBALL PLAYER AND AFTER THE SCENES HE PLAYS A GAME THIS NIGHT AND HE PRETENDS HE IUS NOT WESLEY SNIPES AND AXTUALLY SITS WITH US IN THE AUDINCE. I KNEW IT WAS HIM AND TALKED TO HIM ABOUT STUFF LIKE MUSIC AND KARATE AS WELL AS BASEBALL BUT NOT ABOUT ACTING. I LEARNED NOT TO TALK TO ACTORS ABOUT ACTING UNLESS THEY BRING IT UP FIRST. ITS SORT OF A RESPECT ISSUE THING.

WELL, EVERYONE GUESSED IT WAS WESLEY IN THE AUDIENCE THAT NIGHT AND WE ALL HAD A GOOD TIME. I GOT AN AUTOGRAPH THAT NIGHT FOR MY DAUGHTER AND MY MANAGER LAILAH WHO IS A FAN OF WESLEY SNIIPES BUT MY DAUGHTER WASNT ONLY BECAUSE SHE IS IN GAILS STOMACH AT THIS TIME IN 1995. THIS WAS SOMEWHERE IN EARLY 1995 AND MY DAUGHTER WASNT BORN UNTIL OCTOBER 27TH 1995.

AND WHEN MY DAUGHTER WAS BORN IT WAS EXTREMELEY SPECIAL.

MY DAUGHTERS NAME IS CHEYENNE AND NOW SHE IS MY VIDEO EDITOR AND SHE IS CAMERA PERSON WHEN I DO

MUSIC LIVE AND NEED IT TO BE FILMED AND PUT ON U TUBE.

WESLEY SEEMED LIKE A COOL GUY THAT NIGHT AS WELL AS WAS ROBERT DENERO EXCEPT DENERO HAD A LARGER EGO THEN THE REST OF US. I GUESS THAT EGO COMES WITH GREATNESS AS AN ACTOR.

151. ALICE COOPER 152. THE BAND WARRENT 153. STEPHEN OF GREAT WHITE.

151. ALICE COOPER

I SEEN HIM TWO TIMES. ONE WAS IN LAS VEGAS AND ONE WAS IN HOLLYWOOD ON THE SUNSET STRIP.

BOTH TIMES HE WAS ACTING WEIRED LIKE HE DIDNT LIKE BEING KNOWN.

I SAW HIM WITH HIS WIFE ON SUNSET BLVD IN HOLLYWOOD AND YELLED HEY ALICE COOPER AND HE RAN OFF SCARED THEN WHEN I SAW HIM IN LAS VEGAS NEVADA IN A CASINO HE WAS GOING TO THE ALL YOU CAN EAT RESTRAUNT.

I ASKED HIM IF HE NEEDED A SINGER OR A GUITARIST AND HE SAID NO HE WAS NICER HERE AND DIDNT ACT AS WEIRD ABOUT BEING WELL KNOWN AND NOTICEABLE.

`152. WARRENT THE BAND.

AT THE GREEN DOOR IN MONTCLARE WE OPENED FOR WARRENT WHICH WAS IN 1987 BEFORE THEY HAD MADE IT BIG.

THEY WERE GOOD AND I REMEMBER THE LEAD SINGER JAMIE LANE WAS QUITE CHARASMATIC.

ANYWAYS WE PLAYED GOOD THAT NIGHT AND IT WAS A GOOD SHOW.

THE GREEN DOOR WAS A GREAT SPOT FOR BANDS THAT START OUT FOR THE FIRST GIG OR IT CAN BE GREAT BANDS LIKE WARRENT AND MOTLEY CRUE AND BB KING AND ROBIN TROWER TO PLAY ON THE CIRCUIT TOUR CALLED THE CHITLINS CIRCUIT IN WHICH THE GREEN DOOR WAS PART OF THAT CIRCUIT.

153. STEPHEN OF GREAT WHITE.

STEPHEN USED TO WORK AT HANNACHS MIUSIC AND WAS TJHE ENGENEER AT THE STUDEO THERE AND HE WS TELLLING ME AND LAILAH THART HE WRITES MUSIC FOR GREAT WHITE AND IS A MEMBER OF GREAT WHITE WHICH I DIDNT KNOW WHO THEY WERE AND THIS WAS IN 1986 AND I BELEIVE ACCORDING TO MY FRIEND AND DRUMMER OF GREAT WHITE AUDIE DESBROW HE SAID HE WAS THE ORGIONAL DRUMMER STARTING OUT PLAYING WITH GREAT WHITE IN 1984.

STEPHEN WAS A NICE GUY WITH QUITE AND EGO AND THOUGHT HE WAS A SUPERIOR MUSICIAN AND INTIMIDATING FOR ME SINSE IT WAS 1986 AND I AT THIS TIME WAS ONLY ON MY 7TJH YEAR PLAYING IN BANDS.

154. GWEN STAPHANI OF NO DOUBT. 155. ELGIN BAYLOR.

GWEN STPHANI OF NO DOUBT. THE BAND NO DOUBT WAS BOOKED ON ONE OF MY CONCERTS I WAS THROWING BACK IN 1988 AT THE D AND S HALL IN CHINO AND I GOT PICTURES OF GWEN STAPHANI WITH A BOYFRIEND SITTING ON HIS LAP AND SHE LOOKED REAL YOUNG LIKE ABOUT 16-18 YEARS OLD. THE BAND WAS NEW THEN AND AT THIS TIME HAD NOT BEEN SIGNED TO A RECORD CONTRACT. THEY AT THIS TIME WAS IN THE MINOR LEAGIUES AND WE ALL FELT THEY WERE REAL GOOD AND FELT THAT HAD A GOOD SHOT AT GETTING A RECORD DEAL AND OF COURSE

AS HISTROY AND DESTENY HAD IT THEY DID GET SINGED AND FEW YEARS LATER IN THE 1990S.

155. ELGIN BAYLOR.

WE MET ELGIN BAYLOR AT SEARS AS HE WAS DOING A SIGNING OF AUTOGRAPHS AND MEET AND GREET AT SEARS. THIS WAS IN THE EARLY 1970S AND I REMEMBER MY BROTHER JOHN DIDNT LIKE HIM FOR NO REASON AND CALLED HIM ELGIN BUMLER. JOHN MY BROTHER WAS AROUND 10 YEARS OLD AND IT WAS PROBABLEY AROIUND 1971 OR 72 AND JOHN MY BROTHER WAS BORN IN 1962.

ELGIN LAUGHED WHEN MY LITTLE 9 OR 10 YEAR OLD BROTHER CALLED HIM ELGIN BUMLER AND IT WAS ALL FUNNY AND NO BAD VIBES CONSIDERING MY BROTHER WAS ONLY 9 OR TEN YEARS OLD. ALL IN ALL IT WAS A GOOD TIME.

156 PETER FRAMPTON 157 . DAVID LEE ROTH. 158 ROBIN TROWER.

IT WAS THE YEAR OF 1993 AND I HAD JUST MET A FRIEND NAMED JAMIE A GUY ON NEW YEARS NIGHT 1993. DURING THAT WEEK I WAS SINGLE AND HAD BEEN SINGLE SINSE NOVEMBER OF 1992. I WAS LONLEY BECAUSE I AM THE TYPE OF A GUY THAT ALWAYS NEEDS A GIRLFRIEND OR ENGAGED OR MARRIED.

SINSE 1985 OCTOBER I HAD HAD A GIRLFRIEND OR WIFE OR ENGAGEMENT EVERY MONTH EXCEPT SEPTEMBER 1992 TO JANUARY 1993 FROM SEPTEMBER 1985 TO NO WHICH IS AUGUST 29TH 2020.SO IN THE LAST 35 YEARS I HAVE HAD A RELATIONSHIP EVERY MOMENT EXCEPT 4 MONTHS IN 1992.

PRAISE JESUS FOR THIS.

SO JAMIE WAS HANGING OUT WITH ME SINSE NEW YEARS NIGHT WHERE I MET HIM AFTER MIDNIGHT ON NEW YEARS DAY BUT IT WAS THE NIGHT BEFORE BEING STILL JAN 1 BUT AFTER MIDNIGHT THAT DAY I WAS OUT WITH A DATE BUT SHE WASNT A RELATIONSHIP NAMED KAREN WHO WAS A NURSE BUT I DIDNT WANT TO HAVE A BOY GIRLFRIEND RELATIONSHIP WITH HER AND THAT NIGHT WHILE OUT WITH HER AT HER APARTMENT IN POMONA SHE SAID SHE WANTS A RELATIONSHIP OR SHE CANT AND DOESNT WANT TO SEE ME ANYMORE AS JUST A DATE AND CASUAL ACQUANTANCE AND FRIEND. SO WE PARTED ON NEW YEARS OF 1993.

AS I WAS WALKING HOME I PASS THE HA PENNY INN WHICH IS ON THE SOUTH SIDE OF FOOTHILL BLVD IN POMONA AND AS I WALK BY THIS GUY FROM OUT OF THE DARKNESS IN AND NEAR SOME BUSHES AT THE FRONT OF THE HOTEL SAYS HELLO TO ME AND IT IS JAMIE WHO LOOKS LIKE A CRIMINAL BUT ONLY HAD THAT LOOK AT THE BEGENNING OF OUR FRIENDSHIP. JAMIE SAID HE HAD A CAR AND ASKED ME IF I WANTED TO CRUISE TO MEXUCO MEANING TIJUANA. I SAID SURE SO ME AND JAMIE BECAME FAST FRIENDS BUT ONLY FOR A A SHORT TIME AND BY THE END OF OUR FRIENDSHIP WHICH ONLY ENDED BECAUJSE I NEVER SAW HIM AGAIN BUT BY THE END OF OUR FAST FRIENDSHIP WE WENT TO TIJUANA AND THEN FROM THERE WENT TO HOLLYWOOD BY 5 A.M. ALL THIS IN LESS THEN 6 HOURS AMAZING. THEN THE NEXT DAY WE WENT TO LAGOONA BEACH AND WITH 4 GIRLS. ME AND JAMIE WERE DOING REAL GOOD WITH THE LADIES ON THAT WEEKEND WHICH ALSO WENT INTO DAY THREE ME PEFORMING AT THE LIL CLUB WHICH WAS THE NAME OF THE CLUB OWNED BY LOU GRAMM OF FOREIGNER IN MONTCLARE. AT LEAST THIS IS WHAT THE RUMER WAS AND WE WERE PLAYING UP ON STAGE WITH MUSICIANS I KNEW AS WELL AS THE

HOUSE BAND WHICH THIS WAS HOW IT WAS BEFORE KEROKI BECAME WELL KNOWN IN THE EARLY 2000S.

SO IN THE NIGHTS WE ME AND JAMIE WENT TO THE LIL CLUB AND TIJUANA, HOLLYWOOD AS WELL AS A DATE TO LAGOONA BEACH WITH 4 GIRLS AND THEN ON DAY 4 I TOLD HIM ABOUT CLUBS NEAR VINEYARD AVENUE NAMED THE RED LION INN SO WE WENT THERE ALL BECAUSE JAMIE REALLY WANTED TO GO THERE AND THAT DAY 4 I MEET MY FUTURE WIFE AND MOTHER OF MY NOW 25 YEAR OLD CHEYENNE AND ME AND MY WIFE WHO I MET ON DAY 4 WAS NAMED GAIL AND WE HAVE BEEN MARRIED OFF AND ON FOR 27 YEARS.

IN OTHER WORDS JAMIE WAS GOOD LUCK. I ALWAYS WANTED JAMIE TO STAY AROUND BUT HE WAS A TRAVELER AND NEVER SAW HIM AGAIN EXCEPT ONE MORE DAY.

THE DAY I WENT TO HOLLYWOOD TO AUDITION FOR THE ARTIST AND ROCK LEGEND PETER FRAMPTON THE SOLO ARTIST AND GUITARIST FOR THE OL BAND HYMBLE PIE.

MY POINT IS JAMIE SEEMED LIKE AN IMPORTANT PERSON BEING HE GUIDED ME TO GET OUT OF MY SLUMP OF NOT HAVING A GIRLFRIEND AS WELL AS SORT OF GUIDED ME TO MEET GAIL THE MOTHER OF MY 3RD CHILD EHEYENNE.

IT WAS JAMIE THAT INSISTED HE WANTED TO GO TO THE RED LION INN AND THANK GOD HE DID THIS OR I WOULD HAVE GONE TO BAXTERS RESTRAUNT WHICH WAS MY FIRST CHOICE FOR THE DAY.

SO BECAUSE JAMIE INSISTED TO GO TO RED LION INN THAT NIGHT I MET GAIL MY FUTURE WIFE OF NOW 27 YEARS AND 28 YEARS IN 3 MONTHS AND WE HAVE A CHILD WHO IS NOW A GROWN UP NAMED CHEYENNE WHO IS 24 AND MORE BEAUTIFUL THEN I EVER ASKED GOD FOR.

SO AFTER THIS EVENING I DIDNT SEE JAMIE FOR ABOUT 1 MONTH AND HERE SHOWS JAMIE. I INVITED HIM TO STAY DOWNSTAIRS AT MOMS AS LONG AS HE NEEDED AND WANTS TO AND HE HUMBLY DECLINED. I TOLD HIM TODAY I WAS AUDITIONING FOR PETER FRAMPTON AND I WAS TO GIVE HIM AN ALBUM OF THE ALBUM ENTITLED "1990 AUTRY ODAY". NOW IT IS FEBUARY 1993 AND I DRIVE TO PETER FRAMPTONS MANAFGEMENT OFFICE. I GAVE THE TAPE TO THE LADY AND ACTUALLY AUDITIONED FOR PETER FRAMPOTON WITHOUT HIM THERE OR MAYBE HE WAS IN THE NEXT ROOM. I SANG THE SONG ACAPELLA. "ALL I WANT TO BE IS BY YOUR SIDE."

I SANG IT AND THE LADY LIKED IT AND SAID I WAS THE BEST SO FAR.

NEXT ONE MONTH LATER IN MARCH OF 1993 I RECREIVED A CALL BY THE MANAGEMENT OF PETER FRAMPTON AND SAID SHE WANTEED ME TO TALK TO PETER RIGHT AT THIS MOMENT AND I WAS SURPRISED BUT READY.

PETER FRAMPTON GETS ON THE PHONE AND THANKS ME FOR MY TIME AND MY SUBMISSION BUT I DIDNT MAKE IT. HE WAS REALY HUMBLE AND SHY ABOUT IT AND I FELT BLESSED TO AT LEAST TALK TO PETER FRAMPTION WHO WAS A BIG PART OF MY ROCK N ROLL LOVING IN THE MIDDLE 1976 AND 1977. I LOVED THEIR SONG "SHOW ME THE WAY" AND OTHER SONGS. IN FACT I LOVED EVERYTHING ON THE ALBUM ENTITLED "FRAMPTON COMES ALIVE". SURE I WAS DISAPPOINTED THAT I COULD BE HIS LEAD SINGR BUT THATS LIFE.

158. DAVID LEE ROTH.

I WAS AT SAM ASH IN ONTARIO AT THE ONTARIO MILLS MALL AND IN FRONT OF ME IN LINE IS DAVID LEE ROTH. NO ONE WAS REALLY PAYING ATTENTION BUT I NOTICED. DAVE

WAS ADMIRING THESE CUTE LITTLE BLACK KIDS IN THE LINE IN FRONT OF HIM AND DID HIS LEGENDARY GIGGLE. I LAUGED TO AND HE SAID TO ME "CUTE". I AGREED AND THAT WAS IT.

AS HE WALKED OFF IT WAS LIKE AN ORA OF ROCK N ROLL HISTORY FOLLOWED HIM OF DAVID LEE ROTH. ITS HARD TO EXPLAIN BUT THIS IS TRUE.

159. ROBIN TROWER

ROBIN TROWER IS KNOWN TO HAVE TAUGHT JIMI HENDRIX A FEW RIFFS.

I BELEIVE IT.

WE WERE PLAYING FENDERS BALLROOM IN 1989 AND WE WERE OPENING UP FOR ROBIN TROWER.

ROBIN TROWER IS ONE OF MY FAVORITE GUITARISTS AND IN MY OPINION UNDERATED.

AFTER THE SHOW I NOTICED ROBIN BACK STAGE AND RECOGNISED HIM. I SAID HELLO TO HIM AND HE SAID HELLO BACK.

I WATCHED THE WHOLE SHOW ROBIN TROWER DID AND REALLY ENJOYED IT WATCHING IT FROM THE BACK STAFGE AS WELL AS FROM THE FRONT OF THE STAGE AS I LATER VENTURED INTO THE AUDIENCE. THE BAND RESPECTED ME AND OUR BAND AFTER PLAYING AND OPENING UP FOR TROWER SO THEY WERE COOL THAT I WATCHED FROM THE FRONT FOW AND THE FRONT OF THE CROWD IN THE AUDIENCE. IT WAS AN HONOR TO MEET ONE OF MY GUITAR HEROES AND I FOIND ROBIN TROWER A VERY NICE PERSON

160. CHARLES (CHARLIE MURPHY)

CHARLIE MURPHY IS AND ALWAYS HAS BEEN THROUGH HIS WHOLE LIFE BROTHER OF THE GREAT COMIDEAN EDDIE MURPHY.

I MET CHARLIE MURPHY WHEN HE WAS GOING BY THE NAME CHARLES AND HE WAS NOT YET KNOWN AS THE COMIDEAN CHARLIE MURPHY.

I FIRST SAW HIM ON THE BUS HEADING TO COURT TO SAN BERNADINO.

I SAW HIM AND FIRST SAID "YOU LOOK LIKE EDDIE MURPHY". HE LAUGHED AND SAID THAT EDDIE WAS HIS BROTHER,

I DIDNT BELEIVE IT BUT HE OF COURSE WAS DEFINATELEY TELLING ME THE TRUTH.

HE GAVE ME A FLYER ABOUT A SHOW HE WAS DOING ON MY VERNON AVENUE IN SAN BERNADINO.

I THEN TOLD HIM I WAS A PROFESSIONAL MUJSICIAN THAT NEEDED A GIG. IT DIDNT PAY BECAUSE IT WAS A BENIFIT AND I SAID OK.

HE THEN BOOKED ME FOR THAT SUNDAY AND I HAD TO WAKE UP AT 8 AM AND TAKE THE BUS ON THE 14 TO THE 5 BUS TO THE 1 BUS AND THEN I HAD TO WALK A COUPLE MILES WITH MY KEYBOARD AND KEYBOARD STAND AND I PLAYED IT.

AS I PLAYED I NOTICED IT WAS ALL BLACK PEOPLE AND IT THE NAME OF THE SHOW WAS FIGHT THE VIOLENCE AND INCREASE THE PEACE AND THIS WAS WHAT I WAS STANDING FOR AND AT THE SAME TIME THE ALL BLACK AUDIENCE DIDNT RESPECT ME AND WAS PREJUDICE AT FIRST BECAUSE I WAS WHITE AND THE ONLY WHITE

PERSON THERE. I STILL WENT ON WITH THE SHOW THOUGH.

AS I PLAYED NO ONE WAS APPLAUDING AND REALLY NOT LISTENING AND I TOOK A BREAK IN BETWEEN SETS .

A MIRICLE AND A CHANGE OF HEART FROM THE AUDIENCE.

I GOT UP TO TAKE MY BREAK AND I FELL OFF THE STAGE BUT TRULY IT WAS LIKE I FLOATED OFF THE STAGE AS I FELL. MANY PEOPLE IN THE AUDIENCE NOTICED THIS AND SAID "YOU HAVE ANGELS TO CATCH YOU ON YOUR SIDE," AND OTHER COMMENTS LIKE THIS. NEXT THING THE FIRST PREJUDICE AUDIENCE STARTED TO LIKE ME AND AFTER THAT MOMENT I WENT BACK ON STAGE AND FINISHED OUT SET TWO IN WHICH THE ALL BLACK AUDIENCE WAS VERY FRIENDLEY AND SUPPORTIVE.

CHARLIE MURPHY WAS THERE ALSO AND SAID HE WAS SORRY FOR THE TREATMENT THAT HE SAW IN THE FIRST SET AND I SAID NO PROBLEM AND TOLD HIM THAT THE AUDIENCE WAS ALOT MORE FRIENDLER ON THE SECOND SET AND TOLD HIM THE MIRICULAS STORY ABOUT HOW I FLOATED OFF THE STAGE AS I FELL AND I TRULY BELEIVED TOO WITH THE AUDIENCE THAT IT WAS ANGELS FROM GOD MAKING SURE I DIDNT KILL OR HURT MYSELF FROM THE FALL AND YES, THAT ANGELS WERE THERE TO CATCH ME.

THIS WAS IN 1997 AND CHARLIE MURPHY WAS NOT YET WELL KNOWN AND/OR FAMOUS YET.

FROM THIS SHOW I ALSO DID ANOTHER STOP THE VIOLENCE INCREASE THE PEACE WITH ANOTHER SHOW ON THE OTHER SIDE OF RIALTO IN RIALTO PARK WHERE THIS TIME IT WAS MEXICAN CHOLOS WHO BASICALLY WERE THE AUDIENCE AND IF IT WERENT FOR THE ANGELS HELPING ME ON THAT FALL I WOULD HAVE TO SAY THEN THAT THOSE TWO SHOWS THE ONE WITH THE MEXICAN

CHOLOS AT RIALTO PARK AS WELL AS THE SHOW ON MT VERNON WITH THE PREJUDICE BLACK PEOPLE WOULD BE THE TWO WORSE RECIEVED SHOWS I EVER PLAYED IN MY LIFE.

PREJUDICE COMES IN ALL COLORS

161. GARY MOORE, THE LEAD GUITARIST OF THE BAND THIN LIZZY.

WE WERE TO PLAY A CLUB IN ANAHEIM CALLED JEZEBELS. IT WAS A CLASSY CLUB AND ALOT OF LEGENDARY ESTABLISHED ARTISTS HAS AND DO ON A REGULAR BASIS PLAY THERE.

WE WERE NAMED FREE WILL. THIS WAS THE NAME OF OUR BAND AND WE PLAYED 80S HARD AND HEAVY ROCK NOT HEAVY METEL BUT HEAVY ROCK.

THERE IS A DIFFERENCE. HEAVY METEL IS SORT OF LIKE METALLICA AND HEAVY ROCK IS LIKE VAN HALEN.

WE WERE 1/2 HEAVY ROCK AND 1/4 HEAVY METEL.

THIS WAS THE BAND IN WHICH I HAD FRST PLAYED WITH AND MET RAUEL "CHINA" RANOA.

RAUEL WOULD PLAY WITH ME IN THIS BAND AND THEN PLAY IN AUTRY ODAY UP UNTIL AUGUST OF 1990.

SO RAUEL AND ME PLAYED IN THE SAME BANDS FOR AROUND THREE YEARS AND 4 MONTHS FROM APRIL 16TH 1987, MY 26TH BIRTHDAY UP UNTIL AUGUST 1990 WHEN OUR LAST SHOW WAS ON A TELEVISED CABLE SHOW CALLED "GIG PRODUCTIONs". IN WHICH WE PLAYED TWO SONGS, ONE WRITTEN BY ME AND MIKE CORRIERE CALLED SUZIE CIRCLES AND THE OTHER SONG ENTITLED LONG LIVE LOVE WRITTEN BY ME AND SCOTT JONES IN WHICH SCOTT JONES WROTE THE MUSIC AND ME THE LYRICS

OTHER THEN THE FIRST 1/2 OF VERSE 1. AND THE REST OF THE LYRICS I HAD WROTE FROM THAT FIRST VERSE AND THE CHORUS ALSO WAS WRITTEN BY SCOTT JONES WHICH SAID OVER AND OVER "LONG LIVE LOVE" AND THERE I ADDED "GO GO" ONTO THE CHORUS MAKING THE CHORUS SAY "LONG LIVE LOVE GO GO LONG LIVE LOVE GO GO". THAT IDEA TO PUT GO GO ON IT WAS FROM BURL TIFELICIA JOHNSON, A GOOD FRIEND AT THE TIME.

THIS SHOW AT JEZIBELS WAS A GOOD ONE AND WE WERE ALL NERVOUS DUE TO THE REASON THAT WE WERE TO OPEN FOR AN ESTABLISHED ARTIST NAMED GARY MOORE WHO WAS THE LEAD GUITARIST ON THE THIN LIZZY ALBUMS AND WAS THE MAIN GUJITARIST.

I WAS BLESSED ENOIUGH TO MEET HIM IN THE BACK STAGE OF JEZEBELS WHERE HE WISHED ME GOOD LUCK AND I WISHED HIM THAT TOO.

HE WAS A NICE AND HUMBLE GUY WHO DIDNT THINK HE WAS THE STUFF.

ALL IN ALL GARY MOORE WAS A NICE GUY AND VERY HUMBLE AND COOL.

162. STEVE ADLER, THE ORIGIONAL DRUMMER FOR GUNS N ROSES BAND.

ME AND LAILAH WERE LOOKING FOR THE SCREEN ACTORS GUILD NEW PLACE THEY MOVED TO.

WE WERE SOMEWHERE IN THE RESIDENTAL AREA OF BEVERLY HILLS AND WE GO TO THIS GUY TO ASK HIM IF HE KJNEW WHERE TH SCREEN ACTORS GUILD IS. HE HAD A GUNS N ROSES HAT ON. AND IT WAS THE ORIGIONAL DRUMMER STEVE ADLER WHO WAS THE GREAT DRUMMER ON THE ALBUM APPITITE FOR DESTRUCTION AS WELL AS ON OTHER GUNS N ROSES ALBUMS DID JHE PERFORM ON.

LAILAH RECOGNISED HIM AND HE SAID TO US THAT HE DIDNT KNOW BUT THAT HE NEEDS TO JOIN IT TOO.

HE WAS NICE AND DOWN TO EARTH AND VERY FRIENDLEY.

LATER I WOULD SEE STEVE IN UPPER UPLAND BY THE CAMPUS STORES AND HE WAS AGAIN VERY FRIENDLEY AND ACTUALLY REMEMBERED WHEN WE ASKED HIM ABOUT THE GUILD WAY BACK. HE TOLD ME THANKS THAT IT REMINDED HIM TO JOIN THE GUILD AND HE DID IT FROM THERE ON. BECAUSE WE REMINDED HIM. HE LATER WAS ON A REHAB SHOW. A REALITY SHOW WITH VERIOUS CELEBRATIES WHO ARE A LITTLE OR ALOT MESSED UP ON DRUGS OR ALCOHOL.

HE ONCE SAID TO ME AFTER I ASKED HIM IF HE WAs WORKING ON DRUMS AND HE SAID "NOT RIGHT NOW BUT I ALWAYS HAVE MY FRIEND THAT CAN HELP ME. I SAID "WHO AXL ROSE?" HE SAID YES.

I HAVENT SEN STEVE IN ABOUT 5 YEARS OR SO BUT HE WAS A REAL DOWN TO EARTH GUY AND VERY FRIENDLEY AND DOESNT SEEM LIKE HE HAS A DRUG PROBLEM AT ALL. HIS TALKING WAS QUITE INTELLEGENT AND HE WAS AGAIN LIKE I SAID VERY FRIENDLEY.

163. TAWN MASTRY DISC JOCKY FOR 105.5 KNAC ROCK NROLL LONG BEACH.

ME AND LAILAH WENT TO THIS CLUB CALLED RED LION AND I WAS TO AJUDITION FOR A BUDWEISER COMMERCIAL HOSTED BY THE TALENTED AND BEAUTIFUL DISC JOCKY FOR 105.5 KNAC NAMED TAWN MASTRY. ME AND LAILAH MET HER AND SHE WAS TO BE QUITE A FRIENDLEY PERSON AND WAS THE HOST OF THE NIGHT AND VERY FUNNY. SHE WAS FLIRTING WITH ME BUT OF COURSE AT THIS TIME LAILAH WAS MY GIRLFRIEND AND FIANCEE AND WE LATER DID SOME LIVE MUSIC AND I FOR THE AUDITON

HAD TO SING A BUDWEISER SONG THAT THEY GAVE ME LYRICS TO AND I DID THAT BUT I DID NOT GET GET THE JOB THAT I WAS TRYING TO GET FOR THE AUDITION. ALL IN ALL THE NIGHT WAS ALOT OF FUN AND TAWN WAS A VERY COOL PERSON. THIS WAS AROUND 1988 OR 1989.

THE CLUB WAS IN WEST COVINA.

164 BILL GAZZARI. OWNER AND FOUNDER OF THE LEGENDARY HOLLYWOOD NIGHTCLUB CALLED GAZZARIS.

WE PLAYED THE NIGHTCLUB GAZZARIS N MY SECOND BAND CALLED CROSSFIRE AND MY FORTH BAND CALLED ROULETTE WHEN I PLAYED IN THE BAND CROSSFIRE AT GAZZARIS I FIRST REMEMBER MEETING AND TALKING TO BILL GAZZARI RIGHT WHEN YOU COME TO HIS CLUB.. TO THE LEFT OF THE DOOR WHEN COMING THROUGH THE DOOR IS THIS LITTLE OFFICE HE HAD WHICH WAS REAL REAL SMALL. I DO REMEMBER THAT. I DONT REMEMBER HIM THAT MUCH OTHER THEN THE COOL WHITE HAT HE WORE. AFTER THE FIRST TIME I PLAYED THERE WE ACTUALLY WON A BATTLE OF THE BANDS THAT NIGHT AND I REMEMBER BILL COMING TO ME AND SAYING "YOU CROSSFIRE YOU WON HERE IS 75 DOLLORS. HERES YOUR WINNINGS" I TOOK THE 75 DOLLORS PROUDLEY AND AND SAID SOME SMALL TALK TO HIM THAT I DONT REALLY REMEMBER THOUGH I DO REMEMBER TALKING SMALL TALK TO HIM ON THIS INCIDENT.

WE PLAYED THERE A FEW MORE TIMES WITH ROULETTE TOO AND I REMEMBER BILL LETTING US PUT OUR NAME UP ON THE BILLBOARD IN THE FRONT OF HIS CLUB SAYING ROULETTE WHICH I WAS VERY PROUD OF.

WE PLAYED I BELEIVE 3 TIMES WITH CROSSFIRE AND TWO OR THREE TIMES WITH THE BAND ROULETTE. I REMEMBER BILL TALKING TO ME AND RANDY THE DRUMMER OF

ROULETTE AND BILL ASKED WHAT THE DRUMMMERS NAME WAS AND RANDY SAID RANDY AND BILL I REMEMBER SAYING "OK THERE ITS ROULETTE RANDY" AND AFTER BULL GAZZARI SAID THAT THE NAME OF RANDYS WHEN ADSOSSIATED IN WITH THE BAND WAS ROULETTE RANDY.

CREATED BY THE GENIUS BILL GAZZARI.

I REMEMBER WHEN BILL GAZZARI DIED AND I WAS SAD. MY FRIEND AND ONE OF THE PROMOTERS OF THE BAND I WAS IN CALLED AUTRY ODAY NAMEED POP ROCK AKA RON BRADY TOOK OVER FOR A LITTLE WHILE BILLS SPOT AT GAZZARIS UNTIL GAZZARIS FINALLY SOLD OUT TO A CLUB CALLED THE KEY CLUB BUT I REMEMBER RON ALSO OUT OF RESPECT FOR BILL WORE THE WHITE FEDORA HAT ALSO AND HE THEN TOOK OVER BILLS CLUB UNTIL IT WAS SOLD IN I BELEIVE THE LATE 80S SOMEWHERE OR THE EAERLY 90S.

I ALWAYS LIKED BILL AND THOUGHT HE WAS A KIND AND NICE GUY AND HE REALLY LOVED ROCK N ROLL AND ONCE TOLD ME HE LIKED THE NAME CROSSFIRE AND HE SAID HE LIKED THE NAME ROULETTE TOO. ONCE AFTER IA CROSSFIRE SHOW HE SAID HE LIKED THE MUSIC WE WERE DOING.

BILL HAD A DEAL AND THE DEAL WAS YOU GET A FREE TICKET TO GET IN BUT THE RULE OF THAT TICKET AND STIPULATION IS YOU HAVE TO MANDATORY BUY 2 DRINKS AT FULL PRICE. EVERYONE LOVED THIS IDEA BECAUSE EVERYONE WAS GOING TO BUY DRINKS ANYWAYS SO IT WASNT WITH OUT OF POCKET FOR THE FANS. BILL HAD FREE PARKING TOO.

I REMEMEBER ONCE IN GAZZARIS A GUY WHO WAS BARTENDER THERE WAS TALKKING ABOUT HAVING BANDS PAY TO PLAY. THAT GUYS NAME WAS MICHEAL FELL AND

HE WAS THE INVENTOR OF PAY TO PLAY. SOMETHING IN MUSIC I WOULDNT NOT CLAIM TO HAVE DONE PERSONALLY. IT RUINED ALOT FOR MUSIC AND BANDS TRYING TO MAKE IT IN THOSE LATE AND MID 80S.

IN MY OPINION PAY TO PLAY STINKS. IT WOULD BE LIKE A HOUJSE PAINTER PAYING TO PAINT YOIR HOUSE. ITS UNFAIR AND CRAZY.

FINALLY IN 1984 THE BAND I WAS IN CALLED STANGE BEHAVIOR PLAYED GAZZARIS AND BILL KNEW ME AND REMEMBERED ME FROM CROSSFIRE AND ROULETTE.

IN THIS BAND WE HAD SOME VISUAL THINGS WE DID. I BOUGHT A STRAIGHT JACKET FROM ONE OF THOSE HOLLYWOOD STORES. WE USED THIS STRAIGHT JACKET AT THE BEGENNING OF THE SHOWS AND IT WAS FUN. I WOULD COME OUT A MINUTE AFTER MIKE MY GUITARIST WOULD COME OUT. I WOULD COME OUT TRYING TO FIGHT FROM THESE TWO ORDERLEYS HOLDING ON TO ME AND THEN AFTER BREKING LOOSE FROM THE ORDERLEYS I BREAK LOOSE FROM THE STRAIGHT JACKET AND THEN START SINGING.

IT WAS CRAZY AND GOT A WRITE UP IN SOME OF THE LOCAL ROCK MAGAZINES. WE WERE TRYING HARD TO MAKE IT AND GAZZARIS WAS REAL COOL AND I KNEW MR GAZZARI SO WELL AFTER NOW PLAYING IN THREE BANDS AT HIS CLUB FROM 1980 TO 1984 THAT I WAS CALLING HIM BILL AND HE DIDNT MIND AS WELL AS HE CALLED ME CHUCK NOW INSTEAD OF HEY CROSSFIRE OR HEY YOU OR HEY ROULETTE OR HEY BUDDY.

BILL WAS A VERY FRIENDLEY GUY AND I ALWAYS LIKED HIM FROM ALL THREE BANDS. HE WAS A COOL GUY AND I WAS VERY SAD WHEN HE DIED.

165. VINNIE VINCENT THE GUITARIST FOR KISS IN THE 90S AND 80S AND 166. 1. JEFF ENGLAND KEYBOARDIST FOR STEPPENWOLF AND THE OWNER OF MY RECORD COMPANY I WAS SIGNED TO CALLED STATUE RECORDS.

WE WERE GOING WEEKLEY AND AT TIMES ONLY MONTHLY TO BEACH RECORDING STUDEOS AND WHEN IT WAS CALLED BEACH STUDEOS IT WAS AT MY STUDEO MANAGERS HOUSE IN REDONDO BEACH AND HIS NAME WAS JEFF ENGLAND WHO PLAYED KEYBOARDS FOR STEPPENWOLF. JEFF WAS A GREAT KEYBOARD PLAYER AND PLAYED IN STEPPENWOLF AFTER THE ORIGIONAL BAND WAS PLAYING TOGETHER IN STEPPENWOLF.

JEFF PLAYED IN STEPPENWOLF IN THE 1980S AND EARLY 1990S.

JEFF WAS LIKE A FRIEND AND MANY TIMES I WENT TO HIS HOUSE DOING DEALS ON BUYING MASSES OF TAPES OF MY BAND BADDCLOWN AND THE ALBUM BADDCLOWN 1.

JEFF WAS A GREAT GUY AND WE HAD ALOT OF CONVERSATIONS AT ONE TIME HIS EGO WAS PRETTY LARGE ON THE SUCCESS OF STATUE RECORDS. HE SAID ASKING HIM IF HE HAD ENOUGH MONEY WAS LIKE ASKING ROSS PEROT THE SAME QUESTION. I REMEMBER HIM TELLING ME THIS AS I WAS TALKING TO HIM FROM MY MANAGERS LAILAHS MOTHERS HOUSE.

JEFF ONCE GAVE ME THE RED LIGHT TO BE AN A AND R GUY FROM STATUE RECORDS. I DIDNT DO TO GOOD AT THAT BUT THE CARD GOT ME INTO FREE SHOWS IN HOLLYWOOD AND OTHER PLACES.

ALL IN ALL JEFF WAS A GOOD GUY.

OTHER THEN ONE TIME WHEN HE OWED ME SOME TAPES AND I COULDNT REACH HIM OR GET HIM TO COMPLETE

THE DEAL AFTER I ALREADY PAID HIM SO I GOT BIG DEAN WHO WAS A DRUMMER AND MARSHALL ARTIST EXTRODANARE AND I SENT HIM THERE FOR 50 DOLLORS TO TAKE CARE OF BUSINESS MEANING GETTING MY MONEY OR THE DEAL FINISHED AND BIG DEAN DID JUST THAT THOUGH I NEVER DEALT WITH JEFF ENGLAND AGAIN.

I WORKED WITH STATUE RECORDS WHICH WAS JEFFS RECORD COMPANY HE OWNED FROM 1990 TO 1995 AND THEN 1997-99 WHEN THE RECORDING STUDEO WENT FROM VALLEY STUDEOS TO PLANET HOLLYWOOD.

I WORKED WITH THE GREAT ENGENEERING OF TWO FINE ENGENEERS NAMED HOUSTON AND THEN KELLY WHO LEARNED IT ALL FROM HOUSTON AND BECAME JUST AS GOOD AS HOUSTON WAS HIS MENTOR IN THE MID 1990S.

165. VINNIE VINCENT GUITARIST OF THE BAND KISS .

VINNIE WAS THE REPLACEMENT FOR THE ORIGIONAL GUITARIST OF KISS PETER CRISS.

VINNIE GOT THE LARGEST RECORD DEAL AT ONE TIME IN THOSE TIMES AND I BELEIVE IT WAS 5000,000 AND THAT IS IN WRITING 5 MILLION YES 5 MILLION.

WE WERE GOING TO THE RECORDING STUDEO IN THE SAN FERNANDO VALLEY AND OUT OF THE ROOM WALKS VINNIE VINCENT AND ME AND KENNY MEOKLI SAW THIS AND SAID HI TO HIM. WE MET HIM AND HE REALLY HAD NOTHING TO SAY BUT WAS NICE AND FRIENDLEY BUT I DO REMEMBER HAD A WEAK HANDSHAKE. IM ONLY SAYING THIS BECAUSE I REMEMBER THIS BUT ALL IN ALL VINNIE WAS A NICE GUY.

THIS WAS AROUND 1991. HE NAME WAS STUDEO CITY RECORDINGS.

167. BRET MICHEALS AND POISON.

THIS WAS AROUND 1985 AND I WAS WITH THE BAND ATHENZ. WE HAD A SHOW AT THE TIMBERS RESTRAUNT AND DANCE HALL OPENING FOR US WAS AN UNKNOWN BAND AT THAT TIME NAMED POISON.

AFTER THE SHOW I REMEMBER THEM ALL BEING REAL SMALL AND BLONDE AND SQUIRLEY. I REMEMBER ASKING BRET MICHEALS HOWS IT GOING AND HE ANSWERED THAT HE WAS COOL. THEY WERE PRETTY NICE BUT AT THE SAME TIME HAD THIS ROCK STAR ATTITUDE THAT THEY WERE THE BEST AND I GUESS FOR A YEAR OR SO THEY WERE ON TOP OF THE MUSIC SCENE.

CC DIVILLE TRIED TO FIGHT ME AND I DIDNT LIKE CC DIVELLE.

THATS AS MUCH AS I WILL GO ABOUT TALKING ABOUT CC DIVELLE.

IF YOU DONT GOT ANYTHING GOOD TO SAY TO SOMEONE THEN DONT SAY ANYHTHING AT ALL.

168. POLICE CHIEF DARYL GATES, THEN RETIRED.

THIS WAS THE WEIRDEST ENCOUNTER WITH SOMEONE I DO NOT RESPECT OR LIKE T WAS WEIRD. IT WAS RETIRED CHIEF OF POLICE THE LEGENDARY DARYL GATES WHOS LEGACY IS THE FIRST RIOTS OF 1966 AND THEN THE RIOTS OF 1992, THE LEGENDARY RODNEY KING RIOTS.

I DONT KNOW HOW PSYCHOPATHS LIKE DARYL GATES DOESNT HAVE GUILT FOR DESTROYING AND HELPING DESTROY CITIES AND BURN THEM TO THE GROUND THOUGH HE PERSONLLY BURNT THEM TO THE GROUND HE DID LET THE FIRES BURN AND LET THE VIOLENCE TAKE PLACE WITHOUT HIM AND HIS POLICE DOING THEIR JOB.

WHEN I SAW DARYL GATES HE WAS AT, WHAT ELSE? A DONUT SHOP. IT WAS IN CLAREMONT A VERY WHITE PERSON AREA AT THAT TIME AND THIS WAS AROUND THE MIDDLE TO LATE 90S. WHENEVER AFTER DARYL GATES QUIT THE CHIEF JOB.

HE WAS IN THERE GETTING A COFFEE AND DONUTS AND HE ASKS ME WHILE I AM DOING PAPERWORK. OH ARE YOU DOING COLLEGE WORK? I SAID "NO MUSIC WORK" IM IN A BAND".

HE DIDNT LIKE THE ANSWER AND IT SHOWED ON A FROWN ON HIS FACE. HE THEN SAT DOWN WITH AN ATTITUDE OF DISLIKE TOWARDS ME SO BAD AND SO IRRITATING THAT I LEFT.

HE STAYED A WHOLE HOUR BECAUSE I LEFT FOR AN HOUR WALKING BACK TO MOMS HOUSE AND THEN THOUGHT HE MAY BE DONE WITH HIS DONUTS AND COFFEE BUT HE WASNT SO I LEFT DEPRESSED I COUJLDNT BE THERE ANYMORE THAT NIGHT BUT LEFT ME TELL YOU I HAD ONE OF THE MOST UNCOMFORTABLE FEELINGS WITH CHIEF GATES OR SHOULD I SAY THE RETIRED DARYL GATES YOU COULD FEEL. HE WAS A BAD VIBE LIKE PRETTY MUCH ALL COPS ARE TO ME FOR SOME REASON. I GUESS COPS DONT LIKE ENTREAUPANEUR MUSICIANS THAT DO MUSIC PAPERWORK AT THE LOCAL HOME DONUT SHOP. OH WELL. I NEVER SAW HIM AGAIN AND HEARD HE DIED.

169 BOBBY OF TAXI AND 170. RINGO STARR.

169. BOBBY OF TAXI. THIS IS ONE I JUST CAME ACROSS AND DIDNT MEET OR TALK TO. WE WERE DRIVING DOWN SUNSET BLVD AND THIS GUY WAS TRYING TO GET OUR ATTENTION. WHEN HE GOT OUR ATTENTION WE REALIZED IT WAS BOBBY OF TAXI, YOU KNOW THE T.V. SHOW TAXI. HE THEN CHANGED AS WE RECOGNISED HIM AND ACTED

LIKE HE WAS BETTER THEN US AND ACTED STUCK UP. WE THEN LOST INTEREST IN DEALING WITH HIM.

170. RINGO STARR. ANOTHER GUY I DIDNT TALK TO I ONLY CAME ACROSS HIM. WE AGAIN WERE DRIVING DOWN SUNSET BLVD I BELEIVE IN THE LATE 1980S AND HERE IN A BUDGET RENT A CAR WAS RINGO STARR. I TOLD MY MANAGER LAILAH AND SHE WAS AMAZED THAT ONE OF THE BEATLES WERE NEXT TO US. ANOTHER ONE I JUST CAME ACROSS. WE WERE WONDERING WHY HE WAS IN HOLLYWOOD FOR THAT DAY AND THEN A DAY LATER OR SO WE SAW HIM ON THE ARSENIO HALL SHOW.

171. JOE MORTON

I WAS AT THE CASTING AGENCY OF DIC WHICH STANDS FOR THE DISNEY CHANNEL1 iN FRONT OF ME WAS A GUY. I REALLY SAID NOTHING TO HIM UNTIL HE SPOKE TO ME. HE SAID "IVE BEEN ON THE X FILES AND ....BLA BLA BLA.".

AND I WAS NOT REALLY INTERESTED BUT DIDNT WANT TO HURT HIS FEELINGS SO I ACTED LIKE I CARED AND WAS IMPRESSED. HE THEN BECAME LIKE BOBBY OF TAXI. HE CHANGED TO LIKE A SNOBBY GUY. I DONT GET ACTORS BUT IT TURNED OUT TO BE JOE MORTON WHO STAYED WITH THIS FOR YEARS. THIS WAS LIKE THE MID TO EARLY 90S OR MABE EVEN THE LATE 80S . I REALLY CANT REMEMBER BUT I DO KNOW IT WAS BEFORE THEY STOPPED LETTING PEOPLE IN THESE HOLLYWOOD SYSCRAPERS WITHOUT AN APPOINTMENT, YES NOW YOU HAVE TO HAVE HAVE AN APPOINTMENT TO EVEN GET INTO THESE BUILDINGS. BACK THEN YOU COULD JUST WALK IN AND GO ANYWHERE YOU WANT AND THIS IS WHERE I FOUND THE D.I.C. CHANNELL CASTING AREA.

JOE MORTON STAYING WITH IT AND NOW HAVING MORE WORK IN ACTING THEN HE WILL EVER NEED. NOW THAT IM IMPRESSED WITH.

172. TOMMY LASORTA. I RAN INTO TOMMY LASORTA AT THE POMONA VALLEY HOSTBITAL WHICH IS 35 MILES EAST OF LOS ANGELES. WE WERE ALL SITTING IN A WAITING ROOM EITHER TO PICK UP SOMEONE OR TO BE SEEN AND I BELEIVE TOMMIE WAS THERE TO BE SEEN.

AS WE ARE IN THE WAITING ROOM TOMMY STARTS TALKING AND TALKING AND TALKING. HE IS TALKING ABOUT THE BLACK PEOPLE IN THE 50S AND 60S AND 40S AND IT SOUNDS LIKE HES A RACIST SAYING THEY WERE CALLED N------- AND THEY WERE 2ND RATE AD HE WAS ACTING LIKE HE BELEIVES THEY THE BLACK PEOPLE STILL SHOULD BE 2ND. HE MOTIONED TO A COUP;LE OLDER BLACK LADIES AND THEY JUST NODDED WITH HIM OUT OF BEING STAR STRUCK HE IS TOMMY LASORTA BUT ME I DIDNT LIKE IT. I DONT GET STAR STRUCK. TOMMY TO ME SEEMED LIKE A LOUD MOUTH EGOTISTIC RACIST. ALOT OF PEOPLE THAT ARE FAMOIUS TALK AND TALK LIKE ITS A FACET OF WATER THAT DOESNT TURN OFF. TOMMYS MOUTH IS LIKE THAT. HE FELT BECAUSE IHE IS THE FAMOUS TOMMY LASORDA DODGER MANAGER AND COACH EARLIER AND HALL OF FAMER THAT HE CAN JUST TALK AND TALK AS A SELF CENTERED PERSON. I DID NOT LIKE THE MEETING AND TALK I HAD WITH TOMMY OR SHOULD I SAY HIM TALKING ONLY.

YOU PROBABLEY WONDER WHY I MEET SO MANY FAMOUS PEOPLE. WELL 1. IM OLD AND BEEN AROND THE HOLLYWOOD THING FOR 40 YEARS. 2.. BEING IN A PLACE WHERE FAMOUS PEOPLE ARE LIKE VENICE BEACH AND HOLT BLVD AND HOLLYWOOD.

ALSO I BELEIVE ITS SPIRITUAL MEANING GOD SETS IT UP BECAUSE IT SAYS IN THE BIBLE THAT YOU WILL BE AROUND THE PEERS LIKE YOURSELF.

I AM A PROFESSIONL MUSICIAN, AUTHOR, MUSIC ENGENEER MUSIC PRODUCER, KEYBOARDIST, BASE GUITARIST AND GUITARIST.LYRICIST AND LEAD VOCALIST. I BEEN DOING THIS FOR 41 YEARS AND 3 MONTHS.

SO.

THERE IS SOMETHING TO DOING MUSIC 41 YEARS AND THREE MONTHS.

I BELEIVE WHY I MEET SO MANY FAMOUS PEOPLE S I OBSERVE MORE OFTEN AND I DONT THINK THAT THEY ARE LOOK ALIKES. SURE THERE AFE LOOK ALIKES AND I CAN ALWAYS TELL IF ITS A LOOK ALIKE OR THE REAL THING OR THE REAL PERSON.

I ALSO BELEIVE I MEET SO MANY FAMOUS PEOPLE BECAUSE IM NOT STARSTRUCK. I BELEIVE PEOPLE ARE DRAWN TO EACH OTHER AND I BELEIVE FAMOUS PEOPLE FEEL COMFORTABLE AND ARE DRAWN TO ME BECAUSE I MAKE THEM FEEL COMFORTABLE AND I MAKE THEM FEEL GOOD.

ONCE JASON BATEMAN WOULDNT LEAVE BECAUSE HE WANTED TO HEAR MORE OF MY STORIES AND THIS GOES THE SAME WITH KATE HUDSON IN LAS VEGAS. YES, KATE LOVED TO HEAR MY STORIES.

I BELEIVE FAMOUS PEOPLE ARE AROUND ME BECAUSE I AM AN ENTERTAINER AND THEY DONT JUDGE MY SUCCESS WHICH ISNT TOO GOOD AT THIS MOMENT BUT THEY JUDGE MY TALENT AND THEY DONT SAY "ONLY IF YOUR FAMOUS IS YOUR TALENT REAL".

THIS IS HOW STAR STRUCK PEOPLE ARE. THE ONLY THINK YOUR GREAT IF YOU ESTABLISHED IN THE BUSINESS BUT THE PEOPLE WHO ARE FAMOUS IN THE BUSINESS LOOK AT ME FOR MY TALENT AND DONT SEE ME FOR WHAT LEVIL I AM IN THE BUSINESS.

UNLIKE THE STARSTRUCK PEOPLE WHO HATE YOU IF YOUR DOWN AND LOVE YOU IF YOUR UP.

SO AGAIN I AM AROUND FAMOUS PEOPLE ALOT BECAUSE THEY ARE ATTRACTED TO MY ORA AND VIBE AND TALENT.

TO END THIS BOOK I KNOW AND BELEIVE THERE ARE MORE FAMOUS PEOPLE THAT I MET BUT I CANT REMEMBER ANY MORE SO TO END THIS BOOK I WANT TO SAY.

I AM NOT FAMOUS.

Made in the USA
Columbia, SC
21 December 2022